GET FEEDBACK

Giving, Exhibiting, and Teaching Feedback in Special Education Teacher Preparation

GET FEEDBACK

Giving, Exhibiting, and Teaching Feedback
in Special Education Teacher Preparation

Martha D. Elford, PhD
University of Kansas
Lawrence, Kansas

Heather Haynes Smith, PhD
Trinity University
San Antonio, Texas

Susanne James, PhD
Southern Illinois University Edwardsville
Edwardsville, Illinois

SLACK
INCORPORATED

SLACK Incorporated
6900 Grove Road
Thorofare, NJ 08086 USA
856-848-1000   Fax: 856-848-6091
www.slackbooks.com
© 2022 by SLACK Incorporated

Senior Vice President: Stephanie Arasim Portnoy
Vice President, Editorial: Jennifer Kilpatrick
Vice President, Marketing: Mary Sasso
Acquisitions Editor: Tony Schiavo
Director of Editorial Operations: Jennifer Cahill
Vice President/Creative Director: Thomas Cavallaro
Cover Artist: Lori Shields

The procedures and practices described in this publication should be implemented in a manner consistent with the professional standards set for the circumstances that apply in each specific situation. Every effort has been made to confirm the accuracy of the information presented and to correctly relate generally accepted practices. The authors, editors, and publisher cannot accept responsibility for errors or exclusions or for the outcome of the material presented herein. There is no expressed or implied warranty of this book or information imparted by it. Care has been taken to ensure that drug selection and dosages are in accordance with currently accepted/recommended practice. Off-label uses of drugs may be discussed. Due to continuing research, changes in government policy and regulations, and various effects of drug reactions and interactions, it is recommended that the reader carefully review all materials and literature provided for each drug, especially those that are new or not frequently used. Some drugs or devices in this publication have clearance for use in a restricted research setting by the Food and Drug and Administration or FDA. Each professional should determine the FDA status of any drug or device prior to use in their practice.

Any review or mention of specific companies or products is not intended as an endorsement by the author or publisher.

SLACK Incorporated uses a review process to evaluate submitted material. Prior to publication, educators or clinicians provide important feedback on the content that we publish. We welcome feedback on this work.

Library of Congress Cataloging-in-Publication Data

Names: Elford, Martha D., author. | Smith, Heather Haynes, author. | James,
   Susanne (Susanne Marie), 1971- author.
Title: G.E.T. feedback : giving, exhibiting, and teaching feedback in special education teacher preparation /
   Martha D. Elford, Heather Haynes Smith, Susanne James.
Description: Thorofare, NJ : SLACK Incorporated, [2022] | Includes
   bibliographical references and index.
Identifiers: LCCN 2021025921 (print) | LCCN 2021025922 (ebook) | ISBN
   9781630916916 (hardback) | ISBN 9781630916923 (epub) | ISBN
   9781630916930 (pdf)
Subjects: LCSH: Special education teachers--Training of. | Feedback
   (Psychology) | Adult students--Psychology. | Communication in education.
   | BISAC: EDUCATION / Special Education / General
Classification: LCC LC3969.45 .E54 2021 (print) | LCC LC3969.45 (ebook) |
   DDC 371.9/043--dc23
LC record available at https://lccn.loc.gov/2021025921
LC ebook record available at https://lccn.loc.gov/2021025922

Printed in the United States of America.

Last digit is print number: 10   9   8   7   6   5   4   3   2   1

Contents

ACKNOWLEDGMENTS

The feedback I received as a doctoral student at the University of Kansas from Dr. Don Deshler and Dr. Earl Knowlton certainly shaped my understanding of the value of feedback in education. Moreover, the coaching feedback I received from my colleague, Devona Dunekack, from the Kansas Coaching Project provided a model for constructing the language of feedback for adult learners. Jim Knight's foundational work in instructional coaching informed what I believe to be a partnership approach in delivering feedback to adults. Working with Morgan Russell, an interactor for TLE TeachLivE (a mixed-reality classroom with simulated students), taught me how to add feedback into daily practice for students and teachers. The groundbreaking research of Dr. Mary Catherine Scheeler for delivering immediate feedback set me on the path of studying what feedback means in the preparation of special educators. It is with deep gratitude that I acknowledge these individuals on whose knowledge I humbly stand.

On a personal note, I want to express my gratitude to my colleagues and friends, Heather and Susanne. This book would never have been a reality without you. To my family—my mom, children, grandchildren, and siblings—thank you for believing in me, for encouraging me, and for tolerating my impossible schedule. Your feedback means more to me than any other's.

—*Martha D. Elford, PhD*

When I reflect on the impact of feedback, there are numerous specific people across time and experiences who supported my knowledge and thinking through how they gave, exhibited, and taught me about feedback. This work really began during my Master of Arts in Teaching full-year teaching internship at Trinity University when faculty, including Karen Waldron, Master of Arts teachers Carol Coley and Javier Melendez, as well as my cohort, engaged in feedback and support practices that were essential in preparing me to become an effective inclusive elementary school teacher. Several years later, feedback and thought partners from Fort Worth Independent School District in Texas—Marsha Sonnenberg, Clairita Porter, Becki Krsnak, Becky Beegle, and others—contributed to my growth as a recipient and provider of feedback. I am grateful for the continued learning and growth in instructional coaching and technical assistance that I received from the Fort Worth Independent School District, Dale Webster, and the many Texas Reading Technical Assistance Specialists I had the pleasure of working alongside. Working at the University of Texas with Marty Hougen and faculty across Texas in the Higher Education Collaborative was pivotal for me in digging deeper into the role of feedback pertaining to teacher preparation. It inspired and motivated me to pursue my doctorate in special education at the University of Kansas, where I was fortunate to meet Marti and Susanne, thus beginning our explorations of feedback in teacher education and virtual learning. I want to also acknowledge all the other amazing special education teacher preparation faculty and instructors out there. Go team!

I acknowledge my son, A.J.; my husband, Bryan; and my friends for their support. I am grateful to be back at my alma mater, Trinity University, teaching the courses that first inspired me, as well as working alongside colleagues on projects that support deeper learning in teacher preparation and social emotional learning in schools.

—*Heather Haynes Smith, PhD*

Writing a book on giving, exhibiting, and teaching feedback is one of the most rewarding professional endeavors I have experienced. None of this would have been possible without my colleagues, Drs. Martha Elford and Heather Haynes Smith. These strong women have supported me both professionally and personally since we met at the University of Kansas. I am eternally grateful to my family—Aaron, Lindsey, and Lillian—for standing by me through every struggle and accomplishment. You are my heart.

Finally, I would like to thank all of the teachers I have been so lucky to work with in the Lee's Summit R7 School District, the Collinsville Unified School District, and all the other school districts I have worked with in the Metro East Illinois area. You all taught me more than I gave you.

—*Susanne James, PhD*

ABOUT THE AUTHORS

Martha D. Elford, PhD, is a Lecturer and Program Associate in the Department of Special Education at the University of Kansas in Lawrence, Kansas. Dr. Elford is the Program Designer for the online High Incidence Disabilities Teacher Education Practicum program. She has experience as a classroom teacher, a reading specialist, and an instructional coach. Dr. Elford earned her doctorate degree in Special Education at the University of Kansas as a doctoral fellow with L-TEC, Leadership in Teacher Education Core. As a post-doctoral fellow, Dr. Elford supervised the following two research projects: (a) Poses Family Foundation grant studying instructional coaching, and (b) TeachLivE, the use of simulation in teacher-preparation programs. She also has served as Educational Consultant to school districts on co-teaching, instructional coaching, and strategic instruction. Dr. Elford's research interests include the impact of feedback and coaching for pre- and in-service teachers on professional growth, using virtual coaching for teacher preparation and professional development. As a Fulbright Award recipient, Dr. Elford spent 3 months in Finland studying Finnish education and collaborating with faculty at the School of Education at both the University of Jyväskylä and the Niilo Mäki Institute in Jyväskylä, Finland. You can follow her at Vector Virtual Coaching: https://www.vectorcoaching.org/.

Heather Haynes Smith, PhD, is an Associate Professor in the Department of Education at Trinity University in San Antonio, Texas. She teaches undergraduate and graduate courses on high incidence disabilities and reading instruction. Dr. Smith's research, teaching, and service support inclusion, research-based reading instruction, Response to Intervention, Multi-Tiered System of Supports, Social and Emotional Learning, service-learning, and integrated academic and behavioral supports. Prior to completing her doctorate at the University of Kansas, Dr. Smith worked in Texas as an elementary teacher, instructional coach (reading), state-level Reading Technical Assistance Specialist, project coordinator for the Higher Education Collaborative at the Vaughn Gross Center for Reading and Language Arts, and a consultant for the Meadows Center for Prevention of Educational Risk. The United Way of San Antonio and Bexar County honored her as a nominee for the Inaugural Higher Education Innovation Award in 2019. Locally, Dr. Smith serves on the United Way Successful Student Impact Council, SA Reads Board, Winston School Medical and Scientific Advisory Council, and Mahncke Park Community Garden Board. Dr. Smith is a Certified Principal, and an elementary, ESL, and special education teacher and welcomes the opportunity to collaborate on implementing reading-focused multi-tiered systems of support and instruction with schools and districts. You can follow her on Twitter @DrHaynesSmith.

Susanne James, PhD, is an Associate Professor in the Department of Teaching and Learning at Southern Illinois University Edwardsville (SIUE). Dr. James is also the Project Director for the SIUE Virtual Professional Practice Lab (http://www.siue.edu/virtual-practice-lab/). In addition to her work with the SIUE Virtual Professional Practice Lab, she teaches courses in educational research, effective instructional strategies, differentiated instruction, and accommodations of core curriculum. Dr. James serves as the Program Director for the Department of Teaching and Learning Master of Arts in Teaching graduate program for those seeking an alternative route to teacher licensure in Special Education at the graduate level. Prior to completing her doctorate at the University of Kansas, Dr. James was a classroom teacher of students with special needs for 13 years within instructional and inclusion settings in Kansas and Missouri. She also has been an instructional coach and educational consultant to school districts for co-teaching, differentiated instruction, strategic instruction, and effective practices. Dr. James' research, teaching, and service supports virtual learning, co-teaching, teacher preparation, and strategic instruction. You can follow her on the SIUE Virtual Professional Practice Facebook page at https://www.facebook.com/SIUEVPP.

CONTRIBUTING AUTHORS

Reesha Adamson, PhD (Chapter 11)
Associate Professor
Counseling, Leadership, and Special Education
Missouri State University
Springfield, Missouri

Dennis Cavitt, EdD (Chapter 14)
Assistant Professor of Special Education
Midwestern State University
Wichita Falls, Texas

Kyena E. Cornelius, EdD (Chapters 3 and 10)
Associate Professor
Department of Special Education
College of Education Accreditation Coordinator
Minnesota State University
Mankato, Minnesota

Donald D. Deshler, PhD (Foreword)
Williamson Family Distinguished Professor Emeritus of Special Education
Founder and Former Director
Center for Research on Learning
University of Kansas
Lawrence, Kansas

Amy Gaumer Erickson, PhD (Chapter 11)
Associate Research Professor
University of Kansas
Lawrence, Kansas

Lisa A. Finnegan, PhD (Chapter 14)
Associate Professor
Exceptional Student Education
Florida Atlantic University
Boca Raton, Florida

Carlos A. Flores Jr., EdD (Chapter 3)
Assistant Professor
Department of Teacher Education
Angelo State University
San Angelo, Texas

John Hattie, PhD (Foreword)
University of Melbourne
Victoria, Australia

Randa G. Keeley, PhD (Chapter 14)
Assistant Professor
Teacher Education Department
Texas Woman's University
Denton, Texas

Kristin Joannou Lyon, PhD (Chapter 4)
Research Project Coordinator
KU Center on Developmental Disabilities
University of Kansas
Lawrence, Kansas

Katie Martin Miller, PhD (Chapter 9)
Assistant Professor
Exceptional Student Education
Florida Atlantic University
Boca Raton, Florida

Cynthia Mruczek, PhD (Chapter 3)
Lecturer/Program Associate
Leadership in Special and Inclusive Education
University of Kansas
Lawrence, Kansas

Jessica Nelson, EdD, BCBA (Chapter 11)
Assistant Professor
Counseling, Leadership, and Special Education
Missouri State University
Springfield, Missouri

Ruby L. Owiny, PhD (Chapter 10)
Associate Professor
Access Program Director
Director of the Division of Education
Trinity International University
Deerfield, Illinois

Jennifer Porterfield, PhD (Chapter 14)
Senior Lecturer
Department of Curriculum and Instruction
Special Education Program
Texas State University
San Marcos, Texas

Felicity Post, EdD (Chapter 11)
Associate Professor
Special Education
Peru State College
Peru, Nebraska

Anni K. Reinking, EdD (Chapters 12 and 14)
Assistant Professor
Early Childhood Education
Department of Teaching and Learning
Southern Illinois University Edwardsville
Edwardsville, Illinois

Cathy Newman Thomas, PhD (Chapter 14)
Associate Professor of Special Education
Department of Curriculum and Instruction
Texas State University
San Marcos, Texas

Virginia L. Walker, PhD, BCBA-D (Chapter 4)
Associate Professor
Department of Special Education and Child Development
University of North Carolina–Charlotte
Charlotte, North Carolina

Wendy H. Weber, PhD (Chapter 8)
Professor
Southern Illinois University Edwardsville
Edwardsville, Illinois

Margaret Williamson, MEd (Chapter 13)
Senior UX Researcher
UserTesting
Atlanta, Georgia

PREFACE

We live in a world where feedback bombards our daily lives. Corporations request our feedback after almost every encounter. Traffic lights at city intersections provide electronic feedback, with images and numerical countdowns for how much longer we must wait before we can cross the street. In social media, many people rely on feedback to determine how much they are "liked" by counting the quick iconic responses and comments. The GPS navigation systems in handheld devices or in vehicles provide feedback on whether we are taking the correct route and also when we have reached our destination. Persistent emails request feedback by pestering us to respond to a company's "short survey" after buying items online. People who play video and online games depend on feedback to challenge themselves as they move to more complex levels in the game. In some ways, feedback has become the **noise** that we have to filter through to find the message.

How does this **noise** affect us? When prompted for feedback from large corporations like Amazon or Delta Airlines, we can easily delete the unsolicited email. As a pedestrian, we prefer to know how much longer we must wait before the light changes to red, so we can calculate the risk of dashing across the street. On social media, we have been known to experience joy and affirmation from a comment made by someone we respect. We also have reacted with annoyance and disdain when a comment is made by someone whose opinion we do not value. Navigation via GPS has made travel easier by eliminating the struggle to refold a large map or to read it while driving, with it perched on the passenger seat. We even unsubscribe from online retailers to stop receiving emails that clutter our inbox. The feedback in video and online games is designed to keep us coming back for more, and it works remarkably well (says a person who is new to Pokémon Go).

As we sort through the various sources of feedback, commonalities become evident. Large corporations invite tips on how their service or user experiences can be improved. Transportation systems deliver progress information relevant to the walker's or driver's desired destination. Social media motivates individuals through ongoing feedback that entices engagement. GPS navigates travelers from a starting point to the final destination. Video and online games reinforce the participant by rewarding success with access to higher levels of the game or more points.

The bombardment of feedback and its accompanying noise has led us to examine the following three rarely discussed critical components as they relate to education: (a) how feedback occurs in our professional practice in special education, (b) how instructors learn to deliver this feedback, and (c) the role of the recipient of the feedback—the adults who are enrolled in our teacher-preparation programs. This book attempts to address these critical components.

—*Martha D. Elford, PhD*
—*Heather Haynes Smith, PhD*
—*Susanne James, PhD*

FOREWORD

Two of the common threads running through the efforts to change the educational landscape are as follows: (a) standards must be raised to enable students to be prepared to compete in the rapidly changing world of employment and, (b) the achievement gap must be closed for the growing number of struggling learners, including students with disabilities. Not surprisingly, the goals of "raising the bar" and "closing the gap" can be difficult to address simultaneously. Successfully doing so requires, among other things, that the practices used to prepare teachers should be dramatically altered from those traditionally followed so that teachers are better equipped to address the magnitude of this challenge.

This book addresses one topic in the preparation of teachers that has received, at best, only cursory attention. Namely, how should individuals preparing to become teachers be provided with feedback regarding their performance so they can acquire the broad array of skills required to be highly proficient teachers? But, why an entire book on how to provide high-quality feedback to teachers? Research studies have repeatedly underscored that high-quality feedback is one of **the** most powerful variables in the entire learning process—for **both** K-12 students **and** adults.

During the teacher-preparation process, the volume of information and skills that teacher candidates are expected to master is very large and continues to grow. Acquiring the broad array of skills required to continuously assess, monitor, and differentiate instruction to meet the unique learning profiles of students requires a high level of sophistication and is most demanding. Unless teacher candidates become highly proficient in those dimensions of the teaching process, they will not be capable of successfully addressing the "raising the bar/closing the gap" dilemma confronting them. Hence, during their teacher-preparation programs, they must be able to experience high-quality feedback as a learner as well as to learn how give feedback as a teacher.

This book gives feedback the attention it has long deserved but has not received in the teacher-preparation literature. The book is brilliantly conceptualized and organized. The way it is written indicates that the authors are highly seasoned as both K-12 educators and in the preparation of teacher candidates. Not only does this book make a compelling case for the unique and very significant role of high-quality feedback in the teacher preparation process, it does so by articulating a simple, yet elegant, model of the feedback process. This model—G.E.T. Model—represents the main venues by which instructors should embed feedback in teacher-preparation courses. Namely, by **G**iving feedback, **E**xhibiting feedback, and **T**eaching how to deliver feedback.

One of the most powerful aspects of this book is the way the authors have masterfully integrated adult learning theory into their conceptualization and recommendation of how high-quality feedback should be implemented. Their sophisticated treatment of feedback in the context of the realities of adult learning, both cognitively and affectively, greatly enhances the understanding of this important learning variable for those involved in the preparation of teachers.

Finally, there are a host of features of this book that make it a very meaningful and practical learning tool in preparing teachers, including authentic scenarios/vignettes to ground and contextualize the principles being taught, a set of learning objectives that answer the key questions of "what, why, and how," a broad array of practical applications, and personal reflections as well as "lessons learned" by a host of instructors involved in the preparation of teachers. In short, the book is designed to be a very practical and usable resource. In light of the way this book is structured, I am convinced that practitioners will find it to be an extremely valuable resource as they prepare teachers for the challenging world of education they are entering.

In short, this is a very readable book that is written with passion, vivid examples, and numerous practical suggestions that can be readily implemented. It will be a resource to which those involved in teacher preparation will frequently turn. If used as intended, it holds the promise of being a transformative resource in the preparation of tomorrow's teachers.

—*Donald D. Deshler, PhD*

FOREWORD

Feedback is the hot topic of the decade. We are continually invited to like or not like, asked to provide feedback, readily give feedback, social media apps dish out feedback (even when not asked for), and bookcases are full of books about feedback. Maybe feedback is becoming noise, and it is perhaps no wonder than most feedback is not received, heard, or actioned. If feedback fell in a forest, would anyone hear it?

But, there are 20+ meta-analysis studies on feedback (http://www.visiblelearningmetax.com), showing high impact but remarkable variance in the presence of feedback—it is this variance that is the dilemma. Why is some feedback effective and some not, and why does feedback for one student makes a difference but the same feedback to another does not? Given the ever-present occurrence of feedback, this book proposes a model for maximizing the reception of feedback to truly make a difference to the learning lives of students. The model's premise is to focus on the reception of feedback as much as, if not more, than its giving. We need to be more attentive to the giving, exhibiting, and teaching of receiving feedback (the authors' G.E.T. Model), particularly feedback to the teacher about their impact on the learner (which is music to my ears). While the major attention is directed toward special education teachers, the messages are indeed relevant to all. The fundamental definition of feedback emphasizes that feedback is of little consequence until it informs understanding or restructures thinking and beliefs. This is a major change from the usual treatises on how to give feedback, the need to provide more feedback, and the faults of learners who do not appreciate the bounty of feedback.

While the big ideas in this book came from teaching children who receive special education supports and services, the epiphany for the authors came when they asked why the same methods that were working with the students could not also work with adults. The beauty of working with children with special needs is their willingness to talk about what they do not know; their honesty in their struggles with learning; their appreciation that struggle is good, as learning is hard work; and their transparent joy in learning. These are attributes that many other students (and teachers when talking about their own learning) often aim to hide, suppress, or see as irrelevant to successful learning. Too often, learning is seen as easy, not entailing hard work, comes naturally, and is personal. If you went to a physician for a medical problem and they said you had disease X, there is no assumption that you are a lesser or bad person. However, for too many students if they do not learn, they are told it is them that is the problem, and if they are provided with feedback that they are clearly poor learners who need it. Further, many students become encultured to view feedback as not being worthwhile if it confirms their prior beliefs, whereas the G.E.T. Model aims to show that feedback that may question prior beliefs can be the most powerful.

Hence the need for feedback to be purposeful, timely (give corrective feedback now, ponder on deeper feedback timing), specific, and constructive. It should aim to reduce the gap between where the adult is now and where we (and hopefully they too) need to be. It is worthwhile to read about how assessment is a medium for feedback and that the quality of the assessment is more a function of the GET powers of the receiver who is interpreting and actioning the feedback.

The tools, resources, and strategies can then flow with abundance, with the powerful message that feedback—both the giving and receiving of—can be taught. This book is a powerful and rich resource of great ideas that will move the debates about feedback into the most worthwhile areas.

—John Hattie, PhD

The G.E.T. Model

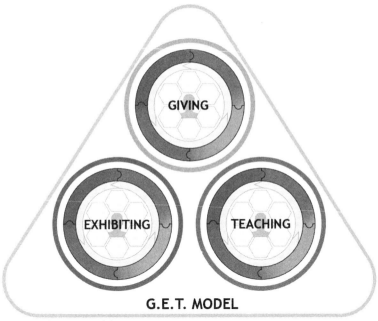

Figure I-1. The G.E.T. Model.

Section I includes Chapters 1 and 2 and provides the necessary basic knowledge on feedback and its intersection with adult learning theory, which is the foundation of the G.E.T. Model. Section I is essential reading in preparation for the reflection and practice in the future chapters on the G.E.T. Model. Chapter 1 introduces readers to the concepts and theories that contribute to the G.E.T. Model (Figure I-1). Chapter 2 describes the organization of the book and its chapters.

Introduction and Conceptual Framework

We learn differently when we are learning to perform
than when we are beginning to understand what is being communicated to us.

—Jack Mezirow

Learning and feedback go hand in hand. Giving feedback to an adult student can present challenges that may cause you to question whether your teaching has produced any learning at all. The disconnect that exists between instructors' feedback and teacher candidates' transformative learning—the disruption of existing schema to create new interpretation, meaning, and habits—may be due to a basic disruption in communication. During course evaluations, the teacher candidates ask for more feedback, yet instructors believe they spend hours giving feedback that is never read or acknowledged (Scott, 2014). Feedback, no matter how frequent, thorough, descriptive, or timely, falls short of its purpose when instructors fail to put the recipient at the center of the feedback they are giving. Understanding who the recipient is (in this case, it is the teacher candidates), where they are on a learning continuum, and how ready they are to receive feedback, contributes to the effectiveness of the feedback. For feedback to be effective and transformative, it must be communicated in a way that the recipient can receive it and use it. Succinctly stated, teacher candidates may not get feedback because instructors give it in ways that work for them but not for the adult who receives it.

This book is a practical guide for instructors to maximize the transformational power of the feedback we give, exhibit, and teach in special education teacher preparation. We begin the book with this chapter to provide an explanation of our conceptual framework and **G.E.T. Model** as a guide for addressing feedback throughout course design, activities, and assignments. The G.E.T. Model represents the three main feedback opportunities that instructors can embed in courses: **G**ive, **E**xhibit, and **T**each. Giving, exhibiting, and teaching feedback is ineffectual if it falls on those who are not ready to learn. We, as instructors in special education teacher preparation, experienced frustration when our teacher candidates failed to change their behaviors despite our dedication to descriptive,

Elford, M. D., Smith, H. H., & James, S.
GET Feedback: Giving, Exhibiting, and Teaching Feedback in
Special Education Teacher Preparation (pp. 3-20).
© 2022 SLACK Incorporated.

timely, and purposeful feedback. Slowly, we began to realize that changing adult behavior required a method different than what we previously used to change the behaviors of students we once taught in the K-12 settings. As we explored our own failures and successes with giving feedback, we realized that we needed to think about our adult learners and how they receive and act on the feedback we give. This chapter describes the intersection of adult learning theory with feedback and introduces the G.E.T. Model.

Feedback intends to focus on both the giver and the receiver, based on what went well and what could be improved around the related experience. Even when responding to a merchandise survey, we are often requested to provide more specific details, to describe our experience, or to provide a suggested improvement. The same is true when delivering feedback in education. The giver of the feedback focuses on what they observed or experienced and tries to describe that information to the receiver. The receiver of the feedback focuses on the feedback and interprets it though their own observations and experiences. When referring to a marketing survey, individual feedback is lumped together with thousands of others, which is then interpreted as trends. In education, the feedback is personal to the learner. We suggest that feedback is an intimate exchange between the giver and the receiver that can empower both individuals to improve their professional performance. As faculty who prepare special education teacher candidates, we are tasked with <u>G</u>iving, <u>E</u>xhibiting, and <u>T</u>eaching feedback in a way that empowers them to meet the competencies of professional practice. In addition, the feedback we provide should inspire special education teacher candidates to grow and improve professionally throughout their careers. This lofty task inspired us to critically examine the research for feedback in special education teacher preparation and to critically examine our own practices for <u>G</u>iving, <u>E</u>xhibiting, and <u>T</u>eaching feedback in our respective programs. Out of that process, the G.E.T. Model emerged.

Chapter 1 lays the foundation for the G.E.T. Model by describing our understanding of adult learning theory and how it informs the feedback we deliver to adult learners. In addition, we craft a framework of four domains that is based on the feedback research as a means of intersecting adult learning theory and feedback. These domains inform the way we examine and explain each aspect of the G.E.T. Model. Finally, after laying this foundational understanding, we move on to Chapter 2, which describes how the book is constructed. Developing an understanding of the intersection of feedback and adult learning theory leads to the application of the G.E.T. Model that is described in the chapters that follow.

INTERSECTION OF FEEDBACK AND ADULT LEARNING THEORY

The G.E.T. Model is the result of intersecting the widely accepted characteristics of feedback from authors such as Hattie (1999), Wiggins (2012), and Brookhart and Moss (2015) with adult learning theory as conceptualized by Knowles (1978). This framework informs the G.E.T. Model as a roadmap for instructors to give, exhibit, and teach feedback to the adults enrolled in their courses as well as when supervising field experiences. In turn, teacher candidates who learn in this manner will be able to give, exhibit, and teach feedback in their K-12 classrooms.

Recognizing the growing emphasis on feedback in special education teacher preparation policy and practice, we examined the current definition and description of feedback in research, high-leverage practice documents, special education teacher certification expectations, and ethical and instructional standards. We then aligned the predominant descriptions with adult learning theory, as explained in the text that follows. For the purpose of this text, we defined feedback as **any information the recipient receives that informs their understanding or restructures their thinking or beliefs related to their performance, knowledge, or skills.** In the section that follows, we summarize the literature on feedback by examining the effectiveness, questions, levels, and characteristics. Next, we describe our synthesis of those items to create four domains for delivering feedback. Then, we summarize the challenges of feedback in special education teacher preparation and describe how we conceptualized the G.E.T. Model. Finally, we describe Knowles' (1984) adult learning theory and how the four domains integrate with it.

Feedback in the Literature

The effectiveness, questions, levels, and characteristics of feedback have been widely discussed in the scholarly literature. We describe the evolution of feedback, based on the literature from scholars who have been studying feedback for 2 decades. First, the extensive meta-analysis by Hattie (1999) established the high effect size that feedback has on student performance, indicating that feedback does not merely improve student performance but does so substantially. In addition, Hattie and Timperley (2007) comprehensively analyzed the feedback literature and created three fundamental questions for determining the types of feedback to give. Furthermore, these questions work in tandem with the three levels of feedback (Hattie, 2012a; Hattie & Timperley, 2007). Finally, Brookhart (2008) and Wiggins (2012) articulated the essential elements and characteristics required for feedback to be effective. An examination of the research on the topic of feedback established some agreement for its effectiveness, the questions it should answer, the various levels, and the multiple characteristics.

Effectiveness of Feedback

Hattie's (1999) meta-analysis established the foundation for the value of feedback pertaining to its effectiveness on student achievement in K-12 education. As an intervention and educational practice, feedback has a statistically significant effect. According to Hattie's (2012b) more recent analysis of more than 1200 studies on student achievement, the effect size of feedback was 0.73 for students achieving higher levels of understanding, indicating that feedback is an effective intervention for producing higher achievement for students who receive it than students who do not. Cohen (1992) described a method for interpreting effect sizes by breaking the statistical analysis into three groups: 0.20 as *small*, 0.50 as *medium*, and 0.80 as *large*. We can conclude that the higher the effect size is the greater the influence of the educational practice on student outcomes. Furthermore, Wiliam (2012) suggested that feedback may double a person's learning rate. Clearly, feedback is a powerful influence on learning.

Questions

In recent years, researchers and leaders in the field of education have developed and expanded descriptive definitions of effective feedback. This expansion starts with the Hattie and Timperley's (2007) distillation of feedback to answer the following three questions: (a) Where am I going?, (b) How am I going?, and (c) Where to next? Each feedback question listed functions at three levels.

Levels

Hattie and Timperley (2007) explained that effective feedback answers the questions related to goals, process, and next steps by answering each question at three levels. These levels are *task*, *process*, and *self-regulation*. These levels emerged from examining the meta-analyses assessing the influences of feedback (Hattie & Timperley, 2007).

The first level—**task**—describes how well tasks are understood and performed. Feedback at this level states the goal, the steps required to reach the goal, and what to do when the goal is reached.

The second level—**process**—describes the procedures needed to understand the task and to perform the task at the expected level of proficiency. Process-level feedback describes the progress made toward the goal and what else is necessary to continue to develop the skills required to reach the goal.

The third level—**self-regulation**—requires students to be able to self-monitor, direct, and regulate their actions to achieve deeper levels of learning. Self-regulation is the deepest level of feedback because it considers the recipient's role in understanding the goal, what they need to know to achieve the goal, and what to do to move forward. In addition, the self-regulation level requires students to evaluate their goal attainment and demands that they personally evaluate their own learning and how this learning affected them as a student.

A fourth level—**self as a person**—is least effective as feedback because it often does not contain task-related information. It is mentioned here because Hattie and Timperley (2007) included it in their seminal article. At this level, teachers can mistakenly give feedback about effort or endurance that sounds more like praise and is frequently attributive. Feedback at this level can sound more like cheerleading. Furthermore, Hattie (2012a) distinguished praise from feedback by stating that praise can get in the way of feedback because students hear the praise phrase ("good job" or "way to go") and then stop listening. Praise may make the recipient feel good, but it does not lead to learning. Praise should not be mistaken as feedback because it does not serve the purpose of improving performance.

In addition, when feedback attributes quality, such as the amount of effort or value ("you worked really hard" or "you're doing your best work"), it transmits a judgment that can be argued. A teacher may ascribe great effort to something a student spent only a few minutes working on, thus devaluing the feedback because the effort attributed is greater than what actually occurred. Students are the ones who truly know how much effort they expended or whether it is their very best work.

Consequently, students who are concerned primarily with their social image in the classroom may seek self-level feedback solely to improve their reputation with their teacher or peers. Students can easily misinterpret the feedback because of their reputational lens, or how they want to be seen (Hattie & Timperley, 2007). This type of feedback can derail the students' self-monitoring and self-evaluation because the teacher has given a value statement that may or may not be accurate. For this reason, self as a person is omitted from our levels of feedback.

Feedback at each of the three levels that we support in the G.E.T. Model—task, process, and self-regulation—informs more than the performance, or skills, of teaching. Feedback at these three levels affects the goals of teaching by informing teacher candidates where they are on the continuum of skills and what needs to happen for them to improve. Hattie and Timperley (2007) suggested that the task, process, and self-regulation levels serve "to reduce the gap between actual performance and desired goal attainment" (p. 86). Acknowledging that these levels of feedback inform where we are going, how we are progressing, and what should happen next is fundamental to the effectiveness of feedback and the way feedback contributes to learning.

Characteristics

What does effective feedback that answers the three questions and involves the three levels look and sound like? Brookhart (2008) suggested six essential elements characterizing feedback that leads to student achievement, whereas Wiggins (2012) described seven essential characteristics of effective feedback. In processing Brookhart's six elements and Wiggins' seven characteristics, we discovered what we think effective feedback looks and sounds like.

Brookhart (2008) suggested that feedback for student improvement and achievement should be (a) timely; (b) focused on one or more strength and at least one suggestion for the next step; (c) focused on the student's work and learning process (descriptive, not focused on the student personally, nonjudgmental); (d) focused on the process, self-referenced; (e) expressed in a few points with small steps; and (f) positive, clear, and specific. These elements can be combined into categories that describe the time, focus, and language. The first element (timely) refers to determining the best moment for delivering feedback. For academic subjects like math, immediate feedback is most timely to prevent continued errors in multistep problems. However, with more complex tasks, such as testing a hypothesis, timely feedback allows students the time to wrestle with the process.

Elements two (focus on strength and offer suggestions), three (focus on student's work and learning process), and four (focus on self-referenced process) describe the focus of the feedback. Brookhart (2008) suggested that the focus should be strength-related and provide at least one suggestion for what to do next. It should focus on the student's work and work progress; the feedback should not be judgmental or about the student personally. The focus of the feedback should be on the process and about what the student has actually done, what learning is demonstrated, or what the student needs to do to improve. The fifth and sixth elements describe the type of language to use—positive, clear, and specific, with only a few points and small steps. These elements guide those giving feedback to describe to students "something about their work that they might not have noticed themselves, but they understand in terms of how it fits with what they are trying to learn and accomplish" (Brookhart, 2008, p. 34).

In an attempt to answer the question, *What is feedback?*, Wiggins (2012) articulated the following seven essential characteristics of effective feedback: (a) goal-referenced, (b) tangible and transparent, (c) actionable, (d) user-friendly (specific and personalized), (e) timely, (f) ongoing, and (g) consistent. He posited that feedback is information about the progress being made toward a reaching particular goal. Wiggins described several ways that feedback is delivered, from nonverbal body language, such as head nods or a snicker, to direct statements about what someone likes or does not like. Wiggins also described the difference between feedback, which guides people toward their goal, and advice, which sounds judgmental. Using Wiggins' characteristics to inform feedback language increases the chance that the words one uses sound more like feedback and less like advice or judgment.

Summary of Effective Feedback

Effective feedback provides essential information about the goal, the progress to the goal, and how to continue toward the goal (Hattie & Timperley, 2007). Feedback leads to changes in effort, engagement, or efficacy when it is related to the learning task. When feedback answers the three major questions of Where? How? Next? and is delivered appropriately for the level required with the descriptive characteristics, then feedback can shrink the gap between where learners/performers are and where they aim to be (Brookhart, 2008, 2012; Brookhart & Moss, 2015; Hattie & Timperley, 2007; Wiliam, 2016).

By examining the characteristics and levels of feedback and the questions one needs to ask when delivering feedback, we strove to synthesize the information into identifiable domains. Hattie and Timperley's (2007) simple three questions were clearly stated, so we examined the characteristics to determine how those descriptors could fit in the structure of these questions. Because the levels of feedback apply for each question, we explored which level might best fit the three questions asked and the characteristics of feedback. This analysis led us to identify and label the following four main domains for delivering feedback: specificity, immediacy, purposefulness, and constructiveness. We define each domain, and a table is provided to illustrate the way Hattie and Timperley's (2007) questions—How? Where? and Next?—fit into each domain.

Specificity Domain

Specificity includes the questions, characteristics, and levels related to the student learning goal. The domain of specificity identifies the language that is specific to the task and uses language that clearly states the learning goal and describes where the student must go to achieve the goal. The characteristics of specificity include the language used when delivering feedback, who is receiving the feedback, and the ways the feedback is clearly stated to be accessible. These characteristics are shown in Table 1-1.

TABLE 1-1. CHARACTERISTICS OF SPECIFICITY DOMAIN

QUESTION	Where am I going?	Hattie & Timperley, 2007
LEVEL	Task	Hattie & Timperley, 2007
CHARACTERISTIC	Goal-referenced	Wiggins, 2012
	User-friendly	Wiggins, 2012
	Specific and personalized	Wiggins, 2012
	Tangible and transparent	Wiggins, 2012
	Descriptive, not student personally, not judgmental	Brookhart, 2008
	Positive, clear, and specific	Brookhart, 2008

TABLE 1-2. CHARACTERISTICS OF IMMEDIACY DOMAIN

QUESTION	How am I going?	Hattie & Timperley, 2007
LEVEL	Process	Hattie & Timperley, 2007
CHARACTERISTIC	Timely	Brookhart, 2008
	Ongoing and consistent	Wiggins, 2012

Immediacy Domain

Immediacy relates to the timing of when feedback is delivered. The domain of immediacy encompasses the idea of appropriately timed feedback to have a bigger effect on student goal attainment. Timing is an integral component of effective feedback (Hattie & Clarke, 2019). The characteristics of immediacy include the type of learning required, whether surface or deep, and the process in which the learning is occurring. These characteristics are shown in Table 1-2.

Purposefulness Domain

Purposefulness describes progress-related characteristics, questions, and levels. In this domain, feedback includes all the language and methods describing what is required to keep moving forward along the learning continuum. The characteristics of purposefulness include actionable steps that are broken into achievable pieces that lead students toward the goal they must complete. These characteristics are listed in Table 1-3.

Constructiveness Domain

Constructiveness is the notion that feedback constructs new meaning, progress information, or improvement suggestions for the learner. This idea is closely linked to the meaning that the recipient makes of the feedback and what that meaning produces. The characteristics of constructiveness include the traits of self-monitoring, intrinsic motivation, and individualized progress monitoring to move the student forward in constructing a new learning goal. These characteristics are listed in Table 1-4.

The four domains create a lens for us to think about how we employ the G.E.T. Model in special education teacher preparation as we work with adult learners. Specificity reminds us to support teacher candidates in setting goals, being descriptive in our feedback and using language that is easily understood, positive, and nonjudgmental. Immediacy challenges us to consider the timing of the feedback we give so that it fits the learning goal. For example, most students are highly motivated by their course grades, but grades do not provide the task or progress feedback required for

TABLE 1-3. CHARACTERISTICS OF PURPOSEFULNESS DOMAIN

QUESTION	How am I going?	Hattie & Timperley, 2007
LEVEL	Process	Hattie & Timperley, 2007
CHARACTERISTIC	Actionable	Wiggins, 2012
	Personalized	Wiggins, 2012
	Focus on the process	Brookhart, 2008
	Few points and small steps	Brookhart, 2008

TABLE 1-4. CHARACTERISTICS OF CONSTRUCTIVENESS DOMAIN

QUESTION	Where to next?	Hattie & Timperley, 2007
LEVEL	Self-regulation	Hattie & Timperley, 2007
CHARACTERISTIC	Focus on one or more strength and at least one suggestion for improvement	Brookhart, 2008
	Self-referenced	Brookhart, 2008
	Differentiated	Brookhart, 2008

improvement. Purposefulness requires us to make decisions about why we are giving the feedback. The purposefulness domain forces us to reflect on the characteristics of the feedback we give related to the progress the student is making toward the goal. Purposefulness encourages us to be mindful of a shared understanding of how the student is feeling about the assignment, the course, and their development as a professional. Brookhart (2008) stated, "Whether or not feedback is effective depends on what students need to hear, not what you need to say" (p. 34). Constructiveness provides an opportunity for us as instructors to partner with the adult learner by giving feedback that can be used intrinsically. In developing these domains, we concluded that all learners (regardless of age) benefit from attention to the characteristics and levels of feedback. Providing effective feedback requires the integration of characteristics, levels, and how we communicate our feedback to the student. Therefore, feedback in teacher preparation should be explicitly taught, consistently modeled, and frequently reinforced.

Feedback in Special Education Teacher Preparation

In a comprehensive review of the literature, we found that despite the acknowledged importance of feedback in the K-12 setting, explicitly teaching how to give feedback in special education teacher preparation is woefully lacking. Recognizing this gap and acknowledging that instructors describe giving feedback that fails to transform teacher candidate practice (Scott, 2014), we suggest that the domains we have identified should also consider that our audience for receiving feedback is adults, not K-12 learners. We also suggest that aligning these domains with adult learning theory will evolve the domains to address the learning needs of older students. In addition, this conceptual framework will support how instructors give, exhibit, and teach feedback in special education teacher candidate preparation.

In higher education, the recipients of feedback are teacher candidates. Being an adult, by definition, indicates physical maturity and a more fully developed frontal lobe. One common rite of passage from adolescence to adulthood is post-secondary learning. In special education teacher preparation, combining scholarship on feedback and adult learning theory enables us to better attend to the unique needs of adult learners.

The audience for feedback in higher education is adult learners—people who, by virtue of age, can enlist in the military, drive, marry, produce children, enroll in higher education programs, and enter into debt (Arnett, 2000). Adult learners possess different characteristics than K-12 students. According to Knowles et al. (1998), child learners have dependent personalities, focus on subject-oriented learning, and require extrinsic motivation to learn; for young learners, prior experience is irrelevant to learning. Pedagogy, which Ozuah (2005) described as the "art and science of teaching children" (p. 83), places the importance on teacher-directed learning. On the other hand, adult learners possess intrinsic motivation and are self-directed, problem-oriented, and independent learners (Merriam et al., 2007). Andragogy, "the art and science of helping adults learn" (Knowles, 1980, p. 43), responds to the difference between children and adults as learners. Because the audience for feedback in teacher preparation is adult learners, the feedback that instructors provide should be tailored to adult learners. Therefore, in addition to integrating characteristics and levels of feedback (summarized previously,) feedback should factor in the core principles of adult learning theory to better support the learning outcomes for the recipients—future special educators.

Getting to the G.E.T. Model

The G.E.T. Model represents the three main opportunities that instructors have to embed feedback in courses: **G**iving feedback, **E**xhibiting feedback, and **T**eaching how to deliver feedback. **Giving** feedback requires instructors to deliver any information to a recipient that informs their understanding or restructures their thinking or beliefs related to their performance, knowledge, or skill. **Exhibiting** feedback requires instructors to explicitly model how feedback should be given through sharing the "why and how" of delivering feedback. **Teaching** feedback requires instructors to explicitly teach what feedback looks like and sounds like in the classroom for K-12 learners. Special educators must understand why feedback is an essential element in teaching, and instructors must be strategic in communicating how to use feedback to increase student outcomes.

The G.E.T. Model is informed by positive psychology, coaching, and change theory. Fundamentally, it comes from the curiosity we had as teachers regarding why the feedback behaviors that made us successful in the K-12 setting did not produce the same results when we started teaching in higher education. The scholars who studied these effective feedback behaviors have given us direction for the questions, levels, and characteristics of feedback. We quickly discovered that each child is different, and effort and intentional behaviors are required to provide feedback to children that will produce the desired results. As special education teachers, we created motivating, experiential learning opportunities that were highly successful in the classroom. We gave feedback to students that was task-orientated, timely, and specific before we even had the language for what we were doing. We were able to provide the feedback without judgment by focusing on student learning and revising for mastery. No one taught us that we should say more than "good job" when giving feedback—we just knew it. Then…we started working with adults. We discovered that the strategies we were using effectively for K-12 students were not working with the adults we were teaching in special education teacher preparation, and we wanted to know why. We set out to discover why the characteristics of feedback we had used successfully in the K-12 setting were not working with the adult learners in special education teacher preparation.

ADULT LEARNING THEORY

Andragogy, the art and science of helping adults learn, provides guidance for designing learner-centered instruction. Knowles et al. (2015) stated, "Our position is that andragogy presents core principles of adult learning that in turn enable those designing and conducting adult learning to build more effective learning processes for adults" (p. 2). Feedback for adult learners, by necessity, requires us to examine our feedback within the context of these core principles. Adult learning theory (Knowles et al., 1998) indicated the following six core principles:

1. Learner's need to know (the "what, why, and how")
2. Self-concept of the learner (autonomous and self-directing)
3. Prior experience of the learner (resources and mental models)
4. Readiness to learn (life-related, developmental task)
5. Orientation to learning (problem-centered, contextual)
6. Motivation to learn (intrinsic value, personal payoff)

We suggest that embedding the domains of feedback within these core principles of andragogy will enable those designing courses in special education teacher preparation to build competency and capacity for giving, exhibiting, and teaching feedback (GET).

Applying Knowles' (1998) adult learning principles to a real-life situation illustrates how each principle impacts the feedback we give teacher candidates. Dr. Elford reflects on the following important lesson from a student's unsolicited feedback during the first semester she taught an online course:

> Each week, teacher candidates were required to build on their assignments, based on the feedback they received. I had one student who was not making any adjustments, based on the feedback I gave. I had even conferenced with this student, asking specific questions about the feedback I had written in the online platform where assignments were posted. Success in the course depended on the teacher candidates' effective use of the feedback they had received on assignments. Finally, in the final week, I received a frantic phone call from this student who realized she would fail the class. I agreed to meet with her, using an online video platform that allowed me to see her face and for her to see mine. At the time, there was no screen-sharing available on the online platform I was using for video conferencing. I had downloaded all her assignments, which included the feedback notations I had made, and I asked her to do the same, so I was sure we were looking at the same documents. I asked her to open the first document and look at the feedback. I could see her face squinting at the computer screen when I asked her if she could see the feedback I had written in a particular section. She said, 'I see some highlighted words and some dots leading to the margin.' I told her to look just beyond the margin to the comments. Her face squinted even more. I said, 'Do you have the review feature on? What software are you using?' She said, 'I have a PC. Is that okay?' This unsolicited feedback I received from the student came in the form of the look of shock she could not hide. This scenario of a student who was not understanding where or why I gave feedback demonstrated that all the feedback I had given was useless. I had not taken into consideration Knowles' et al. (1998) third principle—**prior experience of the learner** (resources and mental models)—because it was clear to me that the student had no experience with the technology of the Microsoft Word track changes function, which allows a reader to offer written comments in the margins of a document. So, I backed up and walked her through how to turn on the review feature in Microsoft Word. When she saw the comments appear on the side of the document, it was an unprecedented "light-bulb" moment for me as a teacher. The look of shock on her face told me everything I needed to know. This student had not incorporated my feedback because she had not received it but not because I had not given it. Although the student **needed to know** how to improve her assignments (principle one), was **motivated** (principle six) to learn, and **ready** to hear my feedback (principle four), she had never seen the feedback. My feedback was ineffective because I had not crafted it based on her prior experience, her orientation to learning (principle five), and her **self-concept as a learner** (principle two). This scenario explicitly demonstrates how feedback must intersect with adult learning theory for transformative learning to occur.

Trying to explain the intersection of feedback and adult learning theory is a little like looking at the transparent overlay of the human body in a biology textbook. Adult learning theory (Knowles, 1984) can be compared to the skeleton—it defines the bones of adult learning, which are different from the bones of children's learning and must be treated differently.

Feedback should lead to change. Prochaska and DiClemente's (1992) stages of change are the circulatory system; it reminds us that change is an ongoing process, much like the way blood is needed for the exchange of oxygen in all the cells. Feedback is essential in producing results toward a desired change. In Prochaska and DiClemente's stages of change, adults are precontemplative, then contemplative, preparing to change, actually making the change, and maintaining the behavioral change or relapsing into old behaviors. This ongoing process is not linear, and oftentimes adults regress and revert to the first stage, even after taking action from the feedback that was given.

Mezirow's (1997) transformational learning theory and Bandura's (1977) social learning theory are the muscles in this overlay. Movement can occur only when the skeleton, circulation, and respiration work in concert with the muscles. Hence, transformational learning theory and social learning theory provide the strength to move and make changes based on the feedback. Mezirow's transformational learning theory posited that adults' assumptions must be disrupted for new learning to occur. Mezirow's theory explained more fully the way andragogy occurs in practice. Bandura's social learning suggested that adults learn from observing others' behaviors and that modeling provides opportunities to learn from watching others before we practice a new skill ourselves. Bandura reminded us that learning does not happen in a vacuum. The feedback we get from others influences the identity we assume and the behaviors we adopt based on that identity (Drake, 2007).

Finally, to continue the textbook overlay metaphor, the skin in the picture is described by Csikszentmihalyi (1975) as "flow" of the optimal experience. In the G.E.T. Model, this skin example illustrates how the four domains hold together the principles of adult learning theory, the components of effective feedback, and the other elements that contribute to the transformation that occurs when feedback is delivered with the recipient in mind. Csikszentmihalyi's contribution to the development of positive psychology, "the study of conditions and processes that contribute to flourishing or optimal functioning of people, groups, and institutions" (Gable & Haidt, 2005, p. 103), influenced the shift from interventions that focused on problems to the solutions-focused interventions. Positive psychology seeks to improve what already exists and extends support by cultivating inner strength. Feedback, by its very nature, tells us where we are in relation to optimal functioning and to our inner strength scale.

The textbook overlay metaphor is one way to think about the intersection of adult learning theory and feedback. More importantly, we want to describe how to create a context for the ways these different theories contribute to the complexity of delivering feedback to adults. We want to shift the context and focus of delivering feedback to children to delivering feedback to adult learners, based on what we know about andragogy, the theories that have informed it, and the practices that andragogy has influenced (Figure 1-1).

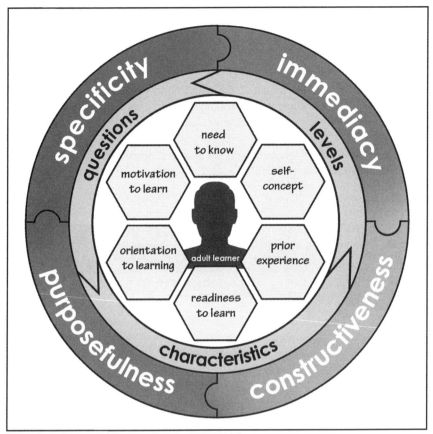

Figure 1-1. Conceptual framework of the G.E.T. Model.

Adult Learning Theory Intersection With Feedback Domains

To make explicit the intersection between the core principles of andragogy and the four domains of feedback, we must examine the direct relationship of each principle to the various domains. Although all feedback domains are beneficial in satisfying each of the adult learning principles, certain domains are more meaningful for certain principles. In the subsequent paragraphs, we describe the adult learning principle and the feedback domain that are most tightly coupled. Next, we provide a table that illustrates this intersection and connects each domain to the adult learning principle in that section. In addition, we connect the questions, levels, and characteristics to each of the feedback domains. Finally, we provide a summary statement that supports our rationale for the coupling of the stated principle and the specific feedback domain.

Learner's Need to Know (The What, Why, and How)

The first adult learning theory we will intersect with feedback is the learners' need to know and immediacy. Adult learners need to know what they are supposed to learn, why it is important to learn something new, and how that learning will occur. Feedback that meets this need should contain characteristics from each of the domains, the most important of which is immediacy. Feedback to adult learners loses its effectiveness if it comes too late to support the adult learners' "what, why, and how" of this adult learning principle. Table 1-5 illustrates how immediacy intersects with the learners' needs to know.

As one can see, immediacy intersects with the learners' need to know by providing feedback at the appropriate time, based on the learning goal. The timing of the feedback is critical to make it worthwhile to the learner.

TABLE 1-5. ADULT LEARNING PRINCIPLE INTERSECTION WITH IMMEDIACY DOMAIN			
SPECIFICITY	**IMMEDIACY**	**PURPOSEFULNESS**	**CONSTRUCTIVENESS**
Feedback only has value because it meets a personal goal. Adult learners need to be invested in the learning. How will the feedback support the learning goals of the adult learner?	For adult learners especially, feedback will not be effective unless it is something they want to learn right then. Is the timing of the feedback appropriate for the learning goal?	Purpose and expectation of feedback must be shared and clear. Why is this important? Is it important to adult learners?	Feedback constructs new meaning, progress information, or improvement suggestions for the learner. How will adult learners make meaning of the feedback? What self-regulation will it produce?
Question: How am I going?			
Level: Process			
Characteristics: Timely; ongoing and consistent			

Self-Concept of the Learner (Autonomous and Self-Directing)

The second adult learning principle is the self-concept of the learner that intersects with the constructiveness domain of feedback. One of the objectives in special education teacher preparation is to build capacity in our teacher candidates to continuously improve as professionals. To meet this objective, the feedback we provide should include deeper levels and include respect for the identity of the learner as a professional. The key domain for this adult learning principle is constructiveness. Table 1-6 illustrates how constructiveness intersects with the learners' self-concept.

Constructiveness intersects with the self-concept of the learner by providing feedback that honors the autonomy and individuality of the adult learner.

TABLE 1-6. ADULT LEARNING PRINCIPLE INTERSECTION WITH CONSTRUCTIVENESS DOMAIN

SPECIFICITY	IMMEDIACY	PURPOSEFULNESS	CONSTRUCTIVENESS
Is the feedback language goal-referenced, tangible and transparent, positive as well as corrective, and leading to improvement? Can it be delivered in a way that promotes autonomy? Does the use of questions as feedback give the adult learner the confidence to know they can do it?	Does the timing of the feedback meet the needs of the adult learner? Does the adult learner prefer to wrestle with the problem, or does the adult learner need frequent support in knowing that they are on the right track?	Does the feedback consider the adult learner's values? Does the adult learner believe in continual improvement? How comfortable is the adult learner with the messiness of the process?	How does the feedback consider what is the responsibility of the adult learner in the next step? In what way(s) is the feedback differentiated?
Question: Where to next?			
Level: Self-regulation			
Characteristics: Focus on one or more strength and at least one suggestion for improvement; self-referenced; differentiated			

Prior Experience of the Learner (Resources and Mental Models)

The third principle of adult learning—prior experience of the learner—intersects with the domain of purposefulness. You will recall from the story about the teacher candidate that prior experience of the adult learner is critical when giving feedback. Unlike middle school students, who may not respond to feedback for two basic reasons—because they cannot or because they will not—adult learners must have some prior experience or mental model on which to connect the feedback for it to become meaningful. As we contemplate the feedback, we must consider what the learners know and do not know. The key domain for this adult learning principle is purposefulness. Table 1-7 illustrates how purposefulness intersects with the learners' self-concept.

The intersection of the prior experience of the learner and purposefulness requires feedback that specifically identifies the actionable steps that focus on the progress the individual adult learner is making toward the goal.

TABLE 1-7. INTERSECTION OF LEARNERS' SELF-CONCEPT WITH PUROSEFULNESS DOMAIN			
SPECIFICITY	**IMMEDIACY**	**PURPOSEFULNESS**	**CONSTRUCTIVENESS**
Does the feedback describe the actionable steps? Is it focused on the process, and does it include a few main points?	How frequently does the adult learner need feedback to keep making progress?	Where is the adult learner on the learning continuum? What actionable steps are required to move forward? How much scaffolding is needed to lead the adult learner toward the desired goal?	Is the feedback specific to the adult learner? Does it include references that are individualized?
Question: Where to next?			
Level: Self-regulation			
Characteristics: Strength-focused, with one suggestion for improvement; self-referenced; differentiated			

Readiness to Learn (Life-Related and Developmental Task)

The fourth principle of adult learning—readiness to learn—also intersects with constructiveness. Maturing adults have acquired a host of knowledge and experience, often called *frame of reference*. This defines their world according to associations, beliefs, feelings, conditioned responses, and social context. Adults are more ready to learn when the developmental task is oriented to their role in society. Feedback for adult learners should consider their identity, assumptions, and social role. The key domain for this adult learning principle is constructiveness. Table 1-8 illustrates how constructiveness intersects with learners' readiness to learn.

Feedback that is necessary for the intersection of readiness to learn and constructiveness attends to the adult learner's professional learning goals in the context of their current identity. Constructiveness feedback for readiness to learn appropriately addresses the progress the adult learner makes by connecting it to what they already know and have experienced.

TABLE 1-8. INTERSECTION OF READINESS TO LEARN WITH CONSTRUCTIVENESS DOMAIN

SPECIFICITY	IMMEDIACY	PURPOSEFULNESS	CONSTRUCTIVENESS
Is the feedback differentiated to meet the individual identity, societal role, and cultural perspective of the adult learner?	Is the timing of the feedback appropriate for the learning outcomes? Should feedback be delayed while the adult learner makes sense of the learning experience?	Is the feedback contextualized for the identity of the adult learner? Does the feedback consider prior knowledge and professional experience?	Does the feedback connect to prior learning and is it meaningful to the adult learner's current professional improvement? Is it self-referenced and differentiated?
Question: Where to next?			
Level: Self-regulation			
Characteristics: Strength-focused, with improvement mentioned; self-referenced; differentiated			

Orientation to Learning (Problem-Centered and Contextual)

Most adults prefer to learn things they can apply immediately and are less interested in new knowledge or tasks that they may use at a later time. If teachers want to learn something they can use immediately, we can assume that the feedback needs to be as immediate as possible. The key domain for this adult learning principle is immediacy. Table 1-9 illustrates how immediacy intersects with adult learners' orientation to learning.

SPECIFICITY	IMMEDIACY	PURPOSEFULNESS	CONSTRUCTIVENESS
Is the feedback specific to what the adult learner needs to know, understand, and be able to do in their current role or with the desired learning outcome?	Feedback fits the specific outcome that is most pressing. Feedback provides information that can be used immediately.	Feedback connects the adult learner's current stage to progress that is being made toward the goal.	Does the feedback serve to motivate the adult learner to continue making progress?

TABLE 1-9. INTERSECTION OF ORIENTATION TO LEARNING WITH IMMEDIACY DOMAIN

Question: How am I going?

Level: Process

Characteristics: Timely; ongoing and consistent

Motivation to Learn (Intrinsic Value and Personal Payoff)

Mezirow (1997) suggested that we must recognize the adult learner's objectives and goals. For adults, motivation is internal, even when they are being awarded a grade in a program or course. The feedback that addresses this principle of adult learning theory should be differentiated and inform self-regulation. The key domain for this adult learning principle is constructiveness. Table 1-10 illustrates how constructiveness intersects with adult learners' motivation to learn.

TABLE 1-10. INTERSECTION OF MOTIVATION TO LEARN WITH CONSTRUCTIVENESS DOMAIN

SPECIFICITY	IMMEDIACY	PURPOSEFULNESS	CONSTRUCTIVENESS
Does the feedback specifically describe the connection to the adult learner's goals? Is it positive and focused on the next steps to keep the adult learner moving forward?	Is the feedback well timed so it can be absorbed by the adult learner for future improvement?	Is this feedback tailored to the adult learner's motivation? Does the feedback match more than an external outcome? Is the feedback emotionally compelling and specific to the individual's locus of control?	Does the feedback reinforce a partnership between the one person giving the feedback and the one person receiving it? Can the feedback be used to empower the adult learner to create their own process for improvement?

Question: Where to next?

Level: Self-regulation

Characteristics: Focus on one or more strength and at least one suggestion for improvement; self-referenced; differentiated

SUMMARY

Our research and practice identified the need for a framework that connects feedback and adult learning theory to provide guidance in integrating feedback into the preparation of special education teacher candidates. Specifically, we want the feedback we give as instructors of future educators to help in their development and learning as well as to improve their practice in giving, exhibiting, and teaching feedback to peers and to K-12 students. As instructors, we cannot just teach or model feedback; we must integrate it throughout a course or program, clearly explaining the purpose and expectations. For example, a teacher candidate should be expected to incorporate feedback from the instructor at every stage of their project assignments. This book provides teacher educators with an approach to their andragogy that gives attention to the topic and the learner. By integrating adult learning theory and the questions, levels, and characteristics of feedback, we have a framework that allows us to infuse feedback into every aspect of special education teacher preparation. Constructing domains in which to house the questions, levels, and characteristics of feedback make the complexity of effective feedback more manageable. Placing the adult learner at the center of the feedback creates a partnership between the person giving and the person receiving the feedback, so that it meets the needs of the student and truly benefits both the teacher candidate and the instructor. Special education teacher preparation will improve if we attend to the effectiveness of feedback as it supports the continuous development of adult learners.

REFERENCES

Arnett, J. J. (2000). Emerging adulthood. A theory of development from the late teens through the twenties. *The American Psychologist, 55*(5), 469-480.

Bandura, A. (1977). *Social learning theory*. Prentice Hall.

Brookhart, S. M. (2008). Feedback that fits. *Educational Leadership, 65*(4), 54-59.

Brookhart, S. M. (2012). Preventing feedback fizzle. *Educational Leadership, 70*(1), 24-29.

Brookhart, S. M., & Moss, C. M. (2015). How to give professional feedback. *Educational Leadership, 72*(7), 24-30.

Cohen, J. (1992). A power primer. *Psychological Bulletin, 112*(1), 155-159.

Csikszentmihalyi, M. (1975). *Beyond boredom and anxiety: Experiencing flow in work and play*. Jossey-Bass.

Drake, D. B. (2007). The art of thinking narratively: Implications for coaching psychology and practice. *Australian Psychologist, 42*(3), 283-294.

Gable, S. L., & Haidt, J. (2005). What (and why) is positive psychology? *Review of General Psychology, 9*(2), 103-110.

Hattie, J. (1999, August 2). *Influences on student learning. Inaugural Lecture: Professor of Education.* https://dokumen.tips/documents/john-hattie-influences-on-student-learning.html

Hattie, J. (2012a). Know thy impact. *Educational Leadership, 70*(1), 18-23.

Hattie, J. (2012b). V*isible learning for teachers: Maximizing impact on learning*. Routledge.

Hattie, J., & Clarke, S. (2019). *Visible learning: Feedback*. Routledge.

Hattie, J., & Timperley, H. (2007). The power of feedback. *Review of Educational Research, 77*(1), 81-112. https://doi.org/10.3102/003465430298487

Knowles, M. (1984). *The adult learner: A neglected species* (3rd ed.). Gulf Publishing.

Knowles, M. S. (1970). *The modern practice of adult education: Andragogy versus pedagogy*. Association Press.

Knowles, M. S. (1978). Andragogy: Adult learning theory in perspective. *Community College Review, 5*(3), 9-20.

Knowles, M.S., Holton III, E. F., & Swanson, R. A. (1998). *The adult learner* (5th ed.). Gulf.

Knowles, M. S., Holton III, E. F., & Swanson, R. A. (2015). *The adult learner: The definitive classic in adult education and human resource development* (8th ed.). Routledge.

Merriam, S. B., Caffarella, R. S., & Baumgartner, L. M. (2007). *Learning in adulthood: A comprehensive guide*. John Wiley & Sons.

Mezirow, J. (1997). Transformative learning: Theory to practice. *New Directions for Adult & Continuing Education, 74*, 5-12. https://doi.org/10.1002/ace.7401

Ozuah, P. O. (2005). First, there was pedagogy and then came andragogy. *Einstein Journal of Biology and Medicine, 21*(2), 83-87.

Prochaska, J. O., & DiClemente, C. C. (1992). Stages of change in the modification of problem behaviors. *Progress in Behavior Modification, 28*, 183-218.

Scott, S. V. (2014). Practising what we preach: Towards a student-centred definition of feedback. *Teaching in Higher Education, 9*(1), 49-57.

Wiggins, G. (2012). Seven keys to effective feedback. *Educational Leadership, 70*(1), 10-16.

Wiliam, D. (2012). Feedback: Part of a system. *Educational Leadership, 70*(1), 30-34.

Wiliam, D. (2016). The secret of effective feedback. *Educational Leadership, 73*(7), 10-15.

Book and Chapter Organization

There are many ways to engage with the content of this book and weave feedback into course content and objectives by using the G.E.T. Model. You might choose to begin by targeting a specific section or chapter. Although the book follows a linear design and can be read from beginning to end, we recognize that some readers might jump to the model and practical application. The brief summaries in this chapter provide an overview at the section and chapter levels so they can be read in isolation. The format of each chapter is also included. Beginning with Chapter 3, there is a predictable order to the content.

The primary audience is special education teacher preparation instructors, which includes clinical faculty, graduate faculty, adjunct faculty, field supervisors, mentor teachers, and all the others who support preservice educator learning, growth, and development. However, we feel the content and activities are applicable to courses in other disciplines as well, especially to related professional programs with clinical practice. Instructional coaches may find these helpful for work in educational settings, as could K-12 administrators who provide feedback to teachers pertaining to their professional performance.

CHAPTER ORGANIZATION

Chapter 1 provided a detailed explanation of the intersection of adult learning theory and special education teacher preparation as well as introduced the G.E.T. Model for how instructors can comprehensively address feedback in their courses. Beginning with Section II, each chapter explores the concepts and practical applications of the G.E.T. Model. Chapters 3 through 12 aim to go deeper in explaining the important concepts, research, and integration of support for giving, exhibiting, and teaching feedback. The format for these chapters is described in the paragraphs that follow.

Elford, M. D., Smith, H. H., & James, S.
*GET Feedback: Giving, Exhibiting, and Teaching Feedback in
Special Education Teacher Preparation* (pp. 21-28).
© 2022 SLACK Incorporated.

TABLE 2-1. GRAPHIC ORGANIZER		
KNOW (WHAT)	**UNDERSTAND (WHY)**	**DEMONSTRATE (HOW)**
APPLY (TAKE ACTION)		

Feedback Scenario

Every chapter begins with a scenario. This section of the chapter provides at least one example of the feedback concept. These scenarios, or vignettes, are authentic. They are included in anticipation that readers can relate to the presented example. The examples are derived from special education teacher preparation experiences and reflect the unique needs of special education preservice teachers.

Chapter Objectives

The objectives section of each chapter provides a roadmap of the skills and new knowledge for the chapter and ends with a practical application and steps to take action. The G.E.T. Model reflects a backward design, starting with the end in mind. As such, each chapter has developed objectives for the chapter that answer the questions of "what, why, and how" and outlines how readers can take action and apply the concept. Each chapter contains a graphic organizer table (Table 2-1).

Describe and Define

The third (and longest) section of each chapter provides a description and key definitions, some of which are in **boldface** in the text and defined in the glossary. It often contains findings from literature reviews and connections to the theoretical basis and concepts that are useful in dissecting the scenario. The strengths and merits of the concepts are the focus.

Spotlight on Adult Learning

We return to adult learning theory in each chapter. As the G.E.T. Model focuses on the intersection of feedback and adult learning theory, we want to make explicit the research-based connections between these fields. This spotlight provides a pause to reflect on the connections. Each domain of the G.E.T. Model is addressed, and questions are posed for the reader to reflect on the chapter content in each specific domain. In the Spotlight section of every chapter, readers will see a visual display similar to Table 2-2.

TABLE 2-2. SPOTLIGHT ON ADULT LEARNING			
SPECIFICITY	**IMMEDIACY**	**PURPOSEFULNESS**	**CONSTRUCTIVENESS**
Question(s)?	Question(s)?	Question(s)?	Question(s)?

Possible Barriers to Using This Type of Feedback

To balance the focus on the strengths and merits of concepts related to giving, exhibiting, and teaching feedback, we must also recognize the possible barriers to using or implementing the type of feedback. In this section of each chapter, we name and describe possible drawbacks and problems to consider or avoid.

Practical Application

The practical application section of each chapter aims to describe how instructors are integrating feedback. The stories and descriptions shared build on the opening scenarios to aid the reader in seeing multiple opportunities for practical application. They sometimes guide the reader in purposeful reflection, visioning, or planning. The goal is to explain how to do it, providing explicit connections to the characteristics, types, and levels of feedback.

Authentic Example

This section of the chapter offers an elaborated, authentic example of course design, activities, and/or assignments that reflect the chapter focus. We sought contributions from diverse special education programs from public and private universities of varying sizes. These authentic course activities reflect diversity in geographical location, coursework content, and foci on initial licensure and graduate coursework. These contributions are provided to give instructors examples of how others are integrating instruction on giving, exhibiting, and/or teaching feedback. Readers will hear, in our contributors' voices, how this example is part of their feedback. The strength of these examples is how they show variations in characteristics, types, and levels. Context is important, and the contributors each provide a short explanation at the beginning of their example. When possible, we have included the actual documents, rubrics, and resources.

Summary

Each chapter ends with a summary. We include the summary as an opportunity for review and a check for understanding. It can provide feedback to readers on whether they are mastering the content. It might also be used for previewing chapter content and ideas, beginning with the end in mind. Regardless of how the reader uses this section, we hope they will find it helpful.

Opportunity for Going Deeper

If you are like us, sometimes you find yourself wanting to know more about a topic. We included this section to wrap up each chapter so that if you are curious or want to know more about a specific topic or similar topics when you finish reading it, you will have some idea of where to look for additional information. This brief section will provide resources or websites to explore.

Overview by Section

This book is organized into five sections to guide feedback with adult learners.
1. Section I: The G.E.T. Model
2. Section II: Giving Feedback
3. Section III: Exhibiting Feedback
4. Section IV: Teaching Feedback
5. Section V: Resources

Section I

Section I includes Chapters 1 and 2. Section I provides the necessary prior knowledge on feedback and its intersection with adult learning theory—the foundation of the G.E.T. Model. Section I is essential reading in preparation for the reflection and practice in future chapters on the G.E.T. Model. Chapter 1 walks readers through the concepts and theories from which the G.E.T. Model is drawn.

Section II

Section II contains three chapters that focus on how instructors give feedback, specifically in special education teacher preparation. These chapters introduce readers to the recipient of the feedback. With this adult learner-centered view, we examine immediate versus delayed feedback as an important overarching consideration and describe giving feedback, including authentic examples and practical reflection.

Section III

Section III contains two chapters on how instructors exhibit feedback and the effect this feedback has on deeper levels of content acquisition by teacher candidates. In this section, we target deeper learning of the characteristics, levels, and domains of feedback. The narrative serves as a guide for instructors to reflect on where feedback opportunities currently exist in their courses, as well as explores and plans for deepening focus and building on the characteristics of feedback.

Section IV

Section IV includes five chapters on teaching feedback. Each provides description and multiple authentic examples from special education teacher preparation instructors related to course content, activities, and assessment. The introductory chapter addresses the rationale for teaching feedback. The subsequent chapters address teaching feedback in instruction, assessment, support of K-12 students' behavioral needs, and in collaboration.

Section V

Section V presents two chapters of helpful resources in understanding and applying the G.E.T. Model. One chapter covers the findings of a comprehensive review of the literature on feedback in special education teacher preparation that provided a foundation for this work and the G.E.T. Model. The other chapter includes several exemplary authentic special education course assignments and templates for reviewing and reflecting on the G.E.T. Model.

OVERVIEW BY CHAPTER

The G.E.T. Model heavily relies on setting clear goals and objectives. Thus, each chapter covering the aspects of the G.E.T. Model was created to address the "what, why, and how" of feedback and its application. Each content chapter (Chapters 3 through 12) begins with a vignette from special education teacher preparation. These scenarios are included to illustrate the impact of considering feedback and/or opportunities for instructor reflection and growth in feedback. After the scenario is presented, each chapter takes a deep dive into the related research, background knowledge, and/or connections to foundational concepts in the G.E.T. Model. There we describe and define the strengths and merits of the type of feedback covered in the chapter, followed by the recognition of possible barriers to using or implementing the type of feedback. The chapter then shifts to providing examples, ideas, and resources for practical application, followed by authentic examples of course design, activities, and/or assignments from special education teacher preparation. Each chapter ends with a summary and guidance on where the reader can discover more information on the topic.

Chapter 3: Audiences/Recipients of Feedback

This chapter introduces the central focus of the G.E.T. Model and discussions of feedback in special education teacher preparation—the future educator, the recipient of the feedback. Where are they in their learning? What do they need? How ready are they for feedback? What are they expecting? This chapter introduces the idea of giving feedback that should be centered on the learner and explores why it is important to take into account what an instructor knows about the learner. This chapter will describe and provide practical examples of recognizing the learner; their readiness, motivation, and prior knowledge when designing courses; assessment; and activities of taking action.

Chapter 4: Immediate Versus Delayed Feedback

This chapter continues to consider the recipients of feedback and addresses an essential question in giving feedback: Do I give it now or later? The answer is…YES! As we will discuss, in special education teacher preparation, there is the need to **give** immediate (now) feedback as well as delayed (later) feedback. This chapter will describe the research on immediate and delayed feedback approaches and why there is utility in including both in your course. This chapter will also demonstrate how to select the appropriate feedback approach, providing examples and prompts to take action.

Chapter 5: How We Give Feedback

This chapter continues our focus on giving feedback. It considers the myriad of ways in which we can give feedback to preservice teachers, including the use of technology. The chapter will describe the research on the many tools and common practices for giving feedback and will examine why teacher educators should consider emerging tools and practices. The chapter will also demonstrate how to give feedback, using tools and practices that align with your instruction and assessment, with examples and prompts to apply your new learning. This chapter wraps up Section II and focuses on giving feedback.

Chapter 6: Exhibiting Feedback and the Four Domains of the G.E.T. Model

This chapter begins Section III and our exploration of how special education teacher preparation instructors can **exhibit** feedback, or the **E** in our G.E.T. Model. To do this, we build on Sections I and II by describing the characteristics of feedback. We first synthesize themes in the feedback literature, exploring the characteristics, levels, and domains of feedback. Second, we consider these themes and their intersections with adult learning theory. This chapter describes research on the characteristics of feedback, the need for knowledge of the characteristics, and why making evident the characteristics of feedback in a course can enhance preservice teacher understanding and practice of feedback. This chapter demonstrates how to reflect on the characteristics of feedback and provides examples and prompts to evaluate opportunities for improvement in exhibiting feedback in courses.

Chapter 7: Exhibiting Feedback: Reflecting and Planning

This chapter continues our exploration of how special education teacher preparation instructors and other education professionals can reflect and plan to exhibit and model feedback. To achieve the transformational understanding of the importance and impact of feedback, feedback must be integrated across a course. This includes a deep and purposeful connection to course goals and objectives as well as reflection on when and how feedback is used. It goes beyond how we give feedback, considering the recipient, the timing of the feedback, and the tools and common practices. This chapter will connect the research on characteristics of feedback from Chapter 6 and offer opportunities and tools for exhibiting feedback in special education and related courses. This chapter will provide opportunities to reflect on the characteristics of feedback currently in use in your teaching as well as provide examples and prompts to consider in creating or revising a course.

Chapter 8: Rationale for Teaching Feedback

This chapter continues to center the recipients of feedback and provides the rationale for teaching feedback. The characteristics of feedback outlined in the document *High-Leverage Practices in Special Education* (McLeskey et al., 2017), feedback assessed in Teacher Performance Assessment (edTPA; Stanford Center for Assessment, Learning and Equity [SCALE], 2017), and the Candidate Preservice Assessment of Student Teaching (Kaplan et al., 2017) are difficult to align to what Hattie and others have defined. This section provides guidance in considering the alignment in the context of your courses or program.

Chapter 9: Teaching Feedback in Instruction

This chapter builds on the rationale for how we **teach** feedback in special education teacher preparation and examines the knowledge and instructional skills we want teacher candidates to display. For special education teacher candidates to develop their knowledge of what good feedback is and to use feedback in their instruction, it must be explicitly taught, consistently modeled, and routinely reinforced.

Chapter 10: Teaching Feedback in Assessment

This chapter builds on considering the knowledge and instructional skills of feedback in special education teacher preparation and addresses teaching feedback as a part of their assessment. As we will discuss, in special education teacher preparation, there is the need to teach clear connections to how assessment uses feedback to move K-12 students with disabilities to higher levels of goal attainment. This chapter will describe the research on assessment feedback approaches and why feedback in assessment is crucial. This chapter will also demonstrate how to provide feedback on assessments, with examples and prompts to take action.

Chapter 11: Teaching Feedback to Support Students' Behavioral Needs

This chapter builds on assessment feedback and addresses feedback in social, emotional, and behavioral contexts in special education. In special education, instructors should **teach** how to give feedback in social, emotional, and behavioral contexts. This chapter will describe the research on social, emotional, and behavioral feedback approaches and why these types of feedback increase student motivation, engagement, and independence, leading to improved student learning and behavior. This chapter will also demonstrate how to select social, emotional, and behavioral feedback approaches, with examples and prompts to take action.

Chapter 12: Teaching Feedback in Collaboration

This chapter continues to consider feedback in collaboration by addressing collaborations with parents, related service providers, general education teachers, and administrators. Special education teacher preparation should **teach** feedback on how to consider multiple perspectives, promote active listening, as well as to give and solicit feedback that demonstrates collaboration standards. This chapter will describe the research on feedback in collaboration approaches and the utility of teaching how to give and receive feedback in a collaborative relationship in courses. This chapter will also demonstrate how to select collaborative feedback approaches, with examples and prompts to take action.

Chapter 13: Comprehensive Review of the Literature on Feedback in Special Education Teacher Preparation

This chapter is included to provide the foundational comprehensive review of the literature completed. The results of the comprehensive review of the literature provided us with evidence of how feedback had been researched across special education teacher preparation programs and established the need for development of the G.E.T. Model. With the growing emphasis on the ability to give and receive feedback (e.g., performance-based assessments, virtual teaching simulation, high-leverage practices), this chapter suggests pathways to continue to research feedback with adult learners in special education teacher preparation.

Chapter 14: Templates and Additional Opportunities to Apply the G.E.T. Model

This chapter is included to provide additional practical application and reflection on the G.E.T. Model using authentic examples from contributors across the country. In addition to these authentic examples, we also provide templates you can use to review and reflect on one of your own activities or assignments.

FINAL THOUGHTS ON BOOK AND CHAPTER ORGANIZATION

The initial and final chapters of the book follow a unique format to facilitate the introduction and summary of what is learned and how this framework can apply to feedback in special education teacher preparation programmatic planning. Readers will find numerous visuals in these chapters and the opportunity to connect ideas. These chapters serve as bookends, introducing and then reviewing key ideas. The chapters aim to aid the readers in organizing this new information on feedback and prompt them to connect the information to knowledge and experiences they may already have. We recognize that we cannot just tell you what you need to know, but rather you must construct your knowledge through these activities and take the opportunity to practice and apply, much like we believe your practice of exhibiting feedback will provide opportunities for learning, practice, and application for preservice special educators.

REFERENCES

Kaplan, C. S., Brownstein, E. M., & Graham-Day, K. J. (2017). One for all and all for one: Multi-university collaboration to meet accreditation requirements. *SAGE Open, 7*(1). https://doi.org/10.1177/2158244016687610

McLeskey, J., Barringer, M-D., Billingsley, B., Brownell, M., Jackson, D., Kennedy, M., Lewis, T., Maheady, L., Rodriguez, J., Scheeler, M. C., Winn, J., & Ziegler, D. (2017). *High-leverage practices in special education.* Council for Exceptional Children & CEEDAR Center.

Stanford Center for Assessment, Learning and Equity (SCALE). (2017). *Educative assessment and meaningful support: 2016 edTPA Administrative report.*

Giving Feedback

Figure II-1. The G.E.T. Model—giving feedback.

Giving feedback (Figure II-1) requires instructors to deliver any information to a recipient that informs their understanding or restructures their thinking or their beliefs related to their performance, knowledge, or skill. Section II contains three chapters focusing on how instructors give feedback, specifically in special education teacher preparation. These chapters introduce you to the audiences and recipients of the feedback. The audience and recipients must be central to planning and giving feedback. Audiences and recipients who are not ready or interested in feedback will likely not benefit from an instructor's feedback. This section aids in considering how we should be mindful of the adult learner and reflect on how to prepare audiences and recipients to receive the feedback we give. With this adult learner-centered view, we also examine immediate versus delayed feedback as an important overarching consideration and describe giving feedback, including authentic examples and practical reflection.

3

Audiences/Recipients of Feedback

FEEDBACK SCENARIO

Dr. Martin is a new faculty member in the department of special education in a small liberal arts college. Her chair has asked her to teach an online Characteristics of Disabilities course as part of the college's plan to provide an online master's program in special education. Dr. Martin felt confident about teaching the course online because she has taught the material in a face-to-face classroom for 3 years. At the end of the semester, Dr. Martin got feedback from her teacher candidates in the form of a course evaluation. The teacher candidates in the class commented that Dr. Martin "tried too many different things" and that the course was confusing in its organization. Many of the teacher candidates felt that the online discussions assigned were just "busy work" because Dr. Martin gave completion points only instead of responding in the threads. The students also commented that the grade on their assignments did not give them a clear picture of what they did poorly and what they did that demonstrated mastery. This feedback to Dr. Martin was harsh for her read—if only her teacher candidates had given her feedback about their frustrations earlier! Dr. Martin was giving feedback to her adult learners but not receiving feedback from them when it would have been useful to her. Unfortunately, Dr. Martin realized too late that the feedback she was giving was not tailored to the recipient because the feedback from her adult learners came too late.

This scenario is one example demonstrating that feedback has many different audiences. It is not solely the job of the expert to give feedback to novices. Getting feedback from the novice informs the expert about what can be improved. Bransford et al. (2000) indicated that feedback should not be unidimensional and that learners should understand when, where, and why to use new knowledge. We have long recognized that feedback is important for successful learning to occur (Thorndike, 1913). However, knowing how to use the new knowledge gained from feedback depends on the audience to whom the feedback was provided. What are the audiences for feedback in education? Audiences for feedback can include K-12 students, college-aged adult learners, and teachers. All

Elford, M. D., Smith, H. H., & James, S.
GET Feedback: Giving, Exhibiting, and Teaching Feedback in
Special Education Teacher Preparation (pp. 31-56).
© 2022 SLACK Incorporated.

teachers give feedback to their students, but only higher education students are given formal opportunities to provide feedback to their instructors, and this often comes too late for it to be helpful to them. The G.E.T. Model seeks to correct this. In moving beyond this basic view of the audience and focusing on the adult learner as the recipient, as well as the context of each learning opportunity, is where the G.E.T. Model can support instructors in improving the impact of their feedback.

CHAPTER OBJECTIVES

Chapter 3 introduces who we believe to be the initial focus of discussion around feedback in special education teacher preparation (i.e., the future educator). Knowing the recipient—the adult learner—allows instructors to better *give*, *exhibit*, and *teach* feedback. Some questions to consider are: (a) Where are they in their learning? (b) What do they need? (c) How ready are they for feedback? (d) What are they expecting? This chapter will also demonstrate how to select the appropriate feedback domain, with examples and prompts to take action. Many adult learners in special education teacher preparation programs are focused on working as a team to understand course content. They are more confident about their abilities and are optimistic about their levels of achievement (Howe & Strauss, 2007). Knowing this about the generation of candidates in our preparation programs lends itself to giving feedback with the learner in mind.

After reading this chapter you will **know** and **understand** these concepts as well as have the opportunity to **demonstrate** and **apply** your knowledge as illustrated in the Table 3-1 graphic organizer.

DESCRIBE AND DEFINE

Know

Who Are the Recipients?

Feedback can be given and received by anyone. Teachers in the K-12 arena give feedback to their students. Giving feedback requires teachers to deliver any information to a student that informs their understanding, or restructures their thinking or their beliefs, related to their performance, knowledge, or skill. This feedback takes many forms, such as verbal, written, tokens, progress reports, and grades. Students in K-12 settings deliver feedback when they describe their understanding or by performing a task correctly or incorrectly. The body language used by students and the way they demonstrate engagement or participation in a lesson also provides feedback to the teacher. For the purpose of this chapter, we focus on the reciprocal feedback that occurs between the instructor and the special education teacher candidate.

What Is Giving Feedback?

To understand what it means to give feedback, we first must define the meaning of feedback. Drawing from the work of Winnie and Butler (1994), we define feedback as **any information that recipients receive that informs their understanding or restructures their thinking or beliefs, related to their performance, knowledge, or skills**. For instructors in special education teacher preparation, this means that we can provide information on teacher candidates' performance, and/or knowledge, and/or skills. Giving means to present voluntarily, to provide or bestow. This implies that instructors can give feedback but says nothing about those receiving the feedback. Our definition requires instructors who are giving feedback to teacher candidates to place the recipient of the feedback at the center and to tailor their feedback to the individual recipient. Giving feedback must consider who the recipients are as individuals, how they view themselves and their relationship to the one delivering the feedback, and where they locate themselves on the continuum of change. In short, giving feedback must place the one receiving the feedback at the center of focus.

TABLE 3-1. GRAPHIC ORGANIZER		
KNOW (WHAT)	**UNDERSTAND (WHY)**	**DEMONSTRATE (HOW)**
What is giving feedback.	Why giving feedback must consider the recipient.	How to give feedback that recognizes the learners': • Needs • Prior knowledge • Readiness • Motivation • Self-efficacy
APPLY (TAKE ACTION)		
Select feedback appropriate for the recipient in the context of course design, activities, and assignments.		

Understand

Why Should Giving Feedback Consider the Recipient?

Feedback, by implicit definition, is primarily interpreted as an instructor delivering information to a learner. Universities were created with the idea that scholars or experts would impart knowledge to adult students or novices. To fit this ideology, feedback—comments on adult learners' work and performance—represents one of the characteristics of quality teaching and about the learning that is occurring (Carless, 2006). These examples of feedback are teacher-driven. Instructors across a variety of disciplines reported that the feedback they deliver is often not read, not understood, or not used (Scott, 2014). We suggest that feedback that puts the adult learner at the center of focus will have the opposite effect. Instructors who understand the adults they teach discover that effective feedback depends on how aware they are about the complexity of providing feedback to adults. This complexity is grounded in the core concepts of identity, status, and change.

Identity

As adults, teacher candidates have already begun to formulate their identity as teachers. Personal identity is interwoven with professional practice, especially for teachers. How we teach establishes one whorl of the fingerprint that identifies each of us as unique, both personally and professionally. That identity informs how we view ourselves and the story we tell ourselves about who we are and how we teach. Teacher candidates invest themselves emotionally in their learning through the time and effort they dedicate to activities and assignments. The way instructors respond to that investment in the feedback they give represents a "return" on that investment (Carless, 2006). Teacher candidates who are formulating their identity as teachers are framing and reframing their identity, based on feedback from their instructors. For this reason, we suggest that feedback is an identity conversation.

Identity conversations shake our fundamental beliefs about who we are and how we see ourselves. To engage in these emotionally complex conversations requires an environment of psychological safety. A person feels psychologically safe when the opportunity to succeed or fail is offered without judgment. In psychologically safe environments, people are less afraid to take risks and more willing to state ideas, ask questions, verbalize concerns, and even ask for support or instruction (Carmeli & Gittell, 2009). In a psychologically safe environment, failure is just a reason to try again and a way to learn something new. Teacher candidates who feel psychologically safe are more willing to examine their personal and professional story as well as the identity they have created and are crafting for themselves.

Status

Although equality is a foundational principle of instructional coaching (Knight, 2007), status differences inform the teacher–learner relationship, whether explicitly or implicitly, consciously or unconsciously. This can include expressions of both deference and demeanor (Schein, 2013). The rule of deference applies to subordinates' show of respect for superiors. The rule of demeanor applies to the way those who have superior power act, based on their status. These rules are usually unspoken and often taken for granted; they are noticed only when they are broken. In fact, when a subordinate shows disrespect to a superior or when a superior behaves in an undignified or inappropriate manner, discomfort, disorientation, and sometimes anger ensue.

When delivering feedback, instructors can reduce the barriers created by status inequalities by intentionally establishing a tone of equality, even when cultural norms might dictate that teacher candidates must be subordinate. Equality allows people to recognize and accept similarities and differences in individual knowledge, circumstance, and experience while striving to treat one another with equal value for what each has to offer in the exchange. Enacting the principle of equality in delivering feedback prevents the adult learner from rejecting feedback from an instructor because of status inequality. For example, instructors should recognize that they are experts in a specific research area, such as teacher preparation, but, unlike their own adult learners, instructors may not have taught in a K-12 classroom in many years. By acknowledging the expertise of the K-12 classroom teachers, instructors contribute to equality in the exchange. Instructors who operate from a place of equality acknowledge that the teacher candidates with whom they work bring their practical expertise to the conversation, thus creating a culture of dialogue that promotes reciprocal feedback for the instructor and the teacher candidate.

Change

The longer we practice habitual behaviors, the more difficult they are to change. Prochaska and DiClemente's (1992) six stages of change described a cyclical process rather than a linear one. Before the change process begins, people are not aware that any kind of change is needed, and they are unwilling to accept help. Prochaska and DiClemente called this *precontemplation*. Often, at this stage, people point out in others the very change they need to make for themselves. In the next stage, *contemplation*, people recognize that a change is necessary and start to think about what is required to make the change. *Preparation/determination* is the stage where people commit to the change. When people are in this stage, they collect all the information they need and make decisions about how they will carry out the change. Action/willpower is the stage where the hard work of changing behavior occurs. In the *maintenance* stage, people continue the changed behavior consistently and with fidelity. *Relapse* occurs when people return to older behaviors and abandon the new changes. Providing feedback to adult learners requires instructors to assess where the person is in the change process.

Demonstrate

How Can We Give Feedback That Recognizes the Recipient?

With learner-focused feedback, identity, status, and change are not barriers that inhibit feedback but instead are tightly coupled with adult learning theory, becoming information that educators use to tailor instruction and feedback to meet the teacher candidates' most pressing need or interest. In addition, adult learning theory promotes improved communication between the instructor and adult learner by creating a partnership. Instructional content and methods of feedback are learner-focused, thus promoting trust and enhancing self-awareness of the teacher candidate (Chan, 2010; Forrest & Peterson, 2006). "Trust is of great relevance to feedback because of the relational, affective, and emotional sides of feedback" (Carless, 2013, p. 90). Trust increases as instructors cultivate reciprocal communication, and trust allows for the exploration of current practice while pointing toward professional growth. Learner-focused feedback that affirms the principles of adult learning minimizes the threat of judgment surrounding identity, status, and change, and it builds trust that fosters professional growth in teacher candidates.

Needs of the Learner

Adults accept and act on feedback more readily when they understand the value of what they are learning and why they need to learn it. Because teaching is an identity career, the feedback given should acknowledge the contribution that the adult learner is making to education and describe how improving a skill or task will contribute to their growth and continual improvement.

Prior Knowledge

The adage "we don't know what we don't know" is certainly true in special education teacher preparation. Dismantling assumptions about what teacher candidates know and do not know can happen only by engaging in status-eliminating dialogue. Instructors who adopt a stance of equality seek to discover the rich resources the teacher candidates possess that permits them to learn from prior experience. Delivering feedback that respects the prior knowledge and experience of adult learners acknowledges their identity and elevates their status.

Readiness

Being naturally curious or interested in something does not mean a person is ready to learn. Adult learners are usually ready to accept feedback when there is a pressing need to know. Instructors who attend to where the teacher candidate is in the process of change are better able to deliver feedback that will be received and will improve the performance of the teacher candidate.

Motivation

The motivation that adult learners have for accepting and using feedback comes from what matters most to them as well as a clear sense of how they will benefit from the feedback. Adult learners who recognize their identity as teachers and who are ready to make a change that will improve their teaching will respond to feedback. By discovering adult learners' most pressing needs, instructors can frame the feedback to satisfy the intrinsic motivation that is key in this adult learning principle.

Self-Efficacy

Self-efficacy refers to the individual beliefs the adult learners hold regarding their capacity to actually execute the performance behaviors required to reach the goals they have set (Bandura, 1986; Tschannen-Moran & Hoy, 2001). Believing one can achieve a goal is a powerful component of actually achieving the goal. "A teacher's efficacy belief is a judgment of his or her capabilities to bring about desired outcomes of student engagement and learning, even among those students who may be difficult or unmotivated" (Tschannen-Moran & Hoy, 2001, p. 783). This notion of self-efficacy is housed in the adult learning principles of self-concept and orientation to learning. The self-concept of adult learners includes adult learners' autonomy to make decisions and choices for themselves. Adult learners should be given feedback that honors their autonomy as adults who are capable of making their own decisions and choices. Feedback to adult learners should not sound like advice or being told what to do. The self-concept of learners is demonstrated in their ability to be self-directing, which means that they can think for themselves and are able to choose their own path. *Orientation to learning* refers to adult learners' confidence that what they are learning will be beneficial and useful to them in their specific contexts. Adult learners are more likely to receive and act on feedback that meets the need of the problem they are trying to solve. For teacher candidates, this problem could be something as simple as feedback on how to establish and maintain consistent routines in a classroom. The change they need to make must be worth the effort they will expend in making the change, so the feedback must provide the right amount of information to be useful in the moment. Feedback that creates incremental change over time increases self-efficacy.

When we attend to these two principles—self-concept and orientation to learning—in giving feedback, we fuel self-efficacy and thus build capacity in adult learners to reach the goals they set because they believe they can. In short, adult learners must believe they can actually reach their goal before they will build the capacity to achieve the desired goal. Like Yoda says, "Do or do not. There is no try" (Kershner, 1980). For adult learners, there will be no "try" if they do not believe in their capacity to "do." The feedback we give should attend to the power of belief.

Why Instructors Must Recognize the Needs of Adult Learners When Giving Feedback

Recall Dr. Elford's experience with a teacher candidate who was not acting on the feedback she was given, as described in Chapter 1. The special education teacher candidate was not actually receiving the feedback because she did not know how to review comments inserted in a digital document. This situation is a good example of why putting the recipient at the center of the feedback really matters.

Teachers who are enrolled in the same Master in Special Education (MSE) online program as the teacher candidate in this scenario come from all over the United States and from a few foreign countries. Most are already licensed teachers in their states and are seeking further certification in special education. These adult learners fit each principle of adult learning theory. As teacher candidates in this online MSE program, they are motivated and ready to learn. They have a need to know because many of them have students with disabilities in their classrooms. They hold a variety of experiences that contribute to prior knowledge. Most of these teacher candidates are oriented to the learning because they already understand the personal benefit of completing an MSE. Of course, every teacher candidate holds their individual self-concept. Creating a learning environment in an online space that attends to the adult learning principles and respects the variety of teacher candidates requires intentional planning for delivering feedback.

During the practicum experience in this MSE online program, the course author intentionally constructed a feedback process to attend to adult learning principles as well as the four domains of feedback. The teacher candidates' learning experience depends on how they interpret and respond to the feedback they are given by the instructor. To illustrate this process and describe the learning experience, we can examine a multiphased assignment from this practicum experience. Phase one of the process requires teacher candidates to upload teaching videos to an online platform where they and their instructor can provide timestamped feedback at precise moments in the video. The feedback the teacher candidate receives regarding the video falls in the feedback domains of purposefulness and specificity. Phase two of the process occurs after the teacher candidates have watched and commented on their own teaching video and have read their instructor's feedback. In phase two, the teacher candidates write a reflective journal assignment that incorporates the timestamped feedback, research articles they have read, and the meaning they make from connecting the two elements. The instructor provides written feedback to the journal assignment. Phase three—the final phase of this assignment—occurs when the teacher candidate and the instructor meet for an online video conference to discuss the teaching video and work together to set a goal for improvement during the subsequent weeks of the practicum. The feedback in both phase two and phase three falls in the feedback domain of constructiveness. Figure 3-1 illustrates this feedback process.

Another example of how practicum course assignments are constructed with feedback and the teacher candidates' learning experience in mind is the Individualized Education Plan (IEP) Analysis assignment. This assignment begins during the first week of the online practicum course and ends at the last week of the course. The teacher candidate receives and responds to feedback at each of the assignment's six stages. The first stage (a) requires the teacher candidate to begin a case study, with an introduction to a K-12 student who the candidate selected as the target student for this project during practicum. The next stages after stage one are as follows: (b) observe the

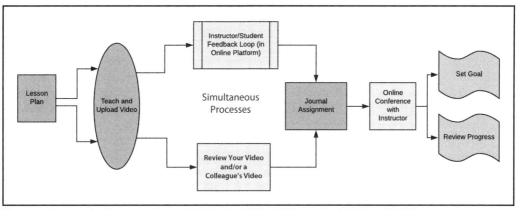

Figure 3-1. Lesson plan flow chart. (Created by Martha D. Elford, PhD and Cynthia Mruczek, PhD.)

student and write an observation summary, (c) plan instruction based on observation and what is written in the IEP, (d) conduct interviews and construct a MAPS (Making Action Plans) document (describe and summarize), (e) submit a draft of the final paper, and (f) submit the final draft. During each stage, the instructor provides written feedback in the document that the teacher candidate is required to incorporate before adding the next stage to the document. In fact, the syllabus clearly states the following:

> Applying feedback from your instructor is an essential requirement of the course. Teacher candidates are required to demonstrate application of instructor feedback throughout the course—both in your written assignments and in the practical classroom application. Assignments that fail to incorporate feedback may not be graded and will result in the unsuccessful completion of the practicum.

This assignment incorporates all four feedback domains (specificity, immediacy, purposefulness, and constructiveness) while attending to all six principles of adult learning theory.

As teacher candidates proceed through the MSE online program, other courses provide multiple opportunities for teacher candidates to provide feedback to one another. One assignment invites teacher candidates to describe their identity using artifacts and captions, based on a variety of domains that are provided in a graphic of some of the aspects of social identity. The teacher candidates upload their artifacts and captions as a presentation, and classmates comment on one another's presentation. The assignment structure provides parameters for peer feedback. Teacher candidates are expected to view and respond to two classmates' presentations for the purpose of better understanding the multiple factors that encompass other's identities. For each presentation, the teacher candidates are instructed to post comments about various aspects of the presentations. They are given these ideas to consider, but their comments are not limited to the following six ideas:

1. Questions you have about the presentation
2. Ways the presentation made you consider aspects of your own identity
3. Aspects of the presentation about which you would like more information or clarification
4. How you interpret artifacts of information in the presentation
5. Ways you are similar to the other person
6. Ways you are different

Peer feedback may prove to be as useful, if not more useful, than instructor feedback when peers are given instructions on how feedback should be delivered. As peers, there is a built-in trust because of their similarity as teaching professionals. Sometimes, teacher candidates may think that instructors' feedback does not quite fit because instructors have not taught in a K-12 classroom in the recent past. However, peer feedback acknowledges common settings, common problems, and a desire for workable solutions. Adult learners are interested in what their peers have to say because, as the orientation to learning principle suggests, they are motivated to learn what is immediately useful. Peers share a common profession and can provide authentic feedback that benefits both the giver and the receiver.

The capstone course of the leadership certificate program at a midwestern university is designed to push the boundaries of traditional online courses in supporting the development of inclusive school and district leaders. Instead of asking graduate students to reflect on what they have learned about inclusive leadership, special education law, systems change, and other program concepts in a final paper or project, graduate students take on avatars of the newly identified leadership team of a virtual school district, Valyria. By reimagining traditional views of learning to incorporate Gee's (2007) gaming principles, the authors of the program created a unique space for Leadership in Special and Inclusive Education students to practice analyzing school policy and implementation by considering not only the letter but the spirit (or intent) of special education law, including the IDEA (Individuals with Disabilities Education Act), ADA (Americans with Disabilities Act of 1990), and 504 (Section 504 of the Rehabilitation Act of 1973). Gameplay creates a myriad of opportunities for practicing educators (adult learners) to engage in thoughtful collaborative leadership while honing the skill sets necessary to lead inclusive schools.

The intention of this capstone course is to create a safe place where future school leaders can challenge themselves to identify, rethink, and even dismantle barriers to equitable implementation of special education law. The stage is set as graduate students are positioned as the newly appointed leadership team of the Valyria School District. First, they begin by engaging in a systems report, which they develop as a team after reviewing and analyzing district data that include teacher-to-student ratios, graduation rates, and even information about the city's failing clean water system. A sense of ambiguity and unease is always palpable in the first days, as graduate students work to distribute leadership and tasks across their team while also trying to determine their first steps. This creates opportunities for these adult learners to take risks with their learning and strive for creative problem-solving. Although there are some specific assignments designed to move the game along, the teams are given the autonomy to decide what they want to accomplish and which of Valyria's numerous needs should first be tackled. In many ways, the first week of the course replicates the reality of what it feels like when one enters a new leadership position within a school district. The situated learning in this simulation addresses all six principles of adult learning theory (see Chapter 1).

During the second stage, graduate students are assigned avatars within the context of Valyria. The avatars reflect typical roles in public school districts in the United States, including a Director of Special Services, Director of Communication, Director of Human Resources, etc. Each of the avatars comes with a rich background and important diverse social identities to encourage the graduate student to stretch their learning beyond their own lived experiences. The melding of the two identities (the "real" self and the "virtual" self) allows for the creation of a "third-space" (Gee, 2007), where the knowledge and background of real and virtual individuals intermingle to create a new identity and therefore new learning.

As the game nears its end in the third stage, the Valyria School District is faced with *doomsday* type tasks that feel overwhelming—a federal mandate to address the disproportionate representation of students of color in the district's special education programs, as well as the high dropout rates for the same group of students. The instructor of this course acts as the Game Master, who responds to the graduate students' efforts and accomplishments in unique and organic ways. This represents feedback that addresses all four domains (see Chapter 1). For example, one recent team decided to make broad sweeping changes across the district, doing away with all self-contained classrooms and moving students with disabilities into the general education classrooms. In this case, the Game Master provided feedback from the domains of specificity, immediacy, purposefulness, and constructiveness in the form of voicemails from angry parents and a letter from the teachers' union challenging the decision.

Course design such as the one described creates an opportunity for adult learners to give and receive feedback in multiple ways from both peers and course instructors at all stages of the course.

Trust is built in the early stage of the game as adult learners figure out how to analyze the data provided for the district and give feedback to one another on the analysis. This trust is essential for stage two when the avatars are assigned and the gameplay begins. During that stage, the team provides feedback organically through the interaction in the game. The choices they make have consequences, and this feedback prompts them to examine those choices as they progress through the game. As Game Master, the course instructor provides situated feedback by introducing obstacles or opening doors for progress. The graduate students provide feedback to the course instructor in many ways, such as situationally by adjusting their gameplay, in emails asking for guidance or expressing frustration, and in frantic texts when the challenge feels too great. This course illustrates Wiliam's (2016) central idea perfectly when he states, "The only thing important about feedback is what students do with it," (p. 10) because the importance of feedback is evident in every decision in the game and in every communication with the instructor.

We asked Dr. Carlos Flores to provide a personal reflection on one way he gives feedback to aspiring special educators. He reflected on how he gives feedback on early classroom teaching opportunities in his program. Read his following reflection, and answer the questions that follow and align with the information in this chapter.

Seniors in my practicum class (the semester before student teaching) observe in self-contained classrooms for a total of 32 hours (16 in elementary and 16 in a secondary). These candidates are now required to teach a lesson in one of these classrooms. The candidates have to follow a few steps before the lesson is taught.

1. Once they are assigned to the classrooms, they choose at which level (elementary or secondary) they wish to teach their lesson.

2. They meet with the classroom teacher to decide what lesson they will teach. Many times, especially in the elementary classrooms, the teacher has a specific IEP goal on which they want the candidate to focus. In secondary classrooms, depending on the way the rooms are set up, they may teach a specific subject or skill.

3. The candidate prepares a lesson plan for me. (Sometimes, however, the lesson plan may go into more detail than what they will do in the classroom due to the requirements or planning accommodations and modifications for all 13 IDEA categories.) Depending on the timing of the semester, they may or may not receive feedback from me on the plan before the lesson is taught in the classroom. There are a variety of factors involving observations that can cause this assignment to be early or late in the semester.

4. The candidate teaches the lesson, which I typically observe. A rubric is used to provide feedback to the teacher candidates. If I am not present to observe the candidate, the classroom teacher uses the same rubric to grade the lesson. The rubric is shared with the candidate.

The candidates may receive feedback in a variety of ways. Occasionally, even the students they taught may give an opinion on the lesson. The candidate may receive feedback from the teacher before, during, or after the lesson. While I try to keep quiet, the classroom teacher is encouraged to offer suggestions and chime in collaboratively during the lesson on how to make something work better. As I observe the lesson, I use a rubric the students are familiar with. At the end of the rubric is a space where I take copious notes during their lessons. I point out things such as when they provided feedback to a student or when they missed a prime opportunity for specific, verbal praise or immediate, corrective feedback. I often provide suggestions on how to revise the lesson to maximize student engagement or provide students more opportunities to respond. I very often run out of room and have to continue in the margins! This does not mean they did anything wrong. Once the candidates receive the completed rubric from me, they make an appointment with me to discuss their lesson. This is done on a voluntary basis, and no one has to come see me if they do not wish to do so. These debrief sessions are helpful for students, many of whom desire clarification or further feedback on their lessons.

While feedback is important in any assignment, I feel it is vital in this case. These candidates are my responsibility to teach, and if they leave my program not knowing how to teach a lesson, not only does it reflect poorly on me and my university, but it can impact every student who will sit in their classroom for years to come. I want to be sure that I provide every possible piece of feedback I can to my teacher candidates to ensure they will be the best teachers they can possibly be.

—*Carlos A. Flores Jr., EdD*

QUESTIONS: DR. FLORES' REFLECTION

- How does Dr. Flores give feedback that recognizes and honors the recipients?

- Reflect specifically on the needs of the adult learner, prior knowledge, motivation, and self-efficacy.

SPOTLIGHT ON ADULT LEARNING

In Table 3-2, we have developed questions designed to guide instructors in the creation and planning of course assignments and activities that attend to the four feedback domains and the six principles of adult learning theory (Figure 3-2).

POSSIBLE BARRIERS TO USING THIS TYPE OF FEEDBACK

There are many possible barriers to giving feedback that is focused on the recipient. One barrier can be connected to the person giving the feedback and their identity, lack of sensitivity, their own habits of practice, and their needs as adults. Another barrier may be that multiple audiences providing feedback to each other may deter adult learners from seeking constructive feedback or acting on it. Fullan (2008) indicated that people often fear judgment and become defensive because they feel it is a critique of their performance. Harley (2014) suggested that trust is essential when giving feedback. In addition, there is a risk of feedback overload. If the feedback comes from multiple sources, it might be difficult to sift through all the noise and glean the value from the feedback that is useful for that task, process, or next step. To prevent misinterpretation when giving feedback, givers should ask themselves the following: (a) What do I hope this feedback will achieve? (b) Do I have enough information to provide feedback? (c) Do I know the recipient well enough to provide feedback? (d) Am I willing to receive feedback in return? Trust, good intent, the language of ongoing regard (Kegan & Lahey, 2001), and thinking of the recipient before the message is delivered can prevent barriers and eliminate the competing noise of too much or the wrong kind of feedback.

TABLE 3-2. SPOTLIGHT ON ADULT LEARNING			
SPECIFICITY	**IMMEDIACY**	**PURPOSEFULNESS**	**CONSTRUCTIVENESS**
Is the feedback task-oriented? Does it move the teacher candidate toward the desired goal? Does the feedback give just the right amount of information so the adult learners' autonomy is respected?	When is the best time to provide feedback? Should feedback be given within 48 hours? Should the feedback be given after the teacher candidate has had time to think through the process?	Will the feedback be given at different stages of the assignment? Does the feedback attend to the process level? What method should be used? Should feedback be written or verbal?	Does the feedback point the teacher candidate toward the next steps? Does the feedback include opportunities for the teacher candidate to construct new meaning from the information? Does the feedback attend to prior knowledge, readiness to learn, and the self-concept of the adult learner?

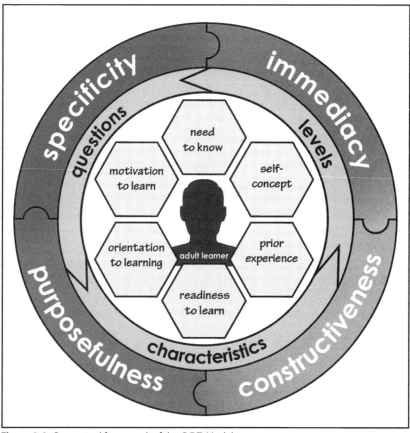

Figure 3-2. Conceptual framework of the G.E.T. Model.

PRACTICAL APPLICATION

The practical application from Smith et al. (2018) demonstrated an instructor giving feedback, as it allows for instructors to deliver feedback to the teacher candidate that informs their understanding or restructures their thinking or their beliefs related to their performance, knowledge, or skill. The Learning Express-Ways (LE) offer an integrated, classroom-scale approach to partnering with students (Cook-Sather et al., 2014) in their learning, positioning future general and special educators to implement this tool in their own classrooms. The LE, an evidence-based instructional communication tool for adolescents with learning disabilities, has been adapted for higher education. The use of LE in a preservice education course on learning disabilities offers a practical example of how feedback can be modeled experientially in a "third space."

The literature supports a need for enhanced experiential learning in higher education, with educator preparation being one example (Kolb & Kolb, 2005). Further, a new epistemology that is focused on creating expanded and innovative opportunities for teachers has emerged, connecting academic coursework and university-based teacher education (Zeichner, 2010). Zeichner (2010) suggested that aspiring educators "frequently do not have opportunities to observe, try out, and receive focused feedback about their teaching methods learned about in their campus courses" (p. 91). Further, "student teachers' learning from experiences is a process involving many interrelated personal and social aspects, including past and present experiences gained in multiple situations and contexts over time" (Leeferink et al., 2015, p. 334). When coursework is carefully constructed and coordinated with field experiences, teacher educators can prepare students who enact evidence-based and high-leverage practices (Hammerness et al., 2005).

This coordination happens at the program and course levels. Zeichner (2010) advocated for "third spaces," where aspiring educator learning is situated in the schools and community, but when this is not achievable as the focus of a specific course, other experiential learning (such as the implementation and practice of LE adapted for higher education) can be an option. Learning Express-Ways is an evidence-based instructional communication tool for adolescents with learning disabilities (Lenz et al., 1994) that was created at the University of Kansas Center for Research on Learning to facilitate student–teacher communication. It involves a written dialogue between student and teacher, where a student can give feedback on a teacher's instruction, reflect on their own attempts at learning the academic content, demonstrate their learning, and provide thoughts and ideas to instructors to enhance their learning. This tool has been adapted for use in educator preparation to model and practice its use.

Researchers who have studied secondary classroom teachers' (grades 6-12) use of LE to connect with individual students in both the general and special education settings reported several benefits. The LE creates a place to record student concerns and improves communication (Adams et al., 2001). Completed at the end of a class or unit, LE enables cueing feedback to address specific student concerns, documents progress monitoring and changes in instruction, and builds trust and a positive relationship (Lenz et al., 2003). The student is responsible for completing the form thoroughly and honestly. The teacher must then read, reflect, and respond to the comments and questions before the next meeting. Although LE was initially developed to support adolescents with learning disabilities in middle and high school in achieving academic goals, the tool has been successfully adapted for use in undergraduate special educator preparation coursework (Smith et al., 2018).

The LE provides a space and framework for written dialogue between student and teacher (Figure 3-3), where a student can give feedback on a teacher's instruction, reflect on their own learning of academic content, and ask questions or make comments about any aspect of instruction or learning (Haynes-Smith, 2013). Similarly, LE offers teachers the opportunity to reflect on their instruction, assess student content mastery, provide feedback and respond to student comments, and revise course content and delivery based on student feedback. Possible benefits to instructors include the encouragement of student voice in pedagogical approaches, opportunities to individualize instruction for a student or group of students, and openings to privately discuss student needs (Smith

	Course name, Instructor
	Semester, Year

Student Name: _____   Date: _____

Message/Comments **to** Instructor:	I rate **my learning** this week as (select your choice):
	0- I didn't learn anything new or relevant.
	1- Learning was minimal.
	2- I learned some new things this week about the chapter(s) and related content.
	3- I learned many new things about the chapter(s) and related content.
	4- I had an outstanding week and learned many new things that will be relevant to my future in education.
Questions/feedback **for** the Instructor:	Message **from** Instructor:

Content Related Writing Prompt: *The question here should be based on content from class and/or materials read or reviewed in preparation for class.*

Student Response to Writing Prompt:

Figure 3-3. Sample Adapted Learning Express-Ways Document for Educator Preparation Course.

et al., 2014). Other instructional tools developed at the University of Kansas Center for Research on Learning, including Strategic Instruction Model Learning Strategies and Content Enhancement Routines, are similarly being taught and modeled in preservice special educator preparation programs (Fisher et al., 1999; Lenz et al., 2003). The introduction of these types of evidence-based tools in special educator preparation offers options to teacher candidates who face the troubling number of students who are at risk for failure in U.S. schools. Aspiring special educators must have the training, practice, and tools to be ready to meet the requirements of students with diverse learning needs, including learners with exceptionalities and students from culturally, economically, and linguistically diverse groups (Darling-Hammond, 2010).

In Table 3-3 we illustrate a sampling of feedback recipients. For the purpose of this book, we are situating the feedback among the following two age groups: (a) K-12 and their teachers and (b) adult learners in higher education and their instructors. We know that giving and receiving feedback in both age groups is reciprocal, whether intended or incidental. Table 3-3 lists a few examples of what feedback might look like and when it might occur, based on the different feedback dyads.

Essentially, the recipient should be at the center of the feedback for it to have a transformational effect because what the person does with it is the most important factor of feedback (Wiliam, 2016). They cannot do anything if it is not appropriate for them and delivered appropriately. Being intentional about employing the domains of feedback adds to its effectiveness. However, we suggest that

TABLE 3-3. EXAMPLES OF FEEDBACK RECIPIENTS			
	BEFORE CLASS	**DURING CLASS**	**AFTER CLASS**
ADULT LEARNERS FROM INSTRUCTORS	Coming to class prepared	Participation in class discussions	Participation and level of knowledge in online discussion boards
INSTRUCTORS FROM COLLEGE-AGED STUDENTS	Review of class content and modifications made to meet the level of proficiency of students	Responding to student answers	Grades on assignments Course evaluations
K-12 STUDENTS FROM TEACHERS	Setting expectations	Checks for understanding	Describing what they did well and what they need to work on
TEACHERS FROM K-12 STUDENTS	Excitement to learn new concepts	Attention and concentration during the lesson	Describing what they liked and did not like about the lesson

focusing on the recipient will add the greatest effect to how that feedback is received and acted upon. To illustrate this idea, consider these feedback recipients and methods. When thinking about the age of the recipient of feedback, one might consider these differences, based on previously cited research regarding feedback questions, levels, and characteristics (Brookhart, 2009; Hattie & Timperley, 2007; Wiggins, 2012). If the audience is an elementary student, feedback should be frequent, direct, and short. If the audience is a middle school or secondary student, feedback may need to be more process-oriented. If the audience is an adult, feedback should take into consideration the adult's motivation to learn. Within these generalized groups, one must remember that each person in that group will respond to feedback differently, based on their personality and preferences. Being careful to consider each individual recipient while attending to the four domains of feedback makes giving feedback worth the time, effort, and intention it requires.

The following questions are provided to guide your review and reflection in the Authentic Example that follows, contributed by Kyena E. Cornelius, EdD.

- In this example, notice how the instructor and peers play a role in giving feedback. Reflect.
- Who are the recipients of feedback in this example?
- What role does the assessment rubric play in providing feedback?

AUTHENTIC EXAMPLE

Contributed by
Kyena E. Cornelius, EdD

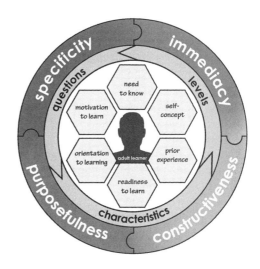

1. Course Details

SPE 413: Professional Growth and Development for Teachers of Diverse Learners. This advanced, undergraduate special education course introduces teacher candidates to methods and strategies for personal and professional growth and development. Teacher candidates in their final semester before student teaching are expected to synthesize and apply previous learning (e.g., theories and content) for better understanding of application. This assignment reflects the material taught in several courses: Due Process and Planning, Instructional Decision-Making, Strategies for Teaching Learners With Special Needs: Reading and Writing, and Strategies for Teaching Learners With Special Needs: Math and Science.

2. Learning Objectives

Course objectives addressed:

a. Develop IEPs for students with mild and moderate disabilities that comply with federal and state statutes.

b. Demonstrate how a student's area of need(s) is aligned with state standards to justify specialized instruction.

c. Understand how learner variance affects IEP writing and the planning process.

d. Understand how communication and collaboration among professionals and parents promote learner success.

3. Assignment Details

This assignment has two phases. During phase one, teacher candidates will create baseline information for a K-12 student with a specific learning disability, demonstrating two areas of need (i.e., math, reading). They will use Hosp's et al. (2016) norm charts about curriculum-based measurement to create current levels of academic performance for their fictional student, considering the grade-level standards for that content/grade as they decide what is applicable for grade-level nondisabled peers. Using this information, as well as examples taken from their real-life field experiences, teacher candidates will write a present levels of academic achievement and functional performance (PLAAFP) statement for their fictional student to clearly identify present levels of academic and functional performance. This statement will be based on the Vanderbilt University IRIS Center's explanation and informed by the principles of IEP writing articulated by Bateman and Herr (2006). During phase two, teacher candidates will revise their PLAAFP as well as draft at least two goals for the K-12 student. To emphasize that IEP teams make final decisions, teacher candidates do not complete the entire template during this assignment. Instead, the assignment carries over into a follow-up class session in which three corrected and revised IEPs are selected at random, and teacher candidates are assigned roles as IEP team members as they conduct mock IEP meetings to determine the remaining components of the IEP.

4. Evaluation Criteria

A sample template and rubric (Table 3-4) are provided.

IEP TEMPLATE

I. Student Information

Student Name: _____

Student ID Number: _____

Grade: _____

DOB: _____

Age: _____

Eligible Disability: _____

Parent's Name: _____

Home Address: _____

Phone Numbers: _____

Date of IEP Meeting: _____

Date of Eligibility: _____

IEP Review Date: _____

II. Current Level of Academic and Functional Performance

A statement of the child's current levels of academic achievement and functional performance, including:

- How the child's disability affects the child's involvement and progress in the general education curriculum (i.e., the same curriculum as for nondisabled children) or for preschool children, as appropriate, how the disability affects the child's participation in appropriate activities (34 CFR §300.320[a][1], 2007).

III. Special Instructional Considerations

Items checked "yes" must be addressed in this IEP:

a. Does the student exhibit behaviors that impeded their learning or the learning of others?
   Yes   No

b. Does the student have limited English proficiency?
   Yes   No

c. Does the student require instruction in Braille and the use of Braille?
   Yes   No

d. Does the student have communication needs (deaf or hearing impaired only)?
   Yes   No

e. Does the student need assistive technology devices and/or services?
   Yes   No

f. Is the student working toward alternate achievement standards assessed via alternate assessments?
   Yes   No

g. Are transition services addressed?
   Yes   No

IV. Annual Goals and Benchmarks

A statement of measurable annual goals, including academic and functional goals designed to:

- Meet the child's needs that result from the child's disability to enable the child to be involved in and make progress in the general education curriculum (34 CFR §300.320[a][2][i] [A], 2007), and
- Meet each of the child's other educational needs that result from the child's disability (34 CFR §300.320[a][2][i][B, 2007]).

PLAAFP statement that is being addressed in this goal: _____

Annual goal:_____

Evaluation method: _____

PLAAFP statement that is being addressed in this goal: _____

Annual goal: _____

Evaluation method: _____

V. Supplementary Aids and Related Services

A statement of the special education, related services, and supplementary aids and services, based on peer-reviewed research to the extent of practicable, to be provided to the child, or on behalf of the child, and a statement of the program modifications or supports for school personnel that will be provided to enable the child to:

- Advance appropriately toward attaining the annual goals (34 CFR §300.320[a][4][i], 2007),
- Be involved in and make progress in the general education curriculum and to participate in extracurricular and other nonacademic activities (34 CFR §300.320[a][4][ii], 2007),
- Be educated and participate with other children with disabilities and nondisabled children in extracurricular and other nonacademic activities (34 CFR §300.320[a][4][iii], 2007), and
- Be provided with a projected date for the beginning of the services and modifications and the anticipated frequency, location, and duration of special education, related services, and supplementary aids and services; and modifications and supports (34 CFR §300.320[a][7], 2007).

SERVICE, AID, OR MODIFICATION	FREQUENCY	LOCATION	BEGINNING DATE

VI. Special Education Delivery

An explanation of the extent, if any, to which the child will not participate with nondisabled children in the regular classroom and in extracurricular and other nonacademic activities (34 CFR §300.320[a][5], 2007).

Special Education

AREA OF NEED	LOCATION OF SERVICE	DURATION	FREQUENCY	SERVICE PROVIDER	BEGINNING DATE

VII. Assessments

A statement of which state and district assessments will be taken.

A statement of any individual appropriate accommodations that is necessary to measure the academic achievement and functional performance of the child on state and districtwide assessments (34 CFR §300.320[a][6][i], 2007).

Reading: (Grades 3, 4, 5, 6, 7, 8, and 10) the student will participate in:

_____STATE Testing _____with _____ *without* accommodations

Explain how accommodations selected are representative of those used in the classroom.

If the IEP Team determines that the child must take an alternate assessment instead of a particular regular state or districtwide assessment of student achievement, a statement of why:

- *The child cannot participate in the regular assessment (34 CFR §300.320[a][6][ii][A], 2007).*
- *The particular alternate assessment selected is appropriate for the child (34 CFR §300.320[a][6][ii][B], 2007).*

_____STATE-Modified, and alternate assessment based on modified achievement standards, Grades 5-8 and 10. If the IEP team determines that the student will take the STATE-Modified, the student's IEP must also include the standard-based goals and objectives. Document the IEP team decision: explain why the assessment option is necessary.

Math: (Grades 3, 4, 5, 6, 7, 8, and 10) the student will participate in:

_____STATE Testing _____with _____ without accommodations

Explain how accommodations selected are representative of those used in the classroom.

If the IEP Team determines that the child must take an alternate assessment instead of a particular regular state or districtwide assessment of student achievement, a statement of why:

- *The child cannot participate in the regular assessment (34 CFR §300.320[a][6][ii][A], 2007).*
- *The particular alternate assessment selected is appropriate for the child (34 CFR §300.320[a][6][ii][B], 2007).*

_____STATE-Modified, and alternate assessment based on modified achievement standards, Grades 5-8 and 10. If the IEP team determines that the student will take the STATE-Modified, the student's IEP must also include the standard-based goals and objectives. Document the IEP team decision: explain why the assessment option is necessary.

Table 3-4. Rubric for Individualized Education Plan With Considerations for Congruency

ITEM	IEP ELEMENT	QUALITY VALUES			
		4	3	2	1
	PLAAFP: *Describes the student's current level of functioning in areas of need*				
P.1.	A statement of student's strength in academic and/or behavioral area of need is provided with evidence.	The PLAAFP includes a statement of the child's strengths. Outcomes from assessments and tools used to measure current level are provided.	A strength is indicated with relation to current performance, but assessment tools used are not mentioned.	A strength is indicated but is poorly evidenced. The PLAAFP is based on nonspecific, qualitative information and is not quantified.	There is not any information included about the child's strengths.
P.2.	The PLAAFP includes a needs statement.	The PLAAFP includes a needs statement that is related to the goal and is student-centered.	The PLAAFP includes a needs statement that is related to goal, but it is not student-centered.	A needs statement is present, but it is not related to the goal.	There is not a needs statement included in the PLAAFP.
P.3.	The area of need is specific, observable, and measurable.	The PLAAFP is specific, observable, and measurable. (The reader "sees" what the writer intended.)	The PLAAFP is specific but may not be measurable.	The PLAAFP is not specific or observable.	The PLAAFP is incomplete.
P.4.	A statement indicating how the disability affects the *progress and involvement* in the general education setting and curriculum.	The PLAAFP states: 1. Student's present level of ability. 2. How the disability affects the student's achievement in the relevant skill area. 3. How it relates to the expectations of the general education curriculum.	The PLAAFP includes two of three elements.	The PLAAFP includes one of three elements.	PLAAFP is limited to naming student's disability category.
Total Score for PLAAFP					

(continued)

TABLE 3-4 (CONTINUED). RUBRIC FOR INDIVIDUALIZED EDUCATION PLAN WITH CONSIDERATIONS FOR CONGRUENCY

ITEM	IEP ELEMENT	QUALITY VALUES			
		4	3	2	1
	Goal: *Describes the student's proposed level of functioning in one specific area of need in one year from the start of IEP*				
G.1.	The goal is meaningful, measurable, and able to be monitored.	Goals are meaningful, measurable, and able to be monitored. Multiple people can agree that the skill has occurred.	Goals are meaningful and measurable, but units of measurement are not conducive to routine monitoring.	Goals are measurable but not meaningful for the stated PLAAFP.	Goals are not meaningful, related to PLAAFP, measurable, or able to be monitored.
G.2.	The goal is rigorous and sets high expectations.	Goals are ambitious enough to drive interventions to allow the child to make meaningful progress.	Goals are somewhat ambitious to allow the child to make progress.	Goals are written such that the student would make progress regardless of the intervention.	Goals are not ambitious enough for the child to make meaningful progress or repeat previous year's IEP.
G.3.	The goal states the condition, the behavior, and the criterion for acceptable performance— *Time frame if goal is to be mastered in less than 1 year.* *Benchmarks/short-term objectives (STOs), if used, should also include time frame if any are to be mastered prior to end of IEP time frame.*	The goal includes: 1. Conditions 2. Behavior 3. Criterion for acceptable performance	The goal contains two of three elements.	The goal contains one of three elements.	Goals lack specificity.

(continued)

TABLE 3-4 (CONTINUED). RUBRIC FOR INDIVIDUALIZED EDUCATION PLAN WITH CONSIDERATIONS FOR CONGRUENCY

ITEM	IEP ELEMENT	QUALITY VALUES			
		4	3	2	1
	Goal: *Describes the student's proposed level of functioning in one specific area of need in one year from the start of IEP*				
G.4.	Related to success in the general curriculum or life skills.	The skill is crucial for participation in general education curriculum or daily life. Lower level skills are precursors to age/grade expectations.	The skill represents a general concept. May be a precursor to necessary element in the acquisition of another skill.	The goal implies importance in general education curriculum or in life skills.	The goal does not pertain to a skill crucial to general education participation or daily life routines.
G.5.	Written in clear and concise language.	The goal is written in clear, jargon-free language and can be elicited by anyone.	The goal is concise, but written with some clinical language.	The goal is written using language only those with specific knowledge can understand.	The language of the goal rambles and contains mostly jargon.
Total Score for Goal					

(continued)

TABLE 3-4 (CONTINUED). RUBRIC FOR INDIVIDUALIZED EDUCATION PLAN WITH CONSIDERATIONS FOR CONGRUENCY

ITEM	IEP ELEMENT	QUALITY VALUES			
		4	3	2	1
Written quality	The IEP has acceptable quality in the following elements: 1. Grammar 2. Spelling 3. Readability	IEP has acceptable quality in all elements.	IEP reflects acceptable quality in two of three elements.	IEP reflects acceptable quality in one of three elements.	IEP reflects poor overall quality for all elements.
	Congruency: The PLAAFP, goals, and benchmarks or STOs are interconnected. The connection between all IEP components is clear.				
C.1.	All areas of need identified in PLAAFP are addressed through a goal. *Consider the connection between P.1. and G.1.*	There is a direct relationship between the PLAAFP and every goal.	There is a direct relationship between the PLAAFP and the goals listed. Some needs addressed in the PLAAFP do not have a goal identified, or a goal does not have an area of need discussed in PLAAFP.	There is some relationship between the PLAAFP and the goals.	There is no relationship between the PLAAFP and the goals.
C.2.	Benchmarks or STOs are related to the annual goal and are measurable (*not needed for all goals, but if you have them, there must be at least two). *If Benchmarks/STOs are included, they will be assessed with same criteria as Goals.*	Objectives or benchmarks are clearly related to the goal and are measurable.	Objectives or benchmarks are clearly related to the goal but are not measurable.	Objectives or benchmarks are somewhat related to the goal but there is room for improvement.	There is no relationship between objectives or benchmarks to the goal, or there are less than two objectives.
Total Score for Congruency					

I. Student Information

Student Name: _____Justin ___Smith_____

Student ID Number:_____   Grade: __2____

DOB: __07/23/2010____ Age* _8___   Eligible Disability : ____Specific Learning Disability_____

Parent's Name: _____Katie Smith_____

Home Address: _____   Phone # _____

_____   Phone # _____

Date of IEP meeting _____10/6/2018_____   Date of Eligibility ____4/23/2018_____   IEP Review Date _____

II. Present Level of Academic and Functional Performance

Justin is an 8 year old 2nd grade student at Washington Elementary School. Justin is a student with low to average ability, whose test scores indicate an area of need in reading and math. Justin was referred for special education in 1st grade for special education and was found eligible under the category of Specific Learning Disability.

In reading, Justin was administered a curriculum based measurement (CBM) reading assessment on (9/13/2018). Justin read 29 words correctly per minute with 70% accuracy on a 2nd grade reading level. Justin is able to decode one syllable words, but struggles with two and three syllable words. Justin is able to distinguish long and short vowels in most one syllable words. Irregular words are a reoccurring problem for him during reading. Compared to his peers, Justin is behind in fluency and decoding multiple syllabic words with a weakness in phonics. When presented with text regarding a scientific subject, Justin is much more engaged and willing to try to decode words he doesn't know. Justin is able to comprehend text that is read to him very well. He enjoys having books about planets read to him and draw pictures about what was read. As Justin is currently only decoding one syllable words he is falling behind his peers and will require intensive instruction to reach the second grade benchmark.

In math, Justin was administered a curriculum based measurement (CBM) math probe on (9/14/2018). Justin is able to complete single digit addition and subtraction problems. When he was given a computation of math problems to complete in two minutes, Justin received 14 correct digits which shows he is at his frustration level. This places Justin in the 25th percentile. When problems are applied to real-world situations, Justin does a better job of understanding what is happening and how to complete the problem. He is also able to distinguish the difference between pennies, nickels, dimes, and quarters. He is unable to add them up when given a combination of coins. Justin will need intensive instruction in addition and subtraction in order to perform at instructional level.

Commented [A1]: Why low? – This may be the case, but typically a student with SLD is going to have average to above average intelligence. Also, don't repeat what would be in the evaluation report. Instead list his area(s) of need.

Deleted: trouble

Commented [A2]: Nice picture!

Commented [A3]: This is awesome – just find the corresponding standard for multisyllabic words

Commented [A4]: Stick with "will require intensive instruction to make progress toward the 2nd grade expectations" – If you say reach you are setting yourself up to have him master the grade level standards and exit out of SPED, or perhaps indicate to others he does not need special education

Deleted: assessment

Commented [A5]: This is above average for his grade level – Try 5 or 7

Commented [A6]: What does this mean to a parent – and 25th percentile is not going to be frustration level. I like the picture you are trying to create, but the skills don't match. Also stay away from money right now – stay with just simple addition and subtraction he has to do that before he can add money anyway

Try this:
Justin scored 5 correct digits. He is able to consistently add and subtract single digit problems but his accuracy decreases when he must regroup and work with place values. His typically achieving peers are working on using place value to describe whole numbers between 10 and 1000 in terms of hundreds, tens, and ones (2.1.1.2) When problems are applied to real-world situations, Justin does a better job of understanding what is happening and how to complete the problem. However, Justin struggles to use place value to describe numbers over 10 he will need intensive intervention to increase his understanding of place value and accuracy of addition and subtraction problems with sums over 18.

Commented [A7]: This is a beautiful example of what he can do. Nicely done.

Figure 3-4. IEP assignment feedback example.

5. Additional Details

Teacher candidates receive feedback during both phases of the assignment. During phase one, teacher candidates submit just the PLAAFP portion of the IEP and receive feedback. This is done through track changes and in-person conferences (if needed). Teacher candidates then use this feedback to revise the PLAAFP and create goals. During phase two, the revised PLAAFP and goals are submitted, and teacher candidates receive feedback that is aligned with the rubric.

A feedback example is shown in Figure 3-4.

6. Feedback Reflection

This feedback becomes very colorful. Each section of the rubric is highlighted in a different color, and then the teacher candidate's submission is similarly highlighted to demonstrate where that component of the rubric is evidenced and how the score was determined. Following the assignments, the teacher candidates are asked to reflect on the project and write a narrative on the most useful feedback they received and how they will use what they learned to improve their professional practice.

SUMMARY

This chapter introduced what we believe to be the initial focus of discussion around feedback in special education teacher preparation as it features the future educator—the recipient of the feedback. The impact of the feedback is improved through recognizing the recipient—the adult learner—at the center of planning and instruction. This focus on the audience, specifically the recipient, in the planning and delivery of feedback in special education teacher preparation reflects a new understanding of the way feedback should be *given, exhibited,* and *taught.*

We think many courses in special education teacher preparation offer opportunities for both experiential learning and application of strategies, alongside explicit instruction of skills that give, exhibit, and/or teach feedback. It is important to learn and take into account what is known about the learner as part of feedback.

OPPORTUNITY FOR GOING DEEPER

The following are resources to support deeper learning on the concepts reflected in Chapter 3:

- Seven keys to effective feedback. This document by Grant Wiggins focuses on the feedback from instructional leaders. http://www.ascd.org/publications/educational-leadership/sept12/vol70/num01/Seven-Keys-to-Effective-Feedback.aspx
- Faculty assessment and feedback plan. This resource by Kristen Sosulski provides an opportunity for deeper learning on faculty and student accountability in the learning process. https://secure.onlinelearningconsortium.org/effective_practices/faculty-assessment-and-feedback-plan-faculty-and-student-accountability-learning
- Author reflections. This resource is the location for a speech given by Sheila Heen. https://www.stoneandheen.com/speaking. She and Douglas Stone are authors of *Thanks for the Feedback: The Science and Art of Receiving Feedback.* https://www.stoneandheen.com/thanks-feedback
- Giving feedback to improve teaching. This 1993 article provides more information on what is effective when giving feedback to improve teaching. Brinko, K. T. (1993). The practice of giving feedback to improve teaching: What is effective? *The Journal of Higher Education, 64*(5), 574-593.

REFERENCES

34 CFR § 300.320. (2006). Definition of individualized education plan. https://www.ecfr.gov/

Adams, G., Lenz, K., Laraux, M., Graner, P., & Pouliot, N. (2001). *The effects of Learning Express-Ways Communication System on students with disabilities in high school settings.* (Research Report). University of Kansas Center for Research on Learning.

Bandura, A. (1986). Fearful expectations and avoidant actions as coeffects of perceived self-inefficacy. *American Psychologist, 41,* 1389-1391.

Bateman, B. D., & Herr, CM. (2006). *Writing measurable IEP goals and objectives.* IEP Resources.

Bransford, J. D., Brown, A. L., & Cocking, R. R. (Eds.). (2000). *How people learn: Brain, mind, experience and school.* National Academy Press.

Brookhart, S. M. (2009). Feedback that fits. In M. Scherer (Ed.), *Engaging the whole child: Reflections on best practices in learning, teaching, and leadership* (pp. 54-59). ASCD.

Carless, D. (2006). Differing perspectives in the feedback process. *Studies in Higher Education, 31*(2) p. 219-233.

Carless, D. (2013). Trust and its role in facilitating dialogic feedback. In D. Boud and E. Molloy (Eds.), *Feedback in higher and professional education: Understanding it and doing it well* (pp. 90-103). Routledge.

Carmeli, A., & Gittell, J. H. (2009). High-quality relationships, psychological safety, and learning from failures in work organizations. *Journal of Organizational Behavior, 30*(6), 709-729.

Chan, S. (2010). Applications of andragogy in multi-disciplined teaching and learning. *Journal of Adult Education, 39*(2), 25-35.

Cook-Sather, A., Bovill, C., & Felten, P. (2014). *Engaging students as partners in learning and teaching: A guide for faculty.* John Wiley & Sons.

Darling-Hammond, L. (2010). Teacher education and the American future. *Journal of Teacher Education, 61*(1-2), 35-47.

Fisher, J. B., Deshler, D. D., & Schumaker, J. B. (1999). The effects of an interactive multimedia program on teachers' understanding and implementation of an inclusive practice. *Learning Disability Quarterly, 22*(2), 127-142.

Forrest, S. P., & Peterson, T. O. (2006). It's called andragogy. *Academy of Management Learning & Education, 5*(1), 113-122.

Fullan, M. (2008). *What's worth fighting for in headship?* McGraw-Hill Education.

Gee, J. P. (2007). *Good video games + good learning: Collected essays on video games, learning and literacy* (2nd ed.). Peter Lang.

Hammerness, K., Darling-Hammond, L., Grossman, P., Rust, F., & Shulman, L. (2005). The design of teacher education programs. In L. Darling-Hammond & J. Bransford (Eds.), *Preparing teachers for a changing world* (pp. 390-441). Jossey-Bass.

Harley, T. A. (2014). *The psychology of language: From data to theory* (4th ed.). Psychology Press.

Hattie, J, & Timperley, H. (2007). The power of feedback. *Review of Educational Research, 77*(1), 81-112. https://doi.org/10.3102/003465430298487

Haynes-Smith, H. (2013, November). *Building positive academic relationships with pre-service teachers utilizing SIM Learning Express-Ways* [Conference presentation]. Teacher Education Division of The Council for Exceptional Children Conference. Fort Lauderdale, FL.

Hosp, M. K., Hosp, J. L., & Howell, K. W. (2016). *The ABCs of CBM: A practical guide to curriculum-based measurement.* Guilford Publications.

Howe, N., & Strauss, W. (2007). *Millennials go to college* (2nd ed.). Paramount Market.

Kegan, R., & Lahey, L. L. (2001). *How the way we talk can change the way we work: Seven languages for transformation.* Jossey-Bass.

Kershner, I. (Director). (1980). *The empire strikes back* [Film]. Lucasfilm Ltd.

Knight, J. (2007). *Instructional coaching: A partnership approach to improving instruction.* Corwin Press.

Kolb, A. Y., & Kolb, D. A. (2005). Learning styles and learning spaces: Enhancing experiential learning in higher education. *Academy of Management Learning & Education, 4*(2), 193-212.

Leeferink, H., Koopman, M., Beijaard, D., & Ketelaar, E. (2015). Unraveling the complexity of student teachers' learning in and from the workplace. *Journal of Teacher Education, 66*(4), 334-348.

Lenz, K., Adams, G., & Fisher, J. (1994). *Learning Express-Ways.* Edge Enterprises.

Lenz, K., Graner, P., & Adams, G. (2003). Learning Express-Ways: Building academic relationships to improve learning. *Teaching Exceptional Children, 35*(3), 70-73.

Prochaska, J. O., & DiClemente, C. C. (1992). Stages of change in the modification of problem behaviors. *Progress in Behavior Modification, 28*, 183-218.

Schein, E. H. (2013). *Humble inquiry: The gentle art of asking instead of telling.* Berrett-Koehler Publishers.

Scott, S. V. (2014). Practising what we preach: Towards a student-centred definition of feedback. *Teaching in Higher Education, 19*(1), 49-57.

Smith, H. H., Peterson, M., & Mitchell, B. B. (2014, October). *Student reflection and feedback: Adapting Learning Express-Ways for teacher preparation* [Conference presentation]. International Council for Learning Disabilities Conference, Philadelphia, PA.

Smith, H. H., Sanchez, A., Peterson-Ahmad, M., Woodbury, C., & Mitchel, B. B. (2018). Using *Learning Express-Ways* in special education teacher preparation: Developing student-faculty relationships as a path to partnership. *Journal of Special Education Apprenticeship, 7*(3), Article 5.

Thorndike, E. L. (1913). *Educational Psychology* (Vol. 1 and 2). Columbia University Press.

Tschannen-Moran, M., & Hoy, A. W. (2001). Teacher efficacy: Capturing an elusive construct. *Teaching and Teacher Education, 17*(7), 783-805.

Wiliam, D. (2016). The secret of effective feedback. *Educational leadership, 73*(7), 10-15.

Winnie, P. H., & Butler, D. L. (1994). Student cognition in learning from teaching. In T. N. Postlethwaite & T. Husen (Eds.), *International encyclopedia of education* (2nd ed., pp. 5738-5745). Pergamon.

Wiggins, G. (2012). Seven keys to effective feedback. *Educational Leadership, 70*(1), 10-16.

Zeichner, K. (2010). Rethinking the connections between campus courses and field experiences in college-and university-based teacher education. *Journal of Teacher Education, 61*(1-2), 89-99.

Immediate Versus Delayed Feedback

FEEDBACK SCENARIO

For the feedback scenario in this chapter, we examine two instructional decisions on whether immediate or delayed feedback would be most appropriate. For both, imagine yourself in the scenario and reflect on the instructional goal and the recipients of the feedback.

For this scenario, you are an instructor of an introductory special education methods course in a teacher education program. The term is about to begin. Based on evidence from the previous time you taught this course, you revised the course to contain an online multiple choice quiz on essential concepts, including accommodations and modifications, as some teacher candidates in the previous term struggled with the concepts. Given in week 4 of the course, the quiz allows teacher candidates to select all the examples from a list that can be considered classroom instructional accommodations.

As the instructor of this course, should you create the quiz items to provide details on whether the response to questions is correct once submitted? Alternatively, should you release the correct answers and explanations of them 4 days later, which would still provide time before the next class session, when the teacher candidates will apply their knowledge to review and revise accommodations in their sample Individualized Education Plans?

In this scenario, the recipient of the feedback is a student—an adult learner. Recent research, as you will learn in this chapter, suggests that delayed feedback can sometimes be more effective for retaining information on knowledge tasks, such as multiple choice assessments, specifically for college students. In this scenario, feedback given by the instructor that is delayed and addresses any incorrect or missing classroom accommodations might be most appropriate because the goal of this task is to demonstrate understanding of new knowledge. Other questions to consider when weighing learning goals and whether to provide immediate or delayed feedback include the following:

Elford, M. D., Smith, H., H., & James, S.
GET Feedback: Giving, Exhibiting, and Teaching Feedback in Special Education Teacher Preparation (pp. 57-80).
© 2022 SLACK Incorporated.

- Will some teacher candidates look only at the grade and not the feedback or correct answers?
- How might delaying the feedback help frame the focus on the learning and content?
- Are there more possible opportunities to learn and apply the content?
- Have you explained the purpose and value of this knowledge in creating Individualized Education Plans?

The choice to deliver immediate or delayed feedback is shaped in part by *what* learning is being assessed, which itself depends on the task and the recipient. In terms of task, immediate feedback is useful to interrupt an error that if it continues to be made could develop into a pattern that is hard to break or if it creates more errors in ongoing work. For example, if the assessment you chose was a performance-based assessment, then immediate feedback might be most appropriate to ensure that the learner does not keep practicing a poor performance. If the assessment reveals an error in understanding surface-level or factual learning of content, then immediate correction can prevent the learner from relying on that information in ongoing work, which would be weakened or invalid if the misunderstanding were not immediately corrected. In contrast, if an assessment seeks to measure deep understanding, including transformative learning and generalization to other contexts, then delayed feedback may be more useful because it provides an opportunity for reflection. In the case of the opening scenario for this chapter, the instructor increases the benefit of delayed feedback by assigning a review of the feedback and responses to prompt preparation for application in an upcoming class session. This assessment and delayed feedback thus provides an opportunity to reflect on and deepen the learning of accommodations and, consequently, according to the research you will review in this chapter, is appropriate for adult learners.

However, the task being assessed is only one factor to consider when deciding whether feedback should be immediate or delayed. The recipient must also be considered. Given that most instructors in special education teacher preparation programs were once K-12 teachers themselves, they have their own expectations of, experiences with, and biases about how feedback should be delivered that may affect their experience of receiving it. However, because these expectations, experiences, and biases were formed in K-12 settings, they may not align with what we know about how adult learners best engage feedback. Remembering the principles of adult learning, recognizing the unique perspectives of K-12 educators, and clearly recognizing the task being assessed are key to delivering appropriately timed feedback.

Chapter Objectives

Chapter 4 builds on the previous chapter and the need to consider the recipients of feedback. This chapter addresses an essential question in giving feedback: Do I give it now or later? The answer is YES! As we will discuss, there is the need to **give** immediate (now) feedback *and* delayed (later) feedback in special education teacher preparation. This chapter describes the research on immediate and delayed feedback approaches and why there is utility to include both in your course. This chapter also demonstrates how to select the appropriate feedback approach, with examples and prompts to take action.

In the last decade, research has suggested that adult learners benefit from delayed feedback on certain assessments (Butler et al., 2008). However, common practice in special education has long supported immediate, corrective feedback as the hallmark of effective instructional practice (Hougen & Smartt, 2012). Nevertheless, immediate feedback is not the only feedback option. Special education teacher preparation instructors should give feedback that considers when immediate versus delayed feedback is most appropriate for adult learners who do or will work in K-12 special education settings.

After reading this chapter you will **know** and **understand** these concepts and will have the opportunity to **demonstrate** and **apply** your knowledge (Table 4-1).

TABLE 4-1. GRAPHIC ORGANIZER		
KNOW (WHAT)	**UNDERSTAND (WHY)**	**DEMONSTRATE (HOW)**
What the research on immediate and delayed feedback suggests, especially for adult learners.	Why giving both immediate and delayed feedback are necessary in special education teacher preparation.	How to give feedback that recognizes: • When immediate feedback is most appropriate • When delayed feedback is most appropriate
APPLY (TAKE ACTION)		
Apply research on immediate and delayed feedback through the appropriate selection of feedback approaches in course design, activities, and assignments.		

Many aspects of giving, exhibiting, and teaching feedback will be discussed in this book to provide instructors an opportunity for comprehensive reflection on all aspects of feedback in special education teacher preparation. This chapter gives attention to a feedback decision that we think should be considered before and across all types of feedback—determining whether the feedback we give should be immediate or delayed.

DESCRIBE AND DEFINE

Giving feedback provides information about expected objectives, what success looks like, and what it would take for teacher candidates to improve their knowledge or performance. As such, feedback is not a value judgment or advice, it is more often information about performance in relation to a specific goal, task, or knowledge and application of theory to support practice. The question of whether to give immediate versus delayed feedback is, to us, preliminary. It ideally occurs during course design and planning. We begin our deeper exploration into giving immediate versus delayed feedback with general definitions. Then, the content of the chapter will address the questions posed in our graphic organizer (see Table 4-1), the "what, why, and how" of selecting the most appropriate format, based on the recipient and the task. The second half of the chapter will address how to apply these ideas and take action.

Immediate feedback is feedback given soon after a task is completed. It can be positive, providing specific details about what a learner has done well and should repeat or build upon, and it can also be corrective, providing an example or details on how to reach an objective. Immediate feedback is often used in response to performance-related tasks.

Delayed feedback is given after considerable time. The delay in the feedback is purposeful and planned. Delayed feedback may provide corrective information, support knowledge objectives, and promote positive progress for the adult learner.

Know

The research on immediate and delayed feedback provides clear guidance regarding differences for adult learners. In higher education, specifically special education teacher preparation, we are dually charged with developing content knowledge and the behavioral practices of preservice educators. Research from other professions with a clinical component, specifically psychology and medicine, suggests a discrepancy between the quality and rate of feedback from the professor or supervisor (Telio et al., 2015). Evidence from clinical practice in medicine suggests that supervisors believe they are giving frequent feedback, but adult students often disagree (Halman et al., 2016; van de Ridder et al., 2008). Before we begin to explore the literature on the phenomenon, first reflect on your practice using the following list of questions:

- What do you think your teacher candidates would say about the feedback you give?
- Do you think they recognize the benefits of immediate or delayed feedback?
- Could teacher candidate reflection assignments be opportunities for explicit instruction in giving feedback?
- What might happen if you explore this topic in class and assist teacher candidates in monitoring progress toward course objectives more explicitly?
- How can reflecting on course design support the giving of feedback?

We start with this reflection because we believe that exploring your ideas and feedback practices is helpful to you as the reader and learner of the G.E.T. Model too. We honor that you are already giving, exhibiting, and teaching feedback. We hope that the prompts, research, practical application, and authentic examples that follow in this and every chapter help you to build from that foundation. We recognize that everyone arriving at this page will be at different stages in their careers, at universities, colleges, and alternative certification programs that range in size, focus (teaching versus research), delivery (face-to-face, online, or hybrid), and are in different states, with varying standards and expectations. These and other considerations will likely have a profound impact on what each reader takes away from this chapter. Recognizing the diversity of readers' experiences with feedback, we now define *immediate* and *delayed* feedback in more depth.

Immediate Feedback

Immediate feedback is feedback given to support, change, or develop preservice teacher behavior and is given immediately or very close to the time of demonstration or practice. Research in special education teacher preparation has established the efficacy of immediate feedback in teacher candidates' learning. Feedback that is as close as possible to the teaching event is best to reduce and correct errors, provides instructors with the chance to model, and provides instruction in less time. In addition, teacher candidates are able to acquire specific teaching behaviors more efficiently and effectively (Rock et al., 2009; Scheeler et al., 2004; Scheeler, 2008; Wiggins & McTighe, 2007) when provided with immediate rather than delayed feedback. Immediate feedback can be delivered through a variety of means, including performance-based (e.g., bug-in-ear; Scheeler et al., 2012), technology-mediated (Dieker et al., 2014), or self-video reflections (Hollingsworth & Clarke, 2017).

Immediate feedback is essential to special education teacher preparation field experiences, placements, and activities (Nagro et al., 2017). Most often, instructors in special education teacher preparation were previously K-12 educators (Hougen & Smart 2012) and have likely experienced the success of immediate feedback teaching and practicing new skills in K-12 special education to support growth and learning toward standards or individualized education plan goals, such as in reading instruction. Because of both a strong evidence-base supporting its use in many situations and instructors' habit of using immediate feedback in their previous careers, it may be viewed as the default timing for feedback delivered. However, immediate feedback cannot always be provided nor is fast delivery always best for adult learning. We must be thoughtful about when and why we use immediate feedback in special education teacher preparation.

Delayed Feedback

Like immediate feedback, delayed feedback is given to support, change, or develop preservice teacher behavior, but it is given at a time farther removed from the moment of assessment to provide teacher candidates with an intentional time span between performing a task and receiving instructor feedback on it.

Use of multiple choice questions is one way that the deep content knowledge required of special educators can be assessed. Whether part of knowledge checks, exit tickets, quizzes, or examples, multiple choice questions can and should go beyond measuring memorization to instead provide opportunities for teacher candidates to apply and demonstrate content. For example, scenario-based multiple choice questions can challenge teacher candidates to apply strategies or demonstrate understanding of K-12 student data in making instructional decisions. Most of all, multiple choice questions should be purposeful, systematic, and intentional. When designed this way, they can be an effective part of special education teacher training and the G.E.T. Model, and adult learners in particular benefit when their multiple choice assignments are given delayed feedback.

Butler and Roediger's (2008) research on the relationship between delayed and immediate feedback on multiple choice assessments for college students suggests that not only is providing feedback on multiple choice assessments important for adult learners but that delayed feedback on these assessments can be more conducive to reflection and learning than immediate feedback because it enhances the positive effects of the feedback and reduces the negative effects of multiple choice testing. Research also suggests that allowing time for reflection on feedback supports retention and deep learning (Butler et al., 2008), delayed feedback on multiple choice assessments is beneficial because of the spaced presentation of information (Butler et al., 2008), and elaborated feedback on the responses are recommended if multiple choice assessments are used (Butler et al., 2013).

Instructors may need to design assignments with delayed feedback to ensure that THEY have time to reflect on what they observed and to manage their own workload; recognizing immediate feedback is not always possible.

Understand

Decisions about the timeliness of feedback require instructors to understand where teacher candidates are on the learning continuum and their readiness to receive feedback. Adult learners in special education teacher preparation can range in age from their late teens to their golden years. The age and experience of an adult learner can have an impact on the need of the learner, prior knowledge, readiness to learn, motivation, and self-efficacy. For more information on these considerations of the recipient, revisit Chapter 3. Although evidence suggests that Millennials are typically used to and prefer immediate feedback from those they see in authority, they are also uncomfortable with peer feedback given in fishbowl activities (Howe & Strauss, 2007; Twenge, 2006). There is less known in teacher education about why, but we purport that it could be connected to concepts of shame and vulnerability described in the research of Brown (2015). This suggests that there may be a meaningful difference in the preference for types of immediate feedback in adult learners, possibly connected to prior experience with this type of feedback, that should be considered in planning or described explicitly and scaffolded into course design and planning. If we choose to use fishbowl activities, we should work to explain the purpose, reflect on the phrasing of our feedback, and work with peers to ensure that the recipient benefits. Further, older students returning to higher education actively seek feedback and are sometimes dissatisfied with the amount of feedback and guidance given in courses (Delahaye & Ehrich, 2008). This is evidence of why instructors in special education teacher preparation programs should consider adult students' demographic background when selecting immediate or delayed feedback. Given new research about the benefits of providing delayed feedback for adult learners, special education instructors should consider how their particular teacher candidates can benefit from both delayed and immediate feedback.

Purposeful practice in considering whether to provide immediate versus delayed feedback as part of the G.E.T. Model begins in course design. As instructors, we work to design courses to maximize the integration of knowledge and theory, often relying on experiential learning, collaborative learning, guided practice, and other evidence-based or high-leverage practices in special education teacher preparation. In designing courses, many also use frameworks such as the Strategic Instruction Model course organizer or Understanding by Design to determine the appropriate course learning objectives and ensure that activities and assessment align with the learning objectives (refer to the Opportunity for Going Deeper section at the end of this chapter for links to these frameworks and related resources). We must communicate feedback in a way that the recipient can receive it and use it. For example, **performance feedback**, in which positive and corrective feedback is delivered immediately through opportunities to respond, verbal expansions, and behavior-specific praise. Performance feedback, as a form of feedback, fits across all areas of the G.E.T. Model to assist you in creating and revising courses, assignments, and activities. Regardless of the framework used, as part of the iterative process of course design, including course revisions, instructors might begin by reflecting on when they are giving feedback and whether this aligns and supports the stated learning objectives for the course. When instructors skip the initial consideration of the timing of feedback and instead leave it to chance, they miss an opportunity to mindfully exploit the full impact of feedback timing on adult learning. The following questions can assist you in reflecting on the timing of feedback during the course design or redesign process:

- Do I currently provide both immediate feedback and delayed feedback?
- What course activities rely on feedback to maximize adult learning?
- What course assignments, including assessments, would benefit from a revised plan for feedback to maximize adult learning?
- Have I considered when immediate and delayed feedback might best support learning in my course activities and assignments?

Demonstrate

Reflecting on current feedback practices gives us the opportunity to determine whether our teaching choices are supporting our goals. First, use Table 4-2 to identify how you give feedback. In Table 4-2, look at the first column. Which feedback formats are you currently using to give feedback? Circle the formats that apply to your course or that you would like to consider. For the formats you identify, then circle in the column to the right whether you use them to provide immediate and/or delayed feedback in that format for adult learners. Then, consider, in the context of YOUR course(s), whether that format is appropriate for providing feedback that is immediate and/or delayed. Note: Because each special education instructor teaches different adult learners, even in classes that seek to teach similar skills or content, there are no right or wrong answers.

The purpose of this reflective exercise is to further examine our current practice and opportunities or interest in addressing immediate or delayed feedback. Now, let us attempt to make sense of the reflection exercise. Read through the following list of questions:

- Do you notice any patterns or preference for one type of feedback?
- Are you happy with these results?
- Do you see any opportunities to explore or expand your immediate or delayed feedback?

Now that you have reflected on your current practice, it is important to consider other factors in determining the appropriateness of immediate versus delayed feedback in special education teacher preparation. These include your teaching load, the student–teacher ratio, state or university policies, graduate teaching assistant support, and more.

We must recognize that sometimes a delay in feedback is unavoidable. For example, grading can take longer than expected. If grading of a particular assignment takes longer than expected in multiple semesters, this could be an indication that the instructor should revise the assignment or clarify expectations for teacher candidates so that more of them more quickly meet the expectations, and thus they will need less corrective feedback. Another possibility is reviewing the assignment and determining what would be needed to complete the feedback as planned, such as revision of the rubric, adapting the assignment to ensure it addresses only the designated learning objective(s), which could then support shortening the length of a paper, length of presentation, or integrating universal design for learning and flexibility of format for an assignment, such as a change to an infographic.

TABLE 4-2. TARGET/FOCUS OF COURSE		
CIRCLE FORMAT	**CIRCLE IMMEDIATE AND/OR DELAYED**	
Online quiz, with feedback included (yes or no)	Immediate	Delayed
Rubrics	Immediate	Delayed
Written on the assignment	Immediate	Delayed
Written as comments in rubrics	Immediate	Delayed
Verbally in instructional coaching conversations	Immediate	Delayed
Written annotation in online assignment	Immediate	Delayed
Grades	Immediate	Delayed
GoReact, video tagging with comments	Immediate	Delayed
Verbally in class, directed to all	Immediate	Delayed
Verbally in class, in response to a question	Immediate	Delayed
Bug-in-ear (Bluetooth or Facebook Live, in-the-moment feedback)	Immediate	Delayed
Virtual teaching simulation (augmented reality) after action review	Immediate	Delayed
Teaching simulation (contrived, role play)	Immediate	Delayed
Teaching simulation in the moment, instructional coaching	Immediate	Delayed
Summative evaluation (feedback on individual results)	Immediate	Delayed
Peer feedback on presentation	Immediate	Delayed
Peer feedback on videos	Immediate	Delayed
Peer feedback on written assignments	Immediate	Delayed
Tuning protocol	Immediate	Delayed
Critical Friends Group protocols on feedback	Immediate	Delayed
Socratic/dialogue	Immediate	Delayed
Self-evaluation	Immediate	Delayed
Other: _____ _____	Immediate	Delayed

TABLE 4-3. SPOTLIGHT ON ADULT LEARNING			
SPECIFICITY	**IMMEDIACY**	**PURPOSEFULNESS**	**CONSTRUCTIVENESS**
Is the adult student invested in learning or behavioral change? Do they see the benefit? How might immediate or delayed feedback fit personal learning needs/goals? How can the feedback go beyond a grade or evaluative judgment?	What is the learning readiness of the adult student(s)? Will the feedback be more effective if given immediately or after some time?	What are the learning objectives for the activity, assignment, or assessment? How would immediate versus delayed feedback best support adult student learning?	Will the adult student(s) be more likely to construct new learning if they receive the feedback on the activity, assignment, or assessment now? Do they have a plan or direction on how to act on the feedback when it is given?

SPOTLIGHT ON ADULT LEARNING

The consideration of immediate versus delayed feedback is necessary in all aspects of the G.E.T. Model. It is appropriate to give, exhibit, and teach feedback. It is also an important consideration of the model's four domains: purposefulness, immediacy, specificity, and constructiveness. As we have said before, we believe giving, exhibiting, and teaching feedback lacks effect if it falls on those not ready to learn. Feedback, no matter how frequent, thorough, descriptive, or timely, falls short of its purpose when instructors fail to put the recipient at the center of the feedback they are giving. Understanding who the recipients are, where they are on the learning continuum, and how ready they are to receive feedback contributes to the effectiveness of the feedback. Table 4-3 provides some questions for reflection on each domain of the G.E.T. Model in considering whether feedback should be immediate versus delayed for each activity, assignment, or assessment in your course.

The questions in Table 4-3 are designed to help you reflect on the specific aspects of giving, exhibiting, and teaching feedback. Again, each chapter will provide additional details for your consideration and deeper learning about feedback in special education teacher preparation.

POSSIBLE BARRIERS TO USING THIS TYPE OF FEEDBACK

Both setting and recipient readiness can present barriers to effectively determining the timing of feedback. The following sections will expand on these barriers.

Setting

Teacher education has multiple settings to consider when weighing the questions of immediate versus delayed feedback. One aspect of teacher preparation is the clinical practice, which includes practicum, student teaching, and other clinical practice opportunities. Clinical education has the added problem of being completed in a workplace setting that is not conducive to providing timely and high-quality feedback to teacher candidates (Boerboom et al., 2015). This often results in feedback being given to teacher candidates via forms (sometimes immediate and sometimes delayed) or final evaluations (often delayed). These types of feedback are often less rich and provide little room for a dialogue and reflection from the teacher candidate than immediate feedback (Boerboom et al., 2015). To overcome this barrier, purposeful attention to immediate versus delayed feedback aligned with the goal of course, activity, and observation should be explained before clinical work begins. A preconference can be helpful in setting expectations. It is important to introduce forms to the preservice teachers early. They need to know how they are being evaluated and the connection to the assignment, performance, or task. Further, forms for feedback are not always grounded in solid theory and understanding of the recipient, so instructors should provide explicit connections between the feedback and the goal. One example of how the explicit connections can be made is feedback facilitation. Boerboom et al. (2015) suggested that clinical educators engage in "feedback facilitation" (p. 49) to improve the acceptance and understanding of feedback, promote reflection and discussion, minimize negative emotions associated with the feedback, and, finally, construct a plan of action on how to change based on feedback provided.

Readiness

Another barrier to giving feedback that supports teacher candidate learning is consideration of the readiness of the recipient. Who are our recipients? Are your teacher candidates members of Gen Z, Millennials, or older people changing careers later in life? Are they willing to be vulnerable? When we are teaching adult learners, the age span can be 18 to 80 years, and each adult learner is unique. Younger adult learners are often used to immediate feedback, whereas other adults might not be.

In the context of this chapter, this means that we cannot just jump in giving immediate or delayed feedback without knowing our recipients. We need to focus on the strengths and opportunities for growth and development, partnering with teacher candidates in their learning. For example, early social validity research in TLE TeachLivE (University of Central Florida, http://teachlive.org/) taught us about barriers to realizing the transformational growth opportunities for teacher candidates because of fear of peer feedback in fishbowl activities. TLE TeachLivE is a mixed-reality classroom with student avatars that provides teachers the opportunity to develop their pedagogical practice (James et al., 2012). We were so excited to use the technology that we barely considered how our teacher candidates might react to activities where we were giving them feedback immediately and sometimes in front of others. We quickly modified our approach to feedback, based on feedback from our teacher candidates in early studies using TLE TeachLivE by providing exposure to a novel virtual reality classroom. Rather than beginning with the exercise, the teacher candidates needed to get to know the virtual avatar students. We needed to be clearer about expectations and explicit about learning objectives. We had to design and plan for opportunities to debrief with a class or small groups of teacher candidates and to prompt them to reflect on how this environment could be beneficial to them in their learning. When we became systematic in preparing the teacher candidates for feedback and the type of feedback, setting expectations, and building trust, we then saw amazing results and growth in our teacher candidates. Our experience with TLE TeachLivE speaks to the importance of purposeful design and building on the prior experience (see Chapter 3) of the adult recipient of the feedback and trust-building through continued demonstration of respect for our adult learners. If our goal is engaged teacher candidates learning and growing from all kinds of feedback, Brown (2015) also warned us that we can teach explicitly about shame and that adult learners may become disengaged when we espouse values they rarely see us do.

Other Criticisms

Some suggest that stopping a lesson to give immediate feedback may disrupt the lesson more than the value of the feedback provides. Scheeler et al. (2004) contended that this may be so, but immediate feedback is worth the cost; therefore, using technology, such as bug-in-ear, is an appropriate alternative. Studies (Scheeler et al., 2006, 2010, 2012) have shown that using bug-in-ear technology to deliver immediate feedback does not disrupt the flow of the lesson and produces notable special education teacher growth and learning.

In an effort to provide immediate feedback, one other possible barrier is the impact on the quality of the feedback. A quick turnaround may be difficult when there are many teacher candidates in a course or the total number of teacher candidates an instructor is working with across courses is very high. Instructors might find it helpful to ask themselves the following question at the course design level: In considering feedback that can be given immediately, how realistically can each be applied to an assignment?

PRACTICAL APPLICATION

The practical application presented demonstrates giving information to a recipient that informs their understanding or restructures their thinking or their beliefs related to their performance, knowledge, or skill. In this practical application, instructors are asked to consider the recipient of feedback. When considering the recipient of the feedback alongside the learning goal, instructors can consider the following questions in answering the question about selecting immediate versus delayed feedback:

- Do teacher candidates know where to look for feedback (e.g., annotated in an online course management system, written directly on a paper, provided in the comments of an online observation form)?
- Have you told teacher candidates what is coming next and how/why the improvement will benefit them? Do they know how to take action and what that would look like?
- Have you considered how you could increase the number of opportunities to give feedback to your teacher candidates?

There is a need for giving both immediate and delayed feedback in special education teacher preparation. However, the balance of how and when to provide immediate versus delayed feedback lies in the context of the course (Hattie & Timperley, 2007). Instructors should consider the course learning objectives to be purposeful in planning the giving of feedback in course activities, assignments, assessments, and evaluation, considering both immediate and delayed feedback opportunities.

In *Daring Greatly*, Brown (2015) reminded us how giving and soliciting feedback has become rare and that people are desperate for feedback. Her research on shame and vulnerability is especially applicable to education and teachers. We believe we can start even earlier with preservice teachers, introducing these ideas and giving feedback that recognizes strengths and purposefully avoids shame.

Now that you have read much of the chapter, let us revisit some considerations from the beginning of the chapter. The same list from Table 4-2 is again presented in Table 4-4. Without looking back, identify a specific course or learning objective and circle the key activities, assignments, and assessments from the course you are teaching (or would like to teach). For each item circled, indicate whether you intend to provide feedback immediately or after some time has passed.

The following are guided reflection questions:

- Review your responses and how they have changed or stayed the same now that you have read this chapter.
- Did you circle too many or too few, given both the needs of the teacher candidates you will likely be teaching and given the demands on your time and energy that delivering high-quality feedback requires?
- Which activities, assignments, and assessments on the list can you adequately address in an identified course? Circle these using a new color.

The following questions are provided to guide your review and reflection in the Authentic Example starting on page 68, contributed by Kristin Joannou Lyon, PhD and Virginia L. Walker, PhD, BCBA-D.

- In this example, how does the instructor apply knowledge of giving immediate versus delayed feedback? Reflect.
- What is an assignment or activity in one of your courses where you give feedback? Is it immediate or delayed?
- How does reflecting on immediate versus delayed feedback support understanding and support the recipients of the feedback?

TABLE 4-4. TARGET/FOCUS OF COURSE

CIRCLE FORMAT	CIRCLE IMMEDIATE AND/OR DELAYED	
Online quiz, with feedback included (yes or no)	Immediate	Delayed
Rubrics	Immediate	Delayed
Written on the assignment	Immediate	Delayed
Written as comments in rubrics	Immediate	Delayed
Verbally in instructional coaching conversations	Immediate	Delayed
Written annotation in online assignment	Immediate	Delayed
Grades	Immediate	Delayed
GoReact, video tagging with comments	Immediate	Delayed
Verbally in class, directed to all	Immediate	Delayed
Verbally in class, in response to a question	Immediate	Delayed
Bug-in-ear (Bluetooth or Facebook Live, in-the-moment feedback)	Immediate	Delayed
Virtual teaching simulation (augmented reality) after action review	Immediate	Delayed
Teaching simulation (contrived, role play)	Immediate	Delayed
Teaching simulation in the moment, instructional coaching	Immediate	Delayed
Summative evaluation (feedback on individual results)	Immediate	Delayed
Peer feedback on presentation	Immediate	Delayed
Peer feedback on videos	Immediate	Delayed
Peer feedback on written assignments	Immediate	Delayed
Tuning protocol	Immediate	Delayed
Critical Friends Group protocols on feedback	Immediate	Delayed
Socratic/dialogue	Immediate	Delayed
Self-evaluation	Immediate	Delayed
Other:_____ _____	Immediate	Delayed

Authentic Example

Contributed by
Kristin Joannou Lyon, PhD
Virginia L. Walker, PhD, BCBA-D

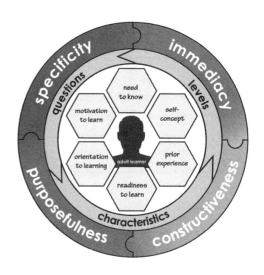

1. Course Details

SPE 4910: Systematic Instruction is an undergraduate course focused on preparing pre-service special education teachers to plan and implement systematic instruction, an evidence-based practice for students with severe disabilities (Spooner et al., 2017). This course was part of a cross-categorical special education teacher preparation program. Prior to implementing systematic instruction with students with severe disabilities in field-based placements, preservice special education teachers submitted demonstrations of various response prompting systems falling under the scope of systematic instruction to receive course instructor feedback.

2. Learning Objectives

Course Objective: Demonstrate, with consistency, procedures associated with systematic instruction.

The course assignment also aligns with the following Council for Exceptional Children Initial Preparation Standards (Council for Exceptional Children, 2015):

a. 1.2. Beginning special education professionals use understanding of development and individual differences to respond to the needs of individuals with exceptionalities.

b. 3.2. Beginning special education professionals understand and use general and specialized content knowledge for teaching across curricular content areas to individualize learning for individuals with exceptionalities.

c. 4.2. Beginning special education professionals use knowledge of measurement principles and practices to interpret assessment results and guide educational decisions for individuals with exceptionalities.

d. 5.6. Beginning special education professionals teach to mastery and promote generalization of learning.

3. Assignment Details

During class time, the course instructor provided written instructions on how to implement different response prompting systems and demonstrated these same response prompting systems. In addition, the instructor provided the preservice teachers with opportunities to rehearse the prompting systems with classmates while receiving instructor feedback. Preservice teachers recorded video demonstrations (original video submissions) of two common response prompting systems—constant time delay and system of least prompts (Collins, 2012). (See Video Application #1 for a sample video assignment description.) The course instructor accessed the video demonstrations using LiveText by Watermark, where she embedded feedback within the videos to describe procedural elements that were implemented correctly or incorrectly. Feedback focused on the following procedural elements: (a) delivery of attentional cue; (b) delivery of instructional cue; (c) use of correct response interval; (d) delivery of correct response prompt, contingent on incorrect student responses; and (e) delivery of reinforcement, contingent on correct student responding. In addition to providing feedback, the course instructor completed an implementation fidelity checklist (Tables 4-5 and 4-6) to calculate an original submission implementation fidelity score. The course instructor requested that preservice teachers review the embedded feedback using LiveText and record the video demonstrations (video resubmissions) a second time, adjusting their implementation based on the feedback received. Again, the course instructor completed an implementation fidelity checklist to calculate a resubmission implementation score to determine the extent of improvement in implementation fidelity.

4. Evaluation Criteria

SPE 4910
Video Application #1

You and your partner will teach (a) one chained cooking task and (b) one discrete academic task to each other. Each person will teach the selected chained and discrete tasks, using constant time delay, while the other acts as the student with a severe intellectual disability. The person acting as a student with a severe intellectual disability will need to wait for the prompt, initiate errors, not respond, and occasionally respond correctly. The instructor will need to provide error correction, feedback, and reinforcement in the appropriate manner and at the appropriate times. Reinforcement will be provided as verbal praise on a continuous reinforcement schedule.

Discrete Academic Task (Table 4-5)

Targeted skill: Verbally identifying coin
Task direction: "Tell me the name of this coin."
Controlling prompt: Verbal
Delay interval: 0 seconds (Video #1), 5 seconds (Video #2)
Trials:

a. Show quarter.

b. Show penny.

c. Show dime.

d. Show nickel.

e. Show penny.

Note: Please label your videos as follows: Last Name_Video#1/Video#2_CTD_0sec/5sec

Table 4-5. Video Application Constant Time Delay Original Assignment

STUDENT: MAGGIE

PROCEDURAL STEPS; TASK ANALYSIS STEP OR TRIAL NUMBER	ORIGINAL/RESUBMISSION: ORIGINAL			ASSESSOR: PROFESSOR LYON	
	1. QUARTER	2. PENNY	3. DIME	4. NICKEL	5. PENNY
0-Second Delay					
Deliver attentional cue	+				
Deliver task direction	+	+	+	+	+
Immediately deliver controlling prompt (verbal)	+	+	+	+	+
• If student responds correctly, reinforce correct response	+	0	+	+	+
• If student responds incorrectly or does not respond, complete step for the student	0	—	0	0	0

(continued)

TABLE 4-5 (CONTINUED). VIDEO APPLICATION CONSTANT TIME DELAY ORIGINAL ASSIGNMENT

STUDENT: MAGGIE	ORIGINAL/RESUBMISSION: ORIGINAL		ASSESSOR: PROFESSOR LYON		
PROCEDURAL STEPS; TASK ANALYSIS STEP OR TRIAL NUMBER	1. QUARTER	2. PENNY	3. DIME	4. NICKEL	5. PENNY
5-Second Delay					
Deliver attentional cue	+				
Deliver task direction	+	+	+	+	+
Wait response interval	+	+	+	+	+
• If student responds correctly, reinforce correct response	+	0	0	+	0
• If student responds incorrectly, deliver controlling prompt (verbal)	0	+	—	0	+

(continued)

Table 4-5 (continued). Video Application Constant Time Delay Original Assignment

STUDENT: MAGGIE	ORIGINAL/RESUBMISSION: ORIGINAL			ASSESSOR: PROFESSOR LYON	
PROCEDURAL STEPS; TASK ANALYSIS STEP OR TRIAL NUMBER	1. QUARTER	2. PENNY	3. DIME	4. NICKEL	5. PENNY
5-Second Delay					
○ If student responds correctly, reinforce correct response	0	+	—	0	+
○ If student responds incorrectly, complete step for the student	0	0	0	0	0
Total number of steps completed correctly				32	
Total number of steps completed				35	
Percentage of steps completed correctly				91%	

+ = step completed by instructor; — = step not completed by instructor; 0 = no opportunity to complete the step; x = did not implement trial/step.

Chained Cooking Task (Table 4-6)

Targeted skill: Preparing a peanut butter and jelly sandwich
Task direction: "Make a peanut butter and jelly sandwich."
Controlling prompt: Gesture
Delay interval: 0 seconds (Video #3), 5 seconds (Video #4)
Task analysis:

a. Place two slices of bread on plate.

b. Open peanut butter jar.

c. Spread peanut butter on one slice of bread.

d. Close peanut butter jar.

e. Open jelly jar.

f. Spread jelly on the other slice of bread.

g. Close jelly jar.

h. Place one slice of bread on the other slice of bread.

Note: Please label your videos as follows: Last Name_Video#3/Video#4_CTD_0sec/5sec

After creating the four videos acting as the teacher, submit videos via LiveText under the corresponding Video Application #1 assignment.

5. Additional Details

We evaluated and provided feedback on the preservice special education teachers' ability to implement the following two response prompting systems: constant time delay and system of least prompts. Constant time delay involves delivering one prompt (i.e., the controlling prompt) after a set interval of time to encourage correct student responding. During initial teaching sessions, a 0-second delay is used, whereby the controlling prompt is immediately delivered before the student has an opportunity to respond to promote errorless learning. In other sessions, the prompt is delivered only if the student does not respond correctly after a predetermined amount of time (e.g., 5 seconds). The system of least prompts is different in that a hierarchy of prompts is used, whereby the least intrusive prompt is delivered initially when the student does not respond correctly. If the least intrusive prompt does not produce the desired response, a more intrusive prompt is delivered until all prompts in the hierarchy have been exhausted or the student responds correctly.

The Modules Addressing Special Education and Teacher Education (MAST; https://mast. ecu.edu/) website offers a learning module where readers can learn more about two response prompting systems with students with significant intellectual disabilities: https://mast.ecu. edu/Students%20with%20Significant%20Intellectual%20Disabilities/Prompting%20Systems/ index.html

6. Feedback Reflection

The video demonstration assignment is an example of **giving feedback** using technology. By embedding feedback within the video demonstrations using LiveText, the course instructor had the opportunity to provide detailed feedback, leaving timestamped comments about specific procedural elements that were or were not implemented correctly. Preservice teachers were able to watch their video demonstrations and carefully review the feedback to determine how to adjust their use of the response prompting systems.

TABLE 4-6. CONSTANT TIME DELAY DISCRETE SKILL EXAMPLE IMPLEMENTATION FIDELITY CHECKLIST

STUDENT: WINSTON	ORIGINAL/RESUBMISSION: RESUBMISSION			
PROCEDURAL STEPS; TASK ANALYSIS STEP OR TRIAL NUMBER	**PLACE BREAD ON PLATE**	**OPEN PEANUT BUTTER JAR**	**SPREAD PEANUT BUTTER**	
Deliver attentional cue	—			
Deliver task direction	+			
Wait response interval: 3 seconds	+	+	+	
• If student responds correctly, deliver reinforcement	0	0	0	
• If student responds incorrectly or does not respond, give the least intrusive prompt in the hierarchy (verbal)	+	+	+	
Wait response interval: 3 seconds	+	+	+	
• If student responds correctly, deliver reinforcement	0	+	0	
• If student responds incorrectly or does not respond, give the next least intrusive prompt in the hierarchy (gesture)	—	0	—	
+ = step completed by instructor; — = step not completed by instructor; 0 = no opportunity to complete the step; x = did not implement trial/step.				

	CLOSE PEANUT BUTTER JAR	OPEN JELLY JAR	SPREAD JELLY	CLOSE JELLY JAR	PLACE SLICES TOGETHER
	+	+	+	+	+
	0	+	0	0	0
	+	0	+	+	+
	+	0	+	+	+
	+	0	0	0	+
	0	0	+	+	0

(continued)

ASSESSOR: PROFESSOR WALKER

TABLE 4-6 (CONTINUED). CONSTANT TIME DELAY DISCRETE SKILL EXAMPLE IMPLEMENTATION FIDELITY CHECKLIST

STUDENT: WINSTON	ORIGINAL/RESUBMISSION: RESUBMISSION			
PROCEDURAL STEPS; TASK ANALYSIS STEP OR TRIAL NUMBER	**PLACE BREAD ON PLATE**	**OPEN PEANUT BUTTER JAR**	**SPREAD PEANUT BUTTER**	
Wait response interval: 3 seconds	—	0	+	
• If student responds correctly, deliver reinforcement	0	0	+	
• If student responds incorrectly or does not respond, give the most intrusive prompt in the hierarchy (model)	+	0	0	
Wait response interval: 3 seconds	+	0	0	
• If student responds correctly, deliver reinforcement	+	0	0	
• If student responds incorrectly or does not respond, complete the step for the student	0	0	0	
Total number of steps completed correctly				
Total number of steps completed				
Percentage of steps completed correctly				
+ = step completed by instructor; — = step not completed by instructor; 0 = no opportunity to complete the step; x = did not implement trial/step.				

| ASSESSOR: PROFESSOR WALKER | | | | |
CLOSE PEANUT BUTTER JAR	OPEN JELLY JAR	SPREAD JELLY	CLOSE JELLY JAR	PLACE SLICES TOGETHER
0	0	+	+	0
0	0	+	0	0
0	0	0	+	0
0	0	0	+	0
0	0	0	+	0
0	0	0	0	0
	40			
	44			
	91%			

Summary

This chapter summarizes the research and application of giving immediate versus delayed feedback in special education teacher preparation in recognition of what is known about adult learners and the needs of K-12 students receiving special education. Immediate, corrective feedback is well established as an effective practice in improving teacher behaviors and K-12 student learning. However, research suggests that delayed feedback on assessments for adult learners may support deeper learning with reflection. Special education teacher preparation instructors should consider their learning objectives and align activities and assessments with objectives to determine where to give immediate versus delayed feedback in practice.

Opportunity for Going Deeper

The following resources support deeper learning on concepts reflected in Chapter 4.

- Multiple choice tests. These links provide more information on Andrew Butler's research studies and projects. For more information on how to word your multiple choice items, visit https://www.chronicle.com/article/5-Tips-for-Using/244718 For more information on his work and collaboration to create this personalized learning tool, visit https://openstax.org/openstax-tutor
- The Strategic Instruction Model. For more information on training and materials to support all learners using content enhancement routines and/or learning strategies visit the University of Kansas, Center for Research on Learning and Strategic Instruction Model webpage: https://sim.ku.edu/sim-curricula The following Content Enhancement Routines specifically come to mind in supporting aligned course design:
  - Strategic Instruction Model: Course Organizer Routine: https://sim.drupal.ku.edu/course-organizer
  - Strategic Instruction Model: Unit Organizer Routine: https://sim.ku.edu/unit-organizer
  - Strategic Instruction Model: Lesson Organizer Routine: https://sim.drupal.ku.edu/lesson-organizer
- Examples of Understanding by Design lessons. In addition to the books on the Understanding by Design framework by Wiggins and McTighe (2011), Trinity University also has an open access repository of K-12 lessons published by master teachers at: https://digitalcommons.trinity.edu/understandingbydesign/
- The features of effective instruction. For more information on the features of effective instruction, specifically immediate, corrective feedback in early reading instruction, visit the Meadows Center for Preventing Educational Risk (MCPER) Library website and search for the 2010 Features of Effective Instruction presentation: https://www.meadowscenter.org/library/resource/features-of-effective-instruction1
- Mastery-focused instruction. This text is helpful for preservice or current educators thinking about the alignment, assessment, and transition to mastery-focused instruction. Frey, N., Hattie, J., & Fisher, D. (2018). *Developing assessment-capable visible learners, grades K-12: Maximizing skill, will, and thrill.* Corwin Press.
- Teaching strategies. For descriptions of teaching strategies read *High-Impact Instruction: A Framework for Great Teaching* by Jim Knight (2013): https://www.instructionalcoaching.com/wp-content/uploads/2016/03/Instructional-Playbook.v4.pdf
- Instruction for students with moderate and severe disabilities. For more ideas and resources for preparing preservice teacher candidates to support students with moderate and severe disabilities read: Collins, B. (2012). *Systematic instruction for students with moderate and severe disabilities.* Brookes Publishing .

- The use of protocols for discussion and feedback. Two resources for selecting and using protocols for discussion and feedback practice are:
  - ◦ School Reform Initiative: https://www.schoolreforminitiative.org/
  - ◦ Critical Friends Groups/National School Reform Faculty protocols: https://nsrfharmony.org/faq-items/cfgvsplc/

REFERENCES

Boerboom, T. B. B., Stalmeijer, R. E., Dolmans, D. H. J. M., & Jaarsma, D. A. C. (2015). How feedback can foster professional growth of teachers in the clinical workplace: A review of the literature. *Studies in Educational Evaluation, 46,* 47-52.

Brown, B. (2015). *Daring greatly: How the courage to be vulnerable transforms the way we live, love, parent, and lead.* Penguin.

Butler, A. C., Godbole, N., & Marsh, E. J. (2013). Explanation feedback is better than correct answer feedback for promoting transfer of learning. *Journal of Educational Psychology, 105*(2), 290-298.

Butler, A. C., Karpicke, J. D., & Roediger, H. L. (2008). Correcting a metacognitive error: Feedback increases retention of low-confidence correct responses. *Journal of Experimental Psychology: Learning, Memory, and Cognition, 34*(4), 918-928.

Butler, A. C., & Roediger III, H. L. (2008). Feedback enhances the positive effects and reduces the negative effects of multiple-choice testing. *Memory & Cognition, 36*(3), 604-616.

Collins, B. C. (2012). *Systematic instruction for students with moderate and severe disabilities.* Brookes Publishing Company.

Council for Exceptional Children. (2015). *What every special educator must know: Professional ethics and standards.* CEC.

Delahaye, B. L., & Ehrich, L. C. (2008). Complex learning preferences and strategies of older adults. *Educational Gerontology, 34*(8), 649-662.

Dieker, L. A., Kennedy, M. J., Smith, S., Vasquez III, E., Rock, M., & Thomas, C. (2014). Use of technology in the preparation of pre-service teachers (Document No. IC-11). http://ceedar.education.ufl.edu/tools/innovation-configurations

Halman, S., Dudek, N., Wood, T., Pugh, D., Touchie, C., McAleer, S., & Humphrey-Murto, S. (2016). Direct observation of clinical skills feedback scale: Development and validity evidence. *Teaching and Learning in Medicine, 28*(4), 385-394.

Hattie, J., & Timperley, H. (2007). The power of feedback. *Review of Educational Research, 77*(1), 81-112. https://doi.org/10.3102/003465430298487

Hollingsworth, H., & Clarke, D. (2017). Video as a tool for focusing teacher self-reflection: Supporting and provoking teacher learning. *Journal of Mathematics Teacher Education, 20*(5), 457-475.

Hougen, M. C., & Smartt, S. M. (Eds.). (2012). *Fundamentals of literacy instruction and assessment, Pre-K-6.* Brookes Publishing Company.

Howe, N., & Strauss, W. (2007). *Millennials go to college* (2nd ed.). Paramount Market.

James, S., Elford, M.D., Haynes, H., (2012, November). *Augmented reality learning environments: A study of educators' understanding of evidenced-based literacy practices* [Conference presentation]. Teacher Education Division of the Council for Exceptional Children Conference, Grand Rapids, MI.

Nagro, S. A., & Cornelius, K. E. (2013). Evaluating the evidence base of video analysis: A special education teacher development tool. *Teacher Education and Special Education, 36*(4), 312-329. https://doi.org/10.1177/0888406413501090

Nagro, S. A., DeBettencourt, L. U., Rosenberg, M. S., Carran, D. T., & Weiss, M. P. (2017). The effects of guided video analysis on teacher candidates' reflective ability and instructional skills. *Teacher Education and Special Education, 40*(1), 7-25.

Rock, M. L., Gregg, M., Thead, B. K., Acker, S. E., Gable, R. A., & Zigmond, N. P. (2009). Can you hear me now? Evaluation of an online wireless technology to provide real-time feedback to special education teachers-in-training. *Teacher Education and Special Education, 32*(1), 64-82.

Scheeler, M. C. (2008). Generalizing effective teaching skills: The missing link in teacher preparation. *Journal of Behavioral Education, 17*(2), 145-159.

Scheeler, M. C., Congdon, M., & Stansbery, S. (2010). Providing immediate feedback to co-teachers through bug-in-ear technology: An effective method of peer coaching in inclusion classrooms. *Teacher Education and Special Education, 33*(1), 83-96.

Scheeler, M. C., McAfee, J. K., Ruhl, K. L., & Lee, D. L. (2006). Effects of corrective feedback delivered via wireless technology on preservice teacher performance and student behavior. *Teacher Education and Special Education, 29*(1), 12-25.

Scheeler, M. C., McKinnon, K., & Stout, J. (2012). Effects of immediate feedback delivered via webcam and bug-in-ear technology on preservice teacher performance. *Teacher Education and Special Education, 35*(1), 77-90.

Scheeler, M. C., Ruhl, K. L., & McAfee, J. K. (2004). Providing performance feedback to teachers: A review. *Teacher Education and Special Education, 27*(4), 396-407.

Spooner, F., McKissick, B. R., & Knight, V. F. (2017). Establishing the state of affairs for evidence-based practices in students with severe disabilities. *Research and Practice for Persons with Severe Disabilities, 42*(1), 8-18.

Telio, S., Ajjawi, R., & Regehr, G. (2015). The "educational alliance" as a framework for reconceptualizing feedback in medical education. *Academic Medicine, 90*(5), 609-614.

Twenge, J. M. (2006). *Generation me: Why today's young Americans are more confident, assertive, entitled—and more miserable than ever before.* Free Press.

van de Ridder, J. M. M., Stokking, K. M., McGaghie, W. C., & ten Cate, O. T. J. (2008). What is feedback in clinical education? *Medical Education, 42*(2), 189-197.

Wiggins, G., & McTighe, J. (2007). *Schooling by design: Mission, action and achievement.* ASCD.

Wiggins, G., & McTighe, J. (2011). *The Understanding by Design guide to creating high-quality units.* ASCD.

How We Give Feedback

FEEDBACK SCENARIO

Four undergraduate students who co-constructed a mini-lesson step into a simulation environment called TLE TeachLivE (University of Central Florida) to teach the lesson using a method called Japanese Lesson Study (Fernandez, 2002). With this method, one person teaches the lesson and the other three observe. At the end of the lesson, the four come together to discuss what went well and what needs to be improved. The three observers give feedback to the person who taught. They have a few minutes to make the necessary changes to the lesson before the second person steps up to teach the same lesson, with its improvements, in the simulation environment. This repeats until all four have taught the lesson, received feedback, and made co-constructed improvements. At the end of the fourth lesson, the four-member team meets with the simulation director, who guides them through an after-action review to process what they have experienced and what they have learned. This feedback is tailored specifically for each group and differentiated for each member. The undergraduate students are encouraged to take notes and share those notes with each another. This concludes the TLE TeachLivE session. However, the assignment includes one more step. Within 24 hours, each undergraduate student receives an email with a link to the video of their teaching. They are required to watch the video and write a reflection on the learning experience as an assignment for the course they are taking.

CHAPTER OBJECTIVES

This chapter continues our focus on giving feedback. It considers the myriad of ways in which we can give feedback to preservice teachers, including the use of technology. As we will discuss, there

Elford, M. D., Smith, H. H., & James, S.
GET Feedback: Giving, Exhibiting, and Teaching Feedback in
Special Education Teacher Preparation (pp. 81-99).
© 2022 SLACK Incorporated.

are many tools and common practices in giving feedback in special education teacher preparation. This chapter will describe research on the tools and practices for giving feedback as well as why to consider emerging tools and practices. The chapter will also demonstrate how to give feedback, using tools and practices that align with your instruction and assessment, with examples and prompts to apply your new learning.

We have many options when selecting tools and practices in giving feedback. There are numerous long-used practices in giving feedback in special education teacher preparation, including written feedback, grades, rubrics, comments on written work, answering questions in class, and written observation notes. Research on emerging practices and tools in giving feedback suggests a greater capacity for preservice teacher change in performance and learning of content. Examples of emerging practices and tools include bug-in-ear (BIE); video platforms, such as GoReact (SpeakWorks, Inc.) and Sibme (Sibme); simulations; after-action reviews; annotated written feedback in course management software; and extended assignments with feedback at multiple turn-in dates.

After reading this chapter you will **know** and **understand** these concepts and have the opportunity to **demonstrate** and **apply** your knowledge (Table 5-1).

DESCRIBE AND DEFINE

Traditionally, feedback on assignments was delivered in written form directly on the assignment document. As the use of technology became more prominent, that written feedback was delivered in whatever digital platform was being used. You will recall the teacher candidate from Chapter 1 who was getting written feedback from the instructor but did not know where to look for it, so she was not acting on the feedback she had been given.

Another traditional feedback method is post-observation conferences. Practicum supervisors observed a lesson, wrote notes, and gave verbal feedback on those notes in a post-observation conference. Now, because of technology, video reduces the need for onsite observation, and video-tagging platforms make it possible for supervisors to tag a video in the very moment they see something they would have previously noted on paper and write a comment that the teacher candidate can see.

In this chapter, we will look at the various tools that are available, describe what they are, examine how each can be used to deliver feedback, and ask why certain tools might be better for different feedback opportunities.

Know

Traditional methods of delivering feedback are well-known to instructors. However, new methods and tools are emerging that provide opportunities to deliver feedback in innovative ways. We will examine four of these methods and will describe different tools that are used to employ them.

First, a method for delivering immediate (in the moment) feedback, commonly known as "bug-in-ear," has been used for decades. As early as 1976, real-time feedback was being delivered remotely via walkie-talkie devices (Bowles & Nelson, 1976). Giebelhaus (1994) did something similar, focusing on classroom management strategies for elementary physical educators. As technology improved, the devices became less bulky and conspicuous. By 2002, when Scheeler and Lee began using BIE for remote teacher supervision, the devices were actually placed in the teacher candidates' ear. Scheeler and Lee (2002) provided immediate feedback to teacher candidates as they taught lessons to elementary-aged students. During the following decade, several scholars tested this method of delivering immediate feedback and reported positive results (Dal Bello et al., 2007; Fry & Hin, 2006; Goodman et al., 2008; Knowlton et al., 2007; Rock et al., 2009; Scheeler & Lee, 2002; Scheeler et al., 2006, 2010, 2012). More recently, emerging research has produced numerous peer-reviewed articles describing the effectiveness, utility, and variety of uses for BIE feedback (Garland & Dieker, 2019; Nottingham, 2019; Ottley et al., 2019; Owens et al., 2019; Regan &

TABLE 5-1. GRAPHIC ORGANIZER		
KNOW (WHAT)	**UNDERSTAND (WHY)**	**DEMONSTRATE (HOW)**
What tools and practices exist for giving feedback.	Why some tools and practices more closely align with specific instruction and assignments techniques.	How to select and implement a tool or practice suited to your feedback goals in: • Instruction • Assignment
APPLY (TAKE ACTION)		
Apply strategies for practicing, selecting, and implementing feedback tools and practices in design, activities, and assignments.		

Weiss, 2020; Schaefer & Ottley, 2018; Scheeler et al., 2018; Schles & Robertson, 2019; Sinclair et al., 2019). Scholars agree that BIE feedback is most effective for performance-based feedback when the person wearing the device understands the expectations and recognizes what the coaching terminology delivered via BIE means. Research has concluded that BIE is generally the following: (a) not disruptive to the teacher receiving the feedback; (b) can be implemented with minimal training; (c) permits immediate feedback; (d) has positive impact on specific teaching practices; (e) can be used onsite or from remote locations; (f) promotes supervisor–student relationship; and (g) is applicable to student teachers, novice teachers, and peer coaches. The study by Scheeler et al. (2012) concluded that "all participants felt comfortable with wearing the BIE, it was not distracting while teaching and all indicated that they actually like receiving feedback on their teaching right away so they knew what to change and knew how to improve" (p. 84). With the improvement in technology for delivering immediate feedback and the increase in research of BIE, this method of delivering immediate feedback is one that can be considered by instructors in special education teacher preparation programs.

The utility and positive results should come as no surprise when we take into account the other arenas in which BIE is used. Law enforcement uses BIE for communication in protection situations, where officers are situated in multiple locations. Clinical psychologists use BIE when training new clinicians. Football coaches standing on the sidelines are seen wearing headphones; they are receiving information from a coach located high above the field. Even store clerks wear BIE devices to better serve their customers by being able to communicate with managers and other clerks in other parts of the store, such as the stockroom. When a more experienced or knowledgeable employee can provide answers and information in the moment, the novice learns and the customer is served more easily. BIE devices effectively deliver information and feedback to the wearer.

With the invention of Bluetooth technology, every person with a cell phone or tablet can connect a listening device and receive messages through that "bug" in their ear. As with all technology, testing different devices and functionality in the setting of use avoids frustration during the delivery of BIE feedback. Using Bluetooth devices requires sufficient Wi-Fi bandwidth for the technology to work seamlessly. However, once the technology is in place and tested, it can be used successfully to deliver immediate feedback to whoever is wearing the device.

Second, video recording now provides new opportunities for instructors to give feedback to teachers in training. Athletic coaches have been using video to provide feedback to players for almost as long as movie film has existed. It is not uncommon for football coaches to review game films the night after the game and then show the film to players during the next practice. This once required expensive movie cameras, projectors, and screens. The films were grainy and in black and white. Despite this rudimentary design, the effectiveness was widely accepted. Many coaches also took advantage of viewing opponents' game film, so they could plan more strategic defense and look for weak areas that could lead to successful offensive plays. Using video in education arrived much later than in sports. However, in recent years, video has emerged as a valuable and effective tool for delivering feedback to teachers.

In an extensive review of the literature, Gaudin and Chaliès (2015) described the reasons video is being used more in teacher education and professional development. The results of this literature review indicated that video viewing in teacher education includes the following categories: (a) the nature of teachers' activity as they view a classroom video, (b) the objectives of video viewing, (c) the nature of classroom videos viewed, and (d) the effects of video viewing. Of these four categories, the most relevant for instructors is the effects of video viewing. We have learned the value of using video as a springboard for feedback in special education teacher preparation. This is consistent with the additional literature that describes improving teacher practice through video recording and constructive feedback (Ostrosky et al., 2013; Tripp & Rich, 2012; West & Turner, 2016).

When using video to observe teachers, instructors need not rely on memory or judgment. Instead, the video creates authenticity for the domain of specificity. Video makes the invisible become visible. Video becomes the means for getting a shared picture of reality, setting meaningful goals, and monitoring progress toward those goals. With the guidance of an instructor who understands the complexities of working with adult learners, teachers are encouraged to view their teaching, based on high-leverage teaching practices (Teaching Works, n.d.), and determine specific areas of improvement. Instructors who partner with teacher candidates use the principles of adult learning theory to provide encouragement for the teacher to grow professionally by focusing on the data provided in the video. The evidence in the video is undeniable and becomes the "third thing" (Palmer, 2009, p. 92) necessary for the teacher and the instructor to equally interpret the video and use it as a "point of departure for all coaching conversations" (Knight, 2014, p. 44). Tkatchov and Pollnow (2012) suggested that job-embedded coaching is needed to support the transfer of teacher learning to classroom practice. By using video, structured coaching conversations, and effective reflective practice, teacher candidates grow professionally.

In recent years, with the advancement of technology, many web-based video platforms have emerged. These video platforms make it possible for the teacher candidate and the instructor to view the video and make comments that are timestamped and visible to both individuals. An asynchronous dialogue can occur that is not unlike the coaches and athletes watching game films together and pointing out what occurred in the contest or how an individual athlete could make different choices to improve their game. The web-based video platforms provide an opportunity for the instructor to "stop the film" by typing a comment at a particular moment when they see something occur that requires a comment. The teacher candidate can read the comment and reply within the video platform. The same opportunity is available for the teacher candidate to write a timestamped comment about something they notice. These asynchronous comments begin the coaching conversations that occur synchronously after both individuals have made comments within the video.

Technology constantly improves, and the variance in the current video platforms offers various options and features. A variety of web-based video platforms exist. The most popular are Edthena (R3 Collaboratives, Inc.), GoReact, TORSH Talent (Torsh, Inc.), and Swivl. The various platforms have different features, but all of them have the fundamental feature of timestamped comments. Although the decision for using this resource will probably be influenced by the individual university's program budget, some choice for which web-based video platform to select rests with the users and their assessment of which features are essential. After having used a variety of web-based video platforms for observation of teacher candidates for more than 5 years, we consider the following features as most important:

- A way to categorize the feedback or specialize it for the observable teaching behaviors to be measured or emphasized.
- Opportunity for the teacher candidate to respond to the comments.
- Some kind of analytics, so the teacher candidate and the instructor can see how many times that comments were made about the different categories.

- Ease of uploading and managing videos.
- Job aids that make the system user-friendly when something appears to not be working.

As with all technologies, more features may be more expensive, and it may not be possible to find all the desired features in one video platform. The availability of video platforms provides a valuable opportunity to observe teaching remotely and coach teacher candidates from a distance. Video combined with video platforms that allow for asynchronous dialogue adds power to the coaching conversations and reflective practice necessary for teacher candidates' professional growth.

Third, simulation—also known as augmented-reality simulation—offers a context for practice that improved technologies have recently made available. Augmented-reality simulation is an environment where real-world physical space is supplemented by computer technology to allow the technology user "to interact with virtual images, using real objects in a seamless way" (Zhou et al., 2008, p. 193). In the vignette at the beginning of this chapter, the four undergraduate students were teaching their lessons in this augmented-reality simulation (TLE TeachLivE). Even though simulation is new in the field of education, it has existed in other disciplines for many years in forms such as flight simulators, physical training simulators for hand–eye coordination, driving simulators, military training simulations, and health care simulations. With increased access to computers, popular virtual reality games allow players to explore difficult situations without fear of harm (Richards et al., 2007). For the purpose of our description of simulation, we will merge the virtual reality and augmented reality simulation. In TLE TeachLivE or Mursion, characters known as avatars behave in typical ways or in ways that are orchestrated, based on an interactive narrative between the user–teacher candidate and the avatar. The simulation itself is an interactive role-play session, where participants (teacher candidates) are given an opportunity to practice classroom management strategies, instructional strategies, and/or relationship-building strategies in a simulated environment (Elford, 2013) in which it is safe to try, fail, and try again.

Feedback can be delivered in many ways in simulation, as illustrated in the opening vignette. The undergraduates received immediate feedback from avatars (controlled by their peers) in simulation. Next, these undergraduate students provided peer feedback to one another at the end of each teaching scenario. Then, the TLE TeachLivE director, a practicum instructor and coach, gave feedback to the group that fit into the domains of Purposefulness and Constructiveness. In addition, there was an opportunity for self-reflective feedback as the undergraduates watched their individual videos and examined their own teaching behaviors. Finally, written comments from the course instructor provided feedback after the reflection assignment was completed. Each of these examples of feedback illustrates how all the domains of feedback can be incorporated into an experiential learning situation such as simulation.

With the advancement and wide availability of virtual reality simulation tools, such as Mursion, all that is required to create a simulation is a computer, an internet connection, and a web camera. A classroom setting depicting an elementary or secondary classroom with five avatars that have well-developed personas engages teacher candidates in "real-life" classroom situations and allows them to practice the skills they need to demonstrate once they enter a classroom with real K-12 students. Teacher candidates participate in teaching scenarios that adapt, based on their actions and responses, using artificial and human interaction. Instructors can then coach the teacher candidates on how to enhance their teaching skills during the simulation and allow them to try again if they want to change their pedagogical decisions—something not available to them when they are in a practicum field experience!

Institutes of higher education have seized the opportunity that virtual simulation has to develop special education teacher candidates. The Southern Illinois University Edwardsville (SIUE) Virtual Professional Practice Lab (https://www.siue.edu/virtual-practice-lab/) has partnered with Mursion to deliver a simulated environment for training teacher candidates. This mixed-reality environment provides opportunities to practice skills in a scaffolded, differentiated, and supported environment, with instructors providing immediate coaching during the sessions and delayed feedback on individual performance in the goals of the teaching scenario.

TABLE 5-2. TECHNOLOGY ALIGNED WITH DOMAIN	
TECHNOLOGY	**FEEDBACK DOMAIN**
Bug-in-ear	Immediacy
Video	Specificity
Simulation	Immediacy Purposefulness Constructiveness
Video reflection	Specificity Purposefulness Constructiveness

Finally, video reflection—recording and watching one's own teaching—is a powerful tool for self-reflective learning because the video provides teachers with the ability to observe themselves doing the work of teaching. Most teachers do not have any idea what it looks like when they teach until they see themselves on video. Therefore, video adds a multidimensional layer to reflective practice. Reflective practice fuels the development of a deeper understanding of the way teachers conduct their work. To become skilled and effective special educators, reflection should involve connecting research to day-to-day practice, uncovering assumptions, and paying attention to the importance of continual improvement. In this way, teachers uncover the what, how, and why of teaching the way they do, allowing them to better understand the choices they make. Loughran (2002) puts it this way, "Effective reflective practice is drawn from the ability to frame and reframe our understanding through action, so that the practitioner's wisdom-in-action is enhanced, and as a particular outcome, articulation of professional knowledge is encouraged" (p. 42).

Video, uploaded to a web-based platform, allows the coach, mentor, or practicum supervisor to deliver transforming feedback using timestamped comments. Feedback in this context meets the criteria of specificity, immediacy, purposefulness, and constructiveness deemed necessary for the improvement process.

Understand

These new methods provide new opportunities for delivering feedback and can be very appealing for their innovation, utility, and availability. However, using the appropriate tool to deliver feedback involves thoughtful planning and intentional design. We will examine four methods described previously and align each to the feedback domain.

Just as each of the adult learning principles is more tightly coupled with different feedback domains so are the different technologies for delivering feedback. Table 5-2 illustrates how we align each technology with each domain. First, as previously mentioned, BIE is best suited for performance-based feedback that is delivered in the moment. Second, video affords the instructor the ability to name exactly what is happening on the video, thus making this technology align most closely with the domain of specificity. Third, simulation provides the opportunity for feedback that suits the domains of immediacy, purposefulness, and constructiveness. Finally, video reflection creates an environment for specificity, purposefulness, and constructiveness.

TABLE 5-3. WHAT IS THE GOAL?	
FEEDBACK PURPOSE	**TECHNOLOGY TOOL**
Instruction	Assessment
Instructional strategy	Video platform
	Simulation
	Bug-in-ear
Classroom management	Video platform
	Simulation
	Bug-in-ear
Unintended bias	Video reflection
Habitual behaviors	Video reflection

Demonstrate

We have explored what tools and practices exist for giving feedback and why some tools and practices more closely align with specific instruction, assignment, and feedback domains. Now it is time to describe how to select and implement a tool or practice suited to the desired feedback goal.

Table 5-3 offers one way to organize the various tools based on the goal for the feedback. In the left column are the categories that are identified as the goal or purpose for the feedback. The right column lists the technology tool that can be used to meet the feedback goal. If the purpose of the feedback is instruction, then the feedback would be delivered in whatever assessment method is available, such as an online grade book. For providing feedback on teacher candidates' proficiency in delivering an instructional strategy, any of the technologies we have mentioned are suitable. Feedback that exposes unintended bias or habitual behaviors is best done through video reflection. Video reflection can be done privately, where the teacher candidate views the video and responds with a personal reflection. It can also be done using personal reflection through a video platform, where the instructor responds to the teacher candidate's reflection on timestamped comments. As with all feedback, it is important to align the tool with the purpose.

TABLE 5-4. SPOTLIGHT ON ADULT LEARNING			
SPECIFICITY	IMMEDIACY	PURPOSEFULNESS	CONSTRUCTIVENESS
Do the adult learner and instructor have an agreed understanding for the feedback language that is being used? Are the words precisely aligned to the goal for the feedback?	What feedback tool best suits the appropriate timing and type of feedback being given? Does the adult learner prefer immediate feedback such as bug-in-ear? In video viewing, does the adult learner want to comment before or after the instructor?	Does the tool being used to deliver feedback suit the purpose of the feedback? Do the instructor and adult learner agree on the purpose and the tool?	What role does the adult learner have in selecting the method for receiving feedback? How does the feedback meet the adult learner's orientation to learning?

SPOTLIGHT ON ADULT LEARNING

As we consider the intersection of feedback and adult learning theory, we should examine how to use the tools we have mentioned in this chapter to fit the desired purpose of the feedback and the person receiving the feedback (Table 5-4). When the technology that can appear invasive or disruptive is introduced as a method for delivering feedback, it is even more important to involve the adult learner in how that feedback will be given.

POSSIBLE BARRIERS TO USING THIS TYPE OF FEEDBACK

The barriers to including these technologies as means of delivering feedback comprise cost, availability, technical support, and readiness by both the instructor and the teacher candidate to learn a new technology. Cost is probably the greatest barrier; yet, as with all technologies, rapid advancement in the industry drives down the price. Many web-based platforms have built-in technical support; however, all technology has the potential to fail at the most inopportune time. In addressing the barrier of instructor and teacher candidate readiness, Knowles' (1984) principle of need to know comes to mind. Although these barriers exist and should be considered, we are convinced that the use of technology in giving feedback adds to its transformational effectiveness.

PRACTICAL APPLICATION

In this section, we offer three different assignments to illustrate how technology can be used to give feedback that informs the performance, knowledge, or skills of the teacher candidate. First, we describe the assignment that is featured in the vignette. Next, we provide an example of a reflection assignment that requires a web-based platform. Finally, we offer an example of feedback incorporated into a co-teaching assignment.

One of the major assignments in a course titled Teaching Exceptional Children and Youth in General Education involved the students creating a lesson plan that contained evidence of Universal Design for Learning (UDL; Rose & Strangman, 2007). One way to enrich the lesson plan assignment was to provide an experience for preservice teachers to use their knowledge from class to prepare a mini-lesson, teach it in TLE TeachLivE platform, and then reflect on their instruction prior to submitting their final lesson plan assignment.

Research supports the use of integrating the UDL framework into course development to enhance preservice educators' understanding of UDL. We know that when educators use multiple representations of material, a broad range of learners have a deeper engagement experience (McGuire et al., 2006). In addition, universally designed lesson plans begin with UDL supports that meet the needs of all learners rather than making adjustments to lesson plans after learners have struggled to gain knowledge (Meo, 2008).

Preparing teacher candidates to develop universal design lesson plans that integrate sound pedagogy with the UDL framework can promote a collaborative co-teaching model between general and special educators (Rose et al., 2006; Rose & Meyer, 2006). General educators, although knowledgeable in content and methods, may need additional preparation for differentiating instruction. Similarly, special educators learn about a variety of differing abilities but may need additional opportunities to employ UDL principles in general education classrooms. Evidence supports the need to design our special education teacher preparation programs to align pedagogy and UDL knowledge with more experience in delivering instruction (Courey et al., 2013). Courey et al. (2013) specifically indicated the need for increased supervised experiences in real classrooms for preservice educators to practice implementing UDL lesson plans. Recently, teacher preparation programs have begun to scaffold the learning process for teacher candidates by offering opportunities for teacher preparation candidates to practice delivering instruction in virtual learning environments before going out into classrooms (Dieker et al., 2008).

You will recall from the vignette that undergraduate students who were enrolled in a preservice education course were given the opportunity to teach a mini-lesson in the virtual learning environment, provide feedback to one another to improve the lesson, receive feedback from the director of TLE TeachLivE, and then watch a video of their teaching. The directions for each phase of that assignment are outlined in the following sections.

Universal Design Lesson Plan Assignment Description

The following are the assignment objectives:

- Students will participate in an interactive simulation to learn to practice UDL strategies to promote engagement and diminish disruptions. The UDL strategies include but are not limited to multiple representation, engagement, and action and expression to meet the students' needs.

- All students will demonstrate planning and preparation by delivering a mini-lesson plan and teaching materials, including PowerPoint slides and/or videos, to the TLE TeachLivE coordinator 2 weeks in advance of the teaching session.

- All students will consider the essential components of a well-executed lesson: advance organizer, explicit instruction, opportunities to respond, direct-specific feedback, check for understanding, monitor progress, and review essential components of the lesson.

- All students will reflect on their teaching by watching the video of their teaching session and submitting a written reflection.

- All students will use what they have learned through the simulation-feedback-reflection process to construct a full lesson plan, based on UDL.

Phase 1: Lesson Planning

Plan the mini-lesson with your peers, based on the knowledge you have gained from course work about UDL.

Phase 2: Lesson Delivery

Teach the mini-lesson in TLE TeachLivE, using the Japanese Lesson Study model.

Teacher 1 teaches the mini-lesson in the virtual learning environment, while three peers observe. At the end of 10 minutes, the group of four has 10 minutes to collectively review the mini-lesson by using structured feedback and then co-construct lesson changes. At the end of 10 minutes, Teacher 2 teaches the mini-lesson with the changes, while three peers observe. This process repeats until all four have taught the mini-lesson. Each teaching session is captured on video.

Phase 3: Lesson Reflection

Watch the video of you teaching the mini-lesson in the virtual learning environment and write a reflection that describes what went well, what did not go as well as you would like, and what accounts for the difference.

Phase 4: Final Universal Design Lesson Plan

Write a full-length lesson, using UDL that reflects the knowledge you have gained from coursework, simulation experience, feedback from peers, and personal reflection.

Reflective Practice

Reflective practice fuels the development of a deeper understanding about the way teachers conduct their work. To become skilled and effective special educators, our reflection should involve connecting research to day-to-day practice, uncovering assumptions, and paying attention to the importance of continual improvement. In this way, we uncover the what, how, and why of teaching the way we do, allowing us to better understand the choices we make. Loughran (2002) put it this way, "Effective reflective practice is drawn from the ability to frame and reframe our understanding through action, so that the practitioner's wisdom-in-action is enhanced, and as a particular outcome, articulation of professional knowledge is encouraged" (p. 42).

Reflective Journal Assignment: Web-Based

The purpose of the weekly journal is to encourage you as a practicum student to become a reflective professional who examines your own instruction, recognizes research-based practices, and in turn improves and modifies your lessons. Each weekly journal is designed to align with a component of the Classroom Observation Rubric, adapted from the Student Teaching Assessment Rubric and/or a high-leverage teaching practice (Ball & Forzani, 2011). This reflective journal assignment requires you to synthesize and connect research to practice. You will develop skills of observation; critical thinking; and clear, concise, and cogent writing. The journals are *not research papers*, but all research referenced should be cited using in-text American Psychological Association (APA) guidelines. Each submission should be thoughtful and reflective and include evidence of what you have learned by observing the teaching video, articulating your own thinking, and reading the research on the weekly topic. Finally, your journal should describe how you plan to apply these ideas in the real context of instructional practice.

One of the important skills necessary for quality educators involves making instructional, management, and professional decisions by combining knowledge of research and evidence of your K-12 students' individual and collective needs. This assignment is designed to assess your competency to synthesize research, reflect on practice, and describe that process in a clear, concise, and cogent manner through your writing.

TABLE 5-5. REFLECTIVE JOURNAL TEMPLATE		
TEACHING VIDEO NAME:		**DATE:**
OBSERVATION (In this column, make observation notes on this form related to a teaching video uploaded in the video platform [GoReact] 1. Identify/describe three to five observations that relate to **this week's journal topic**.)	**MEANING** (In this column, review the observation notes and write your thoughts about what you observed. In other words, what does what you saw and wrote make you think of?)	**RESEARCH** (In this column, note the research that confirms or refutes your thinking, using APA in-text citations for each thought, comment, and/or observation [e.g., author, date, page].)

The steps for this assignment are as follows:
1. Use the template (Table 5-5) to gather your information. On it, you will:
   - Make observation notes related to a teaching video in GoReact.
   - Choose three to five observations that relate to this week's journal topic and record your reflections about them.
   - After reviewing this week's assigned articles and/or webinar, note the research that confirms or refutes your thinking, using APA in-text citations for each thought, comment, and/or observation (i.e., author, date, page).
2. Using the components of the table, summarize what you have learned in your journal entry. You may submit either:
   - 500 written words (three paragraphs) or
   - A 5- to 7-minute video or narrated PowerPoint presentation.

   Your summary should:
   - Describe your observations and your own thoughts on them.
   - Synthesize this week's research (articles and/or webinars) on the topic, comparing and contrasting how it relates to your observations and your own thoughts.
   - Describe how your thinking has changed and what changes you will make in your teaching because of what you have learned.

Co-Teaching With a General Education Peer

You will work in collaboration with a general education K-12 student in the CI 314 course to develop a lesson plan that communicates each teacher's role in a co-taught lesson. The teams will present a co-taught lesson with a lesson provided by the instructor. The emphasis is on the co-teaching planning process and managing the learning environment collaboratively. Using the SIUE Co-Teaching Lesson Plan to provide evidence of team decision making about the delivery of the lesson is required. All communication with your co-teacher will be on a Google platform. You will submit four planning session videos via Google Hangouts, keep all shared documents in Google Docs, and participate in a blog with all students in these two classes via Google Blog. You will then deliver a 10-minute section of the lesson with your co-teacher in TLE TeachLivE, a virtual simulation classroom.

Phase 1: Lesson Planning

Choose your lesson from a choice of literacy-infused math plans provided by instructors. Plan implementation of a lesson where roles are equitable in the delivery of content and implement best practices in teaching. Input the lesson components into the co-teaching lesson plan template in collaboration with your course co-teaching partner, who is versed in the lesson plan format. The primary emphasis will be to deliver the math content using the co-teaching model of team-teaching and managing the learning environment. You are required to use Google technologies (Google Docs and Google Hangouts) to assist in the planning process. Partners are required to turn in four recorded Google Hangout planning sessions, contribute to the Google Plus blog documenting progress, as well as manage lesson plans and materials in Google Docs. Co-teachers will submit these required materials and assignments to the respective instructor of their course. Literacy materials need to be checked out from the SIUE Literacy Center (located in FH 1317). Math manipulatives can be checked out from the Instructional Materials Center (located in FH 1208).

Your lesson plan and instruction should include the following best instructional practices:

- Wait time
- Higher-order questioning
- Effective communication skills

Phase 2: Collaboration/Delivery

You will be required to attend an TLE TeachLivE session that will be outside the normal class period to deliver a co-taught literacy lesson in the lab and observe your peers. Instructors will monitor your delivery of best instructional practices and will provide feedback on your performance. Your peers will assist you in the reflection process by providing detailed feedback from your TLE TeachLivE simulation.

Collaboration Expectations

- Equitable, respectful dialogue between you and partner.
- Evidence of equitable responsibility and participation.
- Implementation of strategies that promote K-12 student access to the general education curriculum.

Delivery

- Attend the TLE TeachLivE session with co-teaching partner.
- Observe peers in a TeachLivE session and listen attentively.
- Provide feedback to peers via the checklist about the learning environment that was created.

Phase 3: Reflection

After the simulation, you will be asked to write a professional reflection, using the peer and instructor feedback and your personal efficacy in collaboration based on your experience. This reflection is part of your final examination for the class, in addition to the progress made using a Google platform of your collaboration. The reflection is 50% of your grade, and your collaboration documentation is the other 50% of your grade for this assignment. In addition, you will complete an online survey about your experience collaborating with a teacher candidate from another program as well as your simulation experience.

Expectations

- Complete reflection of your experience.
- Complete Co-Teaching Professional Collaboration Survey.

The following questions are provided to guide your review and reflection in the Authentic Example that follows, contributed by Martha D. Elford, PhD.

- In this example, how does the instructor give feedback? Reflect.
- How does this example reflect the research and use of technology?
- What types of technology do you use to give feedback?

AUTHENTIC EXAMPLE

*Contributed by
Martha D. Elford, PhD*

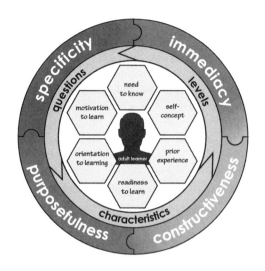

1. Course Details

SPE 775: Practicum With Children and Youth With Disabilities: High Incidence/Adaptive is the initial practicum experience, whereby graduate teacher candidates apply their learning from three previous courses to daily teaching in their practicum setting. Teacher candidates are expected to draw on powerful intervention research in academics and social/emotional supports. They systematically implement personalized learning, based on the needs of the K-12 student, the demands of the curriculum, and the outcomes of the individualized education plans.

2. Learning Objectives

The purpose of this assignment—a guided classroom tour using GoReact, which is an online platform for sharing and critiquing videos—is to introduce your instructor to and heighten your awareness of a classroom setting, its physical surroundings, emotional climate, cultural responsiveness, and visual, auditory, and kinesthetic elements. You should consider these setting characteristics through the lens of whether the environment encourages or inhibits interaction and learning with/for/of students with disabilities. Please use the check sheet (Table 5-6) to evaluate the physical environment of your placement setting.

3. Assignment Description

After you have observed the physical climate of your placement/classroom, develop a 4- to 5-minute video tour, describing what you want the instructor to notice, as if you were a tour guide for an exotic destination. Upload your video to GoReact under the Explorations tab: M1 Guided Classroom Tour. Consider the following checklist (see Table 5-6) that aligns with the evaluation criteria for this assignment as you develop your video.

4. Evaluation Criteria

The evaluation criteria are shown in Table 5-6.

5. Additional Details Regarding Peer Feedback

For this video submission, you will also watch a video of at least one of your peers. The purpose of this feedback activity is to promote professional conversations that result from peer observations because research suggests that learning from peers is a powerful form of professional learning (Kennette & Frank, 2013). You will be observing for the items specific to the checklist. The observational markers are provided in GoReact. It will be up to the teacher providing the guided tour to highlight the area of focus, if there is one. For example, the teacher may say, "Please pay attention to the emotional climate description. I am open to ideas or suggestions." You will offer feedback under the tabs available on GoReact.

6. Feedback Reflection

This assignment is submitted as a video to the online platform GoReact. The instructor has created tags that correspond with each of the categories on the form. The teacher candidate and the instructor leave comments on the video platform in a conversational exchange. The instructor can ask questions to which the teacher candidate can respond. The instructor provides feedback describing the various ways and to what degree the teacher candidate has met the criteria on the checklist. In this way, the instructor is able to get a clearer understanding of the practicum setting, especially when the teacher candidate is in a location outside the instructor's geographic location.

TABLE 5-6. GUIDED CLASSROOM TOUR

√	CATEGORY	DETAILS	
☐	Student descriptions	____ number ____ gender/age ____ race/ethnicity ____ disability ____ general function levels (academic or developmental)	
☐	Physical surroundings	**Setting:** Physical layout, ease of transitions, flow of students, organization of where things occur (whole group, small group, individual) **Schedule:** How much time students spend in this space, how often students are out of the classroom (whole group, small group, individual), include tiered support routines	
☐	Emotional climate	**Expectations:** Classroom rules ____ developmentally appropriate ____ logical and applicable across settings/time, include prosocial behaviors, include behaviors important for success—taught, modeled, and reminded	
		Positive Behavior Supports	
		Increase Positive Behaviors	**Decrease Negative Behaviors**
		• Developmentally appropriate • Tied to class rules • Supports positive teacher-student interactions • Frequent student feedback (verbal and nonverbal) • Imparts value to the student	• Addresses high-frequency behaviors • Differentiates for various problem behaviors • Respects the value of the student • Seeks to understand the cause of the behavior • Avoids power struggles
☐	Cultural responsiveness	How is cultural diversity represented visually? Auditorily? How are students encouraged to explore different cultures and celebrate differences?	
☐	Visual, auditory, and kinesthetic elements	How is technology included? What visual cues are there for instruction and classroom management? How are music, art, and movement used? What evidence is there that students experience information and instruction in a variety of ways?	
☐	Your choice	What would you like to highlight that you think is really great about your classroom?	

SUMMARY

This chapter opens the door to different technologies that can be used to give feedback in special education teacher preparation. The information provided encourages instructors to explore different tools for giving feedback and to develop an understanding of how each tool fits a particular feedback purpose. In addition, we suggest that attending to the intersection of adult learning theory and feedback provides a practical way to decide what feedback tool best fits the desired outcome for giving feedback to teacher candidates. As new technologies for delivering feedback emerge, continuing to focus on the recipient (the adult learner) will ensure that the teacher candidate is able to receive the feedback, regardless of the technology tool being used.

We believe the courses in special education teacher preparation offer opportunities for instructors to plan the immediacy of the feedback given to teacher candidates and that the timing of feedback is critical when considering the adult learners' need to know.

OPPORTUNITY FOR GOING DEEPER

The following resources support deeper learning on the concepts reflected in Chapter 5:

- SIUE Virtual Professional Practice Lab. SIUE's Virtual Professional Practice (VPP) Lab has partnered with Mursio to deliver a simulated environment for the training of professionals in a variety of different fields, including teaching, health care and customer service: https://www.siue.edu/virtual-practice-lab/
- GoReact. GoReact is an interactive platform for feedback, grading, and critiquing of video assignments: https://get.goreact.com/
- Bug-in-ear. In addition to the published research on BIE listed in the references and discussed in this chapter as well as Chapter 13, you can dig deeper with the white paper from Marcia Rock, PhD: https://gtlcenter.org/sites/default/files/Bug-in-ear_Coaching.pdf
- Sibme. A customizable platform of video-enhanced professional learning and coaching to improve professional practice: https://sibme.com/

REFERENCES

Ball, D. L., & Forzani, F. M. (2011). Teaching skillful teaching. *Educational Leadership, 68*(4), 40-45.

Bowles, P. E., Jr., & Nelson, R. O. (1976). Training teachers as mediators: Efficacy of a workshop versus the bug-in-the-ear technique. *Journal of School Psychology, 14*(1), 15-26.

Courey, S. J., Tappe, P., Siker, J., & LePage, P. (2013). Improved lesson planning with universal design for learning (UDL). *Teacher Education and Special Education, 36*(1), 7-27.

Dal Bello, A., Knowlton, E., & Chaffin, J. (2007). Interactive videoconferencing as a medium for special education: Knowledge acquisition in preservice teacher education. *Intervention in School and Clinic, 43*(1), 38-46.

Dieker, L., Hynes, M., Hughes, C., & Smith, E. (2008). Implications of mixed reality and simulation technologies on special education and teacher preparation. *Focus on Exceptional Children, 40*(6), 1-20.

Elford, M. D. (2013). *Using tele-coaching to increase behavior-specific praise delivered by secondary teachers in an augmented reality learning environment* (Publication No. ED553196) [Doctoral dissertation, University of Kansas]. ProQuest Dissertations & Theses Global.

Fernandez, C. (2002). Learning from Japanese approaches to professional development: The case of lesson study. *Journal of Teacher Education, 53*(5), 393-405.

Fry, J. M., & Hin, M. K. T. (2006). Peer coaching with interactive wireless technology between student teachers: Satisfaction with role and communication. *Interactive Learning Environments, 14*(3), 193-204.

Garland, D. P., & Dieker, L. A. (2019). Effects of providing individualized clinical coaching with bug-in-ear technology to novice educators of students with emotional and behavioral disorders in inclusive secondary science classrooms. *Journal of Inquiry and Action in Education, 10*(2), 2.

Gaudin, C., & Chaliès, S. (2015). Video viewing in teacher education and professional development: A literature review. *Educational Research Review, 16*, 41-67.

Giebelhaus, C. R. (1994). The mechanical third ear device: A student teacher supervision alternative. *Journal of Teacher Education, 45*(5), 365-373.

Goodman, J. I., Brady, M. P., Duffy, M. L., Scott, J., & Pollard, N. E. (2008). The effects of "bug-in-ear" supervision on special education teachers' delivery of Learn Units. *Focus on Autism and Other Developmental Disabilities 23*(4), 207-216.

Kennette, L. N., & Frank, N. M. (2013). The value of peer feedback opportunities for students in writing intensive classes. *Psychology Teaching Review, 19*(2), 106-111.

Knight, J. (2014). *Focus on teaching: Using video for high-impact instruction.* Corwin Press.

Knowles, M. (1984). T*he adult learner: A neglected species* (3rd ed.). Gulf Publishing.

Knowlton, E., Israel, M., & Griswold, D. (2007). Effects of interactive video conferencing on teacher education students' knowledge of special education. In R. Carlsen, K. McFerrin, J. Price, R. Weber, & D. Willis (Eds.) *Proceedings of SITE 2007—Society for Information Technology and Teacher Education International Conference* (pp. 3619-3626). Association for the Advancement of Computing in Education.

Loughran, J. J. (2002). Effective reflective practice: In search of meaning in learning about teaching. *Journal of Teacher Education, 53*(1), 33-43.

Mcguire, J. M., Scott, S. S., & Shaw, S. F. (2006). Universal design and its applications in educational environments. *Remedial and Special Education, 27*(3), 166-175.

Meo, G. (2008). Curriculum planning for all learners: Applying universal design for learning (UDL) to a high school reading comprehension program. *Preventing School Failure: Alternative Education for Children and Youth, 52*(2), 21-30.

Nottingham, S. L. (2019). Actual and perceived feedback delivery during athletic training clinical education with and without the use of bug-in-ear technology. *Journal of Allied Health, 48*(1), 38-45.

Ostrosky, M. M., Mouzourou, C., Danner, N., & Zaghlawan, H. Y. (2013). Improving teacher practices using microteaching: Planful video recording and constructive feedback. Y*oung Exceptional Children, 16*(1), 16-29.

Ottley, J. R., Piasta, S. B., Coogle, C. G., Spear, C. F., & Rahn, N. L. (2019). Implementation of bug-in-ear coaching by community-based professional development providers. *Early Education and Development, 30*(3), 400-422.

Owens, T. L., Lo, Y. Y., & Collins, B. C. (2019). Using tiered coaching and bug-in-ear technology to promote teacher implementation fidelity. *The Journal of Special Education, 54*(2), 67-79.

Palmer, P. J. (2009). *A hidden wholeness: The journey toward an undivided life.* Jossey-Bass.

Regan, K., & Weiss, M. P. (2020). Bug-in-ear coaching for teacher candidates: What, why, and how to get started. *Intervention in School and Clinic, 55*(3), 178-184.

Richards, D., Szilas, N., Kavakli, M., & Dras, M. (2007). Impacts of visualisation, interaction, and immersion on learning using an agent-based training simulation. *Research and Development, 28*(45).

Rock, M. L., Gregg, M., Thead, B. K., Acker, S. E., Gable, R. A., & Zigmond, N. P. (2009). Can you hear me now? Evaluation of an online wireless technology to provide real-time feedback to special education teachers-in-training. *Teacher Education and Special Education, 32*(1), 64-82.

Rose, D. H., Harbour, W. S., Johnston, C. S., Daley, S. G., & Abarbanell, L. (2006). Universal design for learning in postsecondary education: Reflections on principles and their application. *Journal of postsecondary education and disability, 19*(2), 135-151.

Rose, D. H., & Meyer, A. (2006). *A practical reader in universal design for learning.* Harvard Education Press.

Rose, D. H., & Strangman, N. (2007). Universal design for learning: Meeting the challenge of individual learning differences through a neurocognitive perspective. Universal Access in the Information Society, 5(4), 381-391.

Schaefer, J. M., & Ottley, J. R. (2018). Evaluating immediate feedback via bug-in-ear as an evidence-based practice for professional development. *Journal of Special Education Technology, 33*(4), 247-258.

Scheeler, M. C., Congdon, M., & Stansbery, S. (2010). Providing immediate feedback to co-teachers through bug-in-ear technology: An effective method of peer coaching in inclusion classrooms. *Teacher Education and Special Education, 33*(1), 83-96.

Scheeler, M. C., & Lee, D. L. (2002). Using technology to deliver immediate corrective feedback to preservice teachers. *Journal of Behavioral Education, 11*(4), 231-241.

Scheeler, M. C., McAfee, J. K., Ruhl, K. L., & Lee, D. L. (2006). Effects of corrective feedback delivered via wireless technology on preservice teacher performance and student behavior. *Teacher Education and Special Education, 29*(1), 12-25.

Scheeler, M. C., McKinnon, K., & Stout, J. (2012). Effects of immediate feedback delivered via webcam and bug-in-ear technology on preservice teacher performance. *Teacher Education and Special Education, 35*(1), 77-90.

Scheeler, M. C., Morano, S., & Lee, D. L. (2018). Effects of immediate feedback using bug-in-ear with paraeducators working with students with autism. *Teacher Education and Special Education, 41*(1), 24-38.

Schles, R. A., & Robertson, R. E. (2019). The role of performance feedback and implementation of evidence-based practices for preservice special education teachers and student outcomes: A review of the literature. *Teacher Education and Special Education, 42*(1), 36-48.

Sinclair, A. C., Gesel, S. A., LeJeune, L. M., & Lemons, C. J. (2019). A review of the evidence for real-time performance feedback to improve instructional practice. *The Journal of Special Education, 54*(2), 90-100.

Teaching Works. (n.d.). High-leverage practices. https://library.teachingworks.org/curriculum-resources/high-leverage-practices/

Tkatchov, O., & Pollnow, S. K. (2012). *A practical guide to teaching and learning*. Roman & Littlefield Education.

Tripp, T. R., & Rich, P. J. (2012). The influence of video analysis on the process of teacher change. *Teaching and Teacher Education, 28*(5), 728-739.

West, J., & Turner, W. (2016). Enhancing the assessment experience: Improving student perceptions, engagement and understanding using online video feedback. *Innovations in Education and Teaching International, 53*(4), 400-410.

Zhou, F., Duh, H. B.-L., & Billinghurst, M. (2008). Trends in augmented reality tracking, interaction and display: A review of ten years of ISMAR. *7th IEEE/ACM International Symposium on Mixed and Augmented Reality*, 193-202. https://doi.org/10.1109/ISMAR.2008.4637362

Exhibiting Feedback

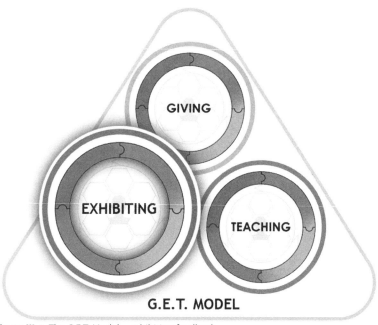

Figure III-1. The G.E.T. Model—exhibiting feedback.

Exhibiting feedback (Figure III-1) requires instructors to explicitly model how feedback should be given through sharing the "why and how" of delivering feedback. Section III comprises two chapters on how instructors can exhibit feedback and the possible effects of this feedback on deeper levels of content acquisition by preservice educators. In this section, we target deeper learning of the characteristics, levels, and domains of feedback. The narrative serves as a guide for instructors to reflect on where feedback opportunities currently exist in their courses and then explore and plan for deepening focus, building on the characteristics of feedback.

Exhibiting Feedback and the Four Domains of the G.E.T. Model

FEEDBACK SCENARIO

Dr. Brooks prided herself on her preparedness for class each day. She thoughtfully analyzed state standards and course objectives, using the textbook and providing instructional materials. Her presentation slides were thorough, and her lecture notes were scripted to make sure she did not forget key aspects of the content associated with each slide. Her students were a vessel that she was ready to fill with knowledge. Her lectures were practiced and polished, ready to impart knowledge, in the hopes that any student's questions were answered within the lecture. She did this for every class, and her students earned decent grades on quizzes and multiple choice exams. However, for the next course in the program sequence, the instructors report that students are not prepared to apply the content learned in Dr. Brooks' course in the previous semester.

Why do you think this is? We do not want you to have the impression that Dr. Brooks is not a good teacher. Many elements of quality course design and content alignment are evident in her teaching. However, there is an opportunity for growth in andragogy and considering the needs of adult learners. After finishing Section II, you are likely recognizing the power of giving feedback—lots of it—and considering the recipient at the center. Think about Dr. Brooks. What feedback is she providing, other than grades? How do learners know if they are learning? Does Dr. Brooks' teaching suggest to students that feedback is important? Does she exhibit feedback?

If you are going to exhibit feedback in your course design and activities, then you have to consider moving beyond a traditional lecture style to present the content. The bold line to draw here about feedback is the fundamental difference between andragogy (Knowles, 1984; see Chapter 1) and pedagogy. Pedagogy is teacher-directed learning, while andragogy is learner-directed. Considering how we exhibit feedback reflects the shift to focus on the adult learner, the future educator.

Elford, M. D., Haynes Smith, H., & James, S.
GET Feedback: Giving, Exhibiting, and Teaching Feedback in
Special Education Teacher Preparation (pp. 103-128).
© 2022 SLACK Incorporated.

This chapter leads us to explore how the shift from pedagogy to andragogy provides opportunities to design coursework in support of adult learners to become special educators. How is what we are exhibiting as teacher educators driven by the specific needs of adult learners? We want to explicitly reiterate that *what we do in higher education is not the same as what we would do when teaching a 4-year old or a seventh-grader.* Our adult learners often care most about grades, whereas we, as instructors in professional programs preparing future special educators, are focused on outcomes-related learning and growth. Believing that learning occurs most efficiently and thus good grades result most easily if course content is "transmitted" via lecture, adult learners resist a more andragogical approach. This chapter is about how we can guide adult learners to deeper learning through exhibiting feedback.

Exhibiting feedback is how instructors can reinforce what is valued in a course. We must be explicit in describing our course learning objectives to our adult learners and explain what our course(s) is about (e.g., professional growth, application of theories). This is why we must exhibit feedback in our actions. In this chapter, you will reflect on your current practice in exhibiting feedback and work through activities to identify your strengths and opportunities for continued growth and development. Chapter 6 will build on your current levels of performance, borrow from our field's language, and provide an opportunity to innovate and revise how you exhibit feedback in course design, activities, and assignments.

Chapter Objectives

This chapter begins our exploration of how special education teacher preparation instructors can exhibit feedback. To do this, we continue our exploration of the four domains of feedback, especially as they help us understand exhibiting feedback. We then consider the intersection with adult learning theory. This chapter will further describe the four domains of the G.E.T. Model of feedback, including the need for knowledge of the domains and why attention to the domains of feedback in a course can enhance preservice teachers' understanding and practice of feedback. This chapter will also offer many opportunities to reflect on the domains of feedback and provide examples and prompts to evaluate opportunities for improvement in exhibiting feedback in courses.

Much has been written about the characteristics of feedback that contribute to our framework in the G.E.T. Model. Once the four domains are clear, understanding a plan for evaluating how the domains are exhibited becomes the next task. We then provide guidance to consider how feedback is exhibited. To assist special education teacher preparation instructors in exhibiting and modeling feedback, we recommend reflecting on the goals and course objectives and making a plan that considers the steps and features related to timing. Special education teacher preparation instructors can use the four domains of the G.E.T. Model in the creation and revision of courses while also recognizing the learning needs of adult learners.

After reading this chapter, you will **know** and **understand** these concepts and have the opportunity to **demonstrate** and **apply** your knowledge (Table 6-1).

Describe and Define

As special education teacher preparation instructors, we have many opportunities to exhibit feedback, including, but not limited to, coursework, field experience, and practica. *Exhibiting* feedback goes a step beyond *giving* feedback. At its most basic level, it is about modeling how feedback should be given and sharing the process of the "why and how" of feedback more explicitly with future educators. The act of giving feedback covered in Section II has important considerations for adult learners. Exhibiting feedback examines the characteristics of the feedback we give—the typical features and distinctive qualities. The systematic and explicit instruction about feedback in lesson

TABLE 6-1. GRAPHIC ORGANIZER		
KNOW (WHAT)	**UNDERSTAND (WHY)**	**DEMONSTRATE (HOW)**
What exhibiting the domains of feedback looks like.	Why special education teacher preparation instructors should examine how feedback is exhibited in course design, activities, and assignments.	How to identify the way the domains of feedback are exhibited in course design, activities, and assignments.
APPLY (TAKE ACTION)		
Apply knowledge of the domains of feedback to evaluate and make recommendations for exhibiting feedback in course design, activities, and assignments.		

design that we are teaching our candidates should not be a mystery in our own practice. We can be explicit about what we do and why we do it to support preservice special educator learning and practice. Serious attention to deeper, transformational change in how to exhibit feedback in our courses and programs is needed. Let us begin by examining our beliefs about how we exhibit feedback in our interactions with preservice special education educators.

> *Note*: We use the term *instructor(s)* to capture a variety of roles, including clinical faculty, academic faculty, site mentors, practicum supervisors, professional development providers, coaches, and others.

The reflection exercise (Table 6-2) examines our beliefs about how we exhibit feedback in our interactions with preservice special education educators.

The four domains of feedback in the G.E.T. Model introduced in Chapter 1 are grounded in research from several fields. We will first explore each of the four domains through a scenario designed to reflect an authentic example of an individualized education plan (IEP) course assignment. We will unpack the scenario, identifying explicitly where the four domains that are central to the G.E.T. Model are exhibited. By the end of the chapter, you will have the opportunity to evaluate and make recommendations on exhibiting feedback. To begin, let us review the following four domains introduced in Chapter 1:

1. **Specificity**. Specificity includes the questions, levels, and characteristics that are goal related. The characteristics of specificity include the language used, who is receiving the feedback, and the ways the feedback is clearly stated and fully accessible.

2. **Immediacy.** Immediacy relates to the timing of when feedback is delivered, based on questions, levels, and characteristics. Timing is an integral component of effective feedback. Wiggins (2012) and Brookhart (2008) both use the word *timely* in their list of characteristics of effective feedback.

3. **Purposefulness**. Purposefulness describes the questions, levels, and characteristics that are progress related. In this domain, feedback includes all the language and methods describing what is required to keep moving forward along the learning continuum.

4. **Constructiveness**. Constructiveness reflects the notion that the learner is a participant in creating new meaning from the feedback received. The questions, levels, and characteristics inform the progress and suggested improvements for the feedback recipient. This idea is closely linked to the meaning the recipient makes of the feedback and what that produces.

TABLE 6-2. REFLECTION EXERCISE	
WHICH DO YOU BELIEVE?	
Column A	*Column B*
1. Instructors should align activities and assessment with learning objectives.	1. Instructors should design activities and assessments based on their preferences.
2. Instructors should provide all the course material to be learned through lecture, video, and reading assignments.	2. Instructors should provide all the course material to be learned, reflecting on Universal Design for Learning and the "what, why, and how" of learning.
3. Instructors should provide feedback on every paper.	3. Instructors should provide feedback on only the papers that are deficient.
4. Instructors should only give performance-based feedback.	4. Instructors should give feedback on a variety of activities and assignments.
5. Instructors should request feedback from adult learners once per semester.	5. Instructors should request feedback from adult learners at multiple points in a semester.
6. Instructors should teach about peer feedback.	6. Instructors should provide opportunities for peer feedback.

What do you notice about the beliefs in Column A or Column B? How can reflecting on your beliefs and practices help you to recognize opportunities for growth in providing feedback to adult learners?

Response:

Know

What is exhibiting feedback? How is it different from giving and teaching feedback? Exhibiting feedback represents a unique conceptualization in the G.E.T. Model. It is necessary and is often overlooked. As special education instructors, we see this missing component as analogous to a research-to-practice gap that many of us have seen in practice, such as K-12 students with learning disabilities who benefit when educators provide explicit instruction and practice in mathematical computation that goes from concrete to representational to abstract (Figure 6-1). Although some K-12 students understand and readily jump from concrete to abstract, research supports representation instruction and practice, especially for K-12 students with learning disabilities. Here we explain and illustrate the similarities between the G.E.T. Model and concrete to representational to abstract models of math for K-12 students with learning disabilities.

The CRA sequence facilitates math learning, although it is rarely used systematically (Mercer & Miller, 1992). Mercer and Miller (1992) first defined the CRA sequence:

- Concrete: The student uses three-dimensional objects to solve computation problems.
- Representational: The student uses drawings to solve computation problems.
- Abstract: The student looks at the computation problem and attempts to solve it without objects or drawings.

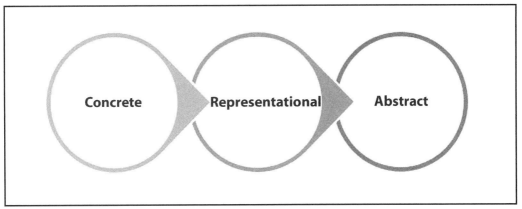

Figure 6-1. Concrete-Representational-Abstract sequence.

Students with learning disabilities have lower computational performance. Practices that support conceptual, procedural, and declarative mathematics knowledge are beneficial for all students, especially students with learning differences (Fuchs et al., 2008; Miller & Hudson, 2007; Powell et al., 2020).

Much like the previous example from special education research and practice, exhibiting feedback is the important connection between giving and teaching feedback to adult learners. Although both the mathematical concepts and feedback can be taught without the middle step, the benefits for all may not be fully recognized without explicit explanation, attention, and reflection on how we exhibit feedback. This is the opportunity for the instructor to explain the "what and why" of giving feedback and how their instruction becomes a model for considering how future special educators will also be purposeful in their work. At the risk of overusing analogies, we offer just one more as a nod to our University of Kansas roots—this is like being the "Great and Powerful Oz." In exhibiting feedback, we are letting our adult learners behind the curtain with us, explaining our application of the G.E.T. Model (Figure 6-2).

What makes exhibiting feedback difficult is that educators cannot reflect on just one specific instructional or design feature, check that box, and then move on. Exhibiting feedback has many layers. To assist in describing and defining what instructors need to know, we share an example of a common special education course topic and assignment—the IEP. The example is followed by an explanation and visuals to assist you in seeing and understanding the layers. In exhibiting feedback, we find all four domains. In the IEP example and description that follows, we suggest that you reflect on how these are **different** from giving feedback.

We recognize that, as readers, your experience and the context of your course and program will influence how you see the connections reflected. This is to be expected, and this example is meant only to be illustrative in describing and defining the domains in exhibiting feedback.

IEP Assignment Description Reflection

The first example to explore is the features of an IEP assignment. The IEP is central to special education instruction. As such, many instructors address IEPs in their courses. This example of demonstrating exhibiting feedback describes an IEP assignment in an online course. This IEP assignment example was designed and scaffolded to teach IEP development in stages. It is tied explicitly to a course learning objective, and the learning goals and expectations were explained at the outset. We will now describe the example, with explicit connections to the domains.

This assignment includes parts of the IEP that are due at each stage. At the first stage, teacher candidates submit details about the child and complete the commonly required fields in an IEP. At future stages, they submit child observations, current levels of performance, appropriate IEP goals

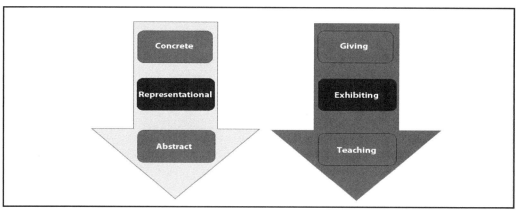

Figure 6-2. Illustrated analogy. The arrow on the left pertains to math computation feedback. The arrow on the right pertains to the G.E.T. Model feedback.

and assistive technology, parent participation, and/or other specific content aligned to the course. At each stage, teacher candidates submit materials for review. The instructor gives feedback at each stage. The instructor also recognizes that other teacher candidates will often have questions about the stage and allots time to online synchronous chat(s) or teacher candidate conferences. In this example, all four domains of exhibiting feedback in the G.E.T. Model are present (Tables 6-3 through 6-6). Each elaborated explanation also examines where feedback is exhibited in the sample IEP assignment description example.

Recognizing Exhibiting Feedback by Domain

Precise evidence of specificity includes conferences and online discussions added in the course design to address questions at all stages of the assignment. Also, the assignment is part of the finished product and is impacted by feedback on each component.

Specific evidence of immediacy—the deliberate choice to offer feedback quickly or after a period for learner reflection—includes planning the conference and online discussion. Thought was given to when feedback would be given and the time needed for teacher candidates to reflect on and revise before moving to the next stage.

Specific evidence of purposefulness includes how the instructor was intentional about chunking feedback alongside stages of assignment submission over time because they wanted to see teacher candidates performing the analysis bit-by-bit and to watch their growth. The instructor explains to the teacher candidates from the very beginning that she will be looking for revisions based on her feedback and that mastery is the expectation at the culmination of the assignment. Does this illustrate to you how one can use the course learning outcomes as the standard and measure learning progress across the semester? Can you see the connections? That might be another way to think about how exhibiting feedback could help to connect the course design, activities, and assignments between giving feedback and teaching feedback.

Specific evidence of constructiveness includes how the teacher candidates were responsible for incorporating the feedback before their IEP submission at the next stage. The instructor selected constructive feedback, realizing that for this assignment it was most important that the feedback was specific and purposeful to assist the teacher candidates in mastery of each stage.

TABLE 6-3. SPECIFICITY IN IEP ASSIGNMENT

COURSE DESIGN	ACTIVITIES	ASSIGNMENT
X		X

Specificity is evident in the IEP assignment description example.

Where do you see specificity in the IEP assignment description example?
Notes:

TABLE 6-4. IMMEDIACY IN IEP ASSIGNMENT

COURSE DESIGN	ACTIVITIES	ASSIGNMENT
X	X	X

Immediacy is evident in the IEP assignment description example.

Where do you see immediacy in the IEP assignment description example?
Notes:

TABLE 6-5. PURPOSEFULNESS IN IEP ASSIGNMENT

COURSE DESIGN	ACTIVITIES	ASSIGNMENT
X		X

Purposefulness is heavily reflected and evident in the IEP assignment description example.

Where do you see purposefulness in the IEP assignment description example?
Notes:

TABLE 6-6. CONSTRUCTIVENESS IN IEP ASSIGNMENT

COURSE DESIGN	ACTIVITIES	ASSIGNMENT
X	X	X

Constructiveness is heavily reflected and evident in the IEP assignment description example.

Where do you see constructiveness in the IEP assignment description example?
Notes:

Understand

To become more proficient and purposeful in exhibiting feedback, you must understand your strengths and practice exhibiting feedback. Prochaska and DiClemente's (1992) stages of change, described in Chapter 1, addresses how we exhibit feedback and recognizes that if we are here, that is, gathering information and beginning to plan, we are likely entering what Prochaska and DiClemente called the *preparation* stage. This stage follows the *precontemplation* and *contemplation* stages, which represent the stages we have moved through or are in the process of moving through. The preparation stage is often considered the most important. For many, skipping this stage will likely mean that the changes attempted in practice will be short-lived. To assist us in giving the necessary attention to understanding, we think that understanding your own practice related to exhibiting feedback is a necessary exercise to catapult into action. Chapter 6 continues with reflection exercises and examples to support our preparation for Chapter 7, where we will guide the reader to action and implementation of exhibiting feedback. The reflection process is also helpful in making actionable plans in implementing the G.E.T. Model in your teaching practice. It is important to focus on what you are already doing as a starting point, which reflects a more strengths-based perspective to this approach to teacher candidate instruction. When possible, think about what you are already doing as a strength versus ticking off a list of what you are not doing.

To understand your strengths and current level of performance in exhibiting feedback, borrowing from our field of special education, we will walk through a strengths-focused checklist. In this activity, you will have the opportunity to free-write your responses as well as utilize checkboxes. It may be that you already recognize how you are doing many of the practices listed here, but which one do you think you do most or is your default domain? Is there one that you value more in preparing future educators? Taking it a step further, what do we tell our teacher candidates when our feedback is heavily aligned with only one or two aspects? Without saying anything, teacher candidates may erroneously think these are the only types of feedback they should be incorporating as teachers or that their interest/practice of another aspect is not acceptable. In this exercise, there is no right answer. In fact, we see how our practices will and should vary, based on a number of factors, including programs, disability category, learner age, geography, teaching format, and more. The goal for this activity or following this activity is the prompt: How do I achieve a balance of exhibiting feedback across these domains in a way that is appropriate to my program and course learning outcomes?

Step 1. Let's begin. Our first step is to reflect on which component of the G.E.T. Model we already incorporate the most. Which domain do you think you do and rely on the most? Although this book has yet to cover each component of the model, please rank and predict the order of the three by indicating the number in the box provided.

☐ Giving feedback

☐ Exhibiting feedback

☐ Teaching feedback

Reflect briefly on why you chose this order. Where is exhibiting feedback and why did you rank it as you did?

Response:

Step 2. Given where exhibiting feedback is in your practice, select at least one learning goal you have for yourself in this section of the book.

☐ Define exhibiting feedback.

☐ Make a list of three new opportunities to exhibit feedback in my course.

☐ Incorporate opportunities for students to provide feedback on how I exhibit feedback.

☐ Identify one activity or assignment to revise to exhibit feedback.

☐ Create my own list of values aligned with exhibiting feedback.

☐ Revise assessments for alignment with course learning objectives.

☐ Revise course learning objectives.

☐ Advocate for program alignment to support exhibiting feedback.

☐ Craft a one-page narrative describing the "what, why, and how" of exhibiting feedback in this course for other instructors.

☐ Indicate two to three dates in my course schedule for explicit presentation on progress toward learning goals and supporting student self-regulation in mastering course content.

☐ Other exhibiting feedback goal: _____

☐ Other exhibiting feedback goal: _____

Step 3. What do you think is your strength in exhibiting feedback? Use the checkboxes to indicate your "go-to" domain strength in exhibiting feedback and brainstorm and reflect on all the ways you do that one, with boxes to the right for other domains that are co-occurring.

Which domain do you think you "exhibit" the most?

☐ Specificity

☐ Immediacy

☐ Purposefulness

☐ Constructiveness

In Table 6-7, circle the domain column you identified in the checklist above. Then add details of evidence from your practice in that domain in the blank space below it, circling whether it is a course design element (CDE), activities (ACT), and/or assignments (AMT). (See Table 6-8 for a completed example.)

TABLE 6-7. DETAILS OF PRACTICE BY DOMAIN

SPECIFICITY			IMMEDIACY			PURPOSEFULNESS			CONSTRUCTIVENESS		
CDE	ACT	AMT	CDE	ACT	AMT	CDE	ACT	AMT	CDE	ACT	AMT
CDE	ACT	AMT	CDE	ACT	AMT	CDE	ACT	AMT	CDE	ACT	AMT
CDE	ACT	AMT	CDE	ACT	AMT	CDE	ACT	AMT	CDE	ACT	AMT
CDE	ACT	AMT	CDE	ACT	AMT	CDE	ACT	AMT	CDE	ACT	AMT
CDE	ACT	AMT	CDE	ACT	AMT	CDE	ACT	AMT	CDE	ACT	AMT

ACT = activities; AMT = assignments; CDE = course design element.

TABLE 6-8. EXAMPLE OF COMPLETED EXERCISE

SPECIFICITY			IMMEDIACY			PURPOSEFULNESS			CONSTRUCTIVENESS		
CDE	ACT	AMT	CDE	ACT	AMT	CDE	ACT	AMT	CDE	ACT	AMT
Ex. IEP—behavioral objectives									X		

ACT = activities; AMT = assignments; CDE = course design element.

Step 4. Now, return to Table 6-7, and in the columns for the remaining domains, place an X to indicate any co-occurring domain(s) for the listed design element, activity, or assignment.

Table 6-8 shows an example of the completed exercise from Step 3.

In the example shown in Table 6-8, specificity is the indicated "go-to" strategy of the instructor. The instructor indicates the multiple rounds of feedback on the IEP assignment, writing behavioral objectives. The instructor checked the constructiveness column as well because the instructor recognized it, along with specificity, as one way that feedback is exhibited in this class. The instructor identified as a value and aspirational goal to be constructive and use the language of ongoing regard.

Step 5. When you have completed the list for your strength, or go-to or preferred domain and co-occurring evidence for each, do the activity again (Table 6-9). In our experience, another domain comes in at a close second. Indicate your next-most strength, go-to, or preferred domain.

Step 6. Now, return to the list in Table 6-9 and in the columns for the remaining domains, place an X to indicate any co-occurring domain(s) for the listed design element, activity, or assignment.

TABLE 6-9. DETAILS OF PRACTICE BY DOMAIN REPEAT EXERCISE

SPECIFICITY			IMMEDIACY			PURPOSEFULNESS			CONSTRUCTIVENESS		
CDE	ACT	AMT	CDE	ACT	AMT	CDE	ACT	AMT	CDE	ACT	AMT
CDE	ACT	AMT	CDE	ACT	AMT	CDE	ACT	AMT	CDE	ACT	AMT
CDE	ACT	AMT	CDE	ACT	AMT	CDE	ACT	AMT	CDE	ACT	AMT
CDE	ACT	AMT	CDE	ACT	AMT	CDE	ACT	AMT	CDE	ACT	AMT
CDE	ACT	AMT	CDE	ACT	AMT	CDE	ACT	AMT	CDE	ACT	AMT

ACT = activities; AMT = assignments; CDE = course design element.

TABLE 6-10. TALLY OF FEEDBACK PRACTICE

PRACTICE	TALLY FROM TABLE 6-7	TALLY FROM TABLE 6-9	TALLY FROM BOTH TABLES
Course design elements			
Activities			
Assignments			

Step 7. Once you have completed two reflection charts, recognizing your practice and strengths in exhibiting feedback, pause to identify what domains and what course design elements, activities, or assignments might be missing. Select a highlighter or different color pen and mark the spaces that are empty. Tally up the number of course design elements, activities, or assignments where you are exhibiting feedback (Table 6-10). Do you see any trends you might balance?

Is there a domain or domains that would benefit from reflection or focus on exhibiting feedback? Describe any action items you have or are considering regarding exhibiting feedback.

Response:

This might be a good time to thank yourself for this reflection on your practice. You may or may not have identified an actionable goal, but you have definitely participated in a scholarly reflection on your practice in a way that can benefit the learners in your course(s).

Other Considerations in Exhibiting Feedback

We exhibit feedback through what we do as instructors—how we plan, explain, model, and reinforce the importance and value of feedback in the learning process. You have worked through examples to support knowing and recognizing the domains in one activity. We need to continue to recognize that the recipients of our feedback are adult learners. Where they are in readiness, prior knowledge, and others will influence how the feedback is received and used. Our role as instructors in exhibiting feedback is **consistently** sending the same message about feedback. For those teacher candidates who are reluctant, instructor behavior regarding consistency in feedback will serve to either encourage or discourage the teacher candidates from acting on the feedback. There are several specific aspects of exhibiting that we need to explore for understanding, beyond the four domains.

It Takes Time!

Exhibiting feedback is a process that can take time. It is important to recognize that a lot of what we are teaching the future special education professionals is not learned overnight; it is a process that occurs over time, enhanced by their reflection as well as course and programmatic design. As instructors, we improve our courses every term, as we incorporate feedback—right? Maybe we are doing a lot in course design but have not considered how explicit we are being about the importance and value of feedback. How do we enhance what we are exhibiting by including talking about it weekly? Maybe we need to be thinking about how our plan is perceived in the day-to-day activities or assessments. Maybe we need to ask the teacher candidates what they think we are trying to do and use that as feedback to tell us whether we are being as clear as we think we are. It takes time to select and refine how we exhibit feedback. There is no one right way to exhibit feedback. You must consider the content of the course and context of your own course, including factors of size, location in the course sequence, and novice versus advanced teacher candidates. However, instructors could have problems here. They might be exhibiting it well, but the teacher candidates do not see or recognize the connection. We need to be explicit and explain often the why and how of our practice.

What Is the Teacher Candidate Perspective?

Having teacher candidates' input is important. They should weigh in. When we are not watching, do we not want our teacher candidates to get it right? We need to be careful to avoid "do what I say, not what I do" in our delivery of instruction and how we exhibit feedback. Why not get feedback from them on what they see in our practice? This could be helpful feedback for instructors' self-efficacy. Try the following: As an exit ticket one day, ask your teacher candidates, "How am I exhibiting feedback?" Do you conduct periodic progress monitoring or offer opportunities for feedback on your teaching? What does or does not say about the role of feedback in your practice? Do the teacher candidates' perspectives match your self-efficacy? An example of a teacher candidate reflection form is shown in Table 6-11.

Demonstrate

How do we exhibit feedback in a classroom versus in a clinical setting or field-based course? How might exhibiting feedback be different in each of these settings? As authors, we endeavor to include diverse examples that reflect the variety of delivery methods in special education teacher preparation programs. How do we respond and pay attention to adult learning? In the moment, how do we determine where the students are, their readiness to learn, as well as their prior knowledge and then respond appropriately by **exhibiting** the feedback we give? For practice, let us now explore a gallery walk activity as an opportunity to exhibit feedback.

TABLE 6-11. EXHIBITING FEEDBACK TEACHER CANDIDATE REFLECTION FORM	
MONTH _____ YEAR _____	EXHIBITING FEEDBACK REFLECTION
On a scale of 1 to 10, with 1 being *almost never* and 10 being *every day*, how often does the course instructor exhibit feedback? 1 ☐ 2 ☐ 3 ☐ 4 ☐ 5 ☐ 6 ☐ 7 ☐ 8 ☐ 9 ☐ 10 ☐ Are you clear on the learning objectives of this course? NO ☐ SOMEWHAT ☐ YES ☐ Can you describe the progress you have made toward the learning objectives of the course? NO ☐ SOMEWHAT ☐ YES ☐	
Reflect on the instruction in this course. Circle one response for each numbered item that you believe most reflects the instructor's beliefs and practices.	
Column A	Column B
1. My instructor aligns activities and assessment with learning objectives	1. My instructor designs activities and assessments based on their preferences.
2. My instructor provides all the course material to be learned through lecture, video, and reading assignments.	2. My instructor provides all the course material to be learned, reflecting on Universal Design for Learning and the "what, why, and how" of learning.
3. My instructor provides feedback on every paper.	3. My instructor provides feedback on only the papers that are deficient.
4. My instructor only gives performance-based feedback.	4. My instructor gives feedback on a variety of activities and assignments.
5. My instructor requests feedback from teacher candidates once a semester.	5. My instructor requests feedback from teacher candidates at multiple points in the semester.
6. My instructor teaches about peer feedback.	6. My instructor provides opportunities for peer feedback.

A gallery walk is an opportunity for teacher candidates (adult learners) to describe what they have learned and explain it to the other people in their group or to a class (a learning community). A gallery walk is part of ongoing learning and progress. Similarly, a jigsaw strategy is an opportunity for organizing instruction and making the text accessible. This example is to demonstrate exhibiting feedback by describing the use of an in-class activity in a face-to-face introductory special education course to deepen foundational knowledge of characteristics and instruction for K-12 students with high-incidence disabilities.

Gallery Walk Description Example

The instructor recognizes that lecturing on the topics is not going to achieve the level of engagement and understanding desired. This gallery walk example begins with the instructor revisiting the course objectives and learning goals aligned to this activity.

Aligned Course Objective. Describe and apply knowledge of high-incidence disabilities (i.e., learning disabilities, emotional and behavioral disorders, communication disorders) and the related appropriate accommodations and evidence-based instructional supports.

Learning Goals. Practice and fluency in describing foundational knowledge of characteristics of high-incidence disabilities.

- Practice and fluency in selecting appropriate accommodations and evidence-based instructional supports.
- Implement feedback and recommendations from peers and the instructor to deepen foundational knowledge.

At this point, the instructor needs to provide an opportunity for practice and feedback on the path to mastery. This activity is clearly not for when learning is finished, and learners should be considering where to go next.

To begin, the instructor chunks specific information (e.g., characteristics, accommodations, instruction for one disability in the high-incidence disability category) across several adult learners, and an infographic is chosen as the product to demonstrate knowledge. The expectation, supported by the long-held belief that the highest level of understanding is when you know it and can teach it to others, is explained alongside the criteria for presentation. Before the day of the presentations, the instructor reviews the products to be shared and gives direct feedback before others walk through or several days in advance to allow for revisions. On the day of the presentation, the instructor says, "As you're viewing one another's infographics, make your feedback specific, descriptive, and accentuate the strengths and make at least one suggestion for improvement." At the same time, the instructor reinforces these directions by following the same guidelines. After the activity, the instructor debriefs the activity and has the class members weigh its utility in their understanding and reflection on how they can improve the connection to the course learning goals. In this example, the criteria for success aligns with the feedback and the expectation for continuing learning by implementing recommendations from peers and the instructor.

Reflecting on the Gallery Walk Example

In this example, all four domains of the exhibiting feedback in the G.E.T. Model are also identifiable (Tables 6-12 through 6-15). Each elaborated explanation notes where exhibiting feedback is evident in the gallery walk activity, including connected implications for course design and related assignments. We have marked an X in the columns we think are most apparent, but there are no right or wrong answers, as your reflection is content- and context-driven. Space is provided for you to reflect on specific evidence or related ideas. Our thoughts follow this space for each of the four domains.

Specificity is evident in the gallery walk activity example because of the precise explanation of expectations and feedback on how those expectations were met. Specific evidence includes how a gallery walk can be adapted for almost any content, given that it aligns with the goals, as the Table 6-11 example shows. It can be taking individual parts of a concept in your course design that build upon each other and having teacher candidates explore, design, and make meaning of each component or concept. In special education courses, alternate examples could include reviewing individual parts of different evidence-based practices in autism spectrum disorder (e.g., exercise, differential reinforcement, and more).

Immediacy is evident in the gallery walk activity example because the feedback is timely and can be delivered both prior to the gallery walk or during the gallery walk. Specific evidence includes decisions about when this activity might fall during the semester. Does the instructor give feedback in advance or model and exhibit feedback during the gallery walk alongside teacher candidates?

Purposefulness is evident in the gallery walk activity because this is a progress-based activity; it fits the process level and answers the question *how am I going*? Specific evidence includes the way the instructor demonstrates that the feedback is ongoing. The teacher candidates are progressing, and this recognizes the continuum of knowledge and the scaffolds needed to build the knowledge toward the selected course learning goals, especially in special education teacher preparation. A gallery walk is a purposeful activity utilized and purposefully planned in course design because teacher candidates are exhibiting what they know and understanding, while a jigsaw strategy allows for more practice and application. In course design, a gallery walk can provide the opportunity for teacher candidates to be purposeful in their learning and being specific in exploring a narrow topic so that it can be presented clearly for other learners.

Constructiveness is evident in the gallery walk activity because the activity requires teacher candidates to use the feedback from peers and from the instructor to construct new meaning or knowledge about the topic. Specific evidence includes the way that the instructor selected constructive feedback, realizing that for this assignment it was most important that the feedback was specific and purposeful to assist the teacher candidates in mastery of each stage.

TABLE 6-12. SPECIFICITY REFLECTION

COURSE DESIGN	ACTIVITIES	ASSIGNMENT
X	X	

Reflection of evidence on specificity:

TABLE 6-13. IMMEDIACY REFLECTION

COURSE DESIGN	ACTIVITIES	ASSIGNMENT
X		X

Reflection of evidence on immediacy:

TABLE 6-14. PURPOSEFULNESS REFLECTION

COURSE DESIGN	ACTIVITIES	ASSIGNMENT
X	X	

Reflection of evidence on purposefulness:

TABLE 6-15. CONSTRUCTIVENESS REFLECTION

COURSE DESIGN	ACTIVITIES	ASSIGNMENT
X	X	

Reflection of evidence on constructiveness:

TABLE 6-16. SPOTLIGHT ON ADULT LEARNING			
SPECIFICITY	IMMEDIACY	PURPOSEFULNESS	CONSTRUCTIVENESS
Are the course design, assignments, and activities clearly described and explicitly connected to the learners' need to know? Does the instructor make clear why feedback is being given and how the feedback moves the teacher candidate forward on the learning continuum?	Do the course design and activities intentionally include opportunities for exhibiting feedback that are timely and responsive to the motivation of the adult learner? Does the way the instructors exhibit feedback consider the prior experience and readiness to learn of the teacher candidate?	Do the course requirements and activities provide opportunity for the instructor to exhibit feedback that is developmentally appropriate for teacher candidates? Is the feedback the instructor exhibits problem-centered and contextual?	In what ways does the course design, assignments, and activities promote self-direction and autonomy? How does the feedback promote teacher candidates' use of new knowledge they are acquiring in a way that is problem-centered and contextual? How do instructors demonstrate their own application of feedback received from teacher candidates?

SPOTLIGHT ON ADULT LEARNING

Table 6-16 demonstrates domain reflection questions. As we have frequently stated, the conceptual model of intersecting feedback with adult learning theory is a layered, complex process. In Chapter 1, we described a biology textbook overlay as one way to think about this complexity. Another way to think about exhibiting feedback and adult learning theory is to picture a beautiful stained glass window. Each of the separate panes are essential to creating the image, but looking at only one pane limits the beauty of the whole picture. Yet, the more we appreciate the color in each pane, the clearer the whole image becomes. In Chapter 5, we concentrated on the adult learner as the recipient—those principles at the center of the G.E.T. Model. In this chapter, we are highlighting the domains of feedback.

POSSIBLE BARRIERS TO USING THIS TYPE OF FEEDBACK

There are many barriers to consider in preparing to change or create new practices around exhibiting feedback. We have organized the discussion of them in this section related to each domain. As we understand our current practice, we think this organization will assist you in preparation because barriers specific to your strengths and opportunities for growth can be easily found. However, we still recommend that you review the barriers for each domain because, as we have demonstrated, they can overlap. General overarching barriers are described at the end of this section.

Barriers to Specificity

Class size may be a barrier to specificity. How can we modify an activity or assignment to exhibit specificity in a way that is manageable for large classes? One opportunity may be incorporating peer feedback to replace some instructor feedback, removing the tasks unrelated to the learning goal or updating a rubric. Another barrier to specificity is the habits of behavior in speech. People use the same words over and over again. It is possible that the meaning of the feedback may not be clear or is idiomatic. There are behavioral considerations as well. If you have historically received one or a few types of feedback, this may be observable in your practice. For example, if you have seen or received behavior-specific praise, you will likely be more proficient in exhibiting this in your practice. Recognizing this can indicate an opportunity to explore other forms of feedback and ways to exhibit it.

Barriers to Immediacy

Decisions about immediacy are visible in assignments, rubrics, and time lines. Expectations about the time between teacher candidate performance and instructor feedback should be clear so that teacher candidates understand the value of both delayed and immediate feedback. While timely feedback—whether delayed or immediate—can involve grades, instructors can also choose to forego offering grades during a teacher candidate-driven formative process and instead "use time more effectively by providing actionable descriptive feedback and giving [teacher candidate] in-class, supervision opportunities to use the feedback to reflect on their progress" (Brookhart, 2019, p. 2).

Barriers to Purposefulness

Impatience can push us to move quickly to action without carefully considering purpose. When our teaching is targeted toward a learning goal that has been aligned with course objectives and thoughtfully articulated in a rubric, and all of this is transparent to teachers so they can clearly understand the "what, why, and how" they will be learning, our teaching is purposive. Yet, creating purposive learning opportunities is difficult and may not feel as exciting as jumping into an activity. In addition, as teachers, we may want to "trust our gut" that a project will produce the results we want rather than carefully defining our goals, accurately measuring teacher candidates' learning, and collecting evidence of our teaching effectiveness. Although our gut may not be wrong, it also may not always be correct, and relying on it rather than being purposeful in our teaching can undermine our success. Purposefulness is not merely course-level, it should inform entire programs and should be visible in the larger alignment of courses.

Another barrier to purposefulness is the length of a semester. What would you do if your university has gone to 10-week blocks to create a trimester versus the previous 15-week semester blocks? Do the course objectives reflect the change? Are they deleted, or are you trying to cram the original learning goals into a shorter time period? Do you fake it until you make it? When time is precious and goals are ambitious, courses should be aligned to eliminate redundancies and ensure that foundational concepts are being taught. We recommend creating a comprehensive course walk or guidance for the order of the courses and will discuss this more in Chapter 9.

Barrier to Constructiveness

One barrier to constructiveness is the need to abandon judgmental language. We have been taught that positive feedback is the best, but so much of the positive language we may have become accustomed to using is attributive. Further, sometimes the examples provided in special education teacher preparation instruction can create cognitive dissonance. For instance, high-leverage practice #8 provides an example of feedback that is evaluative (McLeskey et al., 2017). The example is recommending feedback on effort. This is not what we are trying to do. So, giving judgmental feedback on the effort by saying, "You really worked hard on that," sounds like effort feedback, but those words are really a judgment. Another way to think about this from the recipient's perspective is the receiver could be thinking, "You must be kidding, that took me 10 minutes!", so the feedback could be interpreted as untrustworthy. Attributive or judgmental feedback should be replaced with feedback about specific accomplishments that are evidenced in the actual product. This kind of feedback might include comments such as, "I noticed the attention to detail you have included in this assignment. For example, on page 6 you include…" or "Your drawing demonstrates to me that you were precise and intentional with the colors you've chosen." Specific feedback linked to actual performance builds trust. If adult learners do not trust the feedback they receive or if they receive feedback that is misinterpreted, our feedback may not have an impact, which is a barrier. If the feedback does not align or is not explained explicitly without judgment, it risks impacting an adult learner's readiness to learn.

At the same time, specific feedback may discourage teacher candidates if they generalize their specific errors, weaknesses, or areas for improvement as an inherent lack of worth, which can produce shame (Brown, 2015). Instructors should be careful to focus their feedback on consistent behavior rather than attributing behavior to the character of the adult learners because instructors can be powerful voices in building up or tearing down an adult learner's identity. When instructors fail to consider this aspect of adult learning and impute teacher candidates' performance to something inherent in them rather than identify it as an effort that can be improved, instructors should reflect and apologize. A feedback loop or multiple opportunities for anonymous feedback from the teacher candidates can help instructors see where their values and intentions might not align with their practice and help them articulate their feedback, without inducing shame.

Overarching Barriers

Do you make room for feedback? What about creating assessment-capable learners through purposeful instruction and guidance on how to give self-feedback and guide their feedback and reflection? Sometimes we are, or think we are, exhibiting feedback in a way that should be helpful, but teacher candidates are not ready, lacking background knowledge and understanding that will help them understand the feedback. This is a barrier because not everyone is ready; therefore, application at the next stage misses key information. Differentiation is needed in these situations.

PRACTICAL APPLICATION

Having analyzed a galley walk earlier in this chapter, we now have an opportunity to reflect on how instructional decisions at the course design level explicitly model how feedback should be given through sharing the "why and how" of delivering feedback. This practical application, examining jigsaw versus gallery walk activities, invites you to question how feedback is exhibited in your pedagogy/andragogy. The jigsaw example that follows is a simple activity to support teacher candidates in organizing instruction. In this example, the jigsaw strategy breaks down the reading of the text to make it more accessible and improve teacher candidates' learning and connections.

Jigsaw Activity in Ten Easy Steps

In its simplest form, the following jigsaw instructional strategy is when:

1. Each student receives a portion of the materials to be introduced.
2. Students leave their "home" groups and meet in "expert" groups of other students focusing on the same material.
3. "Expert" groups discuss the material and brainstorm ways to present their understandings to the other members of their "home" group.
4. The experts return to their "home" groups to teach their portion of the materials and to learn from the other members of their "home" group.

In more detail, and written from a teacher's perspective, to conduct a jigsaw activity in your classroom, you would do the following:

5. Assign students to "home" teams of four or five students (generally their regular cooperative learning teams). Have students number off within their teams.

6. Assign study topics to "home" team members by giving them an assignment sheet or by listing their numbers and corresponding roles on the board.

7. Have students move to "expert" groups, where everyone in the group has the same topic as themselves.

8. Students work with members of their "expert" group to read about and/or research their topic. They prepare a short presentation and decide how they will teach their topic to their "home" team. You may want students to prepare mini-posters while in their "expert" groups. These posters can contain important facts, information, and diagrams related to the study topic.

9. Students return to their "home" teams and take turns teaching their team members the material. Students may find it helpful to have team members take notes or record the information in their journals in some way. You may want them to complete a graphic organizer or chart with the new information.

10. Involve the class in a whole-group review of all the content you expect them to master on the assessment. Administer an individual assessment to arrive at individual grades.

Let us now consider how a jigsaw offers instructors an opportunity to exhibit feedback, offering an explicit connection between the feedback given and taught in a course. A jigsaw is a powerful activity, but consider how it might be used during a course to exhibit feedback.

Overall reflection: Can the use of a jigsaw or another activity reinforce how you exhibit feedback through reflection on the activity?

Response:

If you choose a jigsaw for an activity, how do you ensure that the activity reflects the learning objectives?

Response:

If we are intentional in the selection of an activity, such as a jigsaw, then what we have done is created an activity. A possible pitfall here, as with any excellent activity, is that the activity can go awry, with teacher candidate responses reflecting misinformation and, instead of stopping to address it and provide feedback, the course instructor moves on. This is a missed opportunity. This is our opportunity to shift from pedagogy to andragogy and really exhibit feedback.

Let us now work together to identify explicit examples of the four domains in exhibiting feedback.

Specificity

As a reminder, specificity includes the questions, levels, and characteristics that are goal-related. The characteristics of specificity include the language used, who is receiving the feedback, and the ways the feedback is clearly stated and fully accessible.

How can we exhibit specificity in a jigsaw? One way is to plan and predict where possible opportunities for feedback might occur. Archer and Hughes (2011) talk about "assumacide," which occurs when we assume a teacher candidate knows or understands a task or a skill. We should not assume the teacher candidates fully understand the jigsaw activity just because we provided explicit instruction. Exhibiting specificity in feedback could be planning a mini-lesson to demonstrate specifically how the jigsaw task might be completed. A planned think-aloud or metacognitive think-aloud strategy by the instructors could demonstrate how they might think through a problem-based activity before or after guided or independent practice on an activity or task. Do you talk out loud and provide a summary or a model? That could reflect exhibiting immediacy. An instructor might say, "Let's push the pause button. Let me tell you what I am hearing. There is an important first step that some groups are missing…."

> **Reflect:** What is another specific example or opportunity that reflects the specificity domain of exhibiting feedback?
>
> **Response:**

Constructiveness

As a reminder, this domain reflects feedback that is actionable and user-friendly. The instructor and recipient are both important to the impact of this domain. Recall from Chapter 1, there are three considerations for incorporating feedback in coursework: task-related, process-related, and self-regulation. Exhibiting constructiveness feedback is achieved when instructors incorporate course design elements, activities, and assignments that can address all three considerations.

Further, for the adult learner, we can explore the possible responses to actionable, user-friendly feedback that instructors give or exhibit through psychological constructs such as mindset (Dweck, 2006), attribution theory (Weiner, 1972), or goal-orientation (Dweck, 1986). To be effective, exhibiting feedback and constructiveness must address and support failure as well as teacher candidate self-regulation and coping in form or fashion. One popular conversation today in teacher education and K-12 education is about grit. Duckworth (2006) described grit as resilience and strategies to use feedback when improvement is needed. This could be a factor in exhibiting feedback and adult learning. For example, if academic tasks have always been easy for a teacher candidate in special education teacher preparation, but a new emphasis on performance-based assessments and feedback provides evidence that they are struggling, grit will influence their capacity to make changes in practice and impact learning. One example in college-level science, technology, engineering, and mathematics (STEM) is The Factors affecting Learning, Attitudes, and Mindsets in Education network (FLAMEnet). FLAMEnet (https://qubeshub.org/community/groups/flamenet/) is a nationwide network designed to bring together higher education STEM faculty, education researchers, and psychologists to design, deploy, and assess educational interventions that benefit students by promoting academic tenacity and resilience in STEM. Similar to the educational interventions FLAMEnet describes, we believe adding opportunities to reflect on the feedback and completed performance or products in special education teacher preparation explicitly addresses exhibiting constructiveness. Consider implementing an exit ticket reflection after a graded assignment is returned and ask teacher candidates to reflect on their preparation, response, or where they are going next in their learning.

> **Reflect:** What is another specific example or opportunity that reflects the constructiveness domain of exhibiting feedback?
>
> **Response:**

Immediacy

As a reminder, immediacy is not the same as the discussion in Chapter 4 of immediate versus delayed feedback. Immediacy in the G.E.T. Model is about what *timely* means and what adults need. Do adults need wait time the same way that K-12 students do?

Recall in Chapter 4 in which we described how some adults do not want immediate feedback and want to wait until they hear from instructors. Different from learned helplessness (where the learner does not know how to incorporate the feedback), the learner sees the role of the instructor as the guide and facilitator, and when and how the feedback comes is a factor. Immediacy does not always mean immediate in immediacy. It means the timing of the feedback. In some cases, it is immediate. In some cases, it is delayed. In some cases, it begins immediately but continues for some time.

> Reflect: What is another specific example or opportunity that reflects the immediacy domain of exhibiting feedback?
>
> Response:

Purposefulness

As a reminder, this is feedback that is well-planned and connected to the content. It is most helpful when transparent, targeted to a goal (such as course objectives), aligned to evaluation criteria (similar to the processes in the Strategic Instruction Model Course Organizer Routine [Lenz et al., 1998] or Understanding by Design framework [Wiggins & McTighe, 2011]), and competency-based (focused on what standard we are wanting the teacher candidate to meet). Examples of addressing purposefulness includes alignment activities and course design that includes a backwards design. The learning goals or essential questions (see Wiggins & McTighe, 2011) must be central to the instruction, activities, and assessment.

> Reflect: What is another specific example or opportunity that reflects the purposefulness domain of exhibiting feedback?
>
> Response:

The following questions are provided to guide your review and reflection in the Authentic Example that follows, contributed by Susanne James, PhD.

- In this example, how does the instructor apply knowledge of exhibiting feedback? Reflect.
- What is an assignment or activity in one of your courses where you exhibit feedback?
- How does exhibiting feedback support understanding and supporting the recipients of the feedback?

Authentic Example

*Contributed by
Susanne James, PhD*

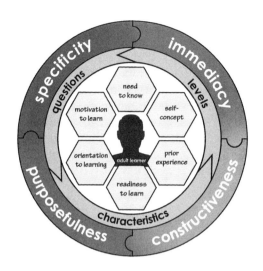

1. Course Details

SPE 511: The Individualized Educational Assessment course provides teachers with advanced knowledge of formal and informal assessment strategies as applied to the identification, evaluation, and ongoing development of an individual's learning progress. Progress monitoring will be a major component of this course so that teachers complete this course with a more in-depth understanding of response to intervention and the necessary skills to successfully monitor student progress. Teachers will use their understanding of the content in this course to make legal and instructional decisions, as well as develop an understanding of formal and informal assessment tools to support students with disabilities.

2. Learning Objectives

Goals for this assignment include the following:

a. To offer a helpful method for students in this class to cooperate more actively to understand class readings.

b. To encourage students to be active readers and apply the text to course objectives.

c. To motivate students to extend their understanding of the required course text and become lifelong learners of assessment.

TABLE 6-17. EVALUATION CRITERIA FORM
CHAPTER: **YOUR NAME:**
Your role in the group (circle one): chapter presenter   chapter participant
1. What positive outcomes did we achieve?
2. What misunderstandings did we encounter about the chapter?
3. What lessons have we learned that could be useful to other groups?
4. What do we do with the information we learned in this chapter?
5. How effective was the handout for this chapter?

3. Assignment Description

The idea of the jigsaw was first presented by Aronson (1978). The jigsaw Data Wise assignment activity is presented in the paragraphs that follow.

During jigsaw, small groups of learners divide a portion of content being covered during the class or session (e.g., information in a textbook like *Data Wise* [Boudett et al., 2013]), with each group presenting a different portion of the text. Following this, new groups are created, with each new group containing at least one member from each original group. In these new groups, participants, in sequence, reinforce the specific information they mastered to the members of the group, answering any specific questions and leading the discussion about the text.

Directions: Ten cooperative groups will form and prepare a 30-minute presentation on a chapter from *Data Wise* (Boudett et al., 2013). After the presentation, each group member will divide into new groups and present an informational handout about the chapter. This handout can consist of items such as double-column notes, concept map, or graphic organizer of the chapter. The group leader will lead a discussion of the chapter, asking thoughtful questions about what was learned and answer any questions from this discussion. If you are not responsible to present a chapter that day, you must still come prepared for the presentation by reading the chapter that will be presented that day and coming with one question or informed comment about what you have read.

4. Evaluation Criteria

The assessment form is shown in Table 6-17. Assessment questions for each session should include the following:
   a. What positive outcomes did we achieve?
   b. What misunderstandings did we encounter about the chapter?
   c. What lessons have we learned that could be useful to other groups?
   d. What do we do with the information we learned in this chapter?
   e. How effective was the handout for this chapter?

5. Additional Details

Resources on different types of handouts (double-column notes, concept maps, and graphic organizers) as well as chapter summaries are provided on Blackboard. A sign-up sheet for cooperative group assignments (Table 6-18) is available in a link to a Google Form.

TABLE 6-18. COOPERATIVE GROUP ASSIGNMENTS

CHAPTER	PRESENTER(S)	DATE OF PRESENTATION
Introduction	Dr. James	
Chapter 1		
Chapter 2		
Chapter 3		
Chapter 4		
Chapter 5		
Chapter 6		
Chapter 7		
Chapter 8		
Chapter 9		
Chapter 10	Dr. James	

6. Feedback Reflection

The goal for this assignment was to take the dense text in *Data Wise* (Boudett et al., 2013) and allow graduate students a cooperative learning opportunity to process the readings and to extend their understanding to their own school report card. The school report card provides families, educators, and communities with an annual informational snapshot of public schools and the progress they are making on a wide range of educational goals. This assignment allows adult learners an opportunity to reinforce the specific information in *Data Wise* by leading the discussion of the specific chapter text and to answer questions from those not presenting. This active engagement and the ability to teach others allows the graduate students to have a deeper level of understanding instead of the instructor just lecturing on the Data Wise process. Graduate students then think about the presentation during a break after the chapter presentation and complete the five questions of the session assessment (see Table 6-17). After the break, graduate students participate in a discussion of the assessment of the graduate students, reflecting on their learning as a chapter presenter or a chapter participant. This allows the presenter to reflect on the presentation and receive both peer feedback and teacher feedback as the assessment is discussed. Finally, the presenter's school report card is displayed to the class during a discussion of the chapter's application to the existing data teams in the school and the presenters' impression of data analysis at their schools. This allows the presenter to get further feedback in the sense-making of collaborative data inquiry to drive continuous improvement.

Summary

This chapter explains why exhibiting feedback is essential and how it supports giving feedback. This chapter sought to demonstrate the complexity of recognizing and describing how feedback is exhibited. Instructors have many opportunities to exhibit feedback, including coursework, field experience, and practica. Instructors reinforce what is valued in a course by exhibiting feedback that considers the four domains of feedback—specificity, immediacy, purposefulness, and constructiveness. Special education teacher preparation instructors can examine how feedback is exhibited in their course design, the activities they do in class, and the assignments they require. Instructors can model how feedback should be given and share the process of the "why and how" of feedback explicitly in their classes. The next chapter will continue to address exhibiting feedback but will provide the opportunity for you to move forward with your action planning and look more closely at values, alignment, course design, and syllabi options.

Opportunity for Going Deeper

The additional resources to support deeper learning on concepts reflected in Chapter 6 are as follows:

- Exhibiting feedback. The following sources address how you can exhibit feedback that encourages adult learners to embrace failure and develop strategies for overcoming challenges.
  - FLAMEnet: https://qubeshub.org/community/groups/flamenet
  - GRIT: https://angeladuckworth.com/
  - Mindset: https://thedecisionlab.com/thinkers/psychology/carol-dweck/
  - Reflection: National Society for Experiential Education: https://www.nsee.org/ or
  - Bassot, B. (2015). *The reflective practice guide: An interdisciplinary approach to critical reflection*. Routledge.
  - Goal Orientations: Woodrow, L. (2012). Goal orientations: Three perspectives on motivation goal orientations. In: Mercer S., Ryan S., Williams M. (Eds.), *Psychology for language learning* (pp. 188-202). Palgrave Macmillan.
  - Attributional Theory: Weiner, B. (1985). An attributional theory of achievement motivation and emotion. *Psychological Review, 92*(4), 548-573.
  - Fear of Failure: Conroy, D. E. (2001). Fear of failure: An exemplar for social development research in sport. *Quest, 53*(2), 165-183. https://doi.org/10.1080/00336297.2001.10491736
- For writing about your teaching. For instructors interested in more information on connecting or explaining their instruction explicitly to scholarly practice, the following resources might be helpful:
  - Bovill, C., Cook-Sather, A., & Felten, P. (2011). Students as co-creators of teaching approaches, course design, and curricula: Implications for academic developers. *International Journal for Academic Development, 16*(2), 133-145. https://doi.org/10.1080/1360144X.2011.568690
  - Darling-Hammond, L., Oakes, J., Wojcikiewicz, S. K., Hyler, M. E., Guha, R., Podolsky, A., Kini, T., Cook-Haravey, C. M., Mercert, C. N. J., & Harrell, A. (2019). *Preparing teachers for deeper learning*. Harvard Education Press.
- Practicing gratitude: The following resources are provided to learn more about the practice of gratitude and the connection to joy for instructors with exhibiting feedback and adult learners.
  - Take the gratitude challenge: https://movingart.com/gratitude-lab-college/
  - Compassionate integrity training: https://www.compassionateintegrity.org/
  - Renshaw, T. L., & Rock, D. K. (2018). Effects of a brief grateful thinking intervention on college students' mental health. *Mental Health and Prevention, 9*, 19-24.

REFERENCES

Aronson, E. (1978). *The jigsaw classroom*. Sage.

Archer, A. L. & Hughes, C. A. (2011). *Explicit instruction: Effective and efficient teaching*. Guilford Press.

Brookhart, S. M. (2008). Feedback that fits. *Educational Leadership, 65*(4), 54-59.

Brookhart, S. M. (2019). A perfect world is one with no grades. *ASCD Express, 14*(31), 1-3.

Brown, B. (2015). *Daring greatly: How the courage to be vulnerable transforms the way we live, love, parent, and lead*. Penguin.

Boudett K. P., City, E. A., & Murnane, R. J. (2013). *Data wise: A step-by-step guide to using assessment results to improve teaching and learning*. Harvard Education Press.

Duckworth, A. (2006). *Intelligence is not enough: Non-IQ predictors of achievement*. Dissertations available from ProQuest. AAI3211063. https://repository.upenn.edu/dissertations/AAI3211063

Dweck, C. S. (1986). Motivational processes affecting learning. *American Psychologist, 41*(10), 1040-1048.

Dweck, C. S. (2006). *Mindset: The new psychology of success*. Random House.

Fuchs, L. S., Fuchs, D., Powell, S. R., Seethaler, P. M., Cirino, P. T., & Fletcher, J. M. (2008). Intensive intervention for students with mathematics disabilities: Seven principles of effective practice. *Learning Disability Quarterly, 31*(2), 79-92.

Knowles, M. (1984). *The adult learner: A neglected species* (3rd ed.). Gulf Publishing.

Lenz, B. D., Schumaker, J. B., Deshler, D. D., & Bulgren, J. A. (1998). *The content enhancement series: The course organizer routine*. Edge Enterprises.

McLeskey, J., Barringer, M. D., Billingsley, B., Brownell, M., Jackson, D., Kennedy, M., Lewis T., Maheady, L., Rodriguez, J., Scheeler, M. C., Winn, J., Ziegler, D. (2017). *High-leverage practices in special education*. Council for Exceptional Children & CEEDAR Center.

Mercer, C. D., & Miller, S. P. (1992). Teaching students with learning problems in math to acquire, understand, and apply basic math facts. *Remedial and Special Education, 13*(3), 19-35.

Miller, S. P., & Hudson, P. J. (2007). Using evidence-based practices to build mathematics competence related to conceptual, procedural, and declarative knowledge. *Learning Disabilities Research & Practice, 22*(1), 47-57.

Powell, S. R., Doabler, C. T., Akinola, O. A., Therrien, W. J., Maddox, S. A., & Hess, K. E. (2020). A synthesis of elementary mathematics interventions: Comparisons of students with mathematics difficulty with and without comorbid reading difficulty. *Journal of Learning Disabilities, 53*(4), 244-276.

Prochaska, J. O., & DiClemente, C. C. (1992). Stages of change in the modification of problem behaviors. *Progress in Behavior Modification, 28*, 183-218.

Weiner, B. (1972). Attribution theory, achievement motivation, and the educational process. *Review of Educational Research, 42*(2), 203-215.

Wiggins, G., & McTighe, J. (2011). *The understanding by design guide to creating high-quality units*. ASCD.

Wiggins, G. P. (2012). Seven keys to effective feedback. *Educational Leadership, 70*(1), 10-16.

Exhibiting Feedback
Reflecting and Planning

FEEDBACK SCENARIO

The instructors at XYZ University are developing a cohesive special education program of study for a new online program. Members of the graduate faculty who would be teaching the coursework form a collaborative group they call "the design studio." They examine the standards that must be met and plan to address them all using case studies across all the courses in the program. By creating case studies—composite K-12 students—from their own teaching experiences, including teaching graduate students in a traditional program, the instructors construct learning opportunities in the different courses and across the entire program. Recognizing that teacher candidates will come to the university from many states and school districts, with limited or no knowledge of specific settings beyond their own personal experiences, the instructors hope that case studies will provide teacher candidates with the opportunity to learn about disabilities, regardless of their previous experiences. They believe that multiple voices in the design studio strengthen adherence to the standards and help to identify the many ways that courses develop a common understanding of curricular and adult learning expectations.

Using the design studio, different groups of instructors build case studies (K-12 student composites) that include rich descriptions, family backgrounds, constructed individualized education plans, and matching of academic and behavioral data. Each team is responsible for developing a case study, then a validity team evaluates those newly created case studies. The validity team evaluates the depth and completeness of each case study, using a rubric they had developed under the scrutiny of the entire design studio. When an initial review reveals gaps in the case studies, they are then expanded to fully meet all the criteria on the form.

Elford, M. D., Smith, H. H., & James, S.
*GET Feedback: Giving, Exhibiting, and Teaching Feedback in
Special Education Teacher Preparation* (pp. 129-147).
© 2022 SLACK Incorporated.

Next, the objectives and assignments in each of the courses are examined to determine where the standards were being met across the program. A rubric co-constructed by instructors helps them to see gaps in the curriculum and develop the scope and sequence for the courses in the program.

Finally, instructors determine how the graduate students will demonstrate their competency in regard to each standard. Rather than submitting a thesis, the graduate students construct an ePortfolio in their capstone course, incorporating signature assignments from each course. Graduate students will revise the signature assignments, based on feedback they had been given by the course instructor, for the ePortfolio. In addition, they write a reflective paper describing the new knowledge they gained and changes in their thinking and understanding over the course of the program. A panel of three faculty/instructors examine the ePortfolio to determine the success of each graduate student in demonstrating competency of the standards.

Although it took many hours of intense work and collaborative conversations, the final program was more cohesive, and the construction of the assignments were more intentional than they would have been without the design studio.

CHAPTER OBJECTIVES

This chapter continues our exploration of how we, as special education teacher preparation instructors and administrators, can exhibit and model feedback through reflection and planning. To achieve the transformational understanding of the importance and impact of feedback, teaching about feedback should be integrated across a course. This includes deep and purposeful connection to course goals and objectives as well as reflection on when and how feedback is used. It goes beyond how we give feedback, considering the recipient, the timing of the feedback, and the tools and common practices. This chapter will build on the information and your ability to identify the domains of feedback from Chapter 6, offering opportunities and tools for exhibiting feedback in your course(s). This chapter is about how to exhibit feedback and will provide opportunities to reflect on the domains of feedback currently in use in your course(s) as well as provide examples and prompts to consider in creating or revising a course.

To assist special education teacher preparation instructors in exhibiting and modeling feedback, we recommend reflecting on goals and course objectives and making a plan for feedback timing. Special education teacher preparation instructors can use these themes in the creation and revision of courses while also recognizing the learning needs of adult learners.

After reading this chapter you will **know** and **understand** these concepts and have the opportunity to **demonstrate** and **apply** your knowledge (Table 7-1).

DESCRIBE AND DEFINE

Effectively exhibiting feedback occurs in course design, activities, and assignments. In Chapter 6, we focused on proficiency in recognizing the opportunities to exhibit feedback and assignments. This chapter focuses most heavily on the course design and planning that are central to applying the G.E.T. Model in practice, specifically for exhibiting feedback. However, we recognize that this opportunity will support giving feedback and prepare you for the next section on teaching feedback. We will reflect on how you exhibit feedback and establish individualized plans for exhibiting feedback by connecting to research on course syllabi.

Ideally, your attention to exhibiting feedback will support teacher candidate self-regulation. Nicol (2010) suggested that assessment and feedback practices should be designed to enable teacher candidates to become self-regulated learners. Just as the K-12 approach to developing assessment-capable learners (Frey et al., 2018) stressed frequent opportunities for teacher candidates to self-assess

TABLE 7-1. GRAPHIC ORGANIZER		
KNOW (WHAT)	**UNDERSTAND (WHY)**	**DEMONSTRATE (HOW)**
What domains of feedback are currently exhibited in your course.	Why exhibiting feedback can be a powerful tool in teacher candidate learning.	How to exhibit feedback in course design, activities, and assignments through reflection and planning.
APPLY (TAKE ACTION)		
Apply what you have learned about feedback and integrate the domains in course design, activities, and assignments.		

and reflect on their own learning, adult learners may fare better when you exhibit feedback that supports teacher candidates gauging their own progress in learning. Sambell (2016) suggested that higher education has some well-developed conceptual models that have been specifically designed to help improve our summative and formative assessment environments and feedback practices as well as recommended research by Gibbs and Simpson (2005), Hounsell (2003), and Nicol (2009). The feedback principles by Nicol and Macfarlane-Dick (2006) include the following:

- Clarifying what good performance is
- Facilitating reflection and self-assessment in learning
- Delivering high-quality feedback information that helps learners self-correct
- Encouraging teacher–learner and peer dialogue
- Encouraging positive motivational beliefs and self-esteem
- Providing opportunities to act on feedback,
- Using feedback from learners to improve teaching

Similarly, McKeachie and Svinicki's (2014) *Teaching Tips: Strategies, Research, and Theory for College and University Teachers* offers a theory of feedback that we find especially useful for instructors who seek to continue to improve their teaching. McKeachie and Svinicki suggested feedback from student performance and from peers, faculty development specialists, and students to continue to grow in practice. We highly recommend this book as a source for support.

Borrowing from the systems change literature, the framework for managing complex change from Knoster et al. (2000) can support our work in exhibiting feedback and course design. Knoster et al. suggested that caring, complex change, such as the integration of the G.E.T. Model in your practice, occurs when the following five features are present: vision, skills, incentives, resources, and an action plan. If any one of the five features are not adequately addressed, then the change does not occur, although unintended consequences, such as confusion and anxiety, might. Similarly, at the individual change level, we recognize the contributions from psychology that support self-efficacy, motivation, and self-regulation. Psychologist Albert Bandura (2001) recognized that efficacy beliefs are important in self-regulation of motivation. He suggested that efficacy beliefs are partly responsible for the challenges we choose to undertake and for how long we continue to engage them. In defining relationships between motivation and learning, psychologist Barry Zimmerman (2013) explained that learning and accompanying motivational beliefs fall into a cycle of forethought, performance, and self-reflection, and this cycle explains the results of repeated efforts to learn. We have attempted to incorporate these understandings of social cognitive theory with research on systems of change to guide you through this chapter on exhibiting feedback. Ultimately, because you will be the person who implements the G.E.T. Model to explicitly address feedback to support teacher candidates' learning in the preparation of future special educators, this chapter includes opportunities to reflect on and explore your motivation and foundational beliefs around teaching and your course content to develop your own action plan.

As you prepare to implement the G.E.T. Model and explicitly address giving, exhibiting, and teaching feedback in a course, we will reflect on your current practice, allowing you the opportunity to establish a plan that is individualized to your interest and motivation. This will build on your reflection from Chapter 6 on your current practice in exhibiting feedback. Answer the questions that follow in the four steps presented. Feel free to write in the book.

Step 1. Let us recognize where you are in your current practice, career, semester, course revision, and exploration of the G.E.T. Model. Revisit Chapter 6 as well as your reflection and perceptions regarding your strengths and preferences in the exhibiting feedback domain.

Where are you? _____

What are your strengths in exhibiting feedback (Table 7-2)? Complete Step 1 by marking the boxes in Table 7-2 with an "X" for your strengths in exhibiting feedback (see Chapter 6).

Step 2. Brown (2015) reminded us that feedback is a function of respect and that actions speak louder than words. What does your practice in exhibiting feedback possibly communicate to teacher candidates? Do you notice a pattern? What opportunities did you identify for exploring or exhibiting feedback?

Response:

What do you want or need to do? Bain (2004) described the impact of personal development and reflecting on course design and revisions to support transformational adult learning. Please use the space below to write down your goal(s) or plan related to exhibiting feedback.

Response:

Step 3. Now, reflect on how you will address these opportunities. Ask yourself: How will I address it? What will it look like? How will I know I have adequately addressed it? For example, if in your self-talk for the second response prompt in Step 2 you find yourself writing, "*I am heavy in immediacy because I am doing a lot of performance-based feedback, but where else am I exhibiting feedback?*", then you might find it helpful to return to the extended discussion of Bandura in Chapter 1. We will continue the exploration Step 4 in the next section.

Response:

Know

This is the actionable part of exhibiting feedback as an instructor. Much research on course design and course syllabi in higher education supports our exploration and planning in this chapter. The G.E.T. Model is supported by a learner-centered approach, specifically adult learners preparing to be special educators, in which the syllabus "reinforces the intentions, roles, attitudes, and

TABLE 7-2. EXHIBITING FEEDBACK			
DOMAIN	**COURSE DESIGN**	**ACTIVITIES**	**ASSIGNMENT**
Specificity			
Immediacy			
Purposefulness			
Constructiveness			

strategies that you will use to promote active, purposeful, and effective learning" (O'Brien et al., 2008, p. 12). Some examples of approaches we have used, both on their own or combined, to support our learner-centered syllabus and course design include backwards design, standards-based alignment, and content-enhancement routines. We based the changes on a number of factors, including but not limited to access/convenience and scholarly, inquiry-based reflection.

The backward design (Wiggins & McTighe, 2011) prompts us to design instructional units with the learning objectives in mind. This practice benefits from reflection and alignment with standards. For some instructors, this is at the program level, and, for others, it is at the course-level design. Further, the creation of a standards crosswalk or alignment document is a helpful step on first assuring that the instructional content as well as demonstration and assessment of learning is aligned (Rapp & Arndt, 2012). The Course Organizer Routine (Lenz et al., 1998), the Unit Planning Routine (Lenz, Shumaker et al., 1993), the Unit Organizer Routine (Lenz et al., 1994), and the Lesson Organizer Routine (Lenz, Marris et al., 1993) are other existing tools that may be helpful in designing and examining alignment. Exhibiting feedback is also a function of seeing yourself as a learner. Scholarly reflection on teaching looks like thinking about why and how you design your course. Does it reflect you as a scholar? Can you explain the rationale for your course or instruction? For more information on developing a syllabus, we recommend the book *The Course Syllabus: A Learning-Centered Approach* (O'Brien et al., 2008).

Using the Course Organizer Routine (Lenz et al., 1998) and the Strategic Instruction Model (University of Kansas Center for Research on Learning, 2011), alignment with several sets of standards, and the purposeful selection of assignments selected through backward design and scholarly inquiry, we present an example of course assignment alignment (Table 7-3) from Dr. Susanne James, based on a course titled "SPE: 405 Foundations of Special Education." In this course, undergraduate students are introduced to problems, characteristics, and issues that impact the development of persons with disabilities.

Step 4. Let's get specific. Do you know how each learning objective is addressed and are all the activities and assignments connected back to the learning objectives? Go back to course design, how will you add feedback here?

Response:

As a program, working to create a crosswalk to align the course expectations and course design elements are part of the effort to create shared values and build teacher candidate skills in self-regulation across courses. Individuals can be powerful catalysts in helping their programs prioritize careful, although time-intensive, work to ensure that theoretical and practical knowledge is being introduced, reviewed, and mastered at multiple places within a program by different instructors. For example, in foundational courses, you might give feedback on only whether teacher candidates are

TABLE 7-3. COURSE ASSIGNMENT ALIGNMENT

ASSIGNMENT	CEC STANDARD	IPTS
Special Education Philosophy Statement: Visual Representation of Special Education Principles	1.1, 1.2, 3.1, 5.1, 6.1, 6.2	1C, 1D, 1E, 1F
Service Learning Writing Project at Maryville Elementary	2.1, 2.2	1C, 1D, 1E, 1F
Concept Map of Service Delivery Models Across Least Restrictive Environments	2.1	1L 3C Planning for Differentiated Instruction
Disability Fact Sheet—Public Service Announcement for Disabilities	5.2, 6.4	2F 1A, 1G Teaching Diverse Students 2E Content and Pedagogical Knowledge
Individualized Education Plan Assignment	2.1, 4.3	3H, 3I, 3K, 3O 5S Instructional Delivery
Individualized Education Plan Meeting in TeachLivE	7.1, 7.3	8S Collaborative Relationships 9A Professionalism, Leadership, and Advocacy
Participation in flipped classroom lectures	7.1, 7.3	8S Collaborative Relationships 9A Professionalism, Leadership, and Advocacy

CEC = Council for Exceptional Children; IPTS = Illinois Professional Teaching Standards.

familiar with the purposes and contents of various special education documents, such as a behavioral intervention plan, while in advanced classes, teacher candidates may be expected to be able to author a behavioral intervention plan. Strong program alignment helps to achieve purposefulness because it recognizes where teacher candidates are on their learning continuum.

Exhibiting feedback is the link between giving feedback and teaching feedback. This action stage, as described by Prochaska and DiClemente (1992), is built on the reflection in Chapter 6. Have you noticed how Section III has attempted to address both Freire's (1970) principle of pedagogy and Knowles' (1984) definition of andragogy and how they align?

Understand

If you are already balanced in how you exhibit feedback, this may be a chapter you skip. Let us take some more time for you to explore and reflect on your understanding of exhibiting feedback and next steps. See the following example of self-talk:

I am heavy in immediacy because I am doing a lot of performance-based feedback, but where else am I exhibiting feedback?

Do you know what your next steps are in designing your course to exhibit feedback? Use the options presented in Table 7-4 to indicate some possibilities. Check all that apply. With your focus on the areas indicated in Table 7-4, let us explore part of a course syllabus and course design.

√	FEEDBACK
	TABLE 7-4. POSSIBLE WAYS TO EXHIBIT FEEDBACK IN COURSE DESIGN
☐	Reflect on exhibiting immediacy.
☐	Reflect on exhibiting specificity.
☐	Reflect on exhibiting purposefulness.
☐	Reflect on exhibiting constructiveness.
☐	Reflect on alignment of activities and course learning goals.
☐	Reflect on alignment of assignments and course learning goals.
☐	Reflect on alignment of assessment(s) and course learning goals.
☐	Identify lessons to incorporate discussion for students on progress toward learning goals.
☐	Start a journal to reflect on use of language of ongoing regard.
☐	Reflect on opportunities for students to provide feedback or reflection on how you exhibit feedback.
☐	Reflect and revise course syllabus to reflect learner-centered values.
☐	Other: _____
☐	Other: _____
☐	Other: _____

Demonstrate

In this section, we will demonstrate what we have learned about exhibiting feedback by using an authentic course example to identify opportunities to exhibit feedback. EDUC 1331: Understanding Learners With Exceptionalities in School and Society is an introductory course offered at Trinity University in San Antonio, Texas, that focused on the legal and theoretical foundations for supporting diverse learners. The course has four major learning requirements. The requirement that has the most time devoted to it is to acquire and demonstrate knowledge of the foundational concepts, characteristics, and strategies in special education and disability studies, including sociocultural and linguistic factors, assessment and instruction, Universal Design for Learning, family involvement, and technology. Further, this course requires teacher candidates to complete a minimum of 15 hours of field experience in a setting that serves individuals with exceptionalities. Teacher candidates are required to attend the Ability Awareness Fair the second week of class to learn about the selected community organizations supporting individuals with disabilities and/or other marginalized groups. Following the Ability Awareness Fair, the instructor meets individually with teacher candidates to create an action plan for their field experience. Using a semi-structured interview format, the course instructor asks teacher candidates about previous experience with individuals with exceptionalities, personal academic interests and hobbies, community group(s) of interest, and their personal reasons for taking the course.

Course readings and instruction address disability studies, equity issues, characteristics of exceptionalities, and effective teaching strategies for K-12 students with exceptionalities. Several in-class opportunities are provided during the semester to discuss experiences and challenges that teacher candidates have encountered during their field-based experiences. Further, teacher candidates are encouraged to come to office hours to discuss their experiences and questions. This program also assesses and supports growth in professional dispositions, reflecting the program's vision and values. Because many state teacher education programs are required to provide only one course on special

TABLE 7-5. COURSE SCHEDULE: EDUC 1331—WEEKS 3-10

DATE	WEEK		OUTLINE	ASSIGNMENT
1/28 and 1/30	3	Select and secure field experiences for service learning	Tuesday—Attend the Ability Awareness Fair in the Fiesta Room (community partners for service-learning will be present to discuss opportunities and design experiences) Tuesday-Friday—Schedule and attend individual, 20-minute, service-learning planning meetings with Dr. Smith; sign up for office hours via the link in the syllabus	Ability Awareness Fair Schedule (attend 40-45 minutes) 9:10 a.m. to 10:40 a.m.
2/4 and 2/6	4		Universal Design for Learning Legal and Theoretical Foundations of Special Education Individualized Education Plans Gallup Strengths 1.0 Presentation	
2/11 and 2/13	5		Issues and Trends in Special Education and Disability Studies Inclusion and Strengths-based Instruction Oral and Visual Communication, Twitter, and Meaningful Social Media	2/13—Select service-learning placement(s) and begin
2/18 and 2/20	6		Supporting Students with High Incidence Disabilities and Accommodations MTSS/RTI PechaKucha Demo	
2/25 and 2/27	7		Supporting Students with High Incidence Disabilities and Accommodations (cont'd.) Learning Strategies, SIOP, English Language Learners and Culturally Responsive Teaching	2/25—Movie Review #1
3/3 and 3/5	8		Spring Break	3/5—Service-learning student updates
3/10 and 3/12	9		Supporting Students with Low Incidence Disabilities and Modifications	
3/17 and 3/19	10		Supporting Students with Autism, Physical Disabilities and Other Health Impairments Gallup Strengths 2.0 Presentation	

MTSS = Multi-Tiered System of Supports; RTI = Response to Intervention; SIOP = Sheltered Instruction Observation Protocol.

education (Fender & Fielder, 1990), the introductory course in special education or other required course must go beyond covering "a disability of the week," with a course outline that communicates a deficit-focused medical model of disability. Instead, we should reimagine special education and address the differences, definitions of normal, and individualization of instruction to move most and some to all students (Florian & Graham, 2014). Given this background information, let us now look through the course schedule for weeks 3 through 10 (Table 7-5).

Nationally recognized as an innovative leader in preparing educators (Koppich, 1999), Trinity University was recently identified by the Learning Policy Institute (Darling-Hammond & Oakes, 2019) as an outstanding teacher preparation program, supporting candidates' ability to:

- Cultivate, practice, and master deep content knowledge
- Develop problem-solving, research and inquiry, communication, and collaboration skills
- Develop metacognitive skills and strategies to guide, regulate, and evaluate their learning
- Attain the social-emotional awareness and academic mindsets necessary to succeed in college and career
- Meaningfully contribute to civic life and our democracy.

Relying on the description and course schedule, we will reflect on current levels of exhibiting feedback and opportunities for revision or elaboration. Given that you do not have all the information about the course, you may draw from your own experiences as you develop your thoughts. There are no right or wrong answers. This exercise is included as an opportunity to demonstrate your knowledge as well as create and practice a short six-step protocol for examining your own practice and opportunities.

Step 1: First Impressions

After reviewing the course description and provided calendar, respond to the questions that follow. This step is an opportunity to think about what you are seeing before we begin reflecting on exhibiting feedback. The goal is not interpretation or judgment but identification and analysis. For example, you might include a note about how only a portion of the course schedule is provided or that there are three assignments due during this 8-week period.

What do you see?
Response:

TABLE 7-6. EXHIBITING FEEDBACK REFLECTION EXERCISE	
WHAT AREA OF EXHIBITING FEEDBACK IS EVIDENT?	**FEEDBACK DOMAIN**
	• Specificity • Immediacy • Purposefulness • Constructiveness
	• Specificity • Immediacy • Purposefulness • Constructiveness
	• Specificity • Immediacy • Purposefulness • Constructiveness

Step 2: Reflection

What are three areas where exhibiting feedback is evident? Using Table 7-6, detail each observation in the column on the left and then use the column on the right to circle one or two of the domains you perceive these examples to most reflect.

Now, take a look at the three areas of exhibiting feedback that you recognized and described. Are there similarities or differences? Is there a theme? Why might these similarities or differences be, or not be, important?

Thinking back to Chapter 6, is there something noticeably missing?
Response:

Which domain do you most recognize?

Which domain(s) are not indicated?

Step 3: Flip the Perspective

Up to this point we were likely using the lens of an instructor. Let us repeat the activities in Steps 1 and 2, attempting to look at the course description and course schedule through the lens of an adult learner in the course. Use Table 7-7 to repeat the reflection activity in Step 2.

TABLE 7-7. EXHIBITING FEEDBACK REFLECTION EXERCISE	
WHAT AREA OF EXHIBITING FEEDBACK IS EVIDENT?	**FEEDBACK DOMAIN**
	• Specificity • Immediacy • Purposefulness • Constructiveness
	• Specificity • Immediacy • Purposefulness • Constructiveness
	• Specificity • Immediacy • Purposefulness • Constructiveness

What do you see?

Response:

Step 4: Compare and Contrast

Compare and contrast the instructor and teacher candidate perspectives on what the description and course schedule are communicating about the course. Again, we realize this is only a slice of information about the course. This exercise is a problem-based opportunity to reflect, interpret, and demonstrate your knowledge, so you can apply it to a course schedule, activity, assignment, assessment, or any other aspect of your course.

What does the perspective suggest about the instructor's commitment to feedback?

What course design elements could be added to further demonstrate a commitment to exhibiting feedback?

What can the instructor say in the course to support exhibiting feedback?

How can exhibiting feedback be more explicit?

TABLE 7-8. SPOTLIGHT ON ADULT LEARNING			
SPECIFICITY	**IMMEDIACY**	**PURPOSEFULNESS**	**CONSTRUCTIVENESS**
What intentional wording and explicit language connects the program and course design to the different ways that instructors exhibit feedback for adult learners?	How is the program and course design intentionally considering the timing of the feedback? How is the timing of feedback aligned with the prior knowledge of the learner, readiness and orientation, and motivation to learn?	Does the program or course design attend to all six adult learning principles when determining the process of feedback that is delivered? How do instructors describe the feedback they give as means of connecting program/course outcomes to what the learners need to know and their orientation to learning?	How does the organization of the program and course design honor the self-concept of the learner? How does it help them be autonomous and self-directing? What opportunities are there for the adult learner to apply the new knowledge to life-related, developmental tasks that are problem-centered and contextual?

SPOTLIGHT ON ADULT LEARNING

Table 7-8 demonstrates domain reflection questions.

POSSIBLE BARRIERS TO USING THIS TYPE OF FEEDBACK

There are multiple barriers to exhibiting feedback. Building on the barriers described in Chapter 6, one issue specifically related to course design and syllabi is how various instructors may teach the same course differently. For example, how can we support a graduate teaching assistant who teaches a course written by another instructor? This is a common occurrence in some special education teacher preparation programs and an opportunity to demonstrate the intellectual and pedagogical, and maybe andragogical, principles and strategies employed during design. Given the importance and individualized nature of the values of different instructors, delivery of a boilerplate syllabus and assignments in a program could be identical but still result in different learner outcomes. One recommendation to overcome this barrier would be to introduce an activity for individual instructors to explore their giving, exhibiting, and teaching of feedback. Instructors could write an abstract or elaborated course overview beyond what is in the course catalogue for the department as an artifact alongside syllabi. The course design description could include how feedback is integrated in the course. This would assist future instructors in understanding the intricacies and integrated scholarly work in the design and ensure alignment to a scope and sequence for the program. Another benefit of an elaborated description would be recognized for new faculty at an institution and first-time instructors. This would support anyone understanding the big picture of a course and a program. Another possible benefit of the elaborated abstract of the course design, akin to an abstract for published research, could be used in annual reviews on teaching, for programmatic design evidence, and more.

AUTHENTIC EXAMPLE

Contributed by
Martha D. Elford, PhD

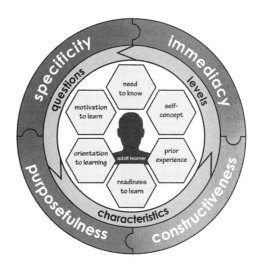

In this Authentic Example, Dr. Martha Elford demonstrates an opportunity for instructors to exhibit feedback and explicitly model how feedback should be given through sharing the "why and how" of delivering feedback when teacher candidates are asked to reflect on a lesson plan they have created.

The following questions are provided to guide your review and reflection in this Authentic Example, contributed by Martha D. Elford, PhD.

- In this example, how does the instructor apply knowledge of exhibiting feedback? Reflect.
- How can you exhibit and model feedback through reflection and planning?
- What activities and assignments in your course(s) do you think impact the ability of your students to exhibit and model feedback in their current or future classrooms with students?

Exhibiting feedback is supported by using a language of ongoing regard (Kegan & Lahey, 2001), language that acknowledges and validates the genuine quality and uniqueness of the teacher candidates in the course. This includes recognizing the strengths and opportunity for growth in exhibiting the four domains in the G.E.T. Model and consistently using, direct, specific, nonattributive feedback. The benefits to future special educators are undermined when judgment or shame is exhibited, or thought to be exhibited, in your teaching or feedback.

1. Course Details

EEX 4066: Teaching Students With Mild/Moderate Disabilities. This course is an undergraduate course with a corequisite practicum. The course is part of the Exceptional Student Education teacher education track. This reflection portion of the assignment is completed after teacher candidates have implemented a comprehensive, detailed lesson plan and provided instruction. Their lesson plan requires an overall reflection; however, this activity requires a deeper reflection that teacher candidates complete, based on a set of questions.

2. *Learning Objectives*

The aligned course objectives are as follows:
a. Demonstrate knowledge of the hierarchy of developmental skills that are prerequisites and requisites for academic, social behaviors, and/or life skills.
b. Implement instructional programs to achieve specific instructional objectives.

3. *Assignment Description*

Teacher candidates will create a lesson and provide instruction, based on the lesson. After the lesson is taught, the teacher candidates will reflect on the instruction delivery and outcomes of their instruction for the components listed in the outline. Teacher candidates should reflect on the specifically provided questions as they complete their responses. The lesson and reflection will be submitted to the faculty/instructor. These lessons cannot be lessons that teacher candidates performed for the purposes of observation by the cooperating teacher or university supervisor, where they received feedback by either of them regarding their instruction that may influence their reflective statements. The instructor will provide feedback on the lesson itself as well as the written reflection. Teacher candidates are to use the form provided and attempt to connect their lesson preparation and instruction by answering each question in the form, providing specific evidence from their lesson and what they observed while teaching the lesson.

4. *Evaluation Criteria*

The evaluation criteria are shown in Table 7-9.

5. *Additional Details*

The rubric for the lesson plan preparation and implementation reflective assignment is shown in Table 7-10.

6. *Feedback Reflection*

This assignment reflects on exhibiting feedback and giving feedback. Teacher candidates evaluate their instruction and management of teacher candidates' engagement after lesson delivery. The instructor reviews both the lesson details and the post-lesson reflection, provides feedback to the teacher candidates by further connecting areas to be addressed in the reflection questions about the course content, and provides suggestions to improve lesson plan preparation and delivery. In addition, the instructor may question other aspects of the lesson to enhance the development of the teacher candidate. The goal is to provide a coherent, connected learning progression, using strategies, resources, and technologies that enhance learning, and establishing a safe, respectful, well-organized learning environment. Teacher candidates are to review the feedback and address the feedback by improving their lesson preparation, instruction, and reflection on their next lesson. Teacher candidates complete four lessons in this format throughout the semester, with a goal of enriching their reflective practices while also improving upon their lesson preparation.

TABLE 7-9. SELF-ASSESSMENT OF LESSON
(MUST INCLUDE ASPECTS OF EFFECTIVE PRACTICES LISTED)

READ, REFLECT AND RESPOND TO THE QUESTIONS WHEN REFLECTING ON YOUR LESSON. QUESTIONS ARE MEANT TO GUIDE YOUR REFLECTION, SO YOU DO NOT NECESSARILY HAVE TO ANSWER EACH ONE.

Effective Practice	Questions for Self-Assessment	Reflective Comments
Intentional instructional practice	How does your instruction provide an attentional cue? In what ways do you confirm students are ready to learn? How is your language clear and explicit to describe the learning objectives? What assessments are planned, both formative and summative, to measure when objectives are met? What learning activities have you planned and how do those align with the learning outcomes?	
Coherent, connected learning progression	How does your lesson provide a coherent learning progression that unites both skills and knowledge? (Is the instruction accurate? Is the lesson clear and logically sequenced with a measurable learning objective?) How well and where is your lesson connected to both the student and the bigger picture? (How is the skill or knowledge connected to another skill or concept or is the skill an isolated skill? How is this learning objective connected to your students' lives?)	

(continued)

TABLE 7-9 (CONTINUED). SELF-ASSESSMENT OF LESSON (MUST INCLUDE ASPECTS OF EFFECTIVE PRACTICES LISTED)

READ, REFLECT AND RESPOND TO THE QUESTIONS WHEN REFLECTING ON YOUR LESSON. QUESTIONS ARE MEANT TO GUIDE YOUR REFLECTION, SO YOU DO NOT NECESSARILY HAVE TO ANSWER EACH ONE.

Effective Practice	*Questions for Self-Assessment*	*Reflective Comments*
Strategies, resources, and technologies that enhance learning	How well do your selected strategies engage all learners? (How did you make learning visual and concrete? How were your learners involved and to what extent? Was it effective?) How do the resources and technologies you use provide purpose, enhance engagement, and potentially transform the learning experiences in your lesson/classroom? (Did the resources/technologies improve the learning or provide an opportunity to be creative? Which SAMR technology/resource was used and why?)	
Safe, respectful, well-organized learning environment	How do you improve the flow of learning in your lesson and in the classroom? (How do you begin and end the lesson? How do you begin and end the day? What are your routines and procedures within the lesson? How can routines, procedures, etc., be improved?) How can interactions in your classroom be improved through better classroom management? (What are the classroom expectations for the lesson? Are they proactive? What is your presence? How can your presence be improved?) Did you see any connection between the design of your lesson, engagement of students, and the behavior and interactions of your students (or a particular student)? Describe.	

SAMR = substitution augmentation modification redefinition: substitution—drill and practice (Quizlet, Google search); augmentation—interactive (Google Docs, PowerPoint slides); modification—narrated animation project (Nearpod, Edmodo, Google+); redefinition—interactive and creative (Padlet, 3D printing, website creation, VoiceThread).

TABLE 7-10. DESCRIPTION OF LESSON PLAN PREPARATION AND IMPLEMENTATION REFLECTION ASSIGNMENT RUBRIC

ASSIGNMENT VALUE	EXEMPLARY (90% TO 100%)	SATISFACTORY (73% TO 89%)	EMERGING (64% TO 72%)	UNSATISFACTORY (0% TO 63%)	NO SUBMISSION
10 points	Teacher makes a thoughtful and accurate assessment of a lesson's effectiveness and the extent to which it achieved its instructional outcomes, citing many specific examples from the lesson and weighing the relative strengths of each. Drawing on an extensive repertoire of skills, the teacher offers specific alternative actions, complete with the probable success of different courses of action. Reflection includes more than one type of specific evidence of: 1. Coherent, connected learning progression 2. Strategies, resources, and technologies that enhance learning 3. Safe, respectful, well-organized learning environment	Teacher makes an accurate assessment of a lesson's effectiveness and the extent to which it achieved its instructional outcomes and can cite general references to support the judgment. Teacher makes a few specific suggestions of what could be tried another time the lesson is taught. Reflection includes at least one type of specific evidence of: 1. Coherent, connected learning progression 2. Strategies, resources, and technologies that enhance learning 3. Safe, respectful, well-organized learning environment	Teacher has a generally accurate impression of a lesson's effectiveness and the extent to which instructional outcomes were met. Teacher makes general suggestions about how a lesson could be improved. Reflection includes some or vague pieces of evidence of: 1. Coherent, connected learning progression 2. Strategies, resources, and technologies that enhance learning 3. Safe, respectful, well-organized learning environment	Teacher does not know whether a lesson was effective or achieved its instructional outcomes, or the teacher profoundly misjudges the success of a lesson. Teacher has no suggestions for how a lesson could be improved. Reflection includes minimal evidence of: 1. Coherent, connected learning progression 2. Strategies, resources, and technologies that enhance learning 3. Safe, respectful, well-organized learning environment	Failed to submit or failed to submit on time.
Comments:					

SUMMARY

This chapter provided the opportunity to demonstrate your understanding of exhibiting feedback, reflect on your practice, and apply and set goals for course revisions. When instructors reflect on the integration of feedback across a course, they can connect feedback directly to course goals and objectives. This chapter provided a four-step reflection protocol to help you identify several areas where you can be more explicit as you attend to the domains of specificity, immediateness, purposefulness, and constructiveness in exhibiting feedback. Instructors need to give feedback, considering the recipient, the timing of the feedback, and the tools and common practices. Exhibiting feedback can be a powerful tool in the preparation of special education teacher candidates. This power will be further discussed in Section IV, which is devoted to how we teach feedback in our courses so that teacher candidates will display feedback in their own practice.

OPPORTUNITY FOR GOING DEEPER

The following resources support deeper learning on the concepts reflected in Chapter 7:
- Strategic Instruction Model. Visit https://kucrl.ku.edu/ and navigate through the tabs on research, resources, people, and events or select any link provided to find interventions/programs to learn more. The interventions/programs link will guide you to the Strategic Instruction Model as well as other programs and interventions.
- Behavioral change research. The Science of Behavior Change (https://scienceofbehaviorchange.org/) is a helpful site in unpacking successful behavioral change research and interventions and goes beyond the social cognitive theory described in this chapter.
- Developing students as partners. The Re-engineering Assessment Practices in Higher Education project (https://www.reap.ac.uk/) describes research and practice in supporting students becoming partners in their own learning.
- Practical advice for effective instruction. Ken Bain's (2004) *What the Best College Teachers Do* provides practical advice for effective instruction, including advice for giving, exhibiting, and teaching feedback in multi-layered instruction.
- Service-learning in teacher education. To learn more about service-learning in teacher education, we recommend *The Handbook on Research in Service-Learning Initiative in Teacher Education* by Tynisha Meidl and Margaret-Mary Sulentic Dowell (2018).
- Reflecting on your course syllabus. If you are looking for a resource to reflect on improvements to your course syllabus, consider *The Course Syllabus: A Learner-Centered Approach* by Judith Grunert O'Brien et al. (2008), which considers the needs of adult learners.

REFERENCES

Bain, K. (2004). *What the best college teachers do.* Harvard University Press.

Bandura, A. (1977). *Social learning theory.* Prentice Hall.

Bandura, A. (1986). Fearful expectations and avoidant actions as coeffects of perceived self-inefficacy. *American Psychologist, 41*(12), 1389-1391.

Bandura, A. (2001). Social cognitive theory: An agentic perspective. *Annual Review of Psychology, 52*(1), 1-26.

Brown, B. (2015). *Daring greatly: How the courage to be vulnerable transforms the way we live, love, parent, and lead.* Penguin.

Darling-Hammond, L., & Oakes, J. (2019). *Preparing teachers for deeper learning.* Harvard Education Press

Fender, M. J., & Fielder, C. (1990). Preservice preparation of regular educators: A national survey of curricular content in introductory exceptional children and youth courses. *Teacher Education and Special Education, 13*(3-4), 203-209.

Florian, L., & Graham, A. (2014). Can an expanded interpretation of phronesis support teacher professional development for inclusion? *Cambridge Journal of Education, 44*(4), 465-478.

Freire, P. (1970). *Pedagogy of the oppressed*. Continuum International Publishing Group.

Frey, N., Fisher, D., & Hattie, J. (2018). Developing "assessment capable" learners. *Educational Leadership, 75*(5), 46-51.

Gibbs, G., & Simpson, C. (2005). Conditions under which assessment supports students' learning. *Learning and Teaching in Higher Education, 1*, 3-31

Hounsell, D. (2003). Student feedback, learning and development. In M. Slowey, & D. Watson (Eds.), *Higher Education and the Lifecourse* (pp. 67-78). Open University Press.

Kegan, R., & Lahey, L. L. (2001). *How the way we talk can change the way we work: Seven languages for transformation*. Jossey-Bass.

Knoster, T., Villa, R., & Thousand, J. (2000). A framework for thinking about systems change. In R. A. Villa, & J. S. Thousand (Eds.), *Restructuring for caring and effective education: Piecing the puzzle together* (pp. 93-128). Brookes Publishing.

Knowles, M. (1984). *The adult learner: A neglected species* (3rd ed.). Gulf Publishing.

Koppich, J. E. (1999). Teacher education at Trinity University: A coherent vision. *American Educator, 23*(2), 24.

Lenz, B. K., Bulgren, J. A., Schumaker, J. B., Deshler, D. D., & Boudah, D. J. (1994). *The content enhancement series: The unit organizer routine*. Edge Enterprises.

Lenz, B. K., Marrs, R. W., Schumaker, J. B., & Deshler, D. D. (1993). *The lesson organizer routine*. Edge Enterprises.

Lenz, B. K., Schumaker, J. B., Deshler, D. D., Boudah, D. J., Vance, M., Kissam, B., Bulgren, J. A., & Roth, J. (1993). *The unit planning routine: A guide for inclusive planning (Research Report)*. University of Kansas Center for Research on Learning.

Lenz, B. K., Schumaker, J. B., Deshler, D. D., & Bulgren, J. A. (1998). *The content enhancement series: The course organizer routine*. Edge Enterprises.

McKeachie, W., & Svinicki, M. (2014). *McKeachie's teaching tips* (14th ed.). Cengage Learning.

Nicol, D. (2009). Assessment for learner self-regulation: Enhancing achievement in the first year using learning technologies. *Assessment and Evaluation in Higher Education, 34*(3), 335-352.

Nicol, D. (2010). From monologue to dialogue: Improving written feedback processes in mass higher education. *Assessment and Evaluation in Higher Education, 35*(5), 501-517.

Nicol, D. J., & Macfarlane-Dick, D. (2006). Formative assessment and self-regulated learning: A model and seven principles of good feedback practice. *Studies in Higher Education, 31*(2), 199-218.

O'Brien, J., Millis, B. J., & Cohen, M. J. (2008). *The course syllabus: A learning-centered approach* (2nd ed.). Jossey-Bass.

Prochaska, J. O., & DiClemente, C. C. (1992). Stages of change in the modification of problem behaviors. *Progress in Behavior Modification, 28*, 183-218.

Rapp, W. H., & Arndt, K. L. (2012). *Teaching everyone: An introduction to inclusive education*. Paul H. Brookes Publishing Company.

Sambell, K. (2016). Assessment and feedback in higher education: Considerable room for improvement? *Student Engagement in Higher Education, 1*(1).

University of Kansas Center for Research on Learning, (2011). *Strategic instruction model*. https://sim.ku.edu/sim-curricula

Wiggins, G. (2012). Seven keys to effective feedback. *Educational Leadership, 70*(1), 10-16.

Wiggins, G., & McTighe, J. (2011). The Understanding by Design guide to creating high-quality units. ASCD.

Zimmerman, B. J. (2013). From cognitive modeling to self-regulation: A social cognitive career path. *Educational Psychologist, 48*(3), 135-147.

Teaching Feedback

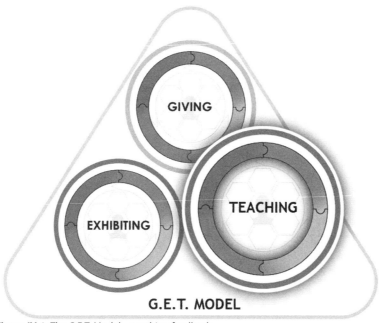

Figure IV-1. The G.E.T. Model—teaching feedback.

Teaching feedback (Figure IV-1) requires instructors to explicitly teach what feedback looks like and sounds like in the classroom for K-12 learners. Special educators must understand why feedback is an essential element in teaching. Instructors must be strategic in communicating how to use feedback to increase student outcomes. Section IV is composed of five chapters on how instructors teach feedback.

Each chapter provides description and multiple authentic examples from special education teacher preparation instructors of course content, activities, and assessment. The narrative serves as a guide for instructors to modeling and teaching the types of feedback we expect teacher candidates to exhibit in their own classrooms. If we do not explicitly teach the expectations for the feedback we require of teacher candidates, how can we expect meaningful and constructive feedback provided in their lessons?

Rationale for Teaching Feedback

FEEDBACK SCENARIO

Dr. King is a new faculty member in a small regional university that is required to comply with the national and accreditation standards of the Council for Exceptional Children (CEC) as well as prepare students to complete the Teacher Performance Assessment (edTPA) prior to licensure. In addition, her department has adopted the Candidate Preservice Assessment of Student Teaching (CPAST), a valid, reliable formative and summative observation protocol during the student teaching practicum. She recently attended a conference, where the High-Leverage Practices (HLPs) for teaching special education were described and explored in many presentations. One consistent word that caught her eye in the standards, edTPA rubrics, CPAST subscales, and in three of the four aspects of the HLPs is *feedback*. Dr. King decided to design a crosswalk that examined each interpretation and expectation for feedback so she could explicitly give, exhibit, and teach feedback to her undergraduate students. What she found was many different interpretations and uses for the word *feedback*. No single use of the word gave her direction on how to give feedback, exhibit feedback in her course assignments, or teach teacher candidates how to give feedback to their future K-12 students. So how can Dr. King improve at teaching about feedback so that her teacher candidates can meet the expectations of the standards and HLPs and pass the high-stakes edTPA?

CHAPTER OBJECTIVES

This chapter continues to consider the recipients of feedback and addresses the rationale of teaching feedback. Considering the high-stakes assessments that many teacher candidates are required to undergo, it behooves instructors to intentionally prepare them for the aspects that are

Elford, M. D., Smith, H. H., & James, S.
*GET Feedback: Giving, Exhibiting, and Teaching Feedback in
Special Education Teacher Preparation* (pp. 151-166).
© 2022 SLACK Incorporated.

specific to feedback. We recall from Knowles (1984) that adult learners need to know why they are being asked to learn new information—the principle called *need to know*. Adult learners are contextual, they need to know why they need to learn what you are teaching—the principle of *orientation to learning* in their learning. Furthermore, adult learners want clarity to understand the meaning of the feedback that instructors give them—the principle called *prior experience*. Even recognizing these adult learning principles, Dr. King felt ill-equipped to meet the demands of preparing special education teacher candidates to deliver feedback to K-12 students because of the variety of interpretations and uses of the word *feedback*. Dr. King's crosswalk sets the stage for examining the different definitions and assessments for giving feedback.

The expectation that special education teachers be able to deliver high-quality feedback effectively has been affirmed repeatedly. Guidance documents for teacher preparation programs are found in the CEC Special Education Professional Preparation Standards for Initial Special Educator Preparation. The CEC is the primary professional organization for those in special education teacher preparation and provides the standards to align special education teacher preparation program goals. In the revised standards of 2015, the CEC has called for special educators to be competent in feedback in the assessment and instruction standards (CEC, 2015). The CEC standards are currently in the revision stage again and will be updated soon to better align to the HLPs. Recently, the HLPs emerged to meet the demand that teacher candidates know effective practices to meet the diverse needs of K-12 students receiving special education services (McLeskey et al., 2017), including mastery of feedback. The HLPs were developed in partnership with the Collaboration for Effective Educator Development, Accountability, and Reform (CEEDAR), and the CEC. This partnership developed and published a set of HLPs for special educators and teacher candidates. The HLPs are organized around four aspects of practice—collaboration, assessment, social/emotional/behavioral, and instruction.

In addition, many states have adopted the high-stakes edTPA for licensure to measure the skills and knowledge that all teachers must possess (Stanford Center for Assessment, Learning, and Equity, 2019). The edTPA is a performance-based, subject-specific assessment and support system used by teacher preparation programs throughout the United States to emphasize, measure, and support the skills and knowledge that all teachers need in the classroom. This assessment was developed by the Stanford Center for Assessment, Learning, and Equity (SCALE), based on the National Board for Professional Teaching Standards and the Interstate Teacher Assessment and Support Consortium Standards portfolio.

Special education teacher preparation programs have sought a valid and reliable measure of student teaching to meet the Council for the Accreditation of Educator Preparation standards and have adopted the CPAST to measure the qualities and behaviors of novice teachers (Arhar et al., 2017). The CPAST form is a valid and reliable formative and summative assessment during the students' teaching practicum.

In each of these documents, feedback is a requirement and is measured. However, a review of how each of these documents describes feedback in assessment, instruction, and social behavioral context reveals that each uses a different definition of the term and has different expectations about what effective feedback looks like.

Furthermore, high-stakes assessments such as the edTPA (SCALE, 2019) and the CPAST (Arhar et al., 2017) articulate different expectations regarding the delivery of feedback that do not easily align to CEC standards or HLPs. The incongruity between various definitions and assessments, combined with the research on feedback, as defined by Hattie and Timperley (2007), creates a conundrum for those in special education teacher preparation. How can we know what to teach to ensure that teacher candidates are prepared to deliver feedback to K-12 students in their professional practice when foundational documents do not agree about the meaning of the term?

TABLE 8-1. GRAPHIC ORGANIZER		
KNOW (WHAT)	**UNDERSTAND (WHY)**	**DEMONSTRATE (HOW)**
What the disciplinary standards and best practices suggest for feedback as an instructional technique.	Why standard language about feedback is necessary in special education teacher preparation.	How to get ready to teach feedback that reflects what effective feedback constitutes.
APPLY (TAKE ACTION)		
Apply strategies for instructional feedback in course design, activities, and assignments.		

As we will discuss, in special education teacher preparation, there is the need to articulate **what** feedback looks like and sounds like, describe **why** feedback is a crucial element in teaching, and communicate **how** to use feedback to increase K-12 student outcomes. This chapter will align the definitions of feedback from the CEC, HLPs, edTPA, and CPAST and will describe how the research on the questions, levels, and characteristics of feedback apply to teacher preparation. This chapter will also demonstrate how to select the appropriate feedback approach, based on where the recipients are on the continuum of readiness to accept the feedback.

Over the past decade, research emerging from related fields suggested that adult learners benefit from feedback that is task- or process-focused and moves each K-12 student teacher to self-regulate and develop an identity as a special education teacher (Drake, 2007; Hattie & Timperley, 2007). Therefore, special education teacher preparation instructors must give feedback that considers the recipients' readiness to accept the feedback and focuses on the level, task, and process of self-regulation most appropriate for the recipient moving toward the desired outcome. This chapter will align the definitions of feedback from the HLPs, edTPA, and CPAST and will describe the research on feedback as it relates to adult learners.

After reading this chapter you will **know** and **understand** these concepts and have the opportunity to **demonstrate** and **apply** your knowledge (Table 8-1).

DESCRIBE AND DEFINE

Know

Teaching feedback requires instructors to explicitly teach what feedback looks like and sounds like in the classroom for K-12 learners. Special educators must understand why feedback is an essential element in teaching. Instructors must be strategic in communicating how to use feedback to increase K-12 student outcomes. The disciplinary standards and practices suggest feedback as an instructional technique that increases K-12 students' academic and social emotional skills. In the following section, we define and describe the specific terminology or qualities of feedback used in each of these foundational documents that inform special education teacher preparation. At the end, a table will provide details for how each of the terms used fall into the G.E.T. Model's four domains: specificity, immediacy, purposefulness, and constructiveness.

Council for Exceptional Children Standards

In the CEC initial preparation standards, feedback is mentioned in Standard 4.4: Assessment. This performance-based standard states, "Beginning special education professionals engage individuals with exceptionalities to work toward quality learning and performance and **provide feedback** to guide them" (CEC, n.d.). While the mention of feedback in this standard only states that it needs to be provided, it loosely aligns with the constructiveness domain of the G.E.T. Model because it prompts the teacher candidate to make new meaning that will promote the quality of learning and K-12 students' performance. Considering that only one CEC standard for initial preparation focuses on feedback, what emphasis has your special education teacher preparation program placed on feedback? Is there a clearly defined focus on the feedback given to teacher candidates or assessed as they work with K-12 students in the coursework?

High-Leverage Practices

The HLPs in special education (McLeskey et al., 2017) were developed to provide a framework for those who prepare special education teachers on the practices that research has shown effective when working with K-12 students with special needs. These practices provide a model for teacher educators to enhance special education teachers' effectiveness and thus improve their students' learning. When examining these HLPs and other standards, we defer to the authors' term for *student* to mean *K-12 student*.

- *Social Emotional Behavioral—HLP #7 and #8.* These HLPs provide a list of the qualities of feedback as it relates to the social, emotional, and behavioral development of the K-12 students that special education educators teach. In these HLPs, special education educators are tasked with guiding students' learning and behavior by increasing the feedback they provide to students across the three areas. This feedback should be "**strategically delivered and goal-directed**, (McLeskey et al., 2017, p. 21), and should tell the student specifically what to improve and ways to improve . This feedback can be delivered verbally, nonverbally, or in written form. This feedback should be "**timely, contingent, genuine, meaningful, age-appropriate, and at rates commensurate with task and phase of learning (i.e., acquisition, fluency, maintenance)**" (McLeskey et al., 2017, p. 21). Finally, this feedback should be goal-driven. This extensive list of feedback qualities falls in each of the four domains of the G.E.T. Model; however, each of the terms in HLP #7 and #8 have distinct meanings and need specific explanation as instructors give feedback, exhibit feedback, and teach feedback. What do each of these terms mean and how do they relate to the performance and the professional growth of the teacher candidate in their effort to support the social, emotional, and behavioral expectations of the students they teach?

- *Instruction—HLP #17.* In this HLP, "**Positive** and **corrective** feedback to support productive learning" (McLeskey et al., 2017, p. 24) is provided in flexible groups. In addition, teachers are to "monitor and sustain group performance through proximity and **positive** feedback" (McLeskey et al., 2017, p. 24). This kind of feedback falls in the domains of specificity and immediacy of the G.E.T. Model. In this HLP, the feedback qualities are to be positive and corrective. This is grounded in the research by Brookhart (2008), Archer and Hughes (2011), and Wiggins (2012).

- *Instruction—HLP #18.* Teachers are to "monitor student engagement and provide **positive** and **constructive** feedback to sustain performance" (McLeskey et al., 2017, p. 24). This kind of feedback falls in the domain of specificity of the G.E.T. Model because it is goal- and task-related.

- *Instruction—HLP #20.* Within intensive instruction, students have many opportunities to respond and receive "**immediate, corrective**" (McLeskey et al., 2017, p. 25) feedback with teachers and peers to practice what they are learning. The feedback that meets the criteria of HLP #20 falls in the immediacy and specificity domains of the G.E.T. Model.

- *Instruction—HLP #22.* As stated in this HLP, the "purpose of feedback is to **guide student learning and behavior and increase student motivation, engagement, and independence**" (McLeskey et al., 2017, p. 25), leading to improved student learning and behavior. Effective feedback must be "**strategically delivered and goal-directed**"; (McLeskey et al., 2017, p. 25) feedback is most effective when the learner has a goal and the feedback informs the learner regarding areas needing improvement and ways to improve performance. Feedback may be "**verbal, nonverbal, or written and should be timely, contingent, genuine, meaningful, age appropriate, and at rates commensurate with the task and phase of learning (i.e., acquisition, fluency, maintenance)**" (McLeskey et al., 2017, p. 25). Teachers should provide "**ongoing** feedback until learners reach their established learning goals" (McLeskey et al., 2017, p. 25). HLP #22 has the most developed reflection of the feedback domains created in the G.E.T. Model, including specificity, immediacy, purposefulness, and constructiveness. However, once again, each term has a distinct meaning that must be taught to teacher candidates if we expect them to display this kind of feedback in coursework and in observations. How can you and your special education teacher preparation program make sense of all these terms that describe feedback in the HLPs?

Teacher Performance Assessment

- *edTPA Task Two, Instruction Rubric #8—Deepening Learning.* In this task, the teacher candidate is required to "provide the focus learner with **accurate, specific** feedback (verbal or nonverbal) and opportunity to **apply** feedback to subsequent responses" (SCALE, 2019). The qualities of feedback in this edTPA rubric fall in the specificity and purposefulness domains of the G.E.T. Model. Furthermore, this rubric, assessed at the highest level of proficiency, requires teacher candidates to provide feedback that moves the focus-learner toward developmentally appropriate **self-evaluation or self-correction**. The highest expectation for teacher candidates to promote self-evaluation and self-correction learning is found in the constructiveness domain of the G.E.T. Model.

- *edTPA Task Three—Assessment Rubric #12.* In this task, the teacher candidate is required to provide **specific** feedback that is related to the learning goal and focuses on the student's needs or reinforces the student's strengths. This rubric, assessed at the highest level of proficiency, requires teacher candidates to include in their feedback a strategy to address a learning need or make connections to prior learning or experiences to improve learning. The quality of specific feedback focused on individual student needs or strengths is consistent with the domains of specificity and purposefulness in the G.E.T. Model. The highest expectation for teacher candidates to include strategies or make connections to prior learning is found in the constructiveness domain of the G.E.T. Model, which is the most intense level of feedback to deliver because it requires the teacher candidate to differentiate their feedback and requires the student to **self-regulate** by understanding and using the strategy or prior knowledge.

- *edTPA Task Three—Assessment Rubric #13.* This rubric requires the teacher candidate to describe the support they will give the student to **understand and use** feedback related to their strengths and needs related to the learning goal. This rubric is evident in the specificity and purposeful domains of feedback of the G.E.T. Model. It should be noted that in the glossary for the edTPA, the term *feedback* is used in the definitions of two words (*assessment* and *learning* task), but the term *feedback* itself is not defined. Considering the high stakes for teacher candidates regarding passing the edTPA, what can special education teacher preparation programs do to ensure that teacher candidates can provide feedback effectively?

TABLE 8-2. CROSSWALK OF FEEDBACK EXPECTATIONS ACROSS STANDARDS OF PRACTICE

STANDARD OF PRACTICE	SPECIFICITY	
Council for Exceptional Children—Initial Preparation Standard 4: Assessment	—	
High-Leverage Practices—Social/Emotional/Behavioral HLP #7 and HLP #8	Positive, specific, age-appropriate, meaningful, caring, goal-directed, genuine; verbal, nonverbal, or written	
High-Leverage Practices—Instruction HLP #17, HLP #18, HLP #20, and HLP #22	Corrective, positive, constructive, goal-orientated, contingent, genuine, meaningful, age appropriate; verbal, nonverbal, or written	
Teacher Performance Assessment—Instruction Task Two, Rubric 8	Accurate, specific; verbal and nonverbal	
Teacher Performance Assessment—Assessment Task Three, Rubric 12 and Rubric 13	Specific, meaningful; written, audio, video; connects to prior learning	
Candidate Preservice Assessment of Student Teaching—Assessment Domain K: Feedback to Learners	Comprehensible, mini-conferences; accurate and clearly understood; assessment feedback on work samples	
Candidate Preservice Assessment of Student Teaching—Critical Thinking and Reflective Practice	Receptive to feedback, constructive criticism, supervision, and responds professionally	

Candidate Preservice Assessment of Student Teaching

In the CPAST, feedback is measured during student teaching observations in *Domain K— Feedback to Learners.* In this assessment domain, teacher candidates are evaluated according to how well they enable learners to recognize strengths and areas of need through feedback that is **comprehensible**, **descriptive**, and **individualized**. These qualities of feedback fall in the specificity and purposeful domains of the G.E.T. Model.

- *CPAST. Critical Thinking and Reflective Practice Domain U. Responds Positively to Feedback and Constructive Criticism.* In this domain, teacher candidates are assessed on their ability to receive feedback and constructive criticism and respond professionally to this feedback. Furthermore, teacher candidates are assessed according to how they incorporate this feedback to improve their practice and whether and how they seek opportunities for further feedback from other professionals. The CPAST's primary use is during student teaching at the end of the program. Based on this intended use, what can special education teacher preparation programs do backwards to design the expectations of the CPAST into the entire program?

IMMEDIACY	PURPOSEFULNESS	CONSTRUCTIVENESS
—	—	Work toward quality learning and performance and provide feedback to guide their students
Timely, ongoing	Age-appropriate, specific performance feedback; strategically delivered; contingent; at rates commensurate with task and phase of learning	Constructive; informs the learner regarding areas needing improvement and ways to improve performance
Timely, ongoing, strategically delivered	Guide student learning and behavior and increase student motivation, engagement, and independence	Informs the learner regarding areas needing improvement and ways to improve performance
—	—	Moves the focus learner toward self-evaluation and self-correction
—	Explain how feedback (including error prevention) provided to focus-learner addresses their strengths and needs related to learning goal; provides a strategy to address a learning need	Provide focus-learner opportunity to understand and use the feedback
Timely, immediate	Guiding learners on how to use feedback to monitor their own progress; results in a positive change in learning	Descriptive, individualized, specific, and extends learner thinking
—	Incorporates feedback to improve practice	Proactively seeks opportunities for feedback

Understand

Standard language about feedback is necessary in special education teacher preparation so that instructors can effectively teach how feedback should look and sound when instructing students in a K-12 classroom. With so many uses of the term *feedback*, consensus is needed regarding what each of these foundational documents intend when giving, exhibiting, and teaching feedback in our special education teacher education programs.

Table 8-2 aligns the CEC standards, HLPs, edTPA, and CPAST by the elements of their feedback requirements across the domains of the G.E.T. Model. However, what is not easily considered or put in a table is how instructors will teach these attributes of feedback to teacher candidates as they are implemented in the instruction of K-12 students with disabilities. Instructors can give feedback and exhibit feedback in their assignments, but how do we teach feedback to teacher candidates? Ask yourself how you design learning opportunities so that teacher candidates understand timely, ongoing feedback that is performance-based and moves students with disabilities to higher levels of skill attainment. Our analysis of these assessments inspired our commitment to be explicit in teaching special education teacher candidates how to effectively deliver feedback across all the domains of the G.E.T. Model for the purpose of K-12 student improvement, as well as to meet the demands of high-stakes assessments. Our commitment faces immediate challenges when we recognize the multiple measures and variety of terms across the various standards and assessments. For instance, the terms indicated in Table 8-2 could have multiple meanings, depending on the population of students with which we work. If working with students to attain functional skills, we suggest constant time delay or a system of least prompts. How does "timely" relate to these prompting techniques? What is corrective, yet specific feedback? How do we move students to higher levels of performance by using the feedback we provide? Various examples are provided at the end of chapters, but special educator instructors must consider how such different expectations between the standards and practices that inform our field are evaluated.

Demonstrate

The process we use to teach feedback needs to reflect what effective feedback looks like and sounds like. As stated in Chapter 1, we want to support teacher candidates in setting goals by being descriptive in our feedback. If we want them to be able to set goals based on the specific feedback we give them, we need consensus on what each term in the standards and practice documents are required of them. Teacher educators coming to consensus on the characteristics of effective feedback would translate into a purpose for giving and receiving feedback, thus allowing teacher candidates to understand the importance of feedback to their future K-12 students. The following are good examples of adult learning principles: readiness to learn, orientation to learning, and motivation to learn. When teacher candidates understand the purpose, as adults, they are more likely to invest time and energy into the learning task. Teacher candidates who are effective are those who are open to constructive feedback. Yet, most teacher educators are faced with "teaching to the test" in high-stakes summative assessments instead of considering the characteristics, questions, and levels of feedback.

Teaching to the Test Versus Teaching the Test

One criticism of this approach to ensure teacher candidates' success in high-stakes assessments is that it is "teaching to the test." Yet, despite the negative connotation that goes along with that phrase, arguably, teaching to the test is exactly what the role of the instructor should entail. Of course, that does not mean teaching the test itself. Instead, in the spirit of backward design (Wiggins & McTighe, 1998), when a known final test or assessment is required, then design instruction with the end in mind can be a useful way to prepare learners to perform well on the final assessment. A focus on teaching the test and meeting the standards and best practices can be confusing for instructors. Thus, the essential question—how do teacher educators build up the skills sets of teacher candidates so they are confidently prepared?

SPOTLIGHT ON ADULT LEARNING

As previously mentioned, we know that adult learners are invested in learning that is life-related and developmental (adult learning theory principle: readiness to learn) and that it has intrinsic value and personal payoff (adult learning theory principle: motivation to learn). Therefore, teaching feedback to teacher candidates should be situated using a backward design to determine what standard or assessment requirement would be practiced and applied across course work. Knowing the different assessments and standards gives instructors the framework for constructing a curriculum that prepares teacher candidates to deliver feedback effectively to K-12 students. The spotlight on adult learning that follows provides questions that can inform the development of the curriculum.

TABLE 8-3. SPOTLIGHT ON ADULT LEARNING			
SPECIFICITY	**IMMEDIACY**	**PURPOSEFULNESS**	**CONSTRUCTIVENESS**
Which of the standards addresses the feedback the teacher candidate provides related to the goal of the task, assignment, or performance?	Which of the standards describes when feedback should be delivered, considering the developmental learning process and the type of assignment?	Which of the standards addresses how teacher candidates need to provide feedback to their K-12 students based on the progress they are demonstrating?	Which of the standards provides direction to teacher candidates to deliver feedback to K-12 students that will develop their capacity of learning?

The G.E.T. Model for teaching feedback seeks to put adult learners at the center by defining feedback as any information that the recipient receives that informs their understanding, restructures their thinking or beliefs, and is related to their performance, knowledge, or skills. As you remember from Chapter 1, we acknowledge adult learners' contextual need to know why they must learn how to give feedback to their K-12 students, not just to meet the criteria of various assessments but as practical application of Hattie's 0.70 effect size (Visible Learning, 2018) on the scale of teacher practices. As instructors in special education teacher preparation, we must keep our sights on the various assessment measures while teaching teacher candidates how to give feedback to their K-12 students. The questions shown in Table 8-3 serve to bring focus on how to align different assessment standards with the four feedback domains of the G.E.T. Model.

POSSIBLE BARRIERS TO USING THIS TYPE OF FEEDBACK

When teaching feedback to teacher candidates, the multiple expectations by different entities (i.e., CEC, HLPs, states' standards) makes it difficult to have a clear definition of what "constructive" feedback is or what "meaningful" feedback looks or sounds like when delivered in the K-12 classroom. These terms are relative and can have different meanings and expectations based on the instructors' knowledge of feedback. Furthermore, the types of valid and reliable measures of feedback like the CPAST require an inordinate amount of time for instructors that might cause the immediate feedback during the observation appointment to be considered only as a goal for improvement instead of providing guidance on how to improve for the next observation.

Another possible barrier to teaching feedback to teacher candidates is the delay in getting results from the edTPA to make programmatic changes. The edTPA is a high-stakes assessment that occurs at the end of the teacher candidate's program; thus, remediation can occur only for future K-12 students as they are taught in methods courses to deliver feedback that provides the focus-learner an opportunity to understand and use the feedback. In addition, the reliability and validity of the edTPA is under scrutiny for its technical adequacy, and some suggest that it should not be used for licensure decisions (Gitomer et al., 2019). Furthermore, first-year teachers are evaluated on their teaching performance using measures such as Danielson's (2007) framework or the Marzano (2007) Teacher Evaluation that require an entirely different set of expectations on feedback (Table 8-4).

TABLE 8-4. FEEDBACK EXPECTATIONS

STANDARD OF PRACTICE	SPECIFICITY	
Danielson's Framework—Component 3d: Using Assessment in Instruction (student)	Accurate, specific, descriptive, understandable; oral and/or written	
Danielson's Framework—Component 4e: Growing and Developing Professionally (teacher)	Feedback on teaching practice; essential element of rich instructional environment	
Marzano Teacher Evaluation	Concrete, actionable, specific	

Another possible barrier to the teaching of feedback can be the lack of shared understanding for each term used in the HLPs. The terminology in the HLPs is grounded in various research articles on feedback, so the different terms used were listed without consensus on the meaning of the terms. Only corrective feedback (Archer & Hughes, 2011) is included in the glossary for the HLPs. Instructors are to infer the meaning as depicted in video examples and resource tools the HLP materials provide to use in the development of the HLP within coursework, but such resources come with the disclaimer that they are not a "complete resource for training/professional learning" (https://highleveragepractices.org/701-2-3/, para. 5).

When instructors are tasked with so many competing resources to consider when backward designing their coursework from testing outcomes, current standards of practice, and what educational research has described as feedback, the sheer number of disparate and unarticulated definitions may present barriers to teaching feedback effectively.

PRACTICAL APPLICATION

The following practical application from Dr. Wendy H. Weber demonstrates teaching feedback, as the instructors must be strategic in communicating how to use feedback to increase K-12 student outcomes. This was done by creating a crosswalk with the new requirements set by the state and the accrediting body, which warranted that a major program redesign was needed to ensure that all expectations were met.

Approximately 5 years ago, the instructors at Dr. Weber's university were overwhelmed with the many new state mandates for teacher preparation and new Council for Accreditation of Educator Preparation requirements. The undergraduate program director at the time and the chair of the special education department worked with the special education instructors to determine what the key terms from the CEC standards, state standards, edTPA rubrics, and CPAST "look for" that could be taught and measured effectively by multiple field supervisors, instructors, and faculty. They considered what would be taught and evaluated across each practicum and class and created a crosswalk of requirements. In addition, after edTPA scores are reported to the university from Pearson (the

IMMEDIACY	PURPOSEFULNESS	CONSTRUCTIVENESS
Timely	Feedback to students guide next steps; focused on improvement	Substantive
Circulates during small-group or independent work, offering suggestions to groups of students	Actively seeks feedback from supervisors and colleagues	Receptivity to feedback from colleagues
—	Directly aligned to rigorous state standards; diagnostic	—

company that owns, administers, and scores the assessment), the program director analyzes the results and shares them with instructors for further course level changes. Over time, since redesigning the coursework to align to standards, the faculty often find that the teacher candidates score poorly on the feedback prompts in the edTPA and find that clinical observations often focus on providing feedback appropriately to the K-12 students they are teaching. This work by the instructors is under continuous improvement as new information, such as HLPs, is considered as part of the preparation of special education teachers. Feedback will be a major focus of the future redesign of the program due to the poor outcomes of the teacher candidates to understand and apply feedback.

The Illinois Professional Teaching Standards and edTPA alignment crosswalk, specifically page 5 of the document, can be viewed by visiting https://www.isbe.net/Documents/edTPA-IPTS-cross-walk.pdf. The details of the alignment of the CEC standards with the courses in the undergraduate special education program at Southern Illinois University Edwardsville are presented in Figure 8-1.

Practical Application for Backward Design

You may recall the design studio from XYZ University described in Chapter 7. Although the program outcomes were considered in programmatic and course decisions, backward design was not initially employed in creating the online program. Given the variability of assessments for special education licensure and endorsement across the United States and the differing assessments for feedback competency, attending to the tenets of backward design may aid in creating programs and curriculum that do not teach to the test but prepare teacher candidates to be successful on assessments. More importantly, these teacher candidates will be well prepared to actually deliver feedback to their K-12 students. The information in Table 8-5 may be helpful to organize your thinking about program and course design. The Design Key column is adapted from Wiggins and McTighe (1998).

Fundamentally, all programs should have outcomes that are met by courses and curriculum. Being intentional about the design of a program, using backward design, will create an opportunity to teach feedback in a way that is situated, authentic, and more than meets the criteria of an assessment.

2015 CEC Standards	SPE Courses at SIUE																	
Courses when completed	290	415	470	401	450	405	430b	402	417a	416	471	418	412	417b	421	422	499	481
1. Learner Development and Individual Learning Differences **1.0 Beginning special education professionals understand how exceptionalities may interact with development and learning and use this knowledge to provide meaningful and challenging learning experiences for individuals with exceptionalities.**																		
1.1 understand how language, culture, and family background influence the learning of individuals with exceptionalities.	X				X	X		X			X			X	X		X	X
1.2 use understanding of development and individual differences to respond to the needs of individuals with exceptionalities.	X					X		X		X				X	X		X	X
2. Learning Environments **2.0 Beginning special education professionals create safe, inclusive, culturally responsive learning environments so that individuals with exceptionalities become active and effective learners and develop emotional well-being, positive social interactions, and self-determination.**																		
2.1 Beginning special education professionals through collaboration with general educators and other colleagues create safe, inclusive, culturally responsive learning environments to engage individuals with exceptionalities in meaningful learning activities and social interactions.					X	X	X	X	X		X				X		X	
2.2 use motivational and instructional interventions to teach individuals with exceptionalities how to adapt to different environments.						X		X									X	
2.3 know how to intervene safely and appropriately with individuals with exceptionalities in crisis.								X		X							X	
3. Curricular Content Knowledge **3.0 Beginning special education professionals use knowledge of general and specialized curricula to individualize learning for individuals with exceptionalities.**																		
3.1 understand the central concepts, structures of the discipline, and tools of inquiry of the content areas they teach, and can organize this knowledge, integrate cross-disciplinary skills, and develop meaningful learning progressions for individuals with exceptionalities.								X						X	X	X	X	
3.2 Beginning special education professionals understand and use general and specialized content knowledge for teaching across curricular content areas to individualize learning for individuals with exceptionalities.								X						X	X	X	X	X
3.3 Beginning special education professionals modify general and specialized curricula to make them accessible to individuals with exceptionalities.								X	X					X	X	X	X	
4. Assessment **4.0 Beginning special education professionals use multiple methods of assessment and data-sources in making educational decisions.**																		
Courses when completed	290	415	470	401	450	405	430b	402	417a	416	471	418	412	417b	421	422	499	481
4.1 Beginning special education professionals select and use																		

Figure 8-1. Objectives: What to know, understand, and demonstrate in order to apply feedback strategies.

	C1	C2	C3	C4	C5	C6	C7	C8	C9	C10	C11	C12	C13	C14	C15	C16
technically sound formal and informal assessments that minimize bias.			X			X			X			X		X		X
4.2 Beginning special education professionals use knowledge of measurement principles and practices to interpret assessment results and guide educational decisions for individuals with exceptionalities.			X			X			X	X		X		X		X
4.3 Beginning special education professionals in collaboration with colleagues and families use multiple types of assessment information in making decisions about individuals with exceptionalities.			X			X	X	X	X			X			X	X
4.4 Beginning special education professionals engage individuals with exceptionalities to work toward quality learning and performance and provide feedback to guide them.			X			X			X			X		X	X	X
5 Instructional Planning and Strategies																
5.0 Beginning special education professionals select, adapt, and use a repertoire of evidence-based instructional strategies to advance learning of individuals with exceptionalities.																
5.1 consider an individual's abilities, interests, learning environments, and cultural and linguistic factors in the selection, development, and adaptation of learning experiences for individuals with exceptionalities.	X		X			X		X	X	X		X	X	X	X	X
5.2 use technologies to support instructional assessment, planning, and delivery for individuals with exceptionalities.		X			X	X		X	X			X	X		X	X
5.3 are familiar with augmentative and alternative communication systems and a variety of assistive technologies to support the communication and learning of individuals with exceptionalities.		X				X		X	X						X	X
5.4 use strategies to enhance language development and communication skills of individuals with exceptionalities.	X	X						X	X	X				X	X	X
5.5 develop and implement a variety of education and transition plans for individuals with exceptionalities across a wide range of settings and different learning experiences in collaboration with individuals, families, and teams.			X						X		X			X	X	
5.6 Beginning special education professionals teach to mastery and promote generalization of learning.				X					X			X	X	X	X	X
5.7 Beginning special education professionals teach cross-disciplinary knowledge and skills such as critical thinking and problem solving to individuals with exceptionalities.								X	X				X	X	X	X

Figure 8-1 (continued). Objectives: What to know, understand, and demonstrate in order to apply feedback strategies.

6 Prof. Learning & Ethical Practice
6.0 Beginning special education professionals use foundational knowledge of the field and their professional Ethical Principles and Practice Standards to inform special education practice, to engage in lifelong learning, and to advance the profession.

Courses when completed	290	415	470	401	450	405	430 b	402	417a	416	471	418	412	417b	421	422	499	481
6.1 Beginning special education professionals use professional Ethical Principles and Professional Practice Standards to guide their practice.			X			X	X			X	X		X	X			X	
6.2 Beginning special education professionals understand how foundational knowledge and current issues influence professional practice.		X		X		X						X		X			X	
6.3 Beginning special education professionals understand that diversity is a part of families, cultures, and schools, and that complex human issues can interact with the delivery of special education services.			X			X		X			X		X				X	
6.4 Beginning special education professionals understand the significance of lifelong learning and participate in professional activities and learning communities.		X											X				X	
6.5 Beginning special education professionals advance the profession by engaging in activities such as advocacy and mentoring.		X									X	X					X	
6.6 Beginning special education professionals provide guidance and direction to paraeducators, tutors, and volunteers.							X										X	
7 Collaboration																		
7.0 Beginning special education professionals collaborate with families, other educators, related service providers, individuals with exceptionalities, and personnel from community agencies in culturally responsive ways to address the needs of individuals with exceptionalities across a range of learning experiences.																		
7.1 Beginning special education professionals use the theory and elements of effective collaboration.				X	X	X	X			X	X				X	X		
7.2 Beginning special education professionals serve as a collaborative resource to colleagues.							X				X				X	X		
7.3 Beginning special education professionals use collaboration to promote the well-being of individuals with exceptionalities across a wide range of settings and collaborators.					X	X	X	X		X	X				X	X		
Totals	4	6	7	11	6	11	12	9	13	14	10	3	7	10	12	13	28	11
Standards in Program Assessment		3	7				12					3		10			all	11

Figure 8-1 (continued). Objectives: What to know, understand, and demonstrate in order to apply feedback strategies.

TABLE 8-5. ORGANIZATION OF PROGRAM AND COURSE DESIGN				
DESIGN KEY	**ASSESSMENT**	**INFORMING CRITERIA**	**TOPIC OF EMPHASIS**	**DEMONSTRATION OF MASTERY**
Stage 1. Identify desired result	edTPA	CEC, state standards	Feedback	What does the edTPA require?
Stage 2. Determine acceptable evidence of learning	Four feedback domains Tailor feedback to audience	Domains of the G.E.T. Model Questions Levels Characteristics Variability of audiences for feedback	Feedback designed for specific audience	Teacher candidates will be able to observe a scenario and construct effective feedback for the learners
Stage 3. Design experience and instruction	Researched-based repertoire of learning; essential knowledge and skill for delivering effective feedback	Situated learning— simulation • Video • Role play	Connect domains of feedback to learning task and specific audience	Deliver effective feedback in an authentic situation based on the G.E.T. Model and the target audience
CEC = Council for Exceptional Children; edTPA = Teacher Performance Assessment.				

SUMMARY

This chapter on teaching feedback builds on considering the recipients of feedback and addresses the rationale for teaching feedback. The variety of interpretations and uses of the word feedback in the standards of practice and within the high-stakes assessments that teacher candidates are required to be proficient. Instructors diving deeper into understanding feedback provides opportunity for us to teach what feedback looks like and sounds like, describe why feedback is a crucial element in teaching, and communicate how to use feedback to increase K-12 student outcomes. This thoughtful reflection of feedback can be achieved by using a backward design in our course development. This chapter explores each of these concepts for instructors and provides guidance on how to align to the course of study and within our special education programs.

We believe that each definition or interpretation of feedback in the standards of practice for special education teacher preparation can make it difficult for instructors to teach how to give feedback. It is critical for instructors working together in their department to come to consensus on what aspects of feedback are important to teach in each course for special education teacher candidates to understand how to teach feedback to their future K-12 students.

OPPORTUNITY FOR GOING DEEPER

The following resources support deeper learning on the concepts reflected in Chapter 8:

- Understanding by Design. For additional reading, the *Understanding by Design* (UbD) books and workbooks by Grant Wiggins and Jay McTighe can be found at https://www.authenticeducation.org

- Published UbD lessons. Trinity University Professor Dr. Laura Allen has led a Summer Curriculum Writing Institute since 2005, where graduates of the Trinity University Master of Arts in Teaching program and their colleagues publish units that follow the UbD framework. These units are available for free download from Trinity University Digital Commons' web page at https://digitalcommons.trinity.edu/understandingbydesign/

- edTPA reliability and validity. The following article provides details on the reliability and validity of the edTPA assessment: Gitomer, D. H., Martínez, J. F., Battey, D., & Hyland, N. E. (2019). Assessing the assessment: Evidence of reliability and validity in the edTPA. *American Educational Research Journal, 58*(1), 3-31. https://doi.org/10.3102/0002831219890608

REFERENCES

Archer, A. L., & Hughes, C. A. (2011). *Explicit instruction: Effective and efficient teaching.* Guilford Press.

Arhar, J., Beickelman, F., Bendixen-Noe, M., Bode, P., Bowman, C., Brannan, S., Brownstein, E., Crell, A., Day, K., Fresch, M., Gallagher, D., Hendricks, M., Jewell, W., Kahrig, T., Kaplan, C., Patterson, C., Price, A., Turner, S., Stewart, V., . . . Whittington, M. (2017). *Candidate Preservice Assessment of Student Teaching* [Measurement Instrument]. Ohio Association of Colleges of Teacher Education. https://ehe.osu.edu/accreditation-placement-licensure/accreditation/candidate-preservice-assessment-student-teaching-cpast/

Brookhart, S. M. (2008). Feedback that fits. *Educational Leadership, 65*(4), 54-59.

Council for Exceptional Children. (n.d.). *About our initial preparation standards.* https://exceptionalchildren.org/standards/initial-special-education-preparation-standards

Council for Exceptional Children. (2015). *What every special educator must know: Professional ethics and standards* (7th ed.).

Danielson, C. (2007). *Enhancing professional practice: A framework for teaching* (2nd ed.). Association for Supervision and Curriculum Development.

Drake, D. B. (2007). The arc of thinking narratively: Implications for coaching psychology and practice. *Australian Psychologist, 42*(4), 283-294.

Gitomer, D. H., Martínez, J. F., Battey, D., & Hyland, N. E. (2019). Assessing the assessment: Evidence of reliability and validity in the edTPA. *American Educational Research Journal.* https://doi.org/10.3102/0002831219890608

Hattie, J., & Timperley, H. (2007). The power of feedback. *Review of Educational Research, 77*(1), 81-112. https://doi.org/10.3102/003465430298487

Knowles, M. (1984). *The adult learner: A neglected species* (3rd ed.). Gulf Publishing.

Marzano, R. J. (2007). *The art and science of teaching: A comprehensive framework for effective instruction.* Association for Supervision and Curriculum Development.

McLeskey, J., Barringer, M-D., Billingsley, B., Brownell, M., Jackson, D., Kennedy, M., Lewis, T., Maheady, L., Rodriguez, J., Scheeler, M. C., Winn, J., & Ziegler, D. (2017). *High-leverage practices in special education.* Council for Exceptional Children & CEEDAR Center. https://ceedar.education.ufl.edu/high-leverage-practices/

Stanford Center for Assessment, Learning, and Equity. (2019). *Teaching performance assessment.* https://scale.stanford.edu/teaching

Visible Learning. (2018). Hattie ranking: 252 Influences and effect sizes related to student achievement. https://visible-learning.org/hattie-ranking-influences-effect-sizes-learning-achievement/

Wiggins, G. P. (2012). Seven keys to effective feedback. *Educational Leadership, 70*(1), 10-16.

Wiggins, G., & McTighe, J. (1998). What is backward design? In *Understanding by Design* (pp. 7-19). Association for Supervision and Curriculum Development.

Teaching Feedback in Instruction

FEEDBACK SCENARIO

Dr. Mason was deeply concerned for a teacher candidate he was supervising this semester in an early childhood special education classroom. The teacher candidate, Mary, had not responded to his repeated emails about course due dates not being met, even as the second observation date was approaching. At the first observation, Mary did not interact with the students and seemed nervous to be around young students with such diverse needs. During the post-observation feedback, Dr. Mason reviewed with Mary the expectations outlined in the practicum observation protocol. They concluded the post-observation meeting with setting two goals—to interact more with the students, which is a central concern of the protocol, and to improve her email communication. Mary apologized for not responding to emails and said she would start answering emails as soon as possible. After this conference with Mary, the cooperating teacher emailed Dr. Mason before he even got back to his office with concerns that the expectations were too high, considering that Mary was only in her first practicum. Dr. Mason reviewed the feedback he gave Mary. He was concerned that she misinterpreted the feedback and the goals he set because she discussed only the email communication with him, but she seemed to have had a conversation with her cooperating teacher about the other observation expectation of interacting more with the students.

This scenario demonstrates that feedback is easily misinterpreted. In this case, the teacher candidate focused more on the email communication, which is an important but not the most important concern, and not on the actual requirements outlined on the practicum observation protocol. Mary was not ready to improve her teaching performance because she focused on the task of email responsiveness instead of focusing on the skills she needs to be a better teacher to students in an early childhood setting. She was unable to discern what was the most important and what was less important in regard to feedback.

Elford, M. D., Smith, H. H., & James, S.
*GET Feedback: Giving, Exhibiting, and Teaching Feedback in
Special Education Teacher Preparation* (pp. 167-192).
© 2022 SLACK Incorporated.

TABLE 9-1. GRAPHIC ORGANIZER		
KNOW (WHAT)	**UNDERSTAND (WHY)**	**DEMONSTRATE (HOW)**
What the research on teaching feedback suggests, especially for adult learners.	Why teaching feedback is necessary in special education teacher preparation.	How to teach feedback that recognizes: • **What** feedback looks and sounds like • **Why** feedback is a crucial element in teaching • **How** to use feedback to increase student outcomes
APPLY (TAKE ACTION)		
Apply strategies for teaching feedback in course design, activities, and assignments.		

CHAPTER OBJECTIVES

This chapter builds on the rationale for teaching feedback in special education teacher preparation and examines the knowledge and instructional skills we want teacher candidates to display when they teach in their own classrooms someday.

As we will discuss, in special education teacher preparation, there is the need to teach clear descriptions and demonstrations of feedback skills, followed by supported practice in our courses. This chapter will describe the research on teaching feedback techniques and including them as part of your course. This chapter will also demonstrate how to select the appropriate instructional feedback skills, with examples and prompts to take action.

Research suggests that adult learners benefit from performing tasks that are goal-oriented and from exploring expected instructional skills firsthand and to learn from their mistakes. Therefore, special education teacher preparation instructors must provide opportunities for teacher candidates to develop an intrinsic understanding of feedback and practice instructional feedback skills. Instructors must provide feedback to adult learners for them to evaluate the quality of the learning experience and to make adjustments.

After reading this chapter, you will **know** and **understand** these concepts and have the opportunity to **demonstrate** and **apply** your knowledge (Table 9-1).

DESCRIBE AND DEFINE

In special education teacher preparation, the teacher-directed instructional approach of explicit instruction maximizes student achievement for students with disabilities (Brophy & Good, 1986; Christenson et al., 1989; Gersten et al., 2000; Marchand-Martella et al., 2004; Rosenshine, 1997; Rosenshine & Stevens, 1986; Simmons et al., 1995; Swanson, 2001; Swanson & Deshler, 2003). Special education educators consider that instructing teacher candidates in evidence-based strategies and instructional skills is central to their work. Archer and Hughes (2011) acknowledged that explicit instruction is a "direct approach that includes both instructional design and delivery procedures" (p. 1). Instructors focus content area methods courses on the instructional design and delivery in explicit instruction so that K-12 student outcomes will be greater. Because special education teacher preparation is grounded in explicit instruction, we contend that teacher candidates need explicit instruction in giving and receiving feedback.

Know

Feedback has long been considered an effective instructional strategy in explicit instruction. Thorndike (1931) suggested in his behavioral theory that learning is the result of associations forming between stimuli and response. Thorndike (1931) further theorized the Law of Effect, which states that any behavior that is followed by pleasant consequences is likely to be repeated, while any behavior followed by unpleasant consequences is likely to be stopped. Applying Thorndike's Law of Effect to education settings, we see that when teachers give positive feedback to students when learning, they are more likely to repeat the behavior. Thorndike (1905, 1913) was one of the first researchers to apply psychological principles to the area of learning, with extensive dependence on reinforcement when teaching students. This idea that students who receive positive feedback are more likely to repeat the behavior is a well-established instructional technique in special education.

Although Thorndike (1931) argued that unpleasant consequences discouraged unwanted behaviors, a review of literature by Hattie and Timperley (2007) clearly demonstrated that negative feedback can discourage not just unwanted behaviors but student effort and achievement. To move students to a higher level of achievement, teachers need to nurture a student's learning and not have them feel deflated that they will never "get it," which can be the result of negative consequences. For true learning to occur, teacher candidates must tell the students not only what they are doing correctly but also what they are doing that needs correcting; however, this must be done without undermining student effort. This analysis is more than a red check mark designating a wrong answer on a page; it may involve student conferencing and goal setting or reteaching the skills or strategies in small-group instruction. Students will achieve higher levels of skill attainment if they are provided with an explanation of what is accurate and inaccurate as well as given modeling and guided practice on how to do the academic skill accurately, as "corrective feedback can be carried out within the positive student-teacher relationships, especially when the teacher displays a positive and respectful attitude toward student efforts, and communicates that such errors are natural steps along the path to mastery" (Hattie & Yates, 2014, p. 53). The feedback will not be considered negative because the student is motivated by the review and the positive outcomes of the guided practice.

Byrnes (1996) contended that true learning happens when a student is able to transfer what has been learned in one context to new contexts. In special education, explicit, systematic instruction (also known as *direct instruction*) includes modeling, scaffolding, and guided practice and takes up most of the learning sequence. Teacher candidates are taught to model using worked examples and to gradually release responsibility (Pearson & Gallagher, 1983) to the students during guided practice and to scaffold learning opportunities to practice and transfer skills. Bransford et al. (2000) expanded on this idea of transfer, noting that students need feedback to understand the degree to which they know when, where, and how to transfer the knowledge they are learning. Our goal is for students with disabilities to generalize, or transfer, skills in various contexts. Feedback is crucial to assume increased responsibility for their learning and to transfer knowledge to other contexts (Figure 9-1).

The research on providing academic and behavioral feedback during instruction is clear when working with students with special needs. When specific, constructive feedback on performance is given, students with special needs better understand the goal of when and where to exhibit the behavior and how to demonstrate the behavior correctly. Chapter 11 will describe in more detail the feedback needed in social, behavioral, and emotional contexts. Chapter 9 will explore the feedback given in academic instruction. Clearly, even giving explicit instruction with formative assessment throughout, students will still make errors when doing independent practice activities. Just like students with special needs, adult learners benefit from performing tasks that are goal-oriented and from exploring expected instructional skills firsthand as they learn from their mistakes. Instructors need to infuse experiential learning opportunities for applying explicit lesson design with feedback given along the way as we gradually release responsibility of the learning goal to them.

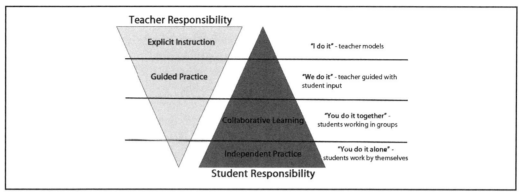

Figure 9-1. Gradual release of responsibility. The most frequent omission is the collaborative learning phase. (Adapted from Fisher, D., & Frey, N. [2014]. *Better learning through structured teaching: A framework for the gradual release of responsibility* [2nd ed.]. ASCD.)

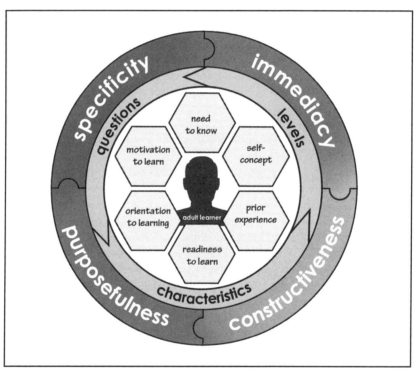

Figure 9-2. Conceptual framework of the G.E.T. Model.

Understand

Learning specific instructional skills in giving feedback is necessary in special education teacher preparation and must be explicitly taught to the teacher candidates. So, how is feedback applied to explicit instruction? Archer and Hughes (2011) stated that explicit instruction has 16 elements, each of which gives instructors in special education teacher preparation a way to GET Feedback. Each element has an opportunity for instructors to apply strategies for teaching feedback in the instructional design process (Figure 9-2).

Let us look at the elements of explicit instruction by Archer and Hughes (2011) and determine where we can teach and model effective feedback as well as what domain(s) of feedback instructors can teach and model (Table 9-2).

TABLE 9-2. INSTRUCTOR FEEDBACK

ELEMENT OF EXPLICIT INSTRUCTION	INSTRUCTIONAL DESIGN PROCESS	DOMAIN OF FEEDBACK TO TEACH AND MODEL FEEDBACK	
1. Focus instruction on critical elements	Planning stage	Specificity	X
		Immediacy	
		Purposefulness	
		Constructiveness	
2. Sequence skills logically	Planning stage	Specificity	X
		Immediacy	
		Purposefulness	
		Constructiveness	
3. Break down complex skills and strategies into smaller instructional units	Planning stage	Specificity	X
		Immediacy	
		Purposefulness	
		Constructiveness	X
4. Design organized and focused lessons	Planning stage	Specificity	X
		Immediacy	
		Purposefulness	X
		Constructiveness	
5. Begin lessons with a clear statement of the lesson's goal and your expectations	Introduction stage	Specificity	X
		Immediacy	
		Purposefulness	X
		Constructiveness	
6. Review prior skills and knowledge before beginning instruction	Introduction stage	Specificity	X
		Immediacy	X
		Purposefulness	X
		Constructiveness	
7. Provide step-by-step demonstrations	Modeling stage	Specificity	X
		Immediacy	X
		Purposefulness	X
		Constructiveness	
8. Use clear and concise language	Modeling stage	Specificity	X
		Immediacy	
		Purposefulness	X
		Constructiveness	
9. Provide an adequate range of examples and non-examples	Modeling stage	Specificity	X
		Immediacy	
		Purposefulness	X
		Constructiveness	

(continued)

TABLE 9-2 (CONTINUED). INSTRUCTOR FEEDBACK

ELEMENT OF EXPLICIT INSTRUCTION	INSTRUCTIONAL DESIGN PROCESS	DOMAIN OF FEEDBACK TO TEACH AND MODEL FEEDBACK	
10. Provide guided and supported practice	Guided practice stage	Specificity	X
		Immediacy	X
		Purposefulness	X
		Constructiveness	X
11. Require frequent responses	Guided practice stage	Specificity	X
		Immediacy	X
		Purposefulness	X
		Constructiveness	X
12. Monitor student performance closely	Guided practice stage	Specificity	X
		Immediacy	X
		Purposefulness	X
		Constructiveness	X
13. Provide immediate affirmative and corrective feedback	Guided practice stage	Specificity	X
	Independent practice stage	Immediacy	X
		Purposefulness	X
		Constructiveness	X
14. Deliver the lesson at a brisk pace	Guided practice stage	Specificity	X
	Independent practice stage	Immediacy	
		Purposefulness	X
		Constructiveness	
15. Help students organize their knowledge	Conclusion stage	Specificity	X
		Immediacy	
		Purposefulness	X
		Constructiveness	X
16. Provide distributed and cumulative practice	Conclusion stage	Specificity	X
		Immediacy	X
		Purposefulness	X
		Constructiveness	X

Demonstrate

Thinking back to Chapter 8, backward design was described in detail to teach feedback in course design, activities, and assignments. When instructors are teaching the lesson plan format for explicit instruction, there are opportunities to teach and model feedback. Consider the assignment used by Dr. James in the instructional planning and collaboration course at her university. Dr. James gradually releases responsibility for teacher candidates to write lesson plans by first providing model lesson plans, leading as the entire class writes a lesson plan together, and then giving teacher candidates the opportunity to write a lesson plan by themselves. At each point, the teacher candidates are asked to reflect on the instructional planning process in small groups. Each phase of the instructional process—(a) planning the focus, (b) embedding strategies, (c) assessment, (d) planning the classroom environment, (e) instructional procedures, (f) consideration of behavioral needs, and (g) planning materials—provide opportunities for instructors to teach feedback and to give, exhibit, and teach **what** feedback looks like and sounds like when delivering instruction, **why** feedback is a crucial element in the instructional process, and **how** to use feedback to increase student outcomes. Consider which domain of feedback can be taught and modeled while teacher candidates are evaluating their own lesson plans during small-group reflection (Table 9-3).

TABLE 9-3. EVALUATING LESSON PLANS

INSTRUCTIONAL PLANNING PROCESS		
CENTRAL FOCUS	**QUESTIONS TO CONSIDER WHEN EVALUATING YOUR EXPLICIT LESSON PLAN**	**WHICH DOMAIN OF FEEDBACK TO TEACH AND MODEL FEEDBACK?**
1. Planning the Learning Central Focus		
	Is the learning objective described in observable and measurable terms? What do you want students to think, know, understand, and/or be able to do?	Specificity _____ Immediacy _____ Purposefulness _____ Constructiveness _____
	Have you determined how the students will demonstrate the lesson objective? Describe observable actions (recommendation: use a backward design).	Specificity _____ Immediacy _____ Purposefulness _____ Constructiveness _____
	Are the Common Core State Standards/Dynamic Learning Maps aligned to lesson objective and grade level expectations?	Specificity _____ Immediacy _____ Purposefulness _____ Constructiveness _____
	Does the lesson address the characteristics of the individual disabilities in the classroom?	Specificity _____ Immediacy _____ Purposefulness _____ Constructiveness _____
	Have the students' IEP goals, supports, and resources been considered?	Specificity _____ Immediacy _____ Purposefulness _____ Constructiveness _____
	Does the lesson consider co-teachers or others collaborating in the classroom?	Specificity _____ Immediacy _____ Purposefulness _____ Constructiveness _____
	Does the lesson reflect understanding of the prerequisite/background knowledge that students need to participate in the lesson?	Specificity _____ Immediacy _____ Purposefulness _____ Constructiveness _____
	A plan for review of prior learning is presented.	Specificity _____ Immediacy _____ Purposefulness _____ Constructiveness _____
	What scaffolds are needed to ensure that all students master the lesson objective?	Specificity _____ Immediacy _____ Purposefulness _____ Constructiveness _____
	What do you, as the teacher, know about this particular concept/topic being taught?	Specificity _____ Immediacy _____ Purposefulness _____ Constructiveness _____

(continued)

TABLE 9-3 (CONTINUED). EVALUATING LESSON PLANS		
INSTRUCTIONAL PLANNING PROCESS		
CENTRAL FOCUS	**QUESTIONS TO CONSIDER WHEN EVALUATING YOUR EXPLICIT LESSON PLAN**	**WHICH DOMAIN OF FEEDBACK TO TEACH AND MODEL FEEDBACK?**
2. Strategies to Ensure Access for All Learners		
	Is the physical environment of the classroom considered?	Specificity _____ Immediacy _____ Purposefulness _____ Constructiveness _____
	Have the prior knowledge, skills, and academic background the students bring to the lesson been considered?	Specificity _____ Immediacy _____ Purposefulness _____ Constructiveness _____
	Is there an agenda provided to the students for the lesson?	Specificity _____ Immediacy _____ Purposefulness _____ Constructiveness _____
	Is there an explanation of the behavioral expectations planned (CHAMPS)?	Specificity _____ Immediacy _____ Purposefulness _____ Constructiveness _____
	Are the necessary materials and equipment ready for lesson presentation?	Specificity _____ Immediacy _____ Purposefulness _____ Constructiveness _____
	Are there any conditions/limitations that might impact the planning and delivery of the lesson?	Specificity _____ Immediacy _____ Purposefulness _____ Constructiveness _____
	How does this lesson fit in the curriculum?	Specificity _____ Immediacy _____ Purposefulness _____ Constructiveness _____
3. Evidence and Assessment of Student Learning		
Student data	How will students' progress be monitored during the lesson? How will you know that the students are learning/working toward the lesson objective?	Specificity _____ Immediacy _____ Purposefulness _____ Constructiveness _____
	Are multiple formative assessments planned at different parts of the lesson? How will students demonstrate their knowledge?	Specificity _____ Immediacy _____ Purposefulness _____ Constructiveness _____

(continued)

Table 9-3 (continued). Evaluating Lesson Plans

INSTRUCTIONAL PLANNING PROCESS

CENTRAL FOCUS	QUESTIONS TO CONSIDER WHEN EVALUATING YOUR EXPLICIT LESSON PLAN	WHICH DOMAIN OF FEEDBACK TO TEACH AND MODEL FEEDBACK?
3. Evidence and Assessment of Student Learning (continued)		
	Is there a clear connection between the summative assessment and the lesson objective?	Specificity _____ Immediacy _____ Purposefulness _____ Constructiveness _____
	Do oral assessments require all students to respond and demonstrate their metacognitive skills?	Specificity _____ Immediacy _____ Purposefulness _____ Constructiveness _____
	Is there a plan to adjust the lesson if formative assessments indicate that students are not ready for the lesson objective?	Specificity _____ Immediacy _____ Purposefulness _____ Constructiveness _____
	How will you record what you see students do and hear them say? How will you analyze these student data and complete error analysis?	Specificity _____ Immediacy _____ Purposefulness _____ Constructiveness _____
	What criteria will you use to determine if students are using critical thinking skills?	Specificity _____ Immediacy _____ Purposefulness _____ Constructiveness _____
	What feedback will you provide on the students' progress? How will your feedback support students in meeting the goals of the lesson?	Specificity _____ Immediacy _____ Purposefulness _____ Constructiveness _____
	How will your students be able to reflect on and self-assess their learning?	Specificity _____ Immediacy _____ Purposefulness _____ Constructiveness _____
	What assessment tools will be used to measure student progress? Have you created a measure or a rubric to document student progress? Are your assessments aligned to the lesson objective?	Specificity _____ Immediacy _____ Purposefulness _____ Constructiveness _____

(continued)

TABLE 9-3 (CONTINUED). EVALUATING LESSON PLANS

INSTRUCTIONAL PLANNING PROCESS

CENTRAL FOCUS	QUESTIONS TO CONSIDER WHEN EVALUATING YOUR EXPLICIT LESSON PLAN	WHICH DOMAIN OF FEEDBACK TO TEACH AND MODEL FEEDBACK?
4. Planning Classroom Environment		
Engagement	Does the lesson include strategies to motivate and engage students with hands-on learning?	Specificity _____ Immediacy _____ Purposefulness _____ Constructiveness _____
Learning activities	Are learning activities age appropriate and challenging to the students?	Specificity _____ Immediacy _____ Purposefulness _____ Constructiveness _____
5. Instructional Procedures		
Introduction	Does the lesson start with strategies to gain student attention and demonstrate the relevance of the lesson objective?	Specificity _____ Immediacy _____ Purposefulness _____ Constructiveness _____
	Did you communicate the learning goals and objectives to the students? Do the students know specifically what they are learning?	Specificity _____ Immediacy _____ Purposefulness _____ Constructiveness _____
	Is there a review of previous learning that is linked to the lesson objective?	Specificity _____ Immediacy _____ Purposefulness _____ Constructiveness _____
	Is there an explanation of behavioral expectations planned that are specific to the lesson activities?	Specificity _____ Immediacy _____ Purposefulness _____ Constructiveness _____
	Are there key teacher questions and prompts that will be used/planned?	Specificity _____ Immediacy _____ Purposefulness _____ Constructiveness _____
Lesson presentation (modeling)	Does the lesson plan pre-teach the vocabulary necessary to complete the academic requirements of the lesson? What do you want students to know, think, and do with the vocabulary?	Specificity _____ Immediacy _____ Purposefulness _____ Constructiveness _____
80% teacher talk, 20% student talk	Are evidenced-based strategies chosen that are the best practice for the lesson objective?	Specificity _____ Immediacy _____ Purposefulness _____ Constructiveness _____

(continued)

TABLE 9-3 (CONTINUED). EVALUATING LESSON PLANS

INSTRUCTIONAL PLANNING PROCESS

CENTRAL FOCUS	QUESTIONS TO CONSIDER WHEN EVALUATING YOUR EXPLICIT LESSON PLAN	WHICH DOMAIN OF FEEDBACK TO TEACH AND MODEL FEEDBACK?
5. Instructional Procedures (continued)		
	Are best practice instructional procedures specific to the disability present in the lesson?	Specificity _____ Immediacy _____ Purposefulness _____ Constructiveness _____
	Are specific think-alouds planned to verbalize the problem solving needed to understand the lesson objective?	Specificity _____ Immediacy _____ Purposefulness _____ Constructiveness _____
	Are opportunities provided to have students self-monitor their understanding/progress?	Specificity _____ Immediacy _____ Purposefulness _____ Constructiveness _____
	How did you model each step with examples and worked problems?	Specificity _____ Immediacy _____ Purposefulness _____ Constructiveness _____
	Are scaffolds present to break up the learning into chunks and provide a tool for students to do the lesson objective?	Specificity _____ Immediacy _____ Purposefulness _____ Constructiveness _____
Guided practice/ monitor practice	Are specific scaffolds in place so the teacher can gradually release the learning to the students?	Specificity _____ Immediacy _____ Purposefulness _____ Constructiveness _____
50% teacher talk, 50% student talk	Are students actively engaged in the lesson? Have you ensured that all students will have equitable opportunities to respond?	Specificity _____ Immediacy _____ Purposefulness _____ Constructiveness _____
	Is adequate practice of new skills sufficient to determine if students understand the overall concept being taught?	Specificity _____ Immediacy _____ Purposefulness _____ Constructiveness _____
	Are questions planned to check for student understanding?	Specificity _____ Immediacy _____ Purposefulness _____ Constructiveness _____
	What kind of explicit feedback of student progress is planned?	Specificity _____ Immediacy _____ Purposefulness _____ Constructiveness _____

(continued)

TABLE 9-3 (CONTINUED). EVALUATING LESSON PLANS		
INSTRUCTIONAL PLANNING PROCESS		
CENTRAL FOCUS	**QUESTIONS TO CONSIDER WHEN EVALUATING YOUR EXPLICIT LESSON PLAN**	**WHICH DOMAIN OF FEEDBACK TO TEACH AND MODEL FEEDBACK?**
5. Instructional Procedures (continued)		
	What kind of feedback is planned for student discourse discussion?	Specificity _____ Immediacy _____ Purposefulness _____ Constructiveness _____
	Adjustments made to instructional processes based on learner feedback?	Specificity _____ Immediacy _____ Purposefulness _____ Constructiveness _____
	What is your plan for error analysis?	Specificity _____ Immediacy _____ Purposefulness _____ Constructiveness _____
Independent practice	Is student self-evaluation of practice provided?	Specificity _____ Immediacy _____ Purposefulness _____ Constructiveness _____
20% teacher talk, 80% student talk	How did you ensure that mastery-level learning is accomplished?	Specificity _____ Immediacy _____ Purposefulness _____ Constructiveness _____
Closure	How will students articulate a review of the lesson objective and key points?	Specificity _____ Immediacy _____ Purposefulness _____ Constructiveness _____
10% teacher talk, 90% student talk	What did you do to ensure that students understand the importance/relevance of the lesson objective(s)?	Specificity _____ Immediacy _____ Purposefulness _____ Constructiveness _____
	What questions or prompts will you use to elicit student articulation of their learning?	Specificity _____ Immediacy _____ Purposefulness _____ Constructiveness _____
	Does the teacher's review meaningfully link to the upcoming lesson?	Specificity _____ Immediacy _____ Purposefulness _____ Constructiveness _____

(continued)

TABLE 9-3 (CONTINUED). EVALUATING LESSON PLANS

INSTRUCTIONAL PLANNING PROCESS

CENTRAL FOCUS	QUESTIONS TO CONSIDER WHEN EVALUATING YOUR EXPLICIT LESSON PLAN	WHICH DOMAIN OF FEEDBACK TO TEACH AND MODEL FEEDBACK?
6. Behavior Considerations		
CHAMPS	Conversation _____ Help _____ Activity _____ Movement _____ Participation _____ Success _____	Specificity _____ Immediacy _____ Purposefulness _____ Constructiveness _____
Social emotional learning	Is there an opportunity to embed social emotional learning into the lesson?	Specificity _____ Immediacy _____ Purposefulness _____ Constructiveness _____
Behavior intervention plan	What specific considerations need to be addressed in behavior intervention plans?	Specificity _____ Immediacy _____ Purposefulness _____ Constructiveness _____
7. Planning Materials		
Lesson materials	Did you only include worksheets that provide only low-level learning?	Specificity _____ Immediacy _____ Purposefulness _____ Constructiveness _____
	What did you do to differentiate lesson materials considering specific student needs?	Specificity _____ Immediacy _____ Purposefulness _____ Constructiveness _____
CHAMPS = Conversation, Help, Activity, Movement, Participation, Success; IEP = individualized education plan.		

Thinking back to the scenario that introduced Chapter 9, how can Dr. Mason use the lesson plan format to instruct the teacher candidates on how to give feedback (Table 9-4)? First, he begins his lesson on feedback with a clear statement of lesson goals and expectations. He gives the teacher candidates an advance organizer that today's class will focus on how we plan to give feedback in the lesson plan. He then provides step-by-step demonstrations of giving feedback by playing a video of a teacher candidate providing an explicit lesson on division and stopping the video at integral moments to demonstrate how a teacher can provide feedback that is timely, constructive, positive, and corrective. Next, he models immediate affirmative and corrective feedback when the teacher candidates identify each of the characteristics of feedback modeled by the instructor. Finally, he requires each teacher candidate to tag the "Glows and Grows" of three peers' lessons that were recorded and uploaded to GoReact (SpeakWorks, Inc.), with the focus on tagging the timely, constructive, positive, and corrective feedback displayed.

TABLE 9-4. SIUE SPE LESSON PLAN TEMPLATE

TEACHER CANDIDATE: _____

DATE: _____

PLANNING	
Prior knowledge: Identify what knowledge and skills students already need to have to be successful in this lesson (**include prerequisites**).	
Baseline data: Describe the instrument and procedures and include the actual data collected.	
Lesson objectives: Observable, measurable. **BOLD** your lesson in this sequence.	**Common core state standard** that aligns to your lesson objective.
1. 2. 3.	
During the lesson: Describe how you will assess student learning during guided practice (formative assessment).	
End of the lesson: How will you use the DAR to determine if they reached the lesson objective? Summative assessment. *Attach DAR to this lesson plan.*	
Communication skill: Identify ONE specific way the learners need to participate or demonstrate their learning.	
Accommodations/modifications from the IEP:	
Planned supports: (i.e., graphic organizer, sentence stems, manipulatives, strategy steps)	
Materials:	

(continued)

TABLE 9-4 (CONTINUED). SIUE SPE LESSON PLAN TEMPLATE

INSTRUCTIONAL PROCEDURES

PROCEDURAL STEPS	SCRIPTED TEACHER EXPLANATIONS AND QUESTIONS	SPECIFIC/POSITIVE/ CONSTRUCTIVE FEEDBACK GIVEN
Introduction: 1. Engage/review 2. CHAMPS 3. Introduce lesson objective 4. Real-life application/rationale		
Modeling: 1. Step-by-step demonstration 2. Think-alouds/explanations 3. CHAMPS (if behavioral expectations change)		
Guided practice: 1. Evidence of gradual release of learning 2. MOTR-choral responses, partner, small group, etc. 3. Remediation for students who struggle 4. CHAMPS (if behavioral expectations change)		
Independent practice: 1. Student demonstration of new knowledge/skill 2. Collect data on DAR 3. CHAMPS (if behavioral expectations change)		
Conclusion: 1. Students summarize learning and provide examples 2. Revisit rationale (student input as appropriate) 3. Make connection to next lesson in sequence		

CHAMPS = Conversation, Help, Activity, Movement, Participation, Success; DAR = Diagnostic Assessments of Reading; IEP = individualized education plan; MOTR = multiple opportunities to respond; SIUE = Southern Illinois University Edwardsville; SPE = special education.

Each of the courses in special education preparation programs present opportunities to teach how to give feedback. As we learned in Chapter 1, adult learners need opportunities to understand and restructure their thinking or beliefs related to their performance, knowledge, or skills. Assignments like those provided previously offer opportunities for instructors to give and model immediate and purposeful feedback.

Now, let us turn to how instructors can give specific and constructive feedback. In Chapter 5, we learned how different technologies can be utilized to provide special education teacher candidates. The ability for teacher candidates to upload videos of themselves teaching using GoReact or Sibme (Dos Terra Limited Liability Company) allows teacher candidates to reflect on their teaching and get feedback from their instructor and peers. The military has long used a process called After-Action Review (AAR; Smith & Allen, 1994) to evaluate performance. An AAR is a structured review process for analyzing what happened, why it happened, and how it can be done differently by the participants. An AAR is centered on the following four questions: (a) What was expected to happen? (b) What actually occurred? (c) What went well and why? and (d) What can be improved and how? As we remember from Hattie and Timperley (2007), similar questions can guide our feedback: (a) Where am I going? (b) How am I going? and (c) Where to next? Those questions provide instructors an opportunity to provide positive and nonjudgmental feedback in the video lessons. When we involve special education teacher candidates to self-evaluate and interact by giving constructive feedback to their peers, a shared understanding of the learning goal is developed by the instructor. Take for example the findings from TeachLivE (University of Central Florida) research that often employs an AAR. Peterson (2014) found in her research review that AAR improved the quality and clarity of instruction because teacher candidates were able to explore their beliefs about the lesson they taught and deepen their understanding of the instructional process. Petersen determined the effect that feedback has on teacher candidate performance of delivering the evidenced-based practice of giving multiple opportunities to respond after practicing in TeachLivE with an AAR. She concluded that participants felt they were more thoughtful during instruction. This demonstrates how thoughtful reflection and guiding questions can help teacher candidates improve their instructional prowess.

When instructors use a backward design to create opportunities to give, exhibit, and teach feedback, teacher candidates learn not only specific teaching skills in the instructional process but also how they can give feedback to the K-12 students they teach.

TABLE 9-5. SPOTLIGHT ON ADULT LEARNING			
SPECIFICITY	**IMMEDIACY**	**PURPOSEFULNESS**	**CONSTRUCTIVENESS**
Is the feedback language being taught consistent with what is being delivered? Are adult learners' mental models about feedback being respected as part of their prior experience? Do these mental models need to be reconstructed with life-related, developmental feedback delivery tasks?	Does the timing of the feedback respect the self-concept of the learner? Does the adult learner need to engage in self-correction before receiving feedback from an instructor?	Do adult learners understand the role that progress plays in feedback? Is there well-defined what, why, and how, so that the adult learning theory principle "need to know" is met? Is the purpose of the feedback grounded in life-related, developmental tasks?	What role do adult learners have in developing their own language and context for delivering feedback? How is the autonomy and motivation of adult learners respected in the feedback they receive and are taught to give?

SPOTLIGHT ON ADULT LEARNING

The practical information for teaching feedback delivered in this chapter emphasizes not only the adult learning principle of need to know but also their readiness to learn and their orientation to learning. When teaching how to give feedback, instructors should deliver life-related, developmental tasks to the teacher candidates that permit them to learn, practice, and perfect the skill of giving feedback to their K-12 students. The G.E.T. Model informs instructors' professional practice of explicitly teaching how to give effective feedback so that special education teacher candidates can apply what they are learning in a way that is problem-centered and contextual (Table 9-5).

POSSIBLE BARRIERS TO USING THIS TYPE OF FEEDBACK

When considering the possible barriers to teaching feedback, we must consider Knowles' (1998) principles of adult learning, especially *need to know*. The teacher candidates have a frame of reference about feedback, based on their own experiences getting feedback. Instructors must consider that teacher candidate identity, assumptions, and social role may impact how they interpret the feedback they see modeled in the instructional process.

In addition, the time required for instructors to use a backward design to provide opportunities for teacher candidates to get, model, and teach feedback in the instructional process might be a possible barrier. Instructors in teacher preparation have experienced much change in their job duties and expectations on their teaching due to increasing government intervention, more stringent licensure requirements, and an expanding research base in teacher preparation. The idea of change fatigue may hinder instructors, as they are in endless improvement cycles.

Another possible barrier to teaching feedback in instruction is that the term *feedback* and related terms are interpreted differently by instructors in the same department, leading the teacher candidates to experience different expectations in the instructional process. Even when interpretations are clear in one course or in interactions with one instructor, they vary across instructors and courses.

And, as explored in Chapter 8, key terms are used differently by different agencies and organizations that participate in the training and credentialing of teachers.

A third barrier to feedback in the instructional process is the difference between teaching and modeling. These terms have different meanings based on the assignment. Teacher candidates early in their learning continuum are emerging teacher candidates. The expectations for them to display the type of feedback that moves K-12 students with disabilities to higher levels of achievement must be scaffolded as they move through their preparation program. The need for a cohesive program of study that situates the expectations for feedback must be developed by program faculty for clear expectations and increasing levels of skill attainment.

PRACTICAL APPLICATION

In this section, we offer an assignment to illustrate how technology can be used to teach feedback that explicitly requires teacher candidates to understand why feedback is an essential element in teaching. Instructors must be strategic in communicating how to use feedback to increase K-12 student outcomes. In this assignment, special education teacher candidates in their first practicum setting are to reflect on how the classroom environment can mediate a positive learning experience for students with disabilities. The teacher candidate completes a video that describes the learning environment and completes a checklist about the classroom environment considerations that were taught in the classroom management course taken in the same semester as the practicum. A cycle of feedback and reflection is encouraged by the faculty supervisor, requiring the teacher candidate to review the video with a checklist and then getting feedback via timestamps in GoReact. The teacher candidate then considers the faculty supervisor's feedback and designs their future classroom environment.

GoReact Video Assignment #1

Goal

The purpose of this assignment is to introduce your faculty supervisor to your practicum setting and heighten your awareness of the classroom, including the following: (a) its physical surroundings, (b) emotional climate, (c) cultural responsiveness, and (d) technology integration. You should consider these setting characteristics through the lens of whether the environment encourages or inhibits interaction and learning for students with disabilities. Please use the checklist (Table 9-6) to evaluate the physical environment of your placement setting.

Assignment Guidelines

Create a 5- to 7-minute video describing what you want the instructor to notice about the classroom environment. Think of yourself as a tour guide for an "exotic destination" by describing in detail the different aspects of the classroom. Upload your video to GoReact and submit the checklist about your classroom setting.

Reflection

The faculty supervisor will watch your video with the checklist you submitted. You will review the feedback given in GoReact timestamps and provide a response about what you would change to encourage interaction and learning for students with disabilities.

Because the teacher candidates are in their first semester of the program, the gradual release of responsibility for reflection and feedback are scaffolded with a checklist format and prompting questions. The instructor plans for timely and specific feedback by providing feedback via timestamps in GoReact. The feedback is purposeful, requiring the teacher candidate to review the timestamp feedback to move toward the goal of creating a positive classroom environment. The feedback is constructive as it moves the teacher candidate to "construct" new meaning about the positive classroom environment.

TABLE 9-6. VIDEO DEVELOPMENT CHECKLIST

√	CATEGORY	DETAIL
☐	Student description	Number of students, gender/age, race/ethnicity, disability categories, general functioning level (academic or functional)
☐	Physical surroundings	**Setting**: physical layout, ease of transitions, flow of students, organization of where things occur (whole group, small group, individual)
☐		**Schedule**: how much time students spend in this space, how often students are out of the classroom (whole group, small group, individual); include tiered support routines
☐	Emotional climate	**Expectations**: classroom rules that are developmentally appropriate and include prosocial behaviors

		Positive Behavior Supports	
		Increase Positive Behaviors	**Decrease Negative Behaviors**
		• Developmentally appropriate	• Addresses high-frequency behaviors
		• Tied to class rules	• Differentiates for various problem behaviors
		• Supports positive teacher-student interactions	• Respects the value of the student
		• Frequent student feedback (verbal and nonverbal)	• Seeks to understand the cause of the behavior
		• Imparts value to the student	• Avoids power struggles

√	CATEGORY	DETAIL
☐	Cultural responsiveness	How is cultural diversity represented visually? Verbally? How are students encouraged to explore different cultures and celebrate differences?
☐	Technology integration	How is technology included? What visual cues are there for instruction and classroom management? How are music, art, and movement used? What evidence is there that students experience information and instruction in a variety of ways?
☐	Your choice	What do you think is really great about your practicum setting?

The following questions are provided to guide your review and reflection in the Authentic Example that follows, contributed by Katie Martin Miller, PhD.

- In this example, how does the instructor apply knowledge of teaching feedback? Reflect.
- Note where explicit instruction in teaching feedback is, or could be, incorporated to teach feedback.
- Can you identify one activity where added explicit instruction in teaching feedback to preservice special educators could be addressed?

Authentic Example

Contributed by
Katie Martin Miller, PhD

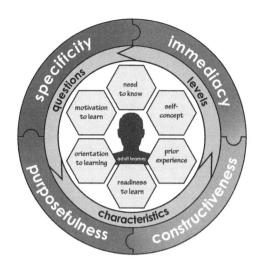

1. Course Details

EEX 4250: Reading Instruction for Special Education. The assignment on direct instruction lesson plans is taught in the course. The EEX 4250 course focuses on the acquisition of knowledge and skills associated with instructing students who experience mild to moderate problems in learning how to become fluent independent readers. The emphasis is on K-12 students in exceptional student education and reading instruction in the areas of phonological awareness, word identification, vocabulary, fluency, and reading comprehension. In addition, this course is the first in which teacher candidates are writing detailed lesson plans on the direct instruction approach to teaching reading interventions. The lesson plan itself is based on Minskoff's (2005) book *Teaching Reading to Struggling Learners*. In addition, they use the Bursuck and Damer (2015) book for more direct instruction routines as well as for knowledge about reading and struggling readers.

2. Learning Objectives

Demonstrate knowledge of the direct instruction model for teaching decoding.

3. Assignment Description

Teacher candidates must write a series of intervention lesson plans focused on one of the five areas of reading (phonics, phonemic awareness, fluency, comprehension, and vocabulary). They align their lessons to one of three fictional studies provided for them.

TABLE 9-7. LESSON PLAN CHECKLIST

☐ Did I include the current level of performance for the current lesson?
☐ Did I use appropriate standard(s)?
☐ Is my objective clear and written in measurable terms?
☐ Does my assessment align to my objective?
☐ Did I include my assessment document (e.g., checklist)?
☐ Did I include an advance organizer (LIP)?
☐ Is modeling included?
☐ Is guided practice included?
☐ Is my independent practice clearly written?
☐ Do I have spelling or grammar errors?

The lesson planning process is discussed in class and is focused on a specific area in reading. Teacher candidates refer to the case study they chose as they identify areas of strength and need for their student. When they have identified an area of specific need, such as phonics, the instructor models an entire direct instruction lesson plan. After the lesson, the instructor shows the lesson plan that was modeled with each component labeled. The components included in this lesson are the advance organizer using LIP (**L**inks to previously learned material, **I**dentifies the objective, and states the **P**urpose of the lesson), modeling, guided practice, and independent practice and assessment.

Next, the instructor and teacher candidates select a routine from the Bursuck and Damer (2015) text, which is aligned to the Minskoff (2005) direct instruction model. The instructor models how to choose a skill area that their case study student needs. The planning process demonstrates how to plan objectives and assessment. The teacher candidate then selects a skill, objective, and, finally, their assessment. The instructor then models how to give feedback to their peers. The teacher candidates in the class then give peer-to-peer feedback. While they are giving peer-to-peer feedback, the instructor is providing feedback to individual teacher candidates regarding their objectives and assessment.

4. Evaluation Criteria

After teacher candidates receive feedback from their peers, they work outside of the classroom setting to structure their lesson plans. In the next class, they share their lesson plans. They use a checklist (Table 9-7) to assess their own work and their peers', and the instructor uses the same checklist to provide feedback. Their final grade is determined using the rubric (Table 9-8).

TABLE 9-8. LESSON PLAN RUBRIC

CRITERIA	SATISFACTORY: 3 POINTS	EMERGING: 2 POINTS	UNSATISFACTORY: 1 POINT	NO ATTEMPT: 0 POINTS
Standards, objective, and current levels	A specific state standard is identified and appropriate for the grade level and content area. The objective states the student's outcome of the lesson. It is measurable and includes what the student will be able to do, under what condition, and at what criterion. Current levels: The content the students are learning in the curriculum is clearly articulated, as it is a snapshot of their current abilities, which is tied to the objective of the current lesson.	A specific state standard is identified and appropriate for the content area. The objective is stated but not clearly measurable. The current levels are stated in general terms and aligned to the objective.	A specific state standard is not identified or is not at the appropriate level for the group of students. The current levels are vague or missing.	Student failed to submit this component of the assignment.

(continued)

TABLE 9-8 (CONTINUED). LESSON PLAN RUBRIC

CRITERIA	SATISFACTORY: 3 POINTS	EMERGING: 2 POINTS	UNSATISFACTORY: 1 POINT	NO ATTEMPT: 0 POINTS
Body of lesson, including advance organizer, modeling, guided practice, and independent practice	Advance organizer is provided, with specific statements, including the LIP. A step-by-step approach for presenting information and incorporation of the "I do, we do, you do" instructional cycle is clear. Engagement strategies and opportunities to respond are provided. The student(s) are able to practice skills or objectives independently.	Advance organizer is included but components are vague. The majority of components are included for the "I do, we do, you do" cycle. Some engagement strategies and opportunities to respond are included.	Advance organizer statement is missing and/or may be vague. Components of the "I do, we do, you do" instructional cycle are missing or incomplete. Engagement strategies and/or opportunities to respond are incomplete or missing.	Student failed to submit this component of the assignment.
Assessment components	The assessment is aligned to the objective and measures the construct intended. A checklist or some type of tracking system is included.	Assessment is aligned to objective and measures the construct intended but may be vague or confusing. Checklist or tracking system is included but may not be clear.	Assessment is missing or does not align to the objective. Checklist or tracking system is not included.	Student failed to submit this component of the assignment.
Grammar, punctuation, and usage	No spelling/grammatical errors.	No more than 3 spelling/grammatical errors.	More than 4 spelling/grammatical errors.	The plan includes so many spelling and grammatical errors that they interfere with meaning.

5. *Additional Details*

Two course texts are important to this assignment. Please review Minskoff (2005) and Bursuck and Damer (2015) for additional details about reading content to support feedback and support in constructing the lesson plans.

6. *Feedback Reflection*

Overall, this assignment works, as the construct of lesson planning is being modeled for teacher candidates through the same lesson planning process they will utilize. Feedback is given across three levels—instructor to teacher candidate, peer to peer, and self-assessment. This helps teacher candidates to construct their lessons appropriately and learn how to give feedback to one another as they will be giving feedback to their K-12 students. It also provides time for them to reflect on their own lesson planning as they utilize the checklist. Teacher candidates are more comfortable receiving feedback from a peer before turning in their feedback to the instructor for a final grade.

SUMMARY

This chapter explored teaching feedback in the instructional process. Instructors must model and teach the instructional skills we want teacher candidates to display when they someday teach in their own classrooms. Instructors teach feedback by giving clear descriptions and demonstrations of feedback skills, followed by supported practice in teacher preparation courses. Research suggests that adult learners benefit from performing tasks that are goal-oriented and from exploring expected instructional skills firsthand and learn from their mistakes. Therefore, special education teacher preparation instructors must provide opportunities for teacher candidates to develop an intrinsic understanding of feedback and practice instructional feedback skills. Instructors must provide feedback to adult learners for them to evaluate the quality of the learning experience and make adjustments.

OPPORTUNITY FOR GOING DEEPER

The following are resources to support deeper learning on the concepts reflected in Chapter 9:

- Quality math instruction. The IRIS Center's (Peabody College Vanderbilt University) "High-Quality Mathematics Instruction: What Teachers Should Know" module includes videos depicting a standards-based curriculum and evidence-based practice; both are components of high-quality mathematics instruction. https://iris.peabody.vanderbilt.edu/module/math/#content
- Inclusion. The SWiFT Education Center's resource page of Inclusive Academic Instruction provides foundational resources for understanding Response to Intervention and implementing MTSS (multi-tiered system of support). http://guide.swiftschools.org/multi-tiered-system-of-support/inclusive-academic-instruction
- Gradual release of responsibility. Douglas Fisher and Nancy Frey's (2014) *Better Learning Through Structured Teaching: A Framework for the Gradual Release of Responsibility* will support continued reflection on your teaching.
- Explicit instruction. Anita Archer and Charles A. Hughes provide video examples of explicit instruction and video guide, with focused questions to answer while watching the video. https://explicitinstruction.org/anita-l-archer-phd/
- High-leverage practices. The CEEDAR Center provides video representations of the high-leverage practices in instruction, including feedback. https://highleveragepractices.org/701-2-2/

REFERENCES

Archer, A. L., & Hughes, C. A. (2011). *Explicit instruction: Effective and efficient teaching*. Guilford Press.

Bransford, J. D., Brown, A. L., & Cocking, R. R. (Eds.). (2000). *How people learn: Brain, mind, experience, and school*. National Academy Press.

Brophy, J., & Good, T. (1986). Teacher behavior and student achievement. In M. C. Wittrock (Ed.), *Handbook of research on teaching* (3rd ed., pp. 328-375). McMillan.

Bursuck, W. D., & Damer, M. (2015). *Teaching reading to students who are at risk or have disabilities: A multi-tier, RTI approach* (3rd ed.). Pearson.

Byrnes, J. P. (1996). *Cognitive development and learning in instructional contexts*. Allyn & Bacon.

Christenson, S. L., Ysseldyke, J. E., & Thurlow, M. L. (1989). Critical instructional factors for students with mild handicaps: An integrative review. *Remedial and Special Education, 10*(5), 21-31. https://doi.org/10.1177/074193258901000505.

Gersten, R., Schiller, E. P., Vaughn, S. (Eds.). (2000). *Contemporary special education research*. Lawrence Erlbaum Associates.

Hattie, J., & Timperley, H. (2007). The power of feedback. *Review of Educational Research, 77*(1), 81-112. https://doi.org/10.3102/003465430298487

Hattie, J., & Yates, G. (2014). *Visible learning and the science of how we learn*. Routledge.

Knowles, M. S., Holton, E. F., & Swanson, R. A. (1998). *The adult learner* (5th ed.). Gulf.

Machand-Martella, N. E., Slocum, T. A., & Martella, R. (2004). *Introduction to direct instruction*. Pearson.

Minskoff, E. (2005). *Teaching reading to struggling learners*. Brookes Publishing.

Pearson, P. D., & Gallagher, M. C. (1983). The instruction of reading comprehension. *Contemporary Educational Psychology, 8*(3), 317-344.

Peterson, M. B. (2014). *Pre-service special education teachers' frequency of opportunities to respond in the TeachLivE virtual classroom* [Doctoral dissertation, Texas Women's University]. https://www.proquest.com/docview/1552714919

Rosenshine, B. (1997, March 28). The case for explicit, teacher-led, cognitive strategy instruction [Conference presentation]. Annual Meeting of the American Educational Research Association, Chicago, IL. http://www.formapex.com/telechargementpublic/rosenshine1997a.pdf

Rosenshine, B., & Stevens, R. (1986). Teaching functions. In M. C. Wittrock (Ed.), *Handbook of research on teaching* (3rd ed., pp. 376-391). Macmillan.

Simmons, D. C., Fuchs, L. S., Fuchs, D., Mathes, P., Hodge, J. P. (1995). Effects of explicit teaching and peer tutoring on the reading achievement of learning-disabled and low-performing students in regular classrooms. *The Elementary School Journal, 95*(5), 387-408.

Smith, R., & Allen, G. (1994). After action review in military training simulations. In M. S. Manivannan, & J. D. Tew (Eds.), *Proceedings of the 26th conference on winter simulation* (pp. 845-849). Society for Computer Simulation International.

Swanson, H. L. (2001). Searching for the best model for instructing students with learning disabilities. *Focus on Exceptional Children, 34*(2), 1-14.

Swanson, H. L., & Deshler, D. (2003). Instructing adolescents with learning disabilities: Converting a meta-analysis to practice. *Journal of Learning Disabilities, 36*(2), 124-135. https://doi.org/10.1177/002221940303600205

Thorndike, E. L. (1905). *The elements of psychology*. A. G. Seiler. https://doi.org/10.1037/10881-000

Thorndike, E. L. (1913). *Educational psychology* (Vols. 1 & 2). Columbia University Press.

Thorndike, E. L. (1931). *Human learning*. Century.

Teaching Feedback in Assessment

Feedback Scenario

Have you ever had one of those moments when you wonder whether what you are teaching in your courses in special education bridges research to practice? Dr. Hernandez was having one of those moments. He has designed specific assignments that address all facets of individualized assessment in special education—screening and identification, eligibility and diagnosis, individualized education plan (IEP) development and placement, instructional planning, and evaluating K-12 student progress. His ultimate goal was to have teacher candidates design, facilitate, and support a comprehensive, multidisciplinary evaluation process, using unbiased assessment measures. Yet, during class discussions and samples of teacher candidates' work, he saw a juxtaposition between what he was teaching in his assessment course and what the teacher candidates were experiencing in the field. At the foundation, a multidisciplinary evaluation process was in place, but he was not seeing how assessment was driving individualized instruction. In addition, the special education teacher candidates at his university consistently received the lowest scores on the Teacher Performance Assessment (edTPA) in Task 3: providing feedback to the focus learner that considers their strengths and continuing needs. They also struggled with the edTPA requirements to provide feedback to the focus learner that moved the learner to higher levels of achievement. Furthermore, teacher candidates were writing practice IEP goals and objectives based only on quarterly global progress monitoring measures, and they were not able to create classroom assessments that determine prerequisite skills for academic decision-making. In discussions with his teacher candidates about their field experiences, it appeared that special education assessment had evolved from measures to ensure that K-12 students with disabilities make meaningful and appropriately ambitious progress to more of a necessary evil so that the IEP was in compliance. Luckily, the Supreme Court agreed with Dr. Hernandez when ruling in the *Endrew F. v. Douglas County School District* (2017)! Dr. Hernandez knew he needed to consider new ways to move the special education teacher candidates to higher

Elford, M. D., Smith, H. H., & James, S.
GET Feedback: Giving, Exhibiting, and Teaching Feedback in
Special Education Teacher Preparation (pp. 193-209).
© 2022 SLACK Incorporated.

TABLE 10-1. GRAPHIC ORGANIZER		
KNOW (WHAT)	**UNDERSTAND (WHY)**	**DEMONSTRATE (HOW)**
What the research on feedback in assessment suggests, especially for adult learners.	Why teaching feedback in assessment is necessary in special education teacher preparation.	How to teach feedback that reflects what effective feedback is and how to use it in assessment.
APPLY (TAKE ACTION)		
Apply strategies for instructional feedback in course design, activities, and assignments.		

levels of understanding pertaining to assessment. He was reinforced in his goal to implement best practices in special education assessment and increase the opportunities for the special education teacher candidates to collect multiple forms of data, analyze patterns of performance, evaluate to determine the strengths and needs of K-12 students with disabilities, determine the impact that disability has on the K-12 student, and recommend a program of individualized instruction.

CHAPTER OBJECTIVES

This chapter builds on considering the knowledge and instructional skills of feedback in special education teacher preparation and addresses teaching feedback as a part of assessment. As we will discuss, in special education teacher preparation, there is the need to **teach** clear connections to how assessment uses feedback to move K-12 students with disabilities to higher levels of academic achievement. This chapter will describe research on the assessment feedback approaches and why feedback in assessment is crucial. This chapter will also demonstrate how to provide feedback on assessments, with examples and prompts to take action.

Feedback is heavily tied to assessment in the Council for Exceptional Children (CEC; 2015) standards and the High-Leverage Practices (McLeskey et al., 2017). Explicit instruction, the edTPA, and the Candidate Preservice Assessment of Student Teaching (CPAST) require teacher candidates to provide feedback to K-12 students on assessment measures. Research suggests that adult learners benefit from learning how to provide feedback compared with learners using performance-based formative and summative measures. The common practice in special education has long supported K-12 students monitoring their performance and providing corrective feedback as the hallmark of effective instructional practice. Therefore, special education teacher preparation instructors must model and teach how to give feedback on assessments while also recognizing the learning needs of adult students.

After reading this chapter you will **know** and **understand** these concepts and have the opportunity to **demonstrate** and **apply** your knowledge (Table 10-1).

DESCRIBE AND DEFINE

Know

The research on feedback in assessment, especially for adult learners, suggests that feedback must engage learners in the content for meaning and deep learning (Hattie & Timperley, 2007). Adult learners may have anxiety about assessments and low self-efficacy understanding the academic, intellectual, psychological, emotional, perceptual, language, cognitive, and medical assessments besides the statistical language of assessment measures. Predominantly, the largest population of teacher candidates in special education teacher preparation programs are adult learners who were born between 1980 and 2000, called Generation Me. This generation is sometimes called Generation Y, the Peter Pan Generation, or the Boomerang Generation (Abbott, 2019). Teacher candidates from this generation are more confident in their technology savviness, are curious, and are accustomed to instant gratification. However, the age of most special education faculty is between 41 and 65 years, called Baby Boomers and Generation X, or those born between 1945 and 1979. The generational differences from these various eras of learners influence feedback cycles in special education assessment courses. College faculty from these eras grew up valuing competition, ambition, and education; thus conflict or tension can be exhibited between them and the teacher candidates they teach from Generation Me (Howe & Strauss, 2007; Sandeen, 2008). Twenge (2014) studied age and birth differences between generations of learners. She described the learners of Generation Me valuing teamwork instead of competition and prefer interactive learning opportunities instead of personal ambition to get the highest grade on an assignment. Generation Me teacher candidates prefer group activities that are relevant to what they already know and what they are experiencing in their own lives. Special education assessment courses provide prime opportunities for learning that develop the knowledge, skills, and values of special education assessment with these kinds of direct experiences.

Many suggestions exist about how to appeal to the special education teacher candidates in the assessment course. One idea is to start with a diagnostic performance assessment, such as a short quiz or mini assignment, to reveal teacher candidates' prior knowledge of assessment for the course lectures to be relevant (Benassi et al., 2014). Alternatively, instructors can use analogies and examples that connect new material to adult students' everyday knowledge so that it is relevant to them (Benassi et al., 2014). Another idea to encourage teacher candidates to engage in deep learning about the content is an assignment that requires them to assess the impact of instructional methods and prerequisite skills of assessment by collaboratively designing a daily assessment record for each topic presented in the special education assessment course. The process of creating the daily assessment record for the instructional goals for each week's class that includes the prerequisite knowledge required, provides teacher candidates with repeated and distributed practice built into the course structure. Finally, an assignment that could be efficiently added in a special education assessment course could include a small-group analysis of a comprehensive assessment report and gradually release teacher candidates to individually complete each section of this kind of report in their field experiences with a K-12 student with a disability. If no students are available or permission is not given, then using technology, such as virtual simulation environments like Mursion, to assess a student's "avatar" with a scenario that incorporates specific error patterns could be an alternative. All these examples of possible assignments in a special education assessment course help teacher candidates to build their self-efficacy for comprehensive assessments and provides them with varied opportunities for instructors to provide feedback on the levels of feedback, task, process, and self-regulation. Considering that most teacher candidates prefer frequent feedback, one must consider the learners' characteristics in the instructional design of content in the assessment course and at what levels of feedback you should engineer.

Twenge (2014) suggested specific strategies that instructors can employ for teaching special education teacher candidates from Generation Me, including frequent and honest feedback on performance and the need for explanation on why assignments are important. As we remember from Chapter 1, feedback that addresses attributes of quality or effort only transmits a judgment that can be misinterpreted. Generation Me teacher candidates may have spent only a few minutes on any one assignment and are likely multitasking as well as attending to social media and instant messaging while completing the assignment, so when instructors give feedback on quality or effort, the students do not value the feedback (Twenge, 2014). Generation Me teacher candidates often have inflated self-perceptions because grades were the primary form of feedback they received in their early educational experiences; thus, increasing formative feedback within special education assessment assignments is needed to move them to higher levels of understanding.

Understand

Special education assessment is a multifaceted learning opportunity for special education teacher candidates. Knowledge requirements in special education assessment range from formal standardized testing to functional behavioral testing to curriculum-based measures. Considering these multiple forms of assessment, special education teacher candidates are required to understand the screening and identification process to identify K-12 students who may be experiencing learning problems and diagnosing whether a child has a disability and is eligible for special education services. In addition, assessment is used in IEP development and placement as well as for further instructional planning and evaluation of student progress. At each point in this special education assessment process, instructors have opportunities to provide experiential learning and feedback to teacher candidates.

The CEC professional standards for initial teacher preparation require special education teacher candidates to use multiple forms of assessment to make placement and instructional decisions in collaboration with other service providers (CEC, 2015). Specifically, in the CEC standards for assessment, feedback is provided to students with exceptionalities to move them toward quality learning and performance. In addition, the High-Leverage Practices (HLPs) in the assessment domain assert that educational assessment is the foundation of special education and requires teachers to understand that multiple assessment sources to determine students with disabilities, strengths, and needs are necessary to provide specially designed instruction collaboratively with other service providers and monitor progress to specific goals (McLeskey et al., 2017). Although feedback in the HLPs is not specifically stated, assessment measures are to be part of discussions with students to design instructional programs; thus, feedback is inferred as you conference with the student. Furthermore, feedback is foundational as an instructional practice in explicit instruction and the edTPA Task 3 prompts, and it is an important "look fors" in the CPAST pedagogy and instruction subscales. Therefore, it is critical for instructors to teach special education candidates how to give feedback on assessment performance and to understand the feedback given to them on assessment tasks within special education teacher preparation courses.

Demonstrate

Instructors have multiple opportunities to teach special education teacher candidates feedback that reflects what effective feedback is and how to use feedback in the assessment process. As this book has established in the G.E.T. Model, the four domains of effective feedback are specificity, immediacy, purposefulness, and constructiveness. Each of these domains of effective feedback can be taught and modeled by instructors in special education teacher preparation in the assessment coursework.

Screening and Identification

In the screening and identification of special education individualized assessment, teacher candidates are taught the process to screen children and identify those who may be experiencing delays or learning problems. Instructors can teach the idea of appropriately timed feedback to prompt teacher candidates to higher levels of goal attainment. In schools, when K-12 students who are experiencing behavioral and/or learning problems are screened, often the student may feel anxious about their performance and have lower levels of self-efficacy unless timely and positive feedback is given. Just like the student being screened, special education teacher candidates need appropriately timed feedback to motivate them. Instructors can use small quizzes or mini assignments at the beginning or end of any class about the assessment topic taught that day and give the teacher candidate immediate feedback on what areas they need to focus their attention in future tasks. This can be done with learning game apps such as Kahoot, Poll Everywhere, or Quizlet (refer to the Going Deeper section). These frequent formative assessments help the adult learner understand "*How am I going?*" and understand the processes involved in the screening and identification of students with suspected behavioral or learning problems.

Eligibility and Diagnosis

The next step in the special education individualized assessment process is determining whether a child has a disability and is eligible for special education services, as well as to diagnose the specific nature of the K-12 student's problems or disability. Using team or group activities, instructors can teach purposeful feedback. Purposeful feedback in the G.E.T. Model focuses on the processes to learn comprehensive and unbiased assessment techniques. Giving special education teacher candidates actionable steps, broken into achievable chunks toward the goal of understanding all the types of assessments that might be used in a comprehensive evaluation, is one assignment that could be done in an assessment course. The types of assessments—academic, intellectual, psychological, emotional, perceptual, language, cognitive, and medical—are divided among the teacher candidates in groups of eight for each kind of assessment and then a jigsaw approach is used to understand each type of assessment (see Chapter 7 for more information on jigsaws). A set of closed responses are given to each teacher candidate to fill in the specific characteristics of that type of assessment. The teacher candidates then break into homogeneous groups of each type of assessment and study the characteristics and measurement specifics, such as testing components and assurances, for validity used in the evaluation. During this fact-finding to fill in the closed-response fact sheet, the instructor circulates around the room to answer questions and give specific feedback that identifies the language that is specific to the type of assessment and uses language that clearly states the learning goal. The instructor will also provide specific feedback to teacher candidates that describes where the students must go to achieve the goal of the type of assessments. Then the teacher candidates break into heterogeneous groups to share with each other all eight types of assessment. The instructor circulates to provide constructive feedback to the groups to move the teacher candidates forward in constructing a new learning goal—applying this knowledge to the identification of specific disability categories. This jigsaw and extension of the different types of assessment domains to disability categories provide opportunities for instructors to model three domains of the G.E.T. Model: specificity, purposeful, and constructive feedback. They allow the teacher candidate to ask *Where am I going?*, *How am I going?*, and *Where do I go next?* Specificity reminds us to support teacher candidates in setting goals to understand special education assessment and use language that is easily understood when we give feedback that is positive and nonjudgmental. Purposeful feedback develops a shared understanding of how the teacher candidate is feeling about the assignment, the types of assessment measures, and their development as a professional on a multidisciplinary evaluation team. Constructiveness provides an opportunity to give feedback that can be used intrinsically for teacher candidates to apply what they know to other contexts. Instructors can use these domains when planning how they will give feedback in the course design and orchestrate when feedback is needed to move the teacher candidates to higher levels of achievement in special education assessment.

IEP Development and Placement

The next phase of the individualized assessment process in special education is to develop an IEP and consider placement in the least restrictive environment. Instructors in assessment courses usually focus on the scores from diagnostic measures and have teacher candidates use these scores to write IEP goals and objectives, with plans for measuring each objective quarterly. Many examples of IEP projects that were presented in previous chapters in this book can be chosen. The types of effective feedback that instructors can teach and model for special education teacher candidates are informed by all four domains of the G.E.T. Model (specificity, immediacy, purposefulness, and constructiveness). Writing IEP goals and objectives based on individual student performance on a variety of educational measures provide opportunities for faculty to teach and model specific feedback on writing goals and objectives by using descriptive language so that they are observable and measurable, which are the hallmarks of a good goal and objective. Teacher candidates learn from the feedback we give them on how to make the goal understandable so the parent can clearly understand the individualized program their child is receiving, based on the areas of needs from the special education comprehensive evaluation. The domain of immediacy is taught and modeled by instructors when they build the distributed practice of assessment by choosing assessment measures and creating daily assessment records that will evaluate the IEP goals and objectives. The timing of the feedback is critical to the learners as they create the IEP goals and objectives so they do not write goals and objectives that are ambiguous and thus not measurable as they describe the educational behaviors measured. Purposefulness in the IEP development is present when instructors focus on the process to consider assessment data to create IEP goals and objectives and provide feedback that is actionable for the teacher candidate. Giving teacher candidates a purpose drives them as they write an entire IEP and participate in IEP team meetings in other classes in their special education program. Finally, writing IEP goals and objectives tied to assessment information gives instructors opportunities for constructive feedback, as it helps the teacher candidate to move from their existing knowledge of assessment to their new identity as a multidisciplinary evaluation team member who will interpret assessment information to formulate an IEP and to make decisions about placement for the student with a disability.

Instructional Planning

The next step in the special education assessment process is to develop and plan instruction that is appropriate to the child's special needs. Chapter 9 detailed how instructors can teach feedback. However, as instructors of assessment, we need to consider how to give feedback so we do not feel like Dr. Hernandez in the scenario that started this chapter. He was concerned that teacher candidates at his university scored lower on the Task 3 assessment rubrics because they had difficulties articulating how they provide feedback that moved the learner to higher levels of achievement. Constructive feedback characteristics that include focusing on one or more strengths and at least one suggestion for improvement are self-referenced and differentiated. Instructors have an opportunity in the assessment course to teach and model constructive feedback when they plan what feedback to give with each assessment assignment. Instructors can intentionally give feedback that possesses each of these characteristics of constructive feedback and then require teacher candidates to describe one or more strengths and at least one suggestion for improvement as part of the curriculum-based measurement (CBM) assessment report.

Evaluation

The last step in the special education assessment process is to evaluate student progress. Instructors have opportunities to teach how to give specific and immediate feedback when teaching formative and summative measurement. The goal of formative assessment is to help students identify their strengths and weaknesses and target the areas that need work. When instructors circulate while teacher candidates are completing direct learning experiences, they can recognize where the candidates are struggling and address problems immediately with specific feedback that is descriptive and tangible. This feedback is relative to the learning experience and teaches the candidates to understand how feedback can be specific and immediate when completing formative assessments.

The goal of summative assessments is to compare candidate progress to some standard or benchmark and is often conducted at the end of an instructional unit. When instructors assign a CBM report as a summative assessment, with planned feedback interleaved into each section, they are modeling and teaching how to give purposeful and constructive feedback. The G.E.T. Model purposeful and constructive feedback requires teacher candidates to reflect on their understanding and performance and moves them forward along the learning continuum.

TABLE 10-2. SPOTLIGHT ON ADULT LEARNING			
SPECIFICITY	**IMMEDIACY**	**PURPOSEFULNESS**	**CONSTRUCTIVENESS**
Does the feedback use the same language as the assessment? Is the feedback goal referenced and task oriented? Does the feedback point the adult learner toward the next steps?	Does the timing of the feedback align with the adult learner's readiness to learn? Is the feedback given at different stages of the assessment process?	Does the feedback clearly focus on the process? Does the feedback describe action steps relevant to assessment? Is the feedback personalized in a way that fits the adult learner's orientation to learning?	How are the assessment assignments and corresponding feedback designed to inform the adult learners of their own self-monitoring? Is the feedback balanced between strengths and improvement areas? Is the feedback differentiated?

SPOTLIGHT ON ADULT LEARNING

Education, by its very nature, tasks one generation with teaching a different generation than its own. The vast difference between the Baby Boomer generation preparing the Generation Me underscores the rationale for placing the recipient at the center of the feedback. Creating feedback that acknowledges the adult learners' orientation to learning, particularly problem-center and contextual, fits well for this generation of adult learners who prefer teamwork. For the feedback to be meaningful that instructors deliver to this generation of adult learners, the feedback must affirm their prior experience, particularly the mental models of this generation, whose education has been influenced by high-stakes standardized testing. Feedback that informs the learning process for mastering assessments in special education may require a paradigm shift for these adult learners. The recipient, more than ever, must receive feedback that informs their understanding, restructures their thinking or beliefs related to their performance, knowledge, and skills. The G.E.T. Model supports this shift by addressing the four domains for teaching feedback when planning instruction and providing feedback on assessments (Table 10-2).

POSSIBLE BARRIERS TO USING THIS TYPE OF FEEDBACK

The barriers inherent to teaching feedback in assessment to teacher candidates is rooted in the self-efficacy of the adult learners, the identity of the adult learner, and their own habits of practice. As we discussed, teacher candidates from Generation Me often have an inflated sense of efficacy and feel that effort should be rewarded, even when knowledge of the assessment is faulty or demonstrates only a surface-level understanding. Many persons in this generation were used to only getting a final grade instead of feedback that addresses their strengths and needs in the area of special education assessment. Considering the complexity of understanding different types of assessment measures and how to interpret the results for instructional planning, teacher candidates may focus on the wrong aspects of lengthy assessment projects. Just like they may witness in their field placements, assessment is focused only on compliance or completion instead of ensuring that students are making meaningful progress. This barrier of moving teacher candidates to higher levels of achievement in the area of assessment can be taught only if instructors are purposeful in designing the feedback they will give, along with the course design.

PRACTICAL APPLICATION

Let us consider a typical assignment in an assessment course. Special education teacher candidates are asked to use CBMs for monitoring K-12 student progress, evaluating the results of instruction, and suggesting modifications and accommodations in learning environments. To structure multiple opportunities for formative feedback before a final grade is given, it is imperative to chunk the assignments, with project-based feedback all along the way. These feedback intervals are not high stakes and do not impact the final grade but allow opportunities for the teacher candidates to improve the assignment as they complete the project. The goal is for the adult learner to complete a summative assessment of assessment skills to evaluate their understanding so they can demonstrate this knowledge in later assignments. Considering the goal that instructors have for teacher candidates to understand different types of CBMs and the purposes for which they are used, planned feedback at integral parts of the assignment will lead to increased proficiency. Consider how the following assignment is structured so these adult learners experience specific, timely, and purposeful feedback that can be designed in the assignment.

Assignment #3: Curriculum-Based Measurement Report

Teacher candidates will develop a written plan to monitor an elementary-age student's progress in specific academic areas. Teacher candidates will administer and score a total of 12 CBM probes across 8 weeks and write an interpretation of the results.

Goals for assignment:
- To become more familiar with different types of CBMs and the purposes for which they are used
- To practice recording baseline data and initial implementation of an intervention
- To graph actual results and interpret findings
- Translate to future instructional planning for a student

Directions:
1. Teacher candidates will work with a parent of an elementary-age student to identify any academic concerns in reading, math, spelling, and writing and receive permission to administer CBM probes. A report of the parent's concern is developed.
2. The teacher candidate will administer the first three CBM probes in **one** of these academic areas, charting the baseline/initial data. You will develop a performance goal for the student and chart the aim line. Initial suggestions for an instructional intervention are considered.
3. Teacher candidates will then administer CBM probes in the other academic areas (reading, math, spelling, and writing). The probes should be spread out over several days and not administered all in one session.
4. Score each protocol, using the procedures outlined in the text, and compare the results to national norms.
5. Chart baseline data and graph the results of the probes, determining a performance goal and aim line.
6. Write a two- to three-page reaction/interpretation, based on the following format:
   - A short description of the student, with grade level and expected academic performance
   - A short description of the probes administered, including the scoring and expected slope norms, based on the student's grade
   - The graph and a short summary of the graph as well as what the aim and trend lines suggest

- ◦ A list/description of recommendations for future instruction, including the feedback the teacher candidate will give to the parent
- ◦ A description of what they will tell the student about their assessment performance that contains one or more strengths and at least one suggestion for improvement

There are six different opportunities for an instructor to give, exhibit, and teach feedback that moves the teacher candidate to inform their understanding of CBMs, restructure their thinking or beliefs of this assessment technique, and relate to their performance, knowledge of administering, and scoring the CBMs.

Giving Feedback

The task feedback that is given to the teacher candidate reinforces the goals for the assignment and the steps they need to take to reach the goals. Process feedback can be given at six different times so that teacher candidates understand the procedures needed to administer and interpret CBMs and to perform the assignment at the expected level of proficiency.

Exhibiting Feedback

By having a clear goal for the desired outcomes, the teacher candidates have specific questions, characteristics, and levels of skill attainment that they must achieve in this CBM assignment. Instructors delivering feedback at each of the six points provides an opportunity for demonstrating how to give performance feedback, thus providing a model of how the teacher candidate should give feedback to the K-12 student they are assessing. When instructors chunk the assignment into six assessment points, the immediate feedback is easier to achieve because the amount of teacher candidate work is in smaller increments. When instructors give actionable steps broken into actionable chunks, it allows the teacher candidate to see a purpose for the assignment. Finally, instructors can construct a new meaning of individualized assessment and improvement suggestions for the learners so they understand how this type of assessment is part of the multiple forms of assessment we use in special education.

Teaching Feedback

The CBM assignment allows instructors to model for teacher candidates how to use assessment data to help their future students to set goals and give descriptive feedback that is easily understood, positive, and nonjudgmental. Considering the emotional dread that many students with disabilities experience when taking tests and assessments, teaching and modeling how to give assessment feedback is a discrete skill.

The following questions are provided to guide your review and reflection in the Authentic Example that follows, contributed by Ruby L. Owiny, PhD and Kyena E. Cornelius, EdD.

- In this example, how does the instructor apply knowledge of teaching feedback? Reflect.
- Why is learning self-efficacy and identity important to understand when designing assignments and activities to teach feedback?
- How does an instructor's ability to teach feedback build on giving and exhibiting feedback? How do all parts of the G.E.T. Model work together?

AUTHENTIC EXAMPLE

Contributed by
Ruby L. Owiny, PhD
Kyena E. Cornelius, EdD

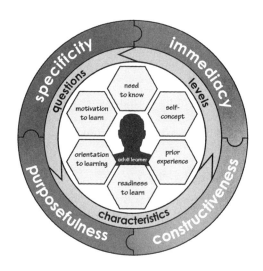

1. Course Details

SPE 413: Professional Growth and Development for Teachers of Diverse Learners. This is an undergraduate course with a targeted field placement in an elementary intervention setting. Teacher candidates spend three sessions each week working with a school intervention specialist to assist in Tier 2 instruction and collect data for the school's student study team. Candidates are expected to use curriculum-based measurement to identify students' academic level and needs, design and deliver instruction using evidence-based practices, and continue to monitor student progress.

This assignment provides candidates with the opportunity to plan and use data collection tools more effectively in the classroom while reflecting on a lesson taught to make informed decisions about future instruction. For the special education teacher candidates, this assignment emphasizes the importance of collecting data related to the lesson, not just the targeted skills. For the general education teacher candidates, this assignment is to help emphasize the importance of collecting data to make informed decisions regarding the effectiveness of the instruction and developing next steps for future instruction.

2. Learning Objectives

The aligned course objectives are as follows:

SPE 413: As a result of this assignment, teacher candidates will be able to:

a. Understand that reflective teaching leads to better teaching as well as personal and professional growth

b. Understand the cultural, social, and other environmental effects on learning and human development

c. Understand what effective lesson planning looks like as well as how it connects and is related to the IEP

3. Activity Description

Teacher candidates write a 2-day lesson plan sequence that includes data collection tools. Teacher candidates implement the first lesson while the university supervisor observes, collecting data on student understanding. Following the delivery of the first lesson, candidates write a reflection of the lesson, using the provided template. As part of the reflection, candidates use the data collected from the first lesson to modify the second lesson.

Preparation for Writing the Lesson Plan

Teacher candidates will participate in a seminar session in which they learn about formative assessment. Multiple examples of formative assessment will be modeled in the lesson. The lesson for the seminar session is outlined as follows:

Seminar Session Lesson Outline: Formative Assessment in Lesson Planning
a. Outcomes:
  - Students will understand the importance of formative assessment data in designing instruction.
  - Students will be able to create a tool to assist in gathering formative assessment data.
b. Measure of Success:
  - Students will produce a data collection tool and explain its use and value in the formative assessment process.
c. Materials:
  - Readings: Blanks (2015) and Cornelius (2013)
  - Post-it notes
  - Poster paper
  - 3x5 cards
  - Laundry Days Activity—four corners activity
d. Preassessment:
  - Making connections
    - T-chart of examples and nonexamples:
      - Students are given two post-it notes and told to write one thing that is true for formative assessment and one thing that is not.
      - Instructors come back at the end of class to "move" post-it notes if needed.
e. Lesson:
  - Based on preassessment activities, adjust lecture/overview of use of formative assessment in lesson planning.
  - Model use of formative assessment:
    - How can one use the preassessment activity to rearrange today's lecture?
    - Discuss how the instructor used various tools in the classroom.
      - Walk through the thought process of planning and using tools.
  - Guided Practice: Give an objective and discuss learning outcomes and measures.
    - Walk students through a discussion:
      - What information do I need?
      - How can I capture it?
      - Why is it important?
    - Create a data collection tool and discuss the data the instructor will collect and what will be done with that information.

TABLE 10-3. LAUNDRY DAY

DETERGENT	WHAT STUDENTS BELIEVE ABOUT THEIR OWN UNDERSTANDING	ACTIVITIES YOU MIGHT SEE TO HELP STUDENT LEARNING
Tide	Students believe the _TID_al wave of information might drown them.	A comprehensive review of the material. Ways to help the learner experience the information in a different way.
Gain	Students understand the basics but need to _GAIN_ a deeper understanding.	Examining text, homework examples, and internet sources to gain more understanding.
Bold	Students are _BOLD_, fairly confident, in their understanding of the topic.	Students create a review activity. Discussion of some finer detail on the topic.
Cheer	Students are certain they understand the topic and can be _CHEER_leaders for other's learning.	Helping students in the Tide corner. Extend the learning to connect to other content or application of topic.

- ○ Group Practice:
  - • Divide students into groups to create collection tools.
  - • Share tool.
  - • On 3x5 card, explain tool and uses (exit ticket).
- ○ Wrap-Up: Laundry Days
  - • Explain 4 corners game and have students complete activities in the "laundry tubs" (a small container with the detergent label).
- ○ Laundry Day: Laundry Day is a formative assessment strategy for students to evaluate their own learning. They group themselves in the classroom around four different laundry detergents: Tide, Gain, Bold, and Cheer (Table 10-3).
  - • Demonstrate how the Laundry Days activity is a formative assessment.
  - • In a blank four-quadrant table, write students' names in the corresponding quadrant to where they self-assessed their knowledge. Based on their work with each group, would the instructor place them in the same quadrant?
  - • As a transition discussion, explicitly point out every formative assessment used in the class session and how that data informed instruction.

4. Evaluation Criteria

The rubric in Table 10-4 provides feedback to candidates on their lesson plan, formative assessment tool, and follow-up lesson.

TABLE 10-4. LESSON PLAN WITH REFLECTION RUBRIC

DESCRIPTION	0 = LITTLE EVIDENCE OF UNDERSTANDING	1 = EVIDENCE OF SOLID LEVEL OF UNDERSTANDING	2 = EVIDENCE OF HIGH LEVEL OF UNDERSTANDING	SCORE
Initial Lesson Plan				
Includes all key components	1-3 components	4-6 components	7-9 components	
Objective/standard/IEP goal/baseline data/opening/model/guided/ unguided/accom or mod				
Data tool	Included	Type Pre/during/post	Completed data tool included	
Reflection				
Answered all questions	No	Partially	Fully	
Judge: • What was successful/ unsuccessful with this lesson?	No	Some examples provided	Details provided that the lesson was successful/ unsuccessful	
Provided details within the answers that guided instructional decision making	No	Discussed decisions without much detail	Discussed decisions with some detail	

(continued)

Table 10-4 (continued). Lesson Plan With Reflection Rubric

DESCRIPTION	0 = LITTLE EVIDENCE OF UNDERSTANDING	1 = EVIDENCE OF SOLID LEVEL OF UNDERSTANDING	2 = EVIDENCE OF HIGH LEVEL OF UNDERSTANDING	SCORE
Reflection of Formative Assessment (last 3 questions)				
Describe: • Tells about the data in detail, no opinion just facts	No	Some opinion or not enough detail to gauge	Only facts and details included	
Analyze: • Why are the data you described important?	No	Some detail on how the data are related to lesson	Provided details on how data are related	
Apply: • What will you do differently in your next lesson?	No	Some examples provided	Details provided that these data will inform instruction	
Follow-Up Lesson Plan				
Incorporated changes based on reflection	No change	Change noted but unaligned or not well aligned	Changes noted and aligned with data	

5. *Additional Details*

Two course texts are important to this assignment. Please review Blanks (2015) and Cornelius (2013) for additional details about assessment and formative assessment. They are assigned readings that need to be completed in preparation for this assignment.

6. *Feedback Reflection*

In this assignment:

- Verbal feedback is provided by the instructor to candidates during the seminar session to ensure that candidates develop a basic level of proficiency in understanding how to plan for formative assessment in all their lesson plans.

- More feedback is provided to candidates on their lesson plan prior to teaching by the university supervisor during a pre-observation conference. This feedback is specific and both positive and corrective. Feedback is provided on all aspects of the lesson plan, including formative assessment measures.

- Finally, feedback is provided to candidates in both written (rubric and comments on documents) and verbal (post-observation conference) form after their lesson is taught.

SUMMARY

In this chapter, feedback as a part of assessment was discussed. The need to teach clear connections to how assessment uses feedback to move K-12 students with disabilities to higher levels of academic achievement was discussed and the research on assessment feedback approaches were described. Feedback as part of the assessment is crucial for instructors to teach because it is a major component of the standards and assessments of teaching that many special education teacher candidates are required to meet. When instructors give feedback often on assessment tasks, it reinforces the goals for the assignment and the steps teacher candidates need to take to reach the goals. When clear goals for the desired outcomes are given, teacher candidates can better answer the specific questions, use the specific characteristics of the assessment process, and achieve higher levels of assessment skill attainment. When instructors teach how to give descriptive feedback in the assessment process that is easily understood, positive, and nonjudgmental, we are modeling for teacher candidates how to use this kind of feedback with their own students. Finally, this chapter demonstrates how to provide feedback on assignments in assessment courses, with examples and prompts to take action.

OPPORTUNITY FOR GOING DEEPER

The following resources support deeper learning on concepts reflected in Chapter 10:

- Revising assessments. Alastair Irons' (2008) *Enhancing Learning Through Formative Assessment and Feedback* provides a helpful perspective, with practical suggestions for revising assessment practices that reflect the teaching of feedback, specifically in assessing written work and peer-assisted and group learning opportunities. Another resource is the High-Leverage Practices (HLP) in assessment. https://highleveragepractices.org/assessment/

- Constructive feedback. The Georgia MTSS webinar series, in partnership with the CEEDAR Center, has a recorded webinar that addresses HLP #8 on providing positive and constructive feedback. This webinar could be used in special education teacher preparation for teachers to consider the standards and practices. At the end of the webinar, there are also considerations for educator preparation providers. https://ceedar.education.ufl.edu/portfolio/the-gift-of-feedback-and-guidance-to-support-student-learning/

- Curriculum-based measurement. Several resources relating to CBM are as follows:
  - Wright, J. (n.d.). *Curriculum-based measurement: A manual for teachers.* http://www.jimwrightonline.com/pdfdocs/cbaManual.pdf
  - Hosp, M. K., Hosp, J. L., & Howell, K. W. (2016). *The ABCs of CBM: A practical guide to curriculum-based measurement.* Guilford Press.
  - easyCBM: *Response to intervention made easy.* https://easycbm.com/

- Candidate Preservice Assessment of Student Teaching (CPAST) Form. https://ehe.osu.edu/accreditation-placement-licensure/accreditation/multi-institutional-collaboration/candidate-preservice-assessment-student-teaching-cpast/

- Student engagement tools:
  - Kahoot! https://kahoot.com
  - Poll Everywhere. https://www.polleverywhere.com/
  - Quizlet. https://quizlet.com/
  - The Jigsaw Method Teaching Strategy. https://www.teachhub.com/jigsaw-method-teaching-strategy

REFERENCES

Abbot, L. (2019, May 8). *11 millennials' traits you should know about before you hire them* [Image attached] [Post]. LinkedIn. https://business.linkedin.com/talent-solutions/blog/2013/12/8-millennials-traits-you-should-know-about-before-you-hire-them

Benassi, V. A., Overson, C. E., & Hakala, C. M. (Eds.) (2014). *Applying science of learning in education: Infusing psychological science into the curriculum* (2014). American Psychological Association.

Blanks, B. (2015). Amazing assessment. In W. W. Murawski, & K. L. Scott (Eds.), *What really works in secondary education* (pp. 216-231). Corwin.

Cornelius, K. E. (2013). Formative assessment made easy: Templates for collecting daily data in inclusive classrooms. *Teaching Exceptional Children, 45*(5), 14-21.

Council for Exceptional Children. (2015). *What every special educator must know: Professional ethics and standards* (7th ed.).

Endrew F. v. Douglas County School District, 137 S. Ct. 988 (2017).

Hattie, J., & Timperley, H. (2007). The power of feedback. *Review of Educational Research, 77*(1), 81-112. https://doi.org/10.3102/003465430298487

Howe, N., & Strauss, W. (2007). *Millennials go to college* (2nd ed.). LifeCourse Associates.

McLeskey, J., Barringer, M-D., Billingsley, B., Brownell, M., Jackson, D., Kennedy, M., Lewis, T., Maheady, L., Rodriguez, J., Scheeler, M. C., Winn, J., & Ziegler, D. (2017, January). *High-leverage practices in special education*. Council for Exceptional Children & CEEDAR Center.

Sandeen, C. (2008). Boomers, Xers, and Millennials: Who are they and what do they really want from continuing higher education? *Continuing Higher Education Review, 72*(Fall), 11-31.

Twenge, J. M. (2014). *Generation me: Why today's young Americans are more confident, assertive, entitled—and more miserable than ever before* (Rev and updated ed.). Atria Books.

Teaching Feedback to Support Students' Behavioral Needs

Reesha Adamson, PhD; Jessica Nelson, EdD, BCBA; and Felicity Post, EdD

To craft teacher feedback that leads to learning, put yourself in the student's shoes.
—Susan Brookhart

FEEDBACK SCENARIO

JoAnna is a new special education teacher candidate preparing for her first practicum to teach in a second-grade classroom. Before entering the classroom, she and her university supervisor, Dr. Martinez, sit down to discuss the goals and desired outcomes for her instruction. They also discuss potential barriers to student growth and receptiveness to instruction. The discussion allows JoAnna to verbalize ways to overcome these barriers. Dr. Martinez encourages JoAnna to undertake an ecological survey about the practicum classroom, gathering information about her students, such as their cultural lens, their behavioral and academic needs, and the availability of instructional and curricular support. Dr. Martinez discusses with JoAnna the university observation expectations and shares the type of feedback that she will provide before, during, and after her instruction. JoAnna feels comfortable and supported in her teaching efforts and is ready to teach her first lesson.

At JoAnna's first practicum observation, Dr. Martinez directly observes her and records feedback that she will later share with the teacher candidate. Dr. Martinez documents evidence of behavior-specific praise, behavior redirection, error correction, supports provided for academic and behavioral growth, interactions with students, and implementation of best practices. Dr. Martinez works to ensure that her observation does not interfere with JoAnna's instruction or student learning, as she is merely an observer within the classroom.

Upon completion of the lesson, Dr. Martinez and JoAnna discuss JoAnna's performance. Before speaking, Dr. Martinez prompts JoAnna to personally reflect on the lesson taught and tell her what went well and what she would change about the lesson. JoAnna shares both her perceived strengths

Elford, M. D., Smith, H. H., & James, S.
*GET Feedback: Giving, Exhibiting, and Teaching Feedback in
Special Education Teacher Preparation* (pp. 211-232).
© 2022 SLACK Incorporated.

and potential areas of development while Dr. Martinez listens. Dr. Martinez then shares her impressions of the lesson observation and details the evidence of observed instructional behavior rates collected during JoAnna's instruction. They are able to discuss the alignment of both the evidence collected by Dr. Martinez and JoAnna's personal reflection. JoAnna is then asked to set informed goals for future lessons, based on what they have both shared, including direct targets of observed instructional behavior rates.

For JoAnna's next practicum observation, she and Dr. Martinez discuss potential models for feedback in her reading lesson. They decide that JoAnna will record her lesson, using provided video software instead of Dr. Martinez visiting the classroom. JoAnna proceeds with the lesson and then shares the video with Dr. Martinez. Both parties review the video independently. While watching, JoAnna personally reflects on her performance, her instruction, and her interactions with students. Dr. Martinez does the same and tags the video for observed instructional behavior rates. When they meet to discuss the feedback derived from the video, Dr. Martinez directly instructs JoAnna to reflect on her goals from the first practicum observation to determine growth and continued areas of improvement.

JoAnna's development continues throughout the course of her practicum experience with Dr. Martinez, utilizing various feedback models for her personal growth as an educator. Dr. Martinez actively works to ensure that goal-based, specific, and timely feedback is delivered strategically and informs JoAnna of the ways she can improve in her implementation of best practices in instructional behavior strategies.

Chapter Objectives

This chapter builds on assessment feedback and addresses feedback in social, emotional, and behavioral contexts in special education, including the need to give feedback in these contexts. This chapter will describe the research on social, emotional, and behavioral feedback approaches and why these types of feedback increase K-12 student motivation, engagement, and independence, leading to improved student learning and behavior. This chapter will also demonstrate how to select feedback approaches, with examples and prompts to take action.

In the past decade, research suggested that adult learners benefit from learning the complexity of how feedback is given for different purposes when considering the social, emotional, and behavioral needs of students with disabilities (Colvin et al., 2009). Special education teacher preparation instructors must teach feedback that considers what type of social, emotional, and behavioral feedback is most appropriate while also recognizing the learning needs of adult students.

After reading this chapter, you will **know** and **understand** these concepts and have the opportunity to **demonstrate** and **apply** your knowledge (Table 11-1).

Describe and Define

Intentional or directed learning within a classroom setting is typically steered toward the completion of a predetermined goal. Feedback is the means by which the learner or person responsible for directing the learning process determines that progress is being made toward the end goal and whether the goal has been reached (Weibell, 2011). In social learning theory (Bandura, 1977), two sources of feedback are typical. The first can be found in the consequences of one's own actions (Vygotsky, 1994). The second type of feedback consists of input from others, such as in the learning of more complex skills (Bandura, 1977). Both types of feedback—the consequences of one's actions and input from others—shape whether a student learns to do something well or poorly. Teachers, the ones directing the learning, are responsible for facilitating both types of feedback in their classrooms.

TABLE 11-1. GRAPHIC ORGANIZER		
KNOW (WHAT)	**UNDERSTAND (WHY)**	**DEMONSTRATE (HOW)**
What the research on social, emotional, and behavioral feedback suggests, especially for adult learners.	Why teaching social, emotional, and behavioral feedback is necessary in special education teacher preparation.	How to teach feedback that recognizes the impact of varied approaches on student motivation, engagement, and independence, leading to improved student learning and behavior.
APPLY (TAKE ACTION)		
Apply research on social, emotional, and behavioral feedback through appropriate selection of feedback approaches in course design, activities, and assessments.		

Considering all the responsibilities and tasks necessary for running a typical classroom, the complexities of teaching are understated. Therefore, ensuring that teacher candidates know the differences between these two types of feedback can minimize some of the complexity in giving feedback to K-12 students. Based on the G.E.T. Model, instructors must give feedback about the social aspects of teaching, exhibit the emotional feedback we can appropriately give the teacher candidates we teach, and teach how to give behavioral feedback. Central to Thorndike's (1913) Law of Effect, which states that repetition in the absence of feedback does nothing to improve performance, instructors must give, exhibit, and teach feedback in social, emotional, and behavioral approaches to teaching.

Know

When assuming a behaviorist perspective, we adhere to the theory of psychology that states that all human behaviors are learned, not innate, and focus on the study of observable and measurable behavior (Watson, 1913). Through feedback, both positive and corrective, we can teach how to give feedback to provide the information and tools necessary for growth in these measurable behaviors. The G.E.T. Model provides a foundation for how feedback can be taught, and no one special education teacher candidate will respond the same to specific, immediate, purposeful, or constructive feedback. In choosing how to give feedback, careful consideration must be paid to the social, emotional, and behavioral feedback approaches in special education, the strengths and developmental preparation of the candidate, as well as potential barriers that could limit the appropriateness and effectiveness of the feedback itself. That is why putting the adult learner at the center as the recipient of the feedback (see Chapter 3) is so important. Regardless, the purpose of feedback should guide teacher candidates' learning and behavior while increasing motivation, engagement, and independence, in turn leading to the improvement of the K-12 students they will teach in the areas of learning and behavior (McLeskey et al., 2017). When verbal, nonverbal, or written, feedback must be delivered strategically and be goal-based, it is most effective when it informs the learner of ways to improve instead of feedback that focuses only on what they did wrong. As stated in the High-Leverage Practices, to maximize effectiveness, feedback must be timely, contingent, genuine, meaningful, age-appropriate, and ongoing until the recipient reaches the intended goal (McLeskey et al., 2017).

Understand

In teacher preparation, as special education teacher candidates move toward mastery of feedback delivery, they must develop an understanding of specific, immediate, purposeful, and constructive feedback in social, emotional, and behavioral contexts. For example, as described in the vignette, Dr. Martinez made explicit the task feedback that JoAnna could expect before, during, and after her instruction. By doing this, Dr. Martinez exhibits feedback and creates a model for JoAnna that she can use as she learns to deliver feedback to K-12 students. Like Dr. Martinez tailors her feedback to the learner as well as to the learning task, she is teaching JoAnna how to give feedback that increases students' levels of achievement. The models described in the following section are those most frequently used in special education teacher preparation, giving instructors the opportunities to give, exhibit, and teach feedback.

Feedback Models

Direct Observation

The most supportive form of feedback can be done using direct observation. This process is typical of traditional teacher candidate observation, where a university supervisor comes to the classroom and observes for specific behaviors or competencies and documents anecdotally their perceptions. However, this process feedback can be less subjective if teacher candidates are given specific feedback that aligns to the data from their classroom practice. To teach candidates how to give feedback after direct observation, instructors can teach feedback that is specific to the data from the students' performance.

An example of this type of task and process feedback is giving teacher candidates ratios of behavior-specific praise. Teacher candidates may feel that they have a supportive and positive classroom environment, but giving them tangible rates of their praise to corrective feedback gives the teacher candidate a baseline of this measure. It also allows the instructor to continually monitor teacher candidates and document their rate of growth and development across time. Another commonly used example is documenting the number of times that students are given opportunities to respond during instruction. This form of feedback can be documented across individuals, such as those demonstrating challenging behaviors, or across the entire class during observations to help determine student engagement or the opportunity for students to become academically engaged.

Video Analysis

You may recall from Chapter 5, direct observation can be achieved with video software and the recording of teacher candidates within their classrooms during instruction. Use of video is one way that many universities gather data and teach reflection, as well as supervise and observe teacher candidates in distance placements. Many programs exist to help universities with such distance teacher candidate programs. Online video platform software, such as those mentioned in Chapter 5, allows for embedded feedback and notes within the observation so that candidates can be directed to observe or reflect on something that an instructor has noted. This can be a powerful tool for feedback and reflection that can make a teacher candidate aware of their behaviors that may be encouraging student behavior—or even misbehavior. By highlighting these behaviors directly, video-based feedback gives teacher candidates direct examples of their own behaviors. It also allows for opportunities to problem-solve specific changes within the teacher candidate's behavior to encourage student success.

Ecological Survey

Creation of a classroom that is conducive to instruction but also is respectful of routines and student needs is a process that takes serious thought on the part of the teacher candidate. Specific understanding of the environment's role on behavior is crucial for instructors to exhibit and teach for creating a classroom setting that supports student learning, provides access to learning for all students, and ensures effective feedback to students. An ecological inventory considers the environmental structure and knowledge of the specific support required for success within the classroom structure for students of all learning needs and abilities. The structure and classroom arrangement are critical to minimizing opportunities for misbehavior. To think about this process critically, an ecological survey can help identify environmental support for behavior. This process can be completed by a teacher candidate and then reviewed with the instructor to problem-solve any potential issues and to process through environmental supports that can prevent problem behaviors from happening. The instructor can provide feedback on these ecological surveys that moves the teacher candidate to understand how important a safe classroom environment can help students with disabilities.

Although there is no standardized form for an ecological assessment, early establishment of the process was created by Fuchs et al. (1994). The proposed format addressed the domains required for student success, including physical environment, teacher/student behavior, posted classroom rules, classroom rules (expectations), and teacher behavior. These domains correspond to discussion around physical arrangement within the classroom, teacher-student interactions and patterns, teacher's classroom management, homework, testing and grading policies, materials required and skills explicitly taught, as well as specific academic and behavioral expectations required for success. In early conception, this process was created to identify important differences between classrooms that could hinder a student's success when transitioning from a special education setting into a general education classroom. However, this same process has been adapted to ensure that a prevention framework, classroom-based universal support for student success is created (Adamson et al., 2019).

Even before candidates begin practice within a classroom, they and their university supervisors can begin to foster effective environments. Advanced planning allows them to be thoughtful about how the environment supports their teaching and student learning. An intentional approach to the environment also allows for in-depth feedback and conversations about the importance of planning for student success and problem-solving through potential barriers. It invites teacher candidates to analyze the effort expended by students as they complete the required routine tasks as well as their own management styles and expectations. When teacher candidates better understand these structural supports, they are better able to articulate and demonstrate to students that the environment is supportive.

At the university level, an assignment to conduct an ecological survey can be completed in combination with any practicum experience. Some specific contexts to consider within an ecological inventory are district, school, classroom, and community. These environments should be explored to analyze a knowledge of the students with whom the teacher candidates will be working and specific factors that may be relevant to the student's culture that teacher candidates will encounter. In addition, within the school context, more specific factors should be examined, including structural arrangement, environmental supports, resources, technology, instructional tools, family support, culture, curriculum, and adult support. These factors may change depending on the environment, but carefully considering each of these components will help determine how to maximize student outcomes and allow candidates to be conscious of the student learning environment. From these factors, a teacher candidate will be able to better insert their own beliefs and assumptions within the existing context and create their own pedagogy and understanding of the classroom community. This understanding allows the teacher candidate to thoughtfully plan and create routines, expectations, and the structural environment around the students' needs while also taking into account the environmental supports and structures.

After candidates conduct an ecological survey, they may need to revisit their inventories to focus on specific student needs within the context and domains as well as to determine any misconceptions or additional considerations to create individualized supports, which ensure that each specific child's needs are being met and that approaches being used to support the individual in combination are appropriate, given the environment. Considerations about individualized academic and behavioral support can be included, which may take some broader adjustments within the larger context. The overall purpose of the ecological survey is to reflect on the factors that may influence student success and ensure that resources and supports are being utilized to their fullest extent to support individual needs, classroom needs, and consideration of the classroom as an entity within the school, district, and community.

Personal Reflection

Reflection is the act of looking back on what we have done as we determine our future course of action. It is a cognitive process or activity (Boud et al., 1985; Dewey, 1933; Langer, 1989; Mezirow, 1991; Seibert, 1999) that involves the emotions of an individual (Boud et al., 1985). This thoughtful planning and realization of the emotional effect that different experiences have on us is at the heart of teacher reflection. Teachers follow a cyclical process when considering what happens in their classrooms each day—they teach a lesson, self-assess the effect of their teaching on student performance, and then consider new ways of teaching to improve student outcomes. This cycle is the reflection process that must be taught to special education teacher candidates, and instructors must give them feedback on their reflection process during each part of the cycle.

Special education teacher candidates must learn to reflect to get the most out of their own learning. In fact, reflection is an integral piece of the learning process and allows teacher candidates to transition from teaching content at a surface level that only covers the content to clear and focused learning before, during, and after application. Unsurprisingly, instructors want their teacher candidates to know how to teach, but candidates must also know how to reflect on their progress to maximize their potential and influence; thus, instructors must teach how to give feedback in this learning cycle. The act of reflection allows teacher candidates to learn more about themselves as educators, their students, and about student–teacher interactions. For example, if a teacher candidate teaches a social skills unit to K-12 students but more than half the class fails to generalize the skill, the candidate would be met with two options: (a) the failure of the group was due to student variables or (b) the candidate needs to stop and reflect on their teaching of the social skill to determine what feedback they could have given to improve student competency of the social skill. In reflecting, the candidate should ask questions that help uncover what factors contributed to a high rate of student failure to generalize. The type of feedback given when teaching a social skill allows instructors an opportunity to give, exhibit, and teach reflection skills. The use of reflection assignments can be utilized in teacher education programs to support teacher candidates in their efforts to learn from their own practice and connect such knowledge to research-generated knowledge, also known as best practice (Korthagen, 2004; Korthagen & Vasalos, 2005; LaBoskey, 2010). Reflection, by definition, is a cognitive process carried out individually or with the assistance of another to elicit knowledge from experiences (Benammar, 2004; Dewey, 1933; Hébert, 2015) and support thoughtful learning (Moon, 2004). Alone, reflection cannot ensure that a teacher candidate will construct new knowledge or understanding (Shulman & Shulman, 2004). Teacher candidates instead need help to formulate knowledge throughout the reflection process (Beijaard et al., 2005).

Most often, teachers engage in two various types of reflection—reflection-in-action and reflection-on-action (Schön, 1983). Reflection-in-action happens as a teacher is actively teaching, resulting in doing and thinking being complementary to one another. When using reflection-on-action, the act of reflection occurs after the teaching experience itself. Teacher candidates must become competent in both if they are to maximize the potential influence of their teaching practices.

Many think of reflection as an event that happens in isolation, perhaps on the drive home or after the classroom has cleared for the day. However, reflection can and should take place while interacting with others (Benammar, 2004; Leijen et al., 2012). Such interaction allows each individual to share personal experiences and learn from those shared by others. This in turn assists teacher candidates in interpreting and developing their own personal perspectives even further. By allowing teacher candidates to reflect with one another, a supportive environment interlaced with critical feedback is created (Danielowich, 2014; Fund, 2010; Lamb et al., 2012). In fact, research has shown that peer feedback can improve the overall quality of reflection (Fund, 2010; Leijen et al., 2012). In addition to leaning on peers to help construct new knowledge, teacher candidates also look to supervisors to provide emotional support, encouragement, advice, suggestions, and evaluation. Such support from both their peers and supervisors assist teacher candidates with the purposeful construction of the knowledge necessary for the application of effective teaching practices.

Another form of reflection that can be utilized through video is video analysis. Video analysis can be more valuable than the traditional forms of reflection that are being used by some universities. In video analysis, teacher candidates record and examine their own teaching (Seidel et al., 2011). Video analysis can be especially beneficial because it provides the unique opportunity to view one's teaching as an outsider looking in. By recording a video of each lesson they teach, teacher candidates have the ability to watch the lesson multiple times to reflect on different parts of the lesson or to compare and contrast changes that they have made in their teaching.

Nagro and Cornelius (2013) suggested three steps for instructing teacher candidates how to perform and use video analysis. They suggested that teacher candidates record a lesson(s) that they are teaching, review the video(s) so that they can evaluate and reflect on the teaching that took place, and, finally, make the necessary changes after evaluation and reflection to ensure that student learning is at the forefront of the lesson.

Research suggests that reflective methods, such as role modeling and use of questions in peer coaching, help individuals to develop skills in reflection and enhance the learning process (Brookfield, 1990; Loughran, 2002; Seibert & Daudelin, 1999; Sparks-Langer & Colton, 1991). Through intentional placement of such activities, instructors can provide feedback that gives critical opportunities for teacher candidates to reflect on their practices. This allows candidates to notice and correct their own errors within teaching, determine behavioral and academic approaches that serve a student population well, and make necessary changes based on evidence.

Role Modeling

Teacher candidates need ample opportunities to practice and receive feedback on critical aspects of teaching while learning about high-quality, evidence-based instruction throughout their teacher preparation programs. Demonstrating a desired behavior using modeling is an evidence-based practice that supports teacher candidates in understanding ways to handle behavior in the classroom (Oliver & Reschly, 2007). Teacher candidates rated effective classroom management, positive rapport and relationships with students, and efficient routines in the classroom as what they most wanted to see modeled and displayed by their classroom teachers (Osunde, 1996). These critical evidence-based strategies provide instructors with avenues to model the practice, as well as model the types of feedback that candidates should give their students when using these strategies.

One example of an evidence-based modeling system in teacher preparation programs is university-constructed teaching environments. Instructors construct classroom situations that candidates may encounter when entering the classroom. Once scenarios have been constructed in the candidates' coursework and candidates have been provided practice with feedback, scenarios are then worked through during the fieldwork portion of their coursework (Benedict et al., 2016). One example of how to ensure that teacher candidates receive proper training is to utilize the "I do, we do, you do" (Fisher & Frey, 2014) modeling system. This system will help strengthen teacher candidates' confidence as they observe the cooperating teacher model the lesson objective—the "I do" part. The instructor and/or cooperating teacher will model how to perform the academic or behavioral task or intervention. This can be thought of as direct instruction for the teacher candidate. After the "I do" model has been shown, the teacher candidate will then model with the instructor, others in the class, and/or the cooperating teacher. This "we do" model can be thought of as guided practice. Once the teacher candidate performs the "we do," the final step requires the teacher candidate to perform the task or intervention on their own while the instructor and/or cooperating teacher observes. This final step can be referred to as independent practice for the teacher candidate. Once the "you do" step has been completed, feedback could be given in the form of peer coaching.

Peer Coaching

The use of peer coaching with teacher candidates is very similar to peer coaching that happens with teachers who have already obtained teaching degrees and are working alongside other teachers in the school environment. Peer coaching can be best summarized as a team of teacher candidates working together professionally by observing each other and providing immediate feedback after a teaching lesson. Some instructors liken this process to Japanese Lesson study (Hiebert et al., 2002)—when teacher candidates are allowed to discuss, reflect, and refine their teaching. Peer coaching should be supportive and not seen as a punitive or judgmental process for improving practice. Teacher candidates should use peer coaching to collaborate with each other on new teaching ideas or thoughts on behavioral interventions.

Four principles are necessary to guide peer coaching (Showers & Joyce, 1996). The principles were designed to ensure that coaching was a collaborative effort among individuals and not seen as punitive. The first principle suggests that teachers agree to engage in a peer coaching team and to develop the criteria for these teams. The criteria that are agreed upon must include the required support of one another's teaching, a willingness to take the feedback and implement necessary changes in teaching, and use of data to support positive change. The second principle indicates that teams must agree to be collaborative. The team as a whole works toward one agreed-upon goal. Third, the team is expected to break into pairs or sometimes small groups for the actual coaching, with pairs or groups determined by the team. Once paired, teams will have a coach and coachee(s). The final principle is to ensure that the team understands that while engaged in peer coaching, the intent is to observe without bias and criticism. Using these four principles, the goal is to collaborate and learn from each other, especially when system-wide change is happening and some team members have unique expertise in it. Peer coaches, who have already been trained in these areas, will work with other teachers in building a plan of action for implementation. At times, peer coaching may be individual, but it can also be in a group format if multiple teachers need support in the same area.

Gottesman (2000) developed a five-step peer coaching model. During phase one, the goal is simply observation. Feedback is not given to the teacher candidate at this time. The second phase in the Gottesman model evolves from simple observation to coaching. The premise of this phase is to give feedback only on what they observed; criticism and suggestions are not given at this time. Peer feedback involves "the request, the visit, the coach's review of the notes, the talk after the visit, and the process review" (Gottesman, 2000, p. 32). The teacher candidate being coached then decides which area of the lesson needs improvement, based on the feedback received from the coach. The two then work on directly addressing the issue and what support is going to be needed. Finally, in step five, the two discuss together how to implement proposed changes and what specific products will result from the coachee's change in instructional behavior.

The five steps of peer coaching can best be summed up as follows: (a) coach comes up with a mutual conducive meeting time to visit coachee, (b) coach observes coachee, (c) coachee reflects on the notes from coach alone, (d) coach and coachee meet and discuss the facts, and (e) coach and coachee examine the peer coaching process and the outcomes from it (Figure 11-1).

One positive aspect of peer coaching is the engagement that occurs between teacher candidates and their supervisor and/or another teacher candidate serving as coach. This process of peer coaching should be a facilitative one, where questions are formed as lessons and teaching are observed and a collaborative conversation helps the teacher candidate to improve in specific targeted areas. When two teacher candidates observe and support each other, candidates practice areas in which feedback was given as well as reflect on not only their own teaching but the teaching being performed by the other teacher candidate.

Another positive that comes from peer coaching is that teacher candidates learn how to collaborate and communicate with others in the educational field (Bowman & McCormick, 2000). Collaboration is valued by other professionals and is a necessary part of the teaching environment.

Demonstrate

When instructors teach feedback that recognizes the impact of varied approaches on student motivation, engagement, and independence, they must address the confounding variable of trauma so not to victimize the students again. In addition, instructors must teach how to give feedback that is culturally responsive in social-emotional learning.

PEER COACHING for EDUCATORS

FIVE STEPS*

1. **REQUEST A VISIT (5 minutes):** the teacher or person to be coached initiates the coaching process by requesting an observation of one skill or problem

2. **VISIT (10 minutes):** observing one skill or problem

3. **REFLECTING ALONE:**
   REVIEW NOTES AND LIST SOME POSSIBILITIES
   (5 minutes)

4. **REFLECTING TOGETHER: TALK AFTER THE VISIT**
   (10 minutes): discussing only the actual facts and the data gathered on the skill requested to be observed

5. **DEBRIEFING: PROCESS REVIEW (3 minutes):** analyzing the deconstruction of the observed skill and the process of coaching itself

Figure 11-1. The five steps of peer coaching. (Reproduced with permission from *Peer Coaching for Educators*, Barbara Gottesman, Rowman and Littlefield, all rights reserved.)

Trauma-Informed Practices

Behavior management is not a one-size-fits-all endeavor. Rather, teacher candidates must understand the importance of individual experiences that work to shape a student's behavior both inside and outside the school environment. Care must be taken on behalf of the instructor and cooperating teacher to discuss, reflect, and give expert input to track and refine their interventions to provide the teacher candidate with feedback related to such experiences. This is especially true regarding a student's confirmed or suspected experience of trauma. Considering that roughly 26% of children in the United States witness or experience a trauma before the age of 4 years (Briggs-Gowan et al., 2010), many educators, including special education teacher candidates, are likely to daily or near-daily encounter a child who has experienced trauma. Of course, teachers and teacher candidates may also have experienced trauma in adulthood or childhood. These traumas may include early loss or lack of consistent caregivers; emotional, physical, or sexual abuse; domestic violence; various forms of neglect; natural disasters; medical and surgical procedures; and serious accidents (Herman 1997; National Child Traumatic Stress Network Schools Committee, 2008; van der Kolk, 2005). In 2012 alone, an estimated 686,000 children were victims of child abuse and neglect (USDHHS, 2013)—just one form of trauma that affects students and their learning.

A child who has survived trauma may experience delays and difficult behaviors in the following areas: language and communication, social and emotional regulation, building relationships, and play (Statman-Weil, 2015). Childhood trauma survivors can both frustrate and overwhelm teachers. Impairments in the developmental domains, including physical, cognitive, social-emotional, and language, are often manifested by difficult and troubling behaviors in the classroom (Koomar, 2009).

Such behaviors can perplex teachers because they are a result of internal processes that the children themselves do not necessarily understand and that the teachers cannot observe or understand (Koplow & Ferber, 2007; van der Kolk, 2005).

Research of the brain has confirmed that when children encounter a perceived threat to their physical or mental safety, their brains trigger a set of chemical and neurological reactions, more commonly known as the stress response. This response activates a child's biological instinct to fight, freeze, fawn, or flee (Porges 2004; Wright, 2014). Experiencing trauma at a young age can cause the stress response to become highly reactive or difficult to end whenever a child perceives threat. Threats can be as simple as a noise, a smell, tone of voice, a word, or an action. Triggers are highly individualized, based on a student's unique experiences.

When addressing the behavioral needs of students in the classroom, teacher candidates must be prepared with feedback regarding any student's experience with trauma. Such information related to the child's previous experiences will allow the teacher candidate to make informed decisions about how best to proceed when dealing with a behavior situation. What works for Johnny will likely not work for Sara, and what works for Sara will probably not work for Jackson. Thus, having the same behavioral expectations for all students would be a mistake. Instead, behavior approaches should be individualized, based on the needs and experiences of each individual student.

Teacher candidates should work to create and maintain consistent daily routines for the classroom to create a feeling of stability and safety (National Child Traumatic Stress Network Schools Committee, 2008). Students should be alerted when events in the classroom will not follow a previously predicted pattern to mitigate feelings of fear and uncertainty (van der Kolk, 2005). Behavioral and academic choices should be developmentally appropriate so that students can take control and build self-esteem (National Child Traumatic Stress Network Schools Committee, 2008). Rather than being reactive to behavior within the classroom, teacher candidates must be proactive and predict difficulty before it occurs so that the student can be given the tools needed to successfully navigate the experience. Using explicit instruction, teacher candidates can work to teach self-regulation, self-awareness, and problem solving. Teacher candidates must ensure that students are given opportunities to practice skills that will replace those already ingrained in their psyche. Positive guidance, nurturing, and affection need to provide the foundation for behavioral approaches chosen. More simply stated, trauma-informed practices need to be provided for all so that students with documented trauma, those whose trauma has not been formally acknowledged, and those who may be affected by the trauma of a current classmate can be supported to the fullest extent (Cole et al., 2005).

Regarding trauma, teacher candidates must also consider the likelihood that they may experience what is known as secondary traumatic stress (STS). Secondary traumatic stress can occur when educators are negatively impacted by their exposure to traumatized students. Secondary traumatic stress is defined as "the natural and consequent behaviors and emotions resulting from knowing about traumatizing events experienced by a significant other [or] the stress resulting from helping or wanting to help a traumatized or suffering person" (Figley, 1995, p. 7). Stamm (1999) defined this kind of trauma as "natural, predictable, treatable, and preventable, unwanted consequence of working with suffering people" (pp. 3-4). Because educators develop empathic and caring relationships with students, STS can be viewed as a natural consequence of their work (Figley, 1995). Thus, university supervisors must actively provide feedback if evidence of such a consequence occurs.

Because such trauma is considered inevitable, it should not be viewed as a weakness of any kind on the part of the teacher. Instead, STS should be acknowledged and immediately addressed. In fact, Yassen (1995) explained that professionals must not ignore the effects of STS but rather should adequately attend to them so that they do not result in harm to the teacher candidate, teacher, their colleagues, family, friends, or any other individual to whom a professional responsibility and/or obligation may exist.

Self-care is a much-needed tool necessary to foster resilience for both the adults and students who may be directly or indirectly affected by trauma. One recommendation for educators to protect themselves from STS is to aim to have a balanced life in which their own needs are taken into account, along with the needs of work, home, family, and friends (Stamm, 1995). Talking with colleagues, attending training workshops, spending time with family or friends, taking vacations, socializing, exercising, limiting workload, and developing spiritual life can all be effective forms of self-care (Pearlman, 1999). Feedback can also include inquiry and instruction on the types of self-care being utilized by the teacher candidate to ensure that the candidate is actively addressing the stress that results from work within the classroom. Note: We want to recognize that we do not support making individuals responsible for managing unreasonable work demands—a criticism of self-care—but introduce a conversation about balance, which could become an opportunity to discuss structural changes that might also build resilience like political influence, unionization, fair compensation, and others.

Social-Emotional Learning

Vast research has provided evidence as to why it is vital for teachers, regardless of school type or level, to develop culturally responsive social-emotional learning (SEL) skills, starting with preservice training (Cruz et al., 2014; Gay, 2001; Hammond, 2015; Hecht & Shin, 2015; Immordino-Yang et al., 2018; Jones et al., 2013; Schonert-Reichl et al., 2017; Villegas & Lucas, 2002). Providing culturally responsive SEL skill development in teacher preparation programs supports the efforts of new teachers to develop foundational competencies in numerous areas, including maintaining their own health, well-being, and emotional resilience to avoid burnout (Jennings, 2019), and fostering students' SEL skills through strength-based, rigorous academic learning (Gay, 2001; Hammond, 2015).

Teacher candidates need time, support, and feedback to develop psychological and emotional resilience to face the ever-growing demands of the teaching profession. Complex diversity of students' backgrounds and needs, high-stakes testing and accountability, lack of quality mentoring, and a small number of professional development opportunities are just the tip of the iceberg. Classroom management challenges often emerge during the first year, and many new teachers feel unprepared to manage their classroom effectively (Intrator, 2006; Koller & Bertel, 2006). Supporting teacher candidates in their efforts to develop their own social-emotional learning skills and agility can help to broaden their capacities for handling the normal yet extremely complex challenges of teaching within a classroom. Sadly, most teacher education programs focus exclusively on instructional skills, with little to no emphasis on teaching teacher candidates how to be aware of their own social and emotional well-being, how to interpret their own emotions, and how to manage personal emotions so they are able to bolster and not interfere with their teaching (Hosotani & Imai-Matsumura, 2011; Intrator, 2006).

The current rate of teacher attrition points to a need for preservice teaching programs to purposefully and explicitly cultivate teacher candidates' psychological and emotional resilience. Such an approach—transformational learning—requires teacher candidates to transform their "frames of reference through critical reflection on the assumptions upon which interpretations, beliefs, and habits of mind or points of view are based" (Mezirow, 1997, p. 7). Such a capacity for transformational self-awareness is imperative to teachers' development of solid social emotional competencies, including self-awareness, self-management, social awareness, responsible decision-making, and relationships management (Jennings & Greenberg, 2009).

The development and nurturing of these competencies when providing behavior feedback will allow teacher candidates to better manage personal emotions, handle conflict constructively, establish positive relationships guided by empathy, engage in perspective taking, make responsible decisions, and handle challenging situations effectively (Durlak et al., 2015). In addition, the development of such social-emotional skills can also enable teacher candidates to provide cognitively challenging and creative instructional practices that optimize meaningful student learning (Donahue-Keegan et al., 2019).

TABLE 11-2. SPOTLIGHT ON ADULT LEARNING			
SPECIFICITY	**IMMEDIACY**	**PURPOSEFULNESS**	**CONSTRUCTIVENESS**
Is the same language being used when delivering feedback as when teaching how to deliver feedback? How is the feedback language addressing the adult learners' need to know and readiness to learn?	Does the feedback respect the autonomy of the adult learner? What is the balance of in-the-moment and reflective feedback? How do different feedback models attend to the prior experience and orientation to learning of the adult learner?	Is the feedback related to the learning task and respectful of the self-concept of the learners, the prior experience of the learners, and their readiness to learn?	How is the practice of reflection for feedback intentionally created to motivate and orient the adult learner? In what ways is feedback sensitive to adult learners' self-concept, prior experience, and readiness to learn?

SPOTLIGHT ON ADULT LEARNING

Preparing special education teacher candidates for giving feedback in the K-12 classroom in social, emotional, and behavioral contexts encompasses every principle of adult learning theory. Because social and emotional learning is included in the K-12 curriculum, all teacher candidates need to know how to deliver feedback in this context. All feedback has the potential to be emotionally charged, so the self-concept and prior experience of the adult learner should be validated as instructors give, exhibit, and teach feedback. Finally, making sure the feedback that instructors give is life-related, contextual, and has a personal payoff to the adult learner is probably more important in the area of social, emotional, and behavioral learning than in other areas (Table 11-2).

POSSIBLE BARRIERS TO USING THIS TYPE OF FEEDBACK

One common barrier to feedback that continuously arises when working with teacher candidates is readiness to hear the instructor feedback. While teacher candidates may be receptive, they do not respond to the feedback and incorporate it into their instruction by the next observation period. If candidates are still not responsive, then the instructor may request a meeting before the next observation time to restate the expectation of the improvement, model appropriate uses of the expectation, have candidates practice with the university supervisor, and give candidates opportunities to brainstorm how they can specifically incorporate feedback within their lesson planning and provide prompts for their own implementation throughout the lesson. If feedback is still not incorporated, the university supervisor may choose to parallel teach with the candidate and even provide in vivo feedback during the lesson.

PRACTICAL APPLICATION

The following practical application demonstrates how teaching feedback requires instructors to explicitly teach what feedback looks like and sounds like in the classroom for K-12 learners. The direct observation form provides instructors a strategy in communicating how to use feedback to increase student outcomes.

Direct Observation Form

A process of direct observation for teacher candidate supervision produces explicit data-driven feedback on performance. The process of supervision can at times be overwhelming, with multiple domains having to be analyzed at once for a candidate. A format that breaks down instructional behaviors into observable and measurable targets can give structure to sometimes ambiguous performance targets. One specific advantage is that teacher candidates' skill performance can be analyzed as a group to identify similar difficulties in instructional techniques across candidates. If they exist, group instruction in coursework can be modified or reviewed to ensure a solid foundation for candidates. Also, the quantitative nature of direct observation lends itself to creating personal goals and performance feedback for candidates that is self-driven rather than supervisor-driven. This mindset makes growth by the candidate more intrinsically valuable and will most likely have lasting impact.

One example of a direct observation form for use with teacher candidates is the classroom observation tool as part of Positive Behavior Interventions and Supports (PBIS), which can be accessed by visiting https://www.pbis.org/resource/positive-behavior-support-classroom-management-self-assessment. This tool incorporates universal components of effective classrooms and combines the literature on foundational management strategies within a simple document and checklist across each component. It also has a specific format for collecting observational data on behavior-specific praise and opportunities to respond. A university supervisor could use this format across observations to give candidates concrete feedback on their teaching behaviors. For instance, if a teacher candidate was not universally engaging students with material or was engaging just a few students, a classroom observation tool could set targets for increasing individual and group opportunities to respond, and the university supervisor and teacher candidate could select instruction targets for lessons and observation. In addition, it could also be used by the candidate for self-monitoring and self-assessment. An advantage of using PBIS-created tools for supervision is that these practices are becoming more prevalent across the country, and numerous free resources and training related to implementation are now available. A record of PBIS classroom observation tools provides evidence to future employers that teacher candidates are familiar with this popular and important approach to intervention. Experience with PBIS observation will also give candidates a solid foundation for implementation of more intensive strategies and has been well-documented to prevent the occurrence of problem behaviors.

Another option for using direct observation and interview to help assist teacher candidates is to use the Classroom Check-Up (CCU; Reinke et al., 2008). With minimal adaptation, a university supervisor can use the model provided by Reinke and colleagues to help teacher candidates understand the current classroom dynamic and move forward with additional support. This can be especially helpful when teacher candidates have a resistant cooperating teacher because they can partner with the candidate within the CCU process. It is also helpful when university supervisors are working with alternatively certified teacher candidates who may already have a classroom in which they are primary instructor but where practices not conducive to effective learning environments are observed. Because the CCU provides more autonomy in practice selection, it may be more compatible with the current classroom and instructional culture. The CCU has six steps: (a) assess classroom, (b) provide feedback, (c) choose intervention, (d) provide choice of practices, (e) engage in action planning, and (f) continue ongoing monitoring. This format takes direct observation to another

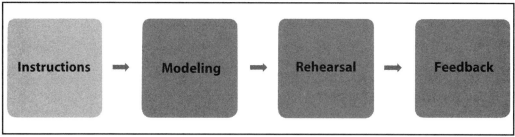

Figure 11-2. Behavior skill training model.

level by also giving the instructor explicit support about the intervention and skills on how to elicit change, using an evidence-based format and construction of performance feedback.

Behavioral Skills Training

Behavioral skills training (BST) is an evidence-based intervention that can help support teacher candidates in understanding how to implement behavioral interventions in the classroom. Two key aspects of BST are modeling skills and meeting a predetermined level of competency (Parsons et al., 2013). With teacher candidates, this would look like the supervisor explaining and teaching the teacher candidate a specific skill. The skill would not be mastered until the teacher candidate demonstrates the skill at a level that was previously agreed upon between the supervisor and teacher candidate. The skill must be observed by the supervisor.

Behavioral skills training can best be described in four steps (Figure 11-2). First, the supervisor must instruct the teacher candidate on the skill they are wanting them to learn. Second, the supervisor will model the skill for the teacher candidate so the teacher candidate can observe exactly how the supervisor expects to see the skill implemented. Third, the supervisor will have the teacher candidate rehearse or demonstrate the skill. Finally, the supervisor will provide specific feedback to the teacher candidate on how they performed the skill.

The use of BST in teacher candidate education programs can be utilized by using the four-step approach to teach at any school. The BST can easily be implemented with video modeling, modeling, direct instruction, and feedback.

Positive Behavior Interventions and Supports
Universal Components

Tier 1 includes universal management strategies that should meet the needs of all students. Utilizing these strategies with teacher candidates are vital because they need to understand the strategies to use and apply them in their own future classrooms. Teacher candidates should be taught how to teach specific behaviors, how to provide positive reinforcement for behaviors that must be seen in the classroom, and how to make sure the learning environment is conducive to learning (Missouri Schoolwide Positive Behavior Support, 2018-2019).

The following questions are provided to guide your review and reflection in the Authentic Example that follows, contributed by Amy Gaumer Erickson, PhD.

- In this example, how does the instructor apply knowledge of teaching feedback to support students' behavioral needs? Reflect.
- How do you teach feedback in the context of behavioral supports and interventions?
- What are some ways an instructor can teach feedback to preservice teachers that reflect the research and evidence-based practices for supporting students with emotional and behavioral support needs in K-12 instruction?

AUTHENTIC EXAMPLE

Contributed by
Amy Gaumer Erickson, PhD

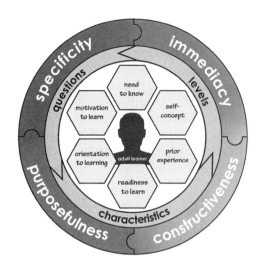

1. Course Details

SPE 707: Adolescents With Disabilities in the Middle/Secondary General Classroom is a course designed for fifth-year teacher candidates after an initial 6-week student teaching experience. Teacher candidates are finishing their teaching license requirements in a dual credit program toward both a bachelor's and master's degree. This course is designed to enable novice teachers to master and apply the instructional and communicative skills that will facilitate appropriate and productive inclusion of middle- and secondary-age students with disabilities within general education classrooms and other school settings. The course facilitates increased knowledge and application of research-based strategies in curriculum content acquisition, behavioral management, collaborative structures, self-determination, and secondary transition planning.

2. Learning Objectives

The aligned course objectives/professional learning standards are as follows:

a. Knowledge about individualized education plan development and participation.

b. Knowledge about individual, class, and school-wide behavior management strategies and programs to create learning environments that encourage positive social interaction, active engagement in learning, and self-motivation.

c. Knowledge about instruction that addresses the varied needs of students (i.e., culturally and linguistically diverse students, students with exceptionalities, and the full range of "typical" learners), including basic principles of universal design, content enhancement tools and routines, and learning strategies.

Purpose

Changing behavior is not an easy endeavor. Teachers often assume that if they set an expectation and tell students to eliminate a behavior that is not conducive to learning, the student will immediately be able to modify the behavior. This assignment teaches early-career educators that behavioral change takes time, effort, and a strong support system. In this assignment, none of the course participants are perfectly successful, and many fail to reach their self-selected goals. Grading is not based on success in behavioral change but rather on following the process and reflecting throughout regarding challenges and successes. This assignment also ensures that teachers understand the functional behavioral assessment protocol and the importance of consistency and ongoing support in implementation of intervention/support plans.

3. Assignment Description

Instructions Provided to Students

This project will help you change a behavior in yourself, and along the way you will become more familiar with behavioral modification techniques used in schools. Select a behavior that you would like to change. This behavior must be within your control and occur often enough that you can monitor the behavior on a daily basis. By changing this behavior, you will become a better teacher (e.g., by becoming healthier, more self-regulated, well-rested). You will receive feedback on your assignment from the instructor and at least one other student in the course. Write a paper that includes the following components: (a) functional behavioral assessment, (b) intervention/support plan, (c) intervention implementation, and (d) reflection.

Part 1. Functional Behavioral Assessment (5 Points). Choose a behavior you would like to change in yourself. Write a brief (one-half page maximum) description of the target behavior. Observe the behavior for one week and then complete the Functional Behavioral Assessment. Almost any behavior will work for this project, but please discuss the behavior with the instructor if you have questions regarding its appropriateness. Identify someone who will act as your support partner in helping you meet your goal and identify the role that person will play. Example forms are provided.

Part 2. Intervention/Support Plan (5 Points). Write a Behavior Intervention Plan or Student Support Plan, based on the Functional Behavioral Assessment. Do not forget that rewards are more effective than punishments and that most behavior change requires both short-term and long-term rewards. Be sure to set a goal and identify the replacement behavior you would like to see. Example forms are provided.

Part 3. Intervention Implementation (5 Points). Implement the plan for two weeks, monitoring your progress each day (e.g., graph, tally). Write a brief journal entry each day, discussing your progress toward reaching your goal, including challenges and effective strategies.

Part 4. Reflection (5 Points). Reflect on the effectiveness of the intervention, describe any setbacks you had along the way, and evaluate the use of behavior intervention techniques in your daily life. Discuss how these techniques can be beneficial to students in your future classroom and how you, as the classroom teacher, can support students' behavioral improvements. This reflection is typically one to two single-spaced pages.

The grading rubric for the paper assignment is shown in Table 11-3.

TABLE 11-3. RUBRIC FOR PAPER ASSIGNMENT			
ASSIGNMENT ELEMENT	**SCORING CRITERIA**	**SCORE**	**FEEDBACK**
Part 1. Functional Behavioral Assessment	• The identified behavior is in the individual's control. • The functions of the behavior are described in detail; all functions are considered, although some functions may not be applicable.	/5	
Part 2. Intervention/ Support Plan	• The replacement behavior is a positive change related to the target behavior. • Interventions are detailed and address the functions of behavior.	/5	
Part 3. Intervention Implementation	• Daily monitoring is recorded. • Journal outlines the challenges and effective strategies, demonstrating reflective practice.	/5	
Part 4. Reflection	• Successes and challenges are summarized. • Intervention techniques are evaluated, demonstrating reflective practice. • The role of the general education teacher is discussed, including techniques the teacher can enact to support behavioral improvements.	/5	

5. Additional Details

Numerous example forms are available for the Functional Behavior Assessment and Behavior Intervention Plan. Ideally, you will utilize forms similar to those that your teacher candidates will encounter in local educational settings. Ensure that the forms facilitate detailed reflection on the function of behavior(s) and identification of positive replacement behavior(s).

6. *Feedback Reflection*

Evidence of feedback: Instructor, peer, and self-reflection feedback are embedded within the assignment. This assignment occurs across six weeks.

a. During Week 1, each student identifies their target behavior. The instructor provides feedback to each student on the description of the target behavior, ensuring that the behavior is in the student's control and occurs at a frequency for which daily monitoring is applicable. Common target behaviors include reducing procrastination of schoolwork, exercising regularly, going to bed earlier, limiting alcohol or tobacco intake, reducing caffeine, increasing water consumption, eating healthier, and studying regularly. Feedback is provided in writing. If the behavior does not meet the criteria, individual meetings are scheduled with students to discuss revisions.

b. During Week 2, each student completes the Functional Behavioral Assessment. In partners during class, students share and discuss their assessments, providing feedback to each other on the strength of the analysis and additional behavior functions to consider. These partners then discuss interventions and implementation steps, brainstorming together.

c. Students can revise their Functional Behavioral Assessments based on peer feedback. Part 1 of the assignment is then uploaded to the learning management system. Feedback (strength of the analysis and additional behavior functions to consider) is provided by the instructor.

d. During Week 3, students complete their intervention/support plans. Students again briefly discuss with their partners, providing each other with feedback regarding the alignment between interventions and functions of behavior. These partners determine how to support each other during the 2-week intervention process. Typically, this support includes reminders, positive persuasion, and check-ins at opportune moments.

e. During Weeks 4 and 5, students implement their plans. During class, partners check in with each other regarding progress and challenges. When necessary, interventions are modified based on reflection and feedback.

f. The complete assignment is due before class on Week 6. During class, students discuss challenges to behavior modification, as well as strategies that supported their progress. This discussion includes an acknowledgment that changing behavior is difficult and takes concerted effort over time. Two weeks is not long enough to sustain a new habit, but students have made positive progress. Effective strategies include having a positive support system that provides encouragement, especially when setbacks have occurred.

g. The instructor reviews, grades, and provides feedback on each assignment. Feedback includes specific praise on behavior change strategies and implementation, explanation of the grade with constructive feedback, positive persuasion to keep moving forward in the behavior change, and denoted lessons learned regarding supporting students to change their behavior.

SUMMARY

Utilization and implementation of effective forms of teacher candidate feedback is a critical component to the successful development of an educator. If the instructor is intentional in their approach to feedback, it will allow for efficient implementation and constructive feedback of best practices in social, emotional, and behavioral feedback. This feedback must be purposeful in its delivery and provide a direct outcome that can be monitored and evaluated by both the teacher candidate and university supervisor.

OPPORTUNITY FOR GOING DEEPER

The following resources support deeper learning on concepts reflected in Chapter 11:

- Positive behavioral interventions and supports. Check the resources from the Technical Assistance Center on the PBIS website to improve the capacity of State educational agencies, local educational agencies, and schools to establish, scale-up, and sustain the PBIS framework. https://www.pbis.org/

- Classroom practices that support PBIS. Check the resources on the Midwest PBIS Network that support PBIS principles in the classroom. http://www.midwestpbis.org/materials/classroom-practices

- Team Workbook for Tier 1 PBIS: See pages 389-398 from this free resource on PBIS Classroom Observation Tools for walk-through and observations in the classroom of PBIS. https://pbismissouri.org/wp-content/uploads/2018/05/MO-SW-PBS-Tier-1-2018.pdf

- Trauma. The National Child Traumatic Stress Network was created by Congress in 2000 as part of the Children's Health Act to raise the standard of care and increase access to services for children and families who experience or witness traumatic events. https://www.nctsn.org/

- Social-emotional well-being. Committee for Children provides resources to positively transform the social-emotional well-being. https://www.cfchildren.org/

- Mounting a camera to observe in a classroom. Swivl is a robotic mount for an iPad (Apple, Inc.), camera, or smartphone that comes with a remote control. https://www.swivl.com/

REFERENCES

Adamson, R. M., McKenna, J. W., & Mitchell, B. (2019). Supporting all students: Creating a tiered continuum of behavior support at the classroom level to enhance schoolwide multi-tiered systems of support. *Preventing School Failure: Alternative Education for Children and Youth, 63*(1), 62-67. https://doi.org/10.1080/1045988X.2018.1501654

Bandura, A. (1977). *Social learning theory*. Prentice Hall.

Beijaard, D. (2005). *Teacher professional development in changing conditions*. Springer.

Benammar, K. (2004). *Conscious action through conscious thinking: Reflection tools in experiential learning. Public seminar.* Amsterdam University Press.

Benedict, A., Holdheide, L., Brownell, M., Foley, A. M. (2016). *Learning to teach: Practice-based preparation in teacher education*. http://ceedar.education.ufl.edu/wp-content/uploads/2016/07/Learning_To_Teach.pdf

Boud, D., Keogh, R., & Walker, D. (Eds.). (1985). *Reflection: Turning experience into learning*. Rouledge.

Bowman, C., & McCormick, S. (2000). Comparison of peer coaching versus traditional supervision effects. *Journal of Educational Research, 93*(4), 256-261. https://doi.org/10.1080/00220670009598714

Briggs-Gowan, M. J., Ford, J. D., Fraleigh, L., McCarthy, K., & Carter, A. S. (2010). Prevalence of exposure to potentially traumatic events in a healthy birth cohort of very young children in the northeastern United States. *Journal of Traumatic Stress, 23*(6), 725-733.

Brookfield, S. (1990). Using critical incidents to explore learners' assumptions. In J. Mezirow (Ed.), F*ostering critical reflection in adulthood: A guide to transformative and emancipatory learning* (pp. 177-193). Jossey-Bass.

Cole, S. F., O'Brien, J. G., Gadd, G., Ristuccia, J, Wallace, L., & Gregory, M. (2005). *Helping traumatized children learn: Supportive school environments for children traumatized by family violence*. Massachusetts Advocates for Children.

Colvin, G., Flannery, K. B., Sugai, G., & Monegan, J. (2009). Using observational data to provide performance feedback to teachers: A high school case study. *Preventing School Failure: Alternative Education for Children and Youth, 53*(2), 95-104.

Cruz, B. C., Ellerbrock, C. R., Vásquez, A., & Howes, E. V. (Eds.). (2014). *Talking diversity with teachers and teacher educators: Exercises and critical conversations across the curriculum*. Teachers College Press.

Danielowich, R. M. (2014). Personalizing science: Four lessons and five strategies for engaging diverse students with socio-scientific issues. *The Science Teacher, 81*(1), 47-52.

Dewey, J. (1933). *How we think: A restatement of the relation of reflective thinking to the educative process*. D. C. Heath & Co.

Donahue-Keegan, D., Villegas-Reimers, E., & Cressey, J. M. (2019). Integrating social-emotional learning and culturally responsive teaching in teacher education preparation programs: The Massachusetts experience so far. *Teacher Education Quarterly, 46*(4), 150-168.

Durlak, J. A., Domitrovich, C. E., Weissberg, R. P., & Gullotta, T. P. (Eds.). (2015). *Handbook of social and emotional learning: Research and practice.* Guilford.

Figley, C. R. (Ed.). (1995). *Compassion fatigue: Coping with secondary traumatic stress disorder in those who treat the traumatized.* Routledge.

Fisher, D., & Frey, N. (2014). *Better learning through structured teaching: A framework for the gradual release of responsibility* (2nd ed.). ASCD.

Fuchs, D., Fernstrom, P., Scott, S., Fuchs, L., & Vandermeer, L. (1994). Classroom ecological inventory: A process for mainstreaming. *Teaching Exceptional Children, 26*(3), 11-15.

Fund, Z. (2010). Effects of communities of reflecting peers on student-teacher development—including in-depth case studies. *Teachers and Teaching: Theory and Practice, 16*(6), 679-701.

Gay, G. (2001). Effective multicultural teaching practices. In C. F. Diaz (Ed.), *Multicultural education in the 21st century* (pp. 23-41). Longman.

Gottesman, B. (2000). *Peer coaching for educators* (2nd ed.). Scarecrow Education.

Hammond, Z. (2015). *Culturally responsive teaching & the brain: Promoting authentic engagement and rigor among culturally and linguistically diverse students.* Corwin.

Hébert, C. (2015). Knowing and/or experiencing: A critical examination of the reflective models of John Dewey and Donald Schön. *Reflective Practice, 16*(3), 361-371. https://doi.org/10.1080/14623943.2015.1023281

Hecht, M. L., & Shin, Y. (2015). Culture and social and emotional competencies. In J. A. Durlak, C. E. Domitrovich, R. P. Weissberg, & T. P. Gullotta (Eds.), *Handbook of social and emotional learning: Research and practice* (pp. 50-64). Guilford.

Herman, J. (1997). *Trauma and recovery: The aftermath of violence—from domestic abuse to political terror* (2nd ed.). Basic Books.

Hiebert, J., Gallimore, R., & Stigler, J. W. (2002) A knowledge base for the teaching profession: What would it look like and how can we get one? *Educational Researcher, 31*(5), 3-15. https://doi.org/10.3102/0013189X031005003

Hosotani, R., & Imai-Matsumura, K. (2011). Emotional experience, expression, and regulation of high-quality Japanese elementary school teachers. *Teaching and Teacher Education, 27*(6), 1039-1048. https://doi.org/10.1016/j.tate.2011.03.010

Immordino-Yang, M. H., Darling-Hammond, L., & Krone, C. (2018). *The brain basis for integrated social, emotional, and academic development: How emotions and social relationships drive learning.* The Aspen Institute.

Intrator, S. M. (2006). Beginning teachers and the emotional drama of the classroom. *Journal of Teacher Education, 57*(3), 232-239. https://doi.org/10.1177/0022487105285890

Jennings, P. A. (2019). *The trauma-sensitive classroom: Building resilience with compassionate teaching.* W. W. Norton.

Jennings, P. A., & Greenberg, M. T. (2009). The prosocial classroom: Teacher social and emotional competence in relation to student and classroom outcomes. *Review of Educational Research, 79*(1), 491-525. https://doi.org/10.3102/0034654308325693

Jones, S. M., Bouffard, S. M., & Weissbourd, R. (2013). Educators' social and emotional skills vital to learning. *Phi Delta Kappan, 94*(8), 62-65. https://doi.org/10.1177/003172171309400815

Koller, J. R., & Bertel, J. M. (2006). Responding to today's mental health needs of children, families and schools: Revisiting the preservice training and preparation of school based personnel. *Education and Treatment of Children, 29*(2), 197-217.

Koomar, J. A. (2009). Trauma- and attachment-informed sensory integration assessment and intervention. *Sensory Integration: Special Interest Section Quarterly, 32*(4), 1-4.

Koplow, L., & Ferber, J. (2007). The traumatized child in preschool. In L. Koplow (Ed.), *Unsmiling faces: How preschools can heal* (2nd ed., pp. 175-193). Teachers College Press.

Korthagen, F. A. J. (2004). In search of the essence of a good teacher: Towards a more holistic approach in teacher education. *Teaching and Teacher Education, 20*(1), 77-97.

Korthagen, F., & Vasalos, A. (2005). Levels in reflection: Core reflection as a means to enhance professional growth. *Teachers and Teaching: Theory and Practice, 11*(1), 47-71.

LaBoskey, V. K. (2010). Teacher education and models of teacher reflection. In P. Peterson, E. Baker, & B. McGaw (Eds.), *International encyclopedia of education* (Vol. 7, pp. 629-634). Elsevier.

Lamb, P., Lane, K., & Aldous, D. (2012). Enhancing the spaces of reflection: A buddy peer-review process within physical education initial teacher education. *European Physical Education Review, 19*(1), 21-38.

Langer, E. J. (1989). *Mindfulness.* Addison-Wesley.

Leijen, Ä., Valtna, K., Leijen, D. A. J., & Pedaste, M. (2012). How to determine the quality of students' reflections? *Studies in Higher Education, 37*(2), 203-217.

Loughran, J. J. (2002). Effective reflective practice: In search of meaning in learning about teaching. *Journal of Teacher Education, 53*(1), 33-43. https://doi.org/10.1177/0022487102053001004

McLeskey, J., Barringer, M-D., Billingsley, B., Brownell, M., Jackson, D., Kennedy, M., Lewis, T., Maheady, L., Rodriguez, J., Scheeler, M. C., Winn, J., & Ziegler, D. (2017). *High-leverage practices in special education.* Council for Exceptional Children & CEEDAR Center. https://highleveragepractices.org/wp-content/uploads/2017/06/Preface.Intro1_.pdf

Mezirow, J. (1991). *Transformative dimensions of adult learning.* Jossey-Bass.

Mezirow, J. (1997). Transformative learning: Theory to practice. *New Directions for Adult & Continuing Education, 74*(Summer), 5-12. https://doi.org/10.1002/ace.7401

Missouri Schoolwide Positive Behavior Support. (2018-2019). *Tier 1 team workbook.* https://pbismissouri.org/wp-content/uploads/2018/05/MO-SW-PBS-Tier-1-2018.pdf

Moon, J. A. (2004). *A handbook of reflective and experiential learning theory and practice.* Routledge Taylor & Francis

Nagro, S. A., & Cornelius, K. E. (2013). Evaluating the evidence base of video analysis: A special education teacher development tool. *Teacher Education and Special Education: The Journal of the Teacher Education Division of the Council for Exceptional Children, 36*(4), 312-329. https://doi.org/10.1177/0888406413501090

National Child Traumatic Stress Network Schools Committee. (2008). *Child trauma toolkit for educators.* National Child Traumatic Stress Network.

Oliver, R. M., & Reschly, D. J. (2007). *Effective classroom management: Teacher preparation and professional development.* National Comprehensive Center for Teacher Quality. https://files.eric.ed.gov/fulltext/ED543769.pdf

Osunde, E. O. (1996). The effect on student teachers of the teaching behaviors of cooperating-teachers. *Education, 116*(4), 612-618.

Parsons, M. B., Rollyson, J. H., & Reid, D. H. (2013). Teaching practitioners to conduct behavioral skills training: A pyramidal approach for training multiple human service staff. *Behavior Analysis in Practice, 6*(2), 4-16.

Pearlman, L. A. (1999). Self-care for trauma therapists: Ameliorating vicarious traumatization. In B. H. Stamm (Ed.), *Secondary traumatic stress: Self-care issues for clinicians, researchers, and educators* (2nd ed., pp. 51-64). Sidran Press.

Porges, S. W. (2004). Neuroception: A subconscious system for detecting threats and safety. *Zero to Three, 24*(5), 19-24.

Reinke, W. M., Lewis-Palmer, T., & Merrell, K. (2008). The classroom check-up: A classwide teacher consultation model for increasing praise and decreasing disruptive behavior. *School Psychology Review, 37*(3), 315-332. https://doi.org/10.1080/02796015.2008.12087879

Schön, D. A. (1983). *The reflective practitioner: How professionals think in action.* Basic Books.

Schonert-Reichl, K. A., Kitil, M. J., & Hanson-Peterson, J. (2017, February). *To reach the students, teach the teachers: A national scan of teacher preparation and social and emotional learning. A report prepared for the Collaborative for Academic, Social, and Emotional Learning.* University of British Columbia.

Seibert, K. W. (1999). Reflection-in-action: Tools for cultivating on-the-job learning conditions. *Organizational Dynamics, 27*(3), 54-65.

Seibert, K. W., & Daudelin, M. W. (1999). *The role of reflection in managerial learning: Theory, research, and practice.* Quorum.

Seidel, T., Stürmer, K., Blomberg, G., Kobarg, M., & Schwindt, K. (2011). Teacher learning from analysis of videotaped classroom situations: Does it make a difference whether teachers observe their own teaching or that of others? *Teaching and Teacher Education, 27*(2), 259-267.

Showers, B., & Joyce, B. (1996). The evolution of peer coaching. *Educational Leadership, 53*(6), 12-16.

Shulman, L. S., & Shulman, J. H. (2004). How and what teachers learn: A shifting perspective. *Journal of Curriculum Studies, 36*(2), 257-271.

Sparks-Langer, G. M., & Colton, A. B. (1991). Synthesis of research on teacher's reflective thinking. *Educational Leadership, 48*(6), 37-44.

Stamm, B. H. (Ed.). (1999). *Secondary traumatic stress: Self-care issues for clinicians, researchers, and educators* (2nd ed.). Sidran Press.

Statman-Weil, K. (2015). Creating trauma-sensitive classrooms. *Young Children, 70*(2), 72-79.

Thorndike, E. L. (1913). *Educational psychology* (Vols. 1-2). Columbia University Press.

U.S. Department of Health and Human Services. (2013). Results from the School Health and Policies and Practices Study 2012. http://www.cdc.gov/HealthyYouth/shpps/index.htm

van der Kolk, B. A. (2005). Developmental trauma disorder: Toward a rational diagnosis for children with complex trauma histories. *Psychiatric Annals, 35*(5), 401-408.

Villegas, A. M., & Lucas, T. (2002). Preparing culturally responsive teachers: Rethinking the curriculum. *Journal of Teacher Education, 53*(1), 20-32. https://doi.org/10.1177/0022487102053001003

Vygotsky, L. (1994). The problem of the environment. In R. van der Veer, & J. Valsiner (Eds.), *The Vygotsky reader* (pp. 338-354). Blackwell.

Watson, J. B. (1913). Psychology as the behaviorist views it. *Psychological Review, 20*(2), 158-277.

Weibell, C. J. (2011). *Principles of learning: 7 principles to guide personalized, student-centered learning in the technology-enhanced, blended learning environment.* https://principlesoflearning.wordpress.com

Wright, T. (2014). Too scared to learn: Teaching young children who have experienced trauma. Research in Review. Y*oung Children, 69*(5), 88-93.

Yassen, J. (1995). Preventing secondary traumatic stress disorder. In C. R. Figley (Ed.), *Compassion fatigue: Coping with secondary traumatic stress disorder in those who treat the traumatized* (pp. 178-208). Routledge.

Teaching Feedback in Collaboration

FEEDBACK SCENARIO

Elsa is a bright, articulate, imaginative first grader. She began reading at 4 years of age and was quickly reading chapter books at levels suited for third graders. Elsa has an advanced vocabulary, an advantage perhaps due to an educated family—her mother has a master's degree and her grandmother has a doctorate degree. Elsa is a sensitive child, with a talented ability and interest in art as well as a desire to help others. She is outgoing and curious. Elsa loves to help and to be included; she enjoys her friends. She learns best when she is engaging hands-on.

About midway through the first semester of first grade, Elsa began having trouble falling asleep at night. She needed extra stories, songs, and comfort at bedtime. Even then, getting to sleep was a real chore. Elsa woke up a little more tired each day, and she would dawdle in the morning, causing conflict with her mother, as they had to rush to get out the door to avoid being late for school and work. Eventually, the dawdling turned to tears and requests to stay home from school. At night, Elsa would cry and beg to not have to go to school the next day. Something was definitely wrong. After the third night of bedtime tears, Ramona, Elsa's mom, finally got more information from Elsa than "I just don't want to go to school." In what seemed like a game of 20 questions, Elsa finally blurted, "*Teacher* yells at us all the time, and I feel scared." That very evening an email came from *Teacher* to all the parents of children in the classroom. The email offered an apology and described how *Teacher* had become overwhelmed and lost her cool with the students, even raising her voice. Ramona decided she would have to schedule a meeting with Elsa's teacher.

Ramona, although well-educated and articulate, loathed conflict of any kind. Having to address this issue with the teacher ranked highly with handling snakes and killing spiders as Ramona's worst nightmare. To bolster her courage and get some strategies, Ramona asked her mother for some advice. After all, her mother had frequent meetings with teachers when Ramona was in school, and

Elford, M. D., Smith, H. H., & James, S.
GET Feedback: Giving, Exhibiting, and Teaching Feedback in Special Education Teacher Preparation (pp. 233-247).
© 2022 SLACK Incorporated.

now her mother worked in the Department of Special Education to prepare future teachers. She was forever talking about parent involvement and parent-teacher collaboration.

Ramona's mother suggested three keys for a successful conversation that would help Ramona see the conversation as collaboration rather than conflict. First, she should approach the conversation with the "generous assumption" that *Teacher* wanted to do what was best for Elsa, just like does Ramona. Second, she should approach the conversation as a Third Space dialogue, where the information about the problem is the focus of the dialogue, thus eliminating taking sides. Instead, both people are working together to solve the problem. Third, she should do her best to employ all her well-honed active listening skills, specifically listening to understand, not to reply. Ramona's mother also suggested that Ramona compose some open-ended, nonthreatening questions in advance, which would lessen her cognitive load and minimize the stress of the situation.

Armed with generous assumptions, problem-centered focus for dialogue, a commitment to listen, and some well-worded questions, Ramona met with the teacher.

This chapter looks at the role of feedback as part of collaborative communication. We will focus on what collaborative conversation can look like, based on the principles of partnership, Third Space dialogue, and active listening, as well as how to use feedback as part of collaboration.

Chapter Objectives

This chapter builds on considering feedback in social, emotional, and behavioral contexts and addresses the role of feedback in collaborations with parents, related service providers, general education teachers, and administrators. As we will discuss, in special education teacher preparation there is the need to teach feedback with the following intentions: considering multiple perspectives, promoting active listening, and demonstrating collaborative practices. This chapter will describe the research on feedback in collaboration approaches and explain why there is utility in teaching how to give and receive feedback in collaborative relationships in your course. This chapter will also demonstrate how to incorporate feedback in collaborative relationships, with examples and prompts to take action.

In the past decade, research has emerged suggesting that adult learners benefit from being actively involved, are responsive to feedback, and are motivated to improve their teaching based on this feedback (Sogrunro, 2015). Common practice in special education has long supported collaboration as a key element of effective instructional practice. Therefore, special education teacher preparation instructors must intentionally teach how to employ feedback in collaborative relationships, as well as consider when collaborative feedback is most appropriate, while also recognizing the learning needs of adult students.

After reading this chapter you will **know** and **understand** these concepts and have the opportunity to **demonstrate** and **apply** your knowledge (Table 12-1).

Describe and Define

Special educators collaborate with a variety of individuals as a regular part of their role.

When we say collaboration, we mean working together toward a common goal, usually related to supports for a child's education. The multiple stakeholders in a child's education each come to the collaboration table with a different lens. Creating an environment of partnership and open authentic communication is essential for all the collaborative voices to be heard in a way that provides the greatest benefit for the child. In keeping with our previously stated definition, feedback is important in collaborative communication because it supplies the information for all stakeholders that informs their understanding and restructures their thinking and beliefs related to their performance, knowledge, or skills as they serve the child they have in common.

TABLE 12-1. GRAPHIC ORGANIZER		
KNOW (WHAT)	**UNDERSTAND (WHY)**	**DEMONSTRATE (HOW)**
What the research on collaboration and feedback suggests, especially for adult learners.	Why teaching feedback for collaborative relationships is grounded in communication skills and dispositions.	How to give feedback that recognizes: • Sharing of multiple perspectives • Active listening • How to give and solicit feedback
APPLY (TAKE ACTION)		
Apply elements of adult learning theory, cultural responsiveness, and collaborative communication in teaching feedback in course design, activities, and assignments.		

Know

Teaching feedback for collaboration is about understanding and using partnership communication. As special education instructors, being intentional about teaching feedback for collaboration is essential in communicating effectively for the best possible outcomes for the children in our care. Research on collaboration and feedback suggests that special educators must be skilled at communicating in ways that honors all stakeholders (Scheeler et al., 2010). This communication requires a partnership approach rather than one that is directive. Communicating as partners requires building trust, promoting autonomy, and embodying coaching behaviors through communication skills. Being able to effectively teach partnership for collaborative communication is the challenge that faces special education instructors. In this chapter, we describe partnership for collaborative communication and how coaching behaviors drive feedback for collaboration as well as explain the importance of developing collaborative relationships with adults.

Partnership for Collaborative Communication

A partnership occurs when two or more people invest their skills and energy in a common goal. The High-Leverage Practices in Special Education suggested that "collaboration allows for varied expertise and perspectives about a student to be shared among those responsible for the student's learning and well-being" (McLeskey et al., 2017, p. 15). When all stakeholders focus on the student's learning and well-being, collaboration is more likely to occur because the student is the center of the conversation. Partnership for collaborative communication can be envisioned as a dialogue that acknowledges, respects, and explores each other's perspectives through interactive, inclusive, and complementary discourse while focused on a common outcome. Achieving partnership for collaborative communication requires building trust, understanding the principles of partnership, and respecting the autonomy of all those involved in the collaboration.

Building Trust

Trust is a fundamental feature of partnership for collaborative communication. To establish trust, collaborators need to demonstrate openness, honesty, and candor (Johnson, 2008). Authentic and active listening is probably the fastest way to build trust. Authentic listening (Stone et al., 1999) includes a genuine curiosity about what the speaker is saying. When we listen to truly understand, we attribute value to a person's thoughts, ideas, perceptions, and feelings. Another important way to build trust is to establish a posture of genuine caring created by a holistic lens (e.g., acknowledging the communication partner as an individual with personal and professional pressures). According to Wheatley (2002), "human conversation is the most ancient and easiest way to cultivate conditions for change…. If we can sit together and talk about what is most important to us, we begin to come alive" (p. 3). These deeper levels of conversations occur only when trust or safety exists, possibly because of the reinforcing aspects of this understanding—we trust those who listen to us, and we speak candidly and vulnerably to those we trust. Trust fuels partnership, and partnership creates the opportunity for true collaborative communication to occur.

Principles of Partnership

Knight (2007) has identified seven principles of partnership for a coaching framework: (a) equality, (b) voice, (c) choice, (d) dialogue, (e) praxis, (f) reflection, and (g) reciprocity. Partnership is essential for collaborative communication. *Equality* allows people to recognize and accept the similarities and differences in individual knowledge, circumstance, and experience, while striving to treat one another as equal in value for what each has to offer to the collaborative exchange. *Voice* is the way individuals are encouraged to express their point of view. In partnership communication, all individuals are awarded the agency to express their opinion. *Choice* provides liberty and autonomy that permits individuals to exercise their own will in making decisions. Extending choice promotes equality. *Dialogue* is the exchange of ideas and perceptions that focuses on interrelated perspectives. It creates an opportunity to combine the strengths of all communicators to develop new approaches for solving problems or examining contexts. *Praxis* merges theory and practice in the action of doing the work. A key component for learning is the opportunity to apply what is being learned and refine it. *Reflection*, as in a mirror, permits viewers to scrutinize their own perspective. While examining the image in a mirror, the viewer retains the capacity to transform the image by changing what is being reflected. Partnership permits reflective thinkers the freedom to adopt or reject ideas. *Reciprocity* comes from empathic listening and responsiveness to the cultural ideas and norms offered by all the collaborators. Reciprocity encourages learning from every conversation, and learning comes from collective understanding (Freire, 1970; Senge, 1990). When these partnership principles are employed to create a Third Space for dialogue, the either/or decisions fade away, and mutual understanding that fosters respect is established. Third Space (Guiterrez, 2008) describes the dialogue that acknowledges, respects, and explores each other's perspectives in an interactive, inclusive, and complementary discourse. Through this dialogue (rather than a directive approach), divergent perspectives merge into a combined viewpoint that honors all the voices at the table. As this occurs, all members of the collaboration feel empowered to contribute to the newly co-constructed understanding, thus promoting transformative ideas and equitable practices.

Respecting Autonomy

In developmental psychology, autonomy is the capacity to make informed uncoerced decisions (Lickerman, 2012). Partnership for collaborative communication fosters autonomy by providing collaborators with different ways to think about topics rather than dictating what to think. Partnership for collaborative communication uses questions to enhance understanding, generate thinking, and honor other individuals' thoughts and ideas. In collaboration, autonomy is respected when there is room for all voices to be heard and when all collaborators are permitted the opportunity for choice. The quickest way to strip someone of autonomy is to silence them and give them no choice in the decisions. This is especially true of adults. As you may recall from Chapter 3, status can create barriers to feedback. The same is true in collaborative conversations. When communicating from a place of partnership, status takes a back seat because all the collaborators are adults whose autonomy is respected because each one is seen as an equal contributor to the collaboration. Each person has the right and opportunity to make decisions based on information not pressure from those in positions of power.

Understand

Why is collaboration important in special education teacher preparation? By the nature of their role, special educators must collaborate with a variety of other related service providers and educators to support K-12 students. Collaboration involves multiple people across different disciplines working together with a single focus—what is best for the student. Members of a collaboration team can include parents or guardians, general educators, special educators, related service providers (occupational therapists, physical therapists, speech pathologists, and psychologists), paraprofessionals, and advocates. With so many different people involved, learning to work together as partners can occur when the partnership principals fuel relationships and communication.

Collaboration driven by partnership looks like the following:

- Equality: Everyone matters, and no one is more important than anyone else.
- Voice: All ideas are valuable and encouraged.
- Choice: Work together in a variety of ways; no one way is dictated.
- Dialogue: Data describes and creates an understanding of current reality.
- Praxis: Goals are born out of what we really want to happen, and we seek to answer the question: *What is the goal?*
- Reflection: Collaborators think about what changes should occur and what it will take to make change happen.
- Reciprocity: Participants are determined to learn from others.

When collaboration is a partnership, no single individual dictates what occurs. Instead, all the collaborators work side-by-side, committed to achieving a common goal—what is best for the child. The 2017 Supreme Court decision in *Endrew F. v. Douglas County School District* (2017) now supports maximum benefit and...

> a new FAPE [free appropriate public education] standard for determining educational benefit. Thus, there is a new, higher benchmark for implementation of a student's IEP [individualized education plan], which now must be designed to confer more than just some educational benefit. New IEPs must be crafted to provide measurable benefit given a student's capabilities.

To focus on what is best for the child, every person involved in the child's IEP must have a voice in how the high benchmark for implementation of the IEP is achieved. The decisions should be informed by what parents and/or guardians can support, as well as input from all other stakeholders. Collaborative conversations, with a dedication to the common goal, will produce a plan that everyone agrees will lead to success for the child.

Demonstrate

How do we live out collaborative relationships? We have already established that successful collaboration is born of partnership. In addition to the principles of partnership, partnership for collaborative communication respects the identity of others, actively honors autonomy, and practices the language of ongoing regard. The following paragraphs will summarize these concepts.

First, personal identity can be described as the narrative we craft for ourselves, based on our own individual sense of self, as well as the nouns and adjectives we use to describe who we are in relationship to the rest of our associations. For instance, we describe relational identity when we use words like *son, daughter, parent,* etc. We define ourselves by reference points of significance when we identify different domains such as religious background; race, ethnicity, or nationality; class; profession; and others. Collective self-esteem adds to the complexity of personal identity. Respecting the identity of others necessitates empathy and the absence of judgment. Abandoning judgment permits collaborators to more readily honor autonomy and identity.

Next, by honoring autonomy, collaborators intentionally encourage all individuals to think for themselves. Third Space dialogue, born out of partnership, does not demand or require anyone to change their mind. Instead, partnership for collaborative communication involves working together through dialogue to reach a shared understanding. Honoring autonomy does not mean that everyone demands their own way. Instead, when autonomy is honored, it provides the agency an opportunity to engage in goal-driven dialogue. In this way, a common goal can be identified for the successful outcome regarding the child for whom the individuals are collaborating.

Finally, Kegan and Lahey (2001) described "the regular expression of genuinely experiencing the value of a coworker's behavior [as] the language of ongoing regard. Ongoing regard has two faces, one of appreciation and the other of admiration" (p. 94). Language of ongoing regard promotes partnership by changing not only how we communicate but how we actually view and feel about others. When we express appreciation, we are saying to the person that we have received something of value, something meaningful, something we feel happy to have. It need not be a material item; it can simply be the experience of working together with someone. Expressing admiration suggests that there is something about the other person's actions or choices that inspires, instructs, or enhances us.

Three criteria, or elements, are required to communicate using the language of ongoing regard. First, speak the words of appreciation or admiration directly to the person, not to others about the person. Second, be specific—describe exactly what you appreciate or admire about the person. Third, be nonattributive in your feedback. Communications of appreciation and admiration are more powerful when they do not describe the other's attributes but rather describe the experience of the speaker. This third criteria is the most complex, but it is essential to mastering the language of ongoing regard. Nonattributive language is the difference between saying, "Alice, you're so sweet to bring cookies to the meeting" and "Alice, I appreciated the cookies you brought to the meeting. The two I ate tasted delicious." The first phrase conveys, albeit unintentionally, a sense of Alice by describing her as sweet for her action of bringing cookies. Alice could argue that she was not behaving sweetly at all, instead she was selfishly trying to rid her house of cookies so she would not eat them. The second phrase conveys the speaker's experience of appreciation and enjoyment. Alice does not have to argue with you or in her head about her sweetness but can just simply accept the appreciation. To simplify this third criteria of nonattributive communication, we can think of the difference between "you statements" and "I statements." "You statements" can provoke pensiveness or argument, whereas "I statements" characterize the speaker's experience not the listener's. According to Kegan and Lahey (2001), "When we practice this non-characterizing, non-attributing form of communication, it inevitably ends up sounding more sincere, more real, more original" (p. 101). Living out collaborative relationships requires deep commitment to behave like partners, respect autonomy, enter into Third Space dialogue, and communicate in a way that honors all collaborators.

Spotlight on Adult Learning

The self-concept of the adult learner is the central principle for collaborative conversations. Autonomy allows the adult learner to make choices and be self-directing. Participating as a partner in collaborative conversations is a life-related, developmental task, thus meeting the readiness to learn principle. Being able to improve one's conversation skills has intrinsic value and a personal payoff, so the adult learner is motivated to learn. Using the G.E.T. Model taps into these areas of adult learning while intentionally planning instruction and feedback to teach the necessary skill of collaborative conversation (Table 12-2).

TABLE 12-2. SPOTLIGHT ON ADULT LEARNING			
SPECIFICITY	**IMMEDIACY**	**PURPOSEFULNESS**	**CONSTRUCTIVENESS**
How does the feedback align with the assignment outcomes?	Does the timing of the feedback meet the adult learner's self-concept?	How will the feedback address the adult learner's prior knowledge?	Does the feedback build capacity for the adult learner to determine next steps?
Does feedback focus on actionable steps or specific behaviors?	How much processing time fits the learning outcome?	Are there manageable steps and processes for practicing the new skills?	How does the feedback empower the adult learner to evaluate their own partnership and collaborative conversation practices?

POSSIBLE BARRIERS TO USING THIS TYPE OF FEEDBACK

Partnership is said to be the most difficult ship to sail. Taking the stance of a partner means mutual respect and humbly accepting someone else's beliefs and opinions as valuable as your own. If actually achieving this is not difficult enough, there are certain cultural expectations about hierarchies that create barriers to partnership necessary for collaboration. Another barrier exists in the reality of power differentials that exist in the educational system. Parents perceive (or fail to acknowledge) teachers as experts. Teachers assume status over paraprofessionals and other service providers. Administrators assign, hire, fire, and promote teachers. Is it possible to build enough trust in collaboration to voice a difference of opinion or make a suggestion that is different than one made by someone with greater power? Forming true partnerships for collaboration requires a concentrated effort and deep commitment to seek solutions, regardless of the magnitude of the barrier.

PRACTICAL APPLICATION

The following practical application provides an example for instructors to explicitly teach what feedback looks and sounds like for teacher candidates who collaborate with stakeholders of K-12 students. The assignment relies on the previous section's research to develop a framework for partnership that leads to collaborative conversation. Now, we will examine what collaborative conversation looks like, sounds like, and how we can create assignments that teach our teacher candidates how to develop this skill.

In a graduate course titled Family and Interprofessional Collaboration in Special Education, teacher candidates learn about collaboration in schools, community systems, and families through a series of assignments geared to building effective relationships among home, school, and community partners. The first assignment requires teacher candidates to describe themselves based on a social construct wheel, using artifacts to illustrate their description. Peers view one another's description and comment on commonalities and things they find interesting. This simulates a "getting to know you conversation" that a special educator might have with a professional colleague or family. After learning about communication from Friend and Cook (2017), teacher candidates analyze a series of videos where communication problems occur. The assignment requires the teacher candidate to describe the problem that results in a breakdown in communication and provide one or two suggestions for resolving the issue by demonstrating what they learned about inter- and intrapersonal communication. The instructor provides feedback through a rubric and written comments.

Armed with some knowledge about effective communication, teacher candidates apply what they have learned about collaborating with families and professional colleagues in an assignment, where the teacher candidate responds to two different scenarios by creating a script of a collaborative conversation. Through this script, the teacher candidate must apply active listening, appropriate use of questions, and dialogue to reach a common goal. The elements of this final assignment are described in the subsequent paragraphs herein. These elements provide the platform for the instructor to give feedback to the teacher candidates because these elements have been explicitly taught and consistently modeled during the course.

First, collaborative conversations require that we listen more than we talk. Listening is more than not talking; it is actually being active in the conversation by listening to understand rather than listening to respond. Active listening is a skill that can be acquired and developed with practice. However, active listening can be difficult to master; therefore, it will take time and patience to develop. Active listening means fully concentrating on what is being said rather than just passively "hearing" the message of the speaker. Active listening involves listening with all the senses as well as giving full attention to the speaker, which is very difficult in our world full of noise in interference and outside interruption. It is important that the active listener is also **seen** to be listening, otherwise the speaker may conclude that what they are talking about is uninteresting to the listener. Nonverbal signs of attentive or active listening include eye contact, nodding your head, smiling, posture, mirroring facial expressions, and saying "yes" or "mmmhmm" to encourage the speaker to continue. Although listening is the most fundamental of intrapersonal skills, it is easy to describe but difficult to master.

Second, collaborative conversations use powerful questions to create a deeper and more comprehensive shared understanding. According to Barkley (2011):

> ...questioning strategies are the educator's mainstay. Whether to influence student behavior; assess student understanding; determine the needs of parents, students, or administrators; or pose reflective inquiries of themselves, teachers use questioning as a life raft for getting through the complexities of any given day. Questions are designed to probe for further information, enhance understanding and generate [student] thinking. (p. 38)

To simplify this questioning strategy, consider the three purposes for asking questions—to clarify, to guide, and for genuine curiosity. Clarification questions are most often closed questions, meaning they can be answered with either yes or no or with a short phrase. Guiding questions or questions originating from genuine curiosity are open-ended questions. Good open questions usually begin with "how" or "what" and invite the conversation partner to give longer, more thoughtful answers. Asking questions promotes dialogue, honors another person's thoughts and ideas, encourages critical thinking, and fuels listening skills. Being intentional in asking questions creates a give-and-take dialogue, where shared understanding emerges.

Finally, collaborative conversations seek to find a solution to whatever problem may be hindering the K-12 student's progress. Szabó et al. (2009) offered the following solution-focused approach with these tenets: (a) everything is easier when we know what we want, (b) small steps bring big changes, and (c) we do not have to change everything. Applying the first tenet focuses the conversation on what is best for the student, thus enabling the collaboration partners to acknowledge a common goal—something they all want. The second tenet encourages collaborators to break the solution into small, manageable steps. Often, when everyone works toward a common goal, each member of the collaborative team has a role in supporting the needed changes. This eliminates the burden of one person being responsible for everything and guarantees investment by all the collaborators in a successful solution. The third tenet keeps the collaborative conversation on track by avoiding broad sweeping changes. Making one meaningful, effective change to which all members of the collaborative team commit is more likely to generate a successful solution to whatever problem the team is addressing. When using collaborative conversations that focus on the solution, less time is spent examining what is not working and more time is spent on what can be achieved.

To teach collaborative conversation skills, instructors should create assignments that situate the teacher candidates as collaborative partners in contextual ways. Some assignment examples include role-playing different stakeholders, conducting interviews, researching cultural differences, generating different types of questions to uncover biases, or forming collaborative teams to use the tenets of solution-focused conversations to create a goal and steps to achieve it. When teaching collaborative conversation, instructors can be aware of their own listening, questioning, and solution-focused skills as they interact with the teacher candidates.

The following questions are provided to guide your review and reflection in the Authentic Example that follows, contributed by Anni K. Reinking, EdD.

- In this example, how does the instructor apply knowledge of teaching feedback to support the importance of collaboration? Reflect.
- How do you teach feedback to foster autonomy?
- What are some ways an instructor can teach feedback to preservice teachers that reflect the research and evidence of partnership?

AUTHENTIC EXAMPLE

Contributed by
Anni K. Reinking, EdD

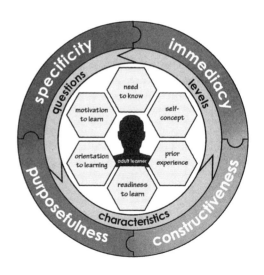

1. Course Details

CIED 318: Collaborative Professional, Family, and Community Relationships: Building Interpersonal and Professional Relationship Skills. This course is part of the early childhood program for teacher licensure and nonlicensure tracks, which include both graduate and undergraduate students. This course focuses on developing professional and mutually respectful relationships with several stakeholders in the field of early childhood education. These two assignments in collaboration reflect the difficult conversations in which teachers and early childhood professionals engage with early childhood parents/guardians, which sometimes include discussions of IEP goals and special services.

2. Learning Objectives

Aligned course objectives:
a. Understand the benefits, barriers, and techniques involved in family relationships and the collaborative process and the skills, which are necessary to implement cooperative relationships.
b. Understand the concerns of parents of individuals with disabilities and know appropriate strategies to collaborate with parents in addressing these concerns.
c. Develop relationships with families to acquire an understanding of the children's lives outside of the school and to support the families in making decisions related to their child's development and learning.
d. Establish and maintain positive collaborative relations with families, colleagues, and other professionals working effectively to support child development, learning, and well-being.

TABLE 12-3. RUBRIC FOR EMAIL COMMUNICATION ASSIGNMENT			
EMAIL/TEXT COMMUNICATION	**BELOW**	**MEETS**	**EXCEEDS**
Responded within 24 hours		5	
Responds with appropriate content			5
Includes research			5
Professional language used (i.e., no "text talk")			5
Displays an understanding of the parents' concern			5
Fully addresses the concern			5

3. Assignment Description

Assignment: Email Communication

a. The goal of this activity is for you to practice communicating with families with appropriate techniques; for example, supporting statements with resources and providing information for collaboration and the healthy development of children.

b. This assignment will be completed in two steps. The first step will be to receive a parent email, created specifically for this course, regarding a concern. You will need to respond professionally, respectfully, and with resources to back your information within 24 hours. When all the responses are received, we will anonymously review the responses to brainstorm and discuss nonverbal and written communication that comes across in emails. The second step will be to apply the information and guidelines discussed in class to respond to a second set of emails, showing your growth and implementation of the guidelines. You must use your SIUE (Southern Illinois University Edwardsville) email address.

Assignment: Virtual Learning Environment: Parent-Teacher Conference

a. The goal of this activity is to provide experiences in a parent-teacher conference setting. You will be given a student profile and will plan the parent-teacher meeting. This will be practiced in the Virtual Professional Practice Lab.

b. The professor will provide the student profiles of students between the ages of birth and second grade (random assignment). You will be given time to plan your parent-teacher meeting. This will be completed in a fishbowl setting.

4. Evaluation Criteria

The rubric for evaluating the email communication assignment is shown in Table 12-3.

The rubric for evaluating the virtual learning environment, parent-teacher conference is shown in Table 12-4.

TABLE 12-4. RUBRIC FOR VIRTUAL LEARNING ENVIRONMENT: PARENT TEACHER CONFERENCE ASSIGNMENT

PARENT/TEACHER CONFERENCE	BELOW	MEETS	EXCEEDS
Show understanding of the student (using the student profile)			5
Clear, respectful, thorough communication with parent			5
Provide information for the parent to "see" and ask questions			5
Reflection of experience			10

5. Additional Details

What is a virtual learning environment? Virtual learning environments (VLE) are rapidly demonstrating utility for expanding experiential learning for early and sustained experiences teaching students in the classroom (Dieker et al., 2008). The VLEs combine the real and virtual worlds in one environment to immerse the teacher candidate in both the physical and social aspects of a classroom (Biocca et al., 2003; Hayes, 2015). This environment combines both human and artificial intelligence to provide authentic experiences in teaching (Blascovich & Bailenson, 2011). The VLEs offer safe, flexible, and appropriate training conditions to practice pedagogical skills.

6. Feedback Reflection

Assignment 1: Email Communication

In this two-part assignment, each round includes feedback. The first time the teacher candidates receive the planned fictive parent email, they are to respond how they believe is appropriate based on course material. After the first round, the professor prints all the email responses, redacts all the names, and engages in a whole-class feedback discussion, based on all the emails. The discussion comprises perceptions of written communication, details included in the communication, tone, and many other aspects that the teacher candidates introduce. After that is discussed, the class develops a round two rubric, which looks very similar to the rubric presented in the Evaluation Criteria section, and is used to provide feedback from the professor during round two.

TABLE 12-5. FEEDBACK FORM

TEACHER CANDIDATE NAME: _____

SCORE LEVEL	PREPAREDNESS	PROFESSIONALISM	NOTES
5	Sources/paperwork are well thought out and varied Has clear goal that is related to the student	Relates to the "parent's" situation (listens) Stays on topic while also sympathizing Uses language that provides information, yet can be understood (i.e., no education jargon)	
3	Sources/paperwork are available, yet seem unrelated Goal is apparent, but not clear	Listens to the "parent" but does not "hear" the parent Stays on topic or sympathizes with parent (but not both) Uses language at times that is more focused on education jargon rather than providing parent information that can been understood or uses slang briefly	
1	No sources/paperwork are provided Has no clear goal	Does not listen to the parent Does not sympathize with the parent and/or does not stay on topic Uses language that is unprofessional (slang) or only education jargon	

Assignment 2: Virtual Learning Environment: Parent-Teacher Conference

The feedback for this assignment happens in two ways. First, the teacher candidates receive real-time feedback during the VLE experience from the professor based on their interactions with the parents, preparedness for the conference, and effectiveness in addressing the parents' concerns/needs. Second, each teacher candidate provides feedback to each other, using a feedback form. This form is given to teacher candidates to take with them and use in their personal reflection of the experience. Teacher candidates complete the form (Table 12-5) for each other. In addition, the professor completes the form to provide detailed feedback on the experience. Furthermore, all sessions are video recorded for teacher candidates to view later and provide self-feedback, if desired.

SUMMARY

In this chapter, the concept of teaching feedback when collaborating was explored. When we collaborate with families, students, and other colleagues, we consider intentions of feedback and acknowledge the multiple perspectives of those with which we are collaborating may possess. Instructors can promote active listening and demonstrate collaborative practices when giving, exhibiting, and teaching feedback. When instructors teach feedback for collaboration, it is important for teacher candidates to understand and use partnership communication and understand how building trust is foundational to collaborative relationships. The principles of partnership, such as equality, voice, choice, dialogue, praxis, reflection, and reciprocity, help to build trusting collaborative relationships so when feedback that might be hard to give is provided, it can be received and appreciated. When instructors teach feedback in collaborative relationships, we model how to respect the identity of others, actively honor autonomy, and practice the language of ongoing regard.

OPPORTUNITY FOR GOING DEEPER

The following resources support deeper learning on concepts reflected in Chapter 12:

- Student learning. If you are looking for more research on student learning, we recommend Arends, R. I., & Kilcher, A. (2010). *Teaching for student learning: Becoming an accomplished teacher*. Routledge. This book could be a useful resource to assist in teaching feedback to preservice special educators or in professional development for current educators.

- Instructional coaching. If you are looking for more research on coaching, we recommend several resources:
  - Cornett, J., & Knight, J. (2009). Research on coaching. In J. Knight (Ed.), *Coaching: Approaches and Perspectives* (pp. 192-216). Corwin Press.
  - Szabó, P., Dierolf, K., & Meier, D. (2009). *Coaching plain & simple: Solution-focused brief coaching essentials.* WW Norton & Company.
  - Van Nieuwerburgh, C. (2017). *An introduction to coaching skills: A practical guide* (2nd ed.). Sage.
  - Coaching with the GROW model. https://www.youtube.com/watch?v=XbkXpdiyNs0
  - Steve Barkley's Coaching model. https://barkleypd.com/blog/podcast-what-is-the-barkley-coaching-model-2/

- Collaborative consultation. The following article on collaborative consultation offers practical suggestions for working with the families of infants and toddlers with or at risk of communication deficits:
  - Woods, J. J., Wilcox, M. J., Friedman, M., & Murch, T. (2011). Collaborative consultation in natural environments: Strategies to enhance family-centered supports and services. *Language, Speech, and Hearing Services in Schools, 42*(3), 379-392.

REFERENCES

Barkley, S. G. (2011). *Questions for life: Powerful strategies to guide critical thinking.* Worth Shorts.

Biocca, F., Harms, C., & Burgoon, J. K. (2003). Toward a more robust theory and measure of social presence: Review and suggested criteria. *Presence: Teleoperators and Virtural Environments, 12*(5), 456-480.

Blascovich, J., & Bailenson, J. (2011). *Infinite reality: Avatars, eternal life, new worlds, and the dawn of the virtual revolution.* HarperCollins.

Dieker, L., Hynes, M., Hughes, C., & Smith, E. (2008). Implications of mixed reality and simulation technologies on special education and teacher preparation. *Focus on Exceptional Children, 40*(6), 1-20.

Endrew F. v. Douglas County School District, 137 S. Ct. 988 (2017).

Freire, P. (1970). *Pedagogy of the oppressed.* Continuum International Publishing Group.

Friend, M., & Cook, L. (2017). *Interactions: Collaboration skills for school professionals* (8th ed.). Pearson.

Guiterrez, K. D. (2008). Developing a sociocritical literacy in the third space. *Reading Research Quarterly, 43*(2), 148-164.

Hayes, S. (2015). *MOOCs and quality: A review of the recent literature.* Quality Assurance Agency MOOCs Network.

Johnson, K. F. (2008). Working as a partner with the adult learner. In J. Knight (Ed.), *Mentoring, coaching and collaboration* (pp. 35-53). Corwin Press.

Kegan, R., & Lahey, L. L. (2001). *How the way we talk can change the way we work: Seven languages for transformation.* John Wiley & Sons.

Knight, J. (2007). *Instructional coaching: A partnership approach to improving instruction.* Corwin.

Lickerman, A. (2012, May 6). The desire for autonomy. *Psychology Today.* https://www.psychologytoday.com/us/blog/happiness-in-world/201205/the-desire-autonomy

McLeskey, J., Barringer, M-D., Billingsley, B., Brownell, M., Jackson, D., Kennedy, M., Lewis, T., Maheady, L., Rodriguez, J., Scheeler, M. C., Winn, J., & Ziegler, D. (2017, January). *High-leverage practices in special education.* Council for Exceptional Children & CEEDAR Center. https://highleveragepractices.org/wp-content/uploads/2017/06/Preface.Intro1_.pdf

Scheeler, M. C., Congdon, M., & Stansbery, S. (2010). Providing immediate feedback to co-teachers through bug-in-ear technology: An effective method of peer coaching in inclusion classrooms. T*eacher Education and Special Education, 33*(1), 83-96.

Senge, P. M. (1990). *The fifth discipline: The art and practice of the learning organization.* Random House.

Sogunro, O. A. (2015). Motivating factors for adult learners in higher education. *International Journal of Higher Education, 4*(1), 22-37.

Stone, D., Patton, B., & Heen, S. (1999). *Difficult conversations: How to discuss what matters most.* Penguin Books.

Szabó, P., Dierolf, K., & Meier, D. (2009). *Coaching plain & simple: Solution-focused brief coaching essentials.* WW Norton.

Wheatley, M. (2002). *Turning to one another: Simple conversations to restore home to the future.* Berrett-Koehler.

SECTION
V

Resources

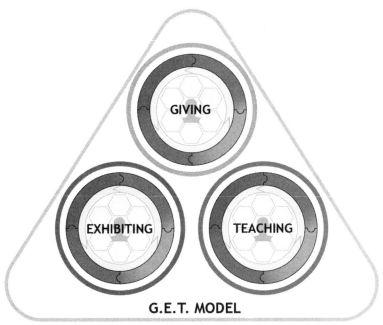

Figure V-1. The G.E.T. Model.

Section V comprises two chapters. The first chapter includes a comprehensive review of the literature, which provided the foundation for the development of the G.E.T. Model. The second chapter contains templates and additional authentic examples for review and reflection to support application of the G.E.T. Model (Figure V-1).

Comprehensive Review of the Literature on Feedback in Special Education Teacher Preparation

BACKGROUND

Several years before we conceptualized the G.E.T. Model, we completed a comprehensive review of the literature on feedback in special education teacher preparation. We had recognized the role of feedback in effective teaching (McLeskey et al., 2017) and that special education teacher preparation programs were compelled to incorporate feedback in their programs to develop the performance and competent decision-making of teacher candidates (Leko et al., 2015). With the growing emphasis on giving feedback and the impact this feedback has on the performance of teacher candidates, as instructors we wanted to understand what the literature suggested about feedback in the preparation of future special education teachers. We soon came to agree that "giving useful feedback is one of the most elusive elements in teaching and learning. Giving effective feedback is a sophisticated, learned skill that requires much modeling and practice—and that also includes feedback to the one learning to give it" (Routman, 2014, p. 73). Because we believe that instructors understand the purpose of feedback in special education teacher preparation and the far-reaching effects this feedback can have for students with disabilities, we seek to find ways to ensure that preparation programs address the multidimensionality of feedback.

The literature review findings suggested that research and practice of feedback in special education teacher preparation needs to move beyond a singular focus on how feedback is given. Further, the analysis of these findings and alignment with adult learning theory (ALT) suggests that attention be given to the context and levels of feedback according to growth in special education teacher preparation. This chapter defines feedback, examines the current empirical evidence, and analyzes how these studies relate to ALT.

Elford, M. D., Smith, H. H., & James, S.
GET Feedback: Giving, Exhibiting, and Teaching Feedback in
Special Education Teacher Preparation (pp. 251-265).
© 2022 SLACK Incorporated.

METHOD

To understand how special education teacher preparation instructors are practicing feedback, we conducted a comprehensive review of the literature on special education teacher preparation and feedback. Then, using findings from the comprehensive review of the literature, we examined the intersection of this literature and ALT.

Search Procedure for Literature Review

Articles included in this review were published in peer-reviewed, English-language journals between 2006 and 2017 and focused on the application and practice of feedback use in special education teachers. The researchers (Susanne James, PhD, Martha D. Elford, PhD, Heather Haynes Smith, PhD, and Margaret Williamson, MEd) used the following databases to complete the search: Academic Search Complete, ERIC (Education Resources Information Center), PsychInfo, JSTOR, and OmniFile. Search terms included *feedback*, *special education*, *teacher preparation*, *teacher education*, *preservice* teachers (and *pre-service teachers*). Search terms and strategies were used consistently across databases to ensure the highest yield of articles and to ensure a replicable search procedure.

Screening and Article Selection Process

The initial search of the five databases using selected keywords yielded a total of 419 articles for review. Initial review of those articles identified 133 studies reporting on feedback in classroom teaching or related assignments in special education teacher preparation. In this initial review of articles, the researchers reviewed the titles and abstracts to eliminate studies in which the participants were not preservice teachers and instructors in institutions of higher education. Further, the preservice teachers needed to be seeking special education licensure, certification, and/or working with students with disabilities. For this initial review, it was determined that any setting was acceptable, provided they met all other inclusion criteria.

The researchers then divided the 133 articles for a secondary in-depth review. Article titles and abstracts were reviewed and studies were eliminated if they were not empirical or the focus was not on studies with special education preservice teachers and institutions of higher education faculty. Qualitative, quantitative, and mixed methods studies were all eligible for inclusion. At this stage, articles were eliminated if the setting was not in special education teacher preparation. Dissertations, literature reviews, and meta-analyses were also excluded at this stage. Duplicate articles across searches were also eliminated. After all inclusion criteria were applied, nine articles remained for final review and coding. The researchers met to approve and verify the final nine articles and to review the screening process before coding the articles that fulfilled the selection criteria.

Coding for Adult Learning Theory and Feedback

According to Knowles (1984), adults learn differently than children; therefore, they should be taught differently. The nine articles identified in the literature review were coded to examine evidence of the principles of ALT in the feedback given to special education teacher candidates. All articles were coded on the basis of whether the following six types of evidence were present:

1. What evidence suggests that participants understood why they should learn the proposed strategy?
2. What evidence suggests that participants became self-directed (independent) in generalizing behavior in response to the feedback?
3. What evidence suggests that the researchers considered the participants' prior experience?

4. What evidence suggests that researchers provided feedback related to developmental tasks of the participants' social roles (i.e., teaching)?
5. What evidence suggests that feedback to the participant provided the opportunity to apply knowledge?
6. What evidence suggests that feedback to the participants promoted internal motivation?

Direct quotations from the text were also recorded and reviewed by the team. Operational definitions and understandings of each type of evidence was established by the research team for internal reliability.

RESULTS

The results of the comprehensive review of the literature identified three types of feedback prevalent in special education teacher preparation literature. These include face-to-face feedback, feedback with demonstrations, and technology-mediated feedback. Table 13-1 provides the results.

TABLE 13-1. COMPREHENSIVE REVIEW OF THE FEEDBACK LITERATURE RESULTS

AUTHOR (YEAR)	DESIGN	PARTICIPANTS	SETTING	
Coogle, C. G., Rahn, N. L., & Ottley, J. R. (2015)	Multiple baseline; single case design	3 UGs, female	Elementary inclusive classroom	
Garland, K. V., Vasquez, E., III, & Pearl, C. (2012)	Multiple baseline; across participants	4 Gs, female	TLE TeachLivE Virtual Lab	
Kennedy, A. S., & Lees, A. T. (2016)	Mixed methods	19 UGs, female	Early childhood classrooms and online modules	
Kennedy, M. J., Newton, J. R., Haines, S. J., Walther-Thomas, C., & Kellems, R. O. (2012)	Case study	11 UGs, males and females	General education classroom course during a summer session	
ABI = activity-based intervention; BIE = bug-in-ear coaching; CLASS = Classroom Assessment Scoring System; DTT = discrete trial teaching; DTTER = Discrete Trials Teaching Evaluation Rubric; G = graduate student; MTSS = Multi-Tiered System of Supports; N/A = not applicable; OTR = opportunities to respond; TCs = teacher candidates; TTC = three-term contingency; UG = undergraduate student.				

TYPE OF FEEDBACK	INDEPENDENT VARIABLE	DEPENDENT VARIABLE (OTHER DATA)	RESULT
Prompt, corrective, and positive	BIE	Teachers' use of communication strategies in ABI framework	Increased use of strategies and found the BIE to be a socially valid way to gain feedback from coaches.
Verbal, positive	TLE TeachLivE coaching	DTT	All participants' DTTER scores increased from baseline to intervention. Participants noted they enjoyed the experience, and their practice of DTT improved with coaching and demonstration.
Written, video feedback	MTSS Supports	Preservice TCs' scores on CLASS assessment	Significant increase in mean scores across all CLASS dimensions pre and post. Peers developed skills in providing reinforcement and formative feedback.
Verbal	N/A: case study	Written reflections, semi-structured interviews, and scored student performance data	Preservice TCs noted that feedback is vital and the 1-1 verbal feedback from instructors was very helpful in improving their final project. As a result of the individualized feedback and goal setting methods, TCs showed success on their final case study projects.

(continued)

TABLE 13-1 (CONTINUED). COMPREHENSIVE REVIEW OF THE FEEDBACK LITERATURE RESULTS

AUTHOR (YEAR)	DESIGN	PARTICIPANTS	SETTING	
McKinney, T., & Vasquez, E. (2014)	Multiple baseline; across participants	3 UGs	Laboratory	
Rock, M., Gregg, M., Gable, R., Zigmond, N., Blanks, B., Howard, P., & Bullock, L. (2012)	Mixed methods	13 Gs, males and females	Special education classrooms grades K-6, with remote coaching	
Rock, M. L., Gregg, M., Thead, B. K., Acker, S. E., Gable, R. A., & Zigmond, N. P. (2009)	Mixed methods	15 Gs, males and females	General and special education classrooms across grades K-12	
ABI = activity-based intervention; BIE = bug-in-ear coaching; CLASS = Classroom Assessment Scoring System; DTT = discrete trial teaching; DTTER = Discrete Trials Teaching Evaluation Rubric; G = graduate student; MTSS = Multi-Tiered System of Supports; N/A = not applicable; OTR = opportunities to respond; TCs = teacher candidates; TTC = three-term contingency; UG = undergraduate student.				

TYPE OF FEEDBACK	INDEPENDENT VARIABLE	DEPENDENT VARIABLE (OTHER DATA)	RESULT
Corrective, positive	BIE	DTT	Steady increases in correct DTT implementation with maintenance. Preservice TCs agree that the DTT is important, and the one-page manual with the BIE was an effective instructional approach.
Immediate corrective, positive	BIE	In-service TCs' rates of OTR	Statistically significant increase in both classroom environment (praise statements and decreased reprimand) and high-access instructional strategies. Technology issues were indicated. BIE experience was positive overall.
Immediate	BIE	In-service TCs' rates of OTR	Statistically significant improvement in all coded student behaviors during the BIE intervention. Overall responses of real-time feedback were positive, empowering, and helpful. Mean level of student engagement increased from baseline.

(continued)

TABLE 13-1 (CONTINUED). COMPREHENSIVE REVIEW OF THE FEEDBACK LITERATURE RESULTS

AUTHOR (YEAR)	DESIGN	PARTICIPANTS	SETTING	
Scheeler, M. C., McAfee, J. K., Ruhl, K. L., & Lee, D. L. (2006)	Multiple baseline; across participants	5 UGs, females	Special education classrooms grades PreK-5	
Scheeler, M. C., McKinnon, K., & Stout, J. (2012)	Multiple baseline; across participants	5 UGs, males and females	General education classroom, elementary	
ABI = activity-based intervention; BIE = bug-in-ear coaching; CLASS = Classroom Assessment Scoring System; DTT = discrete trial teaching; DTTER = Discrete Trials Teaching Evaluation Rubric; G = graduate student; MTSS = Multi-Tiered System of Supports; N/A = not applicable; OTR = opportunities to respond; TCs = teacher candidates; TTC = three-term contingency; UG = undergraduate student.				

TYPE OF FEEDBACK	INDEPENDENT VARIABLE	DEPENDENT VARIABLE (OTHER DATA)	RESULT
Immediate	BIE	TTC trials	Increase for all TCs and maintained. Ceiling effect for students' outcomes. Preservice TCs who initially scored the lowest in baseline measure, gained the most improvement over the course of the intervention. TCs reported that the device and intervention were nonobtrusive and helpful.
Immediate	BIE	TTC	Statistically significant increase in completed TTC trials over a short period of time and most were able to maintain the practice. Preservice TCs felt comfortable with the device, practice, and immediate feedback via BIE.

LITERATURE REVIEW DISCUSSION

The analysis of the results of the comprehensive review of the literature indicated three feedback areas of delivery that are evident in special education teacher preparation research: face-to-face, demonstrations, and technology mediated.

Face-to-Face Feedback

Face-to-face feedback was represented in three of the studies included for review (Garland et al., 2012; Kennedy et al., 2012; Kennedy & Lees, 2016). All three articles indicated improvement in feedback of teacher candidates. In all three studies, special education teacher candidates were able to clarify and ask questions that not only improved understanding of the goals set for each session but allowed for special education teacher candidates to reflect on their practice and make meaningful changes. Across studies, special education teacher candidates perceived the face-to-face sessions as vital and enjoyable, and they felt that such sessions improved their practice. This supported evidence that building relationships in which the expectations and goals are clear and that the feedback provided is clear, positive, and behavior-specific affords teacher candidates with opportunities to reflect on their practice and make long-lasting and generalizable changes. Also, pairing the face-to-face feedback with demonstrations and a written description of discrete trial training procedures allowed for a dynamic relationship between the researcher and the teacher candidate (Garland et al., 2012).

Feedback With Demonstrations

Feedback with physical demonstrations was the least represented type of feedback in the articles reviewed, appearing in only one article (McKinney & Vasquez, 2014). McKinney and Vasquez's (2014) research provided explicit physical demonstrations of discrete trial training procedures. This feedback was also given with a one-page written instructions and verbal bug-in-ear (BIE) prompts. Demonstrating feedback holds promise for empowering teacher candidates by providing a clear example of expected goals and procedures.

Technology-Mediated Feedback

Overwhelmingly, articles included some form of technology to mediate feedback. The BIE technology was the most commonly used method for providing feedback. Six of the nine articles used some version of BIE to provide immediate feedback (see Table 13-1). Examples of technology used across identified articles included use of the TLE TeachLivE lab (Garland et al., 2012), videos of student teaching (Kennedy & Lees, 2016), online modules for content delivery (Kennedy & Lees, 2016), and Content Acquisition Podcasts (Kennedy et al., 2012). These varied approaches of teaching allowed teacher candidates to engage in their learning while following evidence-based Universal Design for Learning principles.

All studies suggested improvement in feedback. Although some special education teacher candidates reported initial distress with technology troubleshooting or the BIE feedback during their teaching (Rock et al., 2012), they reported that over time the BIE feedback became unobtrusive and valuable (Coogle et al., 2015; Rock et al., 2009; Scheeler et al., 2006; Scheeler et al., 2012). Special education teacher candidates even speculated that this technology would be a good way for administrators to provide feedback to teachers and suggested that it may be a useful tool to provide students in the classroom with feedback. This technology is easy to use and is now also an inexpensive option, with only a Bluetooth device and an iPad (Apple, Inc.), tablet, or mobile phone needed for implementation. This BIE feedback strongly underscores the need and importance for immediate feedback. These findings suggest that when special education teacher preparation instructors are designing courses in special education teacher preparation, various forms of emerging and established technologies should be considered.

SECONDARY ANALYSIS: PRESENCE OF ADULT LEARNING THEORY PRINCIPLES

A secondary analysis of the selected articles was also conducted (Table 13-2). The focus of this analysis was the intersection of ALT and feedback and was conducted by us and Margaret Williamson, a research collaborator previously at the University of Kansas. The findings are followed by additional discussion and implications for research and practice.

IMPLICATIONS FOR FUTURE RESEARCH AND PRACTICE

Although special education instructors practice feedback regularly, research on feedback in special education teacher preparation is limited, as seen by the results of the comprehensive review of the literature, and most focus on a few ways that feedback is delivered to teacher candidates: face-to-face, with demonstration, and technology-mediated. Some research suggests that attention is given to the characteristics, questions, and levels of feedback. For example, Hattie and Timperley (2007) suggested that high-quality feedback provides cues or reinforcement, is relevant to performance or task, and relates to the difficulty of the performance or task. Further, Hattie and Timperley suggested that the following three key questions guide the feedback to students: (a) What are the goals for this learning? (b) What progress is being made? and (c) What activities need to be undertaken to make better progress?

Wiggins (2012) posited that if feedback is going to serve the desired purpose, it must be goal-referenced, tangible and transparent, actionable, user-friendly (specific and personalized), timely, ongoing, and consistent. Hattie (2012) organized feedback by the following levels: task > progress > self-regulation > self as a person. The effectiveness of feedback can be measured only by the improvement in student work (Brookhart, 2012) or in improved teaching behaviors of teacher candidates. More research is needed to discover the attention that special education teacher preparation instructors give to these characteristics, questions, and levels in their practice of delivering feedback to teacher candidates, regardless of the method chosen for delivering feedback.

Feedback in special education teacher preparation can be informed by ALT. Attending to the principles and practices of ALT when delivering feedback to teacher candidates may enhance the feedback and create a condition where the feedback is better received and thus more effective. The ALT research suggests that tailoring the feedback to the adult recipient, such as special education teacher candidates, produces a more positive response to the feedback. Although the characteristics, purpose, and levels of effective feedback described previously remain the same, the feedback delivered to special education teacher candidates should intentionally consider the core principles of ALT to fully maximize the effectiveness of the feedback.

Special education teacher preparation instructors must approach their andragogy with attention to the topic and the teacher candidate. Feedback should be explicitly taught, modeled, and integrated throughout the course or program to meet the criteria of ALT. For example, feedback is considered one of the high-leverage practices (i.e., essential activities of teaching; Ball & Forzani, 2011). Therefore, learning how to deliver effective feedback falls under the following core principles of ALT: (a) learners' need to know, (b) readiness to learn, and (c) motivation to learn. It is important to clarify and be explicit about the integration of theory into practice for both the teacher candidate and the instructors who provide feedback to the teacher candidate. By orienting the learner (Knowles et al., 1998) to the research related to effectiveness of feedback and providing explicit instruction, as well as modeling the opportunity to practice delivering feedback, the instructor will be more effective at supporting the teacher candidate in generalization of implementation. This bridge between classroom knowledge and real-world experiences is invaluable and increases teacher candidates' capacity to become learners who are driven by a sense of self-concept and who understand how to deliver

TABLE 13-2. INTERSECTION OF ADULT LEARNING THEORY AND FEEDBACK IN IDENTIFIED STUDIES FROM A COMPREHENSIVE REVIEW OF THE LITERATURE

AUTHOR (YEAR)	Coogle, C. G., Rahn, N. L., & Ottley, J. R. (2015)			Garland, K. V., Vasquez, E., III, & Pearl, C. (2012)			Kennedy, A. S., & Lees, A. T. (2016)			Kennedy, M. J., Newton, J. R., Haines, S. J., Walther-Thomas, C., & Kellems, R. O. (2012			
AREA OF FEEDBACK DELIVERY	Technology-mediated			Face-to-face			Written and technology-mediated			Face-to-face			
ADULT LEARNING THEORY PRINCIPLE	P	D	F	P	D	F	P	D	F	P	D	F	
1. LEARNER'S NEED TO KNOW	Y	N	N	Y	Y	Y	Y	Y	Y	Y	Y	Y	
2. SELF-CONCEPT OF THE LEARNER	Y	Y	Y	Y	N	N	Y	Y	Y	N	Y	Y	
3. PRIOR EXPERIENCE OF THE LEARNER	Y	Y	Y	Y	Y	Y	Y	Y	Y	Y	Y	Y	
4. READINESS TO LEARN	Y	Y	Y	Y	Y	Y	Y	Y	Y	Y	Y	Y	
5. ORIENTATION TO LEARNING	Y	Y	Y	Y	Y	Y	Y	Y	Y	Y	Y	Y	
6. MOTIVATION TO LEARN	N	Y	N	N	N	Y	Y	Y	Y	Y	Y	Y	

ALT = adult learning theory; D = design; F = feedback; N = no; P = present; Y = yes.

McKinney, T., & Vasquez, E. (2014)			Rock, M. L., Gregg, M., Thead, B. K., Acker, S. E., Gable, R. A., & Zigmond, N. P. (2009)			Scheeler, M. C., McAfee, J. K., Ruhl, K. L., & Lee, D. L. (2006)			Scheeler, M. C., McKinnon, K., & Stout, J. (2012)		
Technology-mediated			Technology-mediated			Technology-mediated			Technology-mediated		
P	D	F	P	D	F	P	D	F	P	D	F
Y	Y	Y	Y	N	Y	Y	Y	Y	Y	Y	Y
N	Y	Y	N	Y	Y	Y	Y	Y	N	Y	Y
Y	Y	Y	Y	Y	N	Y	Y	Y	Y	Y	N
Y	Y	Y	Y	Y	Y	Y	Y	Y	Y	Y	Y
Y	Y	Y	Y	Y	Y	Y	Y	Y	Y	Y	Y
Y	Y	Y	N	Y	Y	N	Y	Y	N	Y	Y

and receive feedback as teachers and as professionals (Brookhart & Moss, 2015). As Hattie (2012) recognized, "We all stand to benefit from knowing when to seek feedback, how to seek it, and what to do with it when we get it" (p. 23).

Summary

Feedback is multidimensional and crucial to the development of highly qualified special education teachers. This is evidenced by the number of times and contexts the word feedback is referenced in discussion of high-leverage practices (McLeskey et al., 2017). This review and the analysis of the intersection of feedback and ALT suggest some key elements to be considered in special education teacher preparation. Specifically, more research is needed on feedback, in all its forms, to provide more guidance for use in special education teacher preparation. Feedback may be the key to providing effective special education programs and support.

Learning to give feedback to teacher candidates, like any skill, cannot be fully developed in one reading or one lecture or one workshop. Giving effective feedback requires a clear understanding of the characteristics and levels of feedback as well as the key questions for progress feedback. In addition, well-designed, effective feedback considers the recipient of the feedback, in this case the adult learner (i.e., special education teacher candidate). Learning to give feedback requires knowledge of the language of feedback, understanding how that feedback language will be received and accepted by the teacher candidate, and delivering feedback in a variety of ways (written, oral, face-to-face, virtually) to inform the teacher candidate of progress toward a desired goal or outcome.

The secondary analysis of the intersection of the literature on instructors' feedback in special education teacher preparation and ALT established that most of the ALT principles were evident in the studies. However, there was no indication that the inclusion of these principles was in any way intentional. Our findings suggest that a framework is needed to provide guidance for integration into special education teacher preparation that reflects the multiple contexts and purposes of feedback and connects feedback and ALT. Specifically, the feedback instructors provide should aid in the special education teacher candidate's understanding and ability to give feedback to students and peers. Special education teacher preparation instructors need to go beyond teaching and modeling feedback to integration across a course or program, explicitly teaching how to deliver feedback in a way that satisfies the principles of andragogy. Feedback in special education teacher preparation must be explicitly taught, consistently modeled, and frequently reinforced. Special education teacher preparation instructors need guidance on how to plan and implement feedback, with attention to the topic, the learner, and how the special education teacher candidate will ultimately need to apply feedback in their future classrooms.

References

Ball, D. L., & Forzani, F. M. (2011). Teaching skillful teaching. *Educational Leadership, 68*(4), 40-45.

Brookhart, S. M. (2012). Teacher feedback in formative classroom assessment. In C. F. Webber, & J. L. Lupart (Eds.), *Leading student assessment* (pp. 225-239). Springer Dordrecht.

Brookhart, S. M., & Moss, C. M. (2015). How to give professional feedback. *Educational Leadership, 72*(7), 24-30.

*Coogle, C. G., Rahn, N. L., & Ottley, J. R. (2015). Pre-service teacher use of communication strategies upon receiving immediate feedback. *Early Childhood Research Quarterly, 32*, 105-115. https://doi.org/10.1016/j.ecresq.2015.03.003

*Garland, K. V., Vasquez, E., III., & Pearl, C. (2012). Efficacy of individualized clinical coaching in a virtual reality classroom for increasing teachers' fidelity of implementation of discrete trial teaching. *Education and Training in Autism and Developmental Disabilities, 47*(4), 502-515.

Hattie, J. (2012). *Visible learning for teachers: Maximizing impact on learning.* Routledge.

Hattie, J., & Timperley, H. (2007). The power of feedback. *Review of Educational Research, 77*(1), 81-112. https://doi.org/10.3102/003465430298487

*Kennedy, A. S., & Lees, A. T. (2016). Preparing undergraduate pre-service teachers through direct and video-based performance feedback and tiered supports in Early Head Start. *Early Childhood Education Journal, 44*(4), 369-379.

*Kennedy, M. J., Newton, J., Haines, S. J., Walther-Thomas, C., & Kellems, R. O. (2012). A triarchic model for teaching "introduction to special education": Case studies, content acquisition podcasts, and effective feedback. *Journal of Technology and Teacher Education, 20*(3), 251-275.

Knowles, M. (1984). *The adult learner: A neglected species* (3rd ed.). Gulf Publishing.

Knowles, M. S., Holton, E. F., & Swanson, R. A. (1998). *The adult learner* (5th ed.). Gulf Publishing.

Leko, M. M., Brownell, M. T., Sindelar, P. T., & Kiely, M. T. (2015). Envisioning the future of special education personnel preparation in a standards-based era. *Exceptional Children, 82*(1), 25-43.

*McKinney, T., & Vasquez, E. (2014). There's a bug in your ear!: Using technology to increase the accuracy of DTT implementation. *Education and Training in Autism and Developmental Disabilities, 49*(4), 594-600.

McLeskey, J., Barringer, M-D., Billingsley, B., Brownell, M., Jackson, D., Kennedy, M., Lewis, T., Maheady, L., Rodriguez, J., Scheeler, M. C., Winn, J., & Ziegler, D. (2017, January). *High-leverage practices in special education.* Council for Exceptional Children & CEEDAR Center. https://highleveragepractices.org/wp-content/uploads/2017/06/Preface.Intro1_.pdf

*Rock, M., Gregg, M., Gable, R., Zigmond, N., Blanks, B., Howard, P., & Bullock, L. (2012). Time after time online: An extended study of virtual coaching during distant clinical practice. *Journal of Technology and Teacher Education, 20*(3), 277-304.

*Rock, M. L., Gregg, M., Thead, B. K., Acker, S. E., Gable, R. A., & Zigmond, N. P. (2009). Can you hear me now? Evaluation of an online wireless technology to provide real-time feedback to special education teachers-in-training. *Teacher Education and Special Education, 32*(1), 64-82.

Routman, R. (2014). *Read, write, lead: Breakthrough strategies for schoolwide literacy success.* ASCD.

*Scheeler, M. C., McAfee, J. K., Ruhl, K. L., & Lee, D. L. (2006). Effects of corrective feedback delivered via wireless technology on preservice teacher performance and student behavior. *Teacher Education and Special Education, 29*(1), 12-25.

*Scheeler, M. C., McKinnon, K., & Stout, J. (2012). Effects of immediate feedback delivered via webcam and bug-in-ear technology on preservice teacher performance. *Teacher Education and Special Education, 35*(1), 77-90.

Wiggins, G. (2012). Seven keys to effective feedback. *Educational Leadership, 70*(1), 10-16

*Denotes the articles used in the comprehensive review of the literature.

Templates and Additional Opportunities to Apply the G.E.T. Model

Using the templates provided in this chapter allows you look at the Authentic Examples of assignments collected from instructors in special education teacher preparation from across the United States. These templates could also be used to evaluate one of your own assignments.

The G.E.T. Model defines feedback as any information the recipient receives that informs their understanding or restructures their thinking or beliefs related to their performance, knowledge, or skills. When delivering this feedback on the assignments that teacher candidates are given in special education teacher preparation, there are four main domains for delivering feedback: specificity, immediacy, purposefulness, and constructiveness (Tables 14-1 through 14-4). These four domains create a lens for us to think about how we employ the **G.E.T.** Model in special education teacher preparation.

There are three main opportunities that instructors have to embed the four domains of feedback in courses: **G**iving feedback, **E**xhibiting feedback, and **T**eaching how to deliver feedback. **Giving** feedback requires instructors to deliver any information to a recipient that informs their understanding or restructures their thinking or their beliefs related to their performance, knowledge, or skill. **Exhibiting** feedback requires instructors to explicitly model how feedback should be given through sharing the "why and how" of delivering feedback. **Teaching** feedback requires instructors to explicitly teach what feedback looks like and sounds like in the classroom for K-12 learners. Special education educators must understand why feedback is an essential element in teaching. Instructors must be strategic in communicating how to use feedback to increase student outcomes.

Elford, M. D., Smith, H. H., & James, S.
GET Feedback: Giving, Exhibiting, and Teaching Feedback in
Special Education Teacher Preparation (pp. 267-310).
© 2022 SLACK Incorporated.

TABLE 14-1. TEMPLATE FOR EVALUATING TEACHER CANDIDATE ASSIGNMENTS: SPECIFICITY DOMAIN

Specificity includes the questions, characteristics, and levels related to the learning goal. The domain of specificity identifies the language that is specific to the task and uses language that clearly states the learning goal and describes where the teacher candidate must go to achieve the goal. The characteristics of specificity include the language used when delivering feedback, who is receiving the feedback, and the ways the feedback is clearly stated to be accessible.

GIVING	What evidence suggests that the instructor considered the following questions in the delivery of this lesson? • Are specific directions given that detail why the teacher candidate is doing this assignment so they can be invested in the learning? • If feedback language was given, did it reference the goal of the assignment? • Is the feedback specific to what the teacher candidate needs to know, understand, and be able to do in their current role or with the desired learning outcome?
EXHIBITING	What evidence suggests that the instructor considered the following questions in the design of this lesson? • Was the feedback given on the assignment tangible, transparent, positive, as well as corrective, and leading to improvement? • Is the feedback delivered in a way that promotes autonomy and self-direction for the teacher candidate of the learning outcome? • Is the feedback differentiated to meet the individual identity, societal role, and cultural perspective of the teacher candidate?
TEACHING	What evidence suggests that the instructor considered how to explicitly teach feedback to teacher candidates? • Does the feedback specifically describe the connection to the teacher candidates' goals? • Is the feedback positive and focused on the next steps to keep the teacher candidate moving forward?

You may use the four templates (see Tables 14-1 through 14-4; one for each domain) presented to evaluate the assignments provided in the previous chapters or the additional examples provided in this chapter. These templates may also be useful in analyzing or reflecting on one of your existing syllabi, assignments, or course activities. The key is to practice reflecting on the feedback you provide to your teacher candidates, whether giving, exhibiting, or teaching feedback, and consider if there are additional feedback opportunities.

TABLE 14-2. TEMPLATE FOR EVALUATING TEACHER CANDIDATE ASSIGNMENTS: IMMEDIACY DOMAIN

Immediacy relates to the timing of when feedback is delivered. The domain of immediacy encompasses the idea of appropriately timed feedback to have a bigger effect on student goal attainment.	
GIVING	What evidence suggests that the instructor considered the following questions in the delivery of this lesson? • Does the timing of the feedback meet the needs of the teacher candidate? • Is the timing of the feedback appropriate for the learning outcomes? • Does the feedback provide information that can be used immediately?
EXHIBITING	What evidence suggests that the instructor considered the following questions in the design of this lesson? • Does the feedback fit the specific outcome that is most pressing? • Should the feedback be delayed to support the additional time needed for teacher candidates to make sense of the learning experience? • Does the teacher candidate prefer to wrestle with the problem? • Does the teacher candidate need frequent support in knowing that they are on the right track?
TEACHING	What evidence suggests that the instructor considered how to explicitly teach feedback to teacher candidates? • Is the timing of the feedback appropriate for the learning outcomes? • How frequently does the teacher candidate need feedback to keep making progress? • Is the feedback well-timed so it can be absorbed by the teacher candidate for future improvement?

TABLE 14-3. TEMPLATE FOR EVALUATING TEACHER CANDIDATE ASSIGNMENTS: PURPOSEFULNESS DOMAIN

Purposefulness is the progress-related characteristics, questions, and levels of feedback required to move teacher candidates forward along the learning continuum. The characteristics of purposefulness include actionable steps broken into achievable chunks that lead students toward the goal they must complete.

GIVING	What evidence suggests that the instructor considered the following questions in the delivery of this lesson? • Does the feedback consider the teacher candidates' values? • Is the purpose and expectations for the feedback the instructor will provide shared in the assignment guidelines, and are they clear to understand? • Is this feedback tailored to the teacher candidates' motivation? • Is the feedback emotionally compelling and specific to the teacher candidates' locus of control?
EXHIBITING	What evidence suggests that the instructor considered the following questions in the design of this lesson? • Did the instructor consider where the teacher candidates are on the learning continuum? • How much scaffolding is needed to lead the teacher candidates toward the desired goal? • Is the feedback contextualized for the identity of the teacher candidates? • Does the feedback consider prior knowledge and professional experience of the teacher candidates?
TEACHING	What evidence suggests that the instructor considered how to explicitly teach feedback to teacher candidates? • Does the feedback connect the current stage to the progress that is being made toward the goal? • Are there opportunities for continuous improvement by the teacher candidates? • Does the feedback meet the intrinsic need of the teacher candidates or does it fulfill only an external outcome, such as just getting a passing grade on the assignment?

TABLE 14-4. TEMPLATE FOR EVALUATING TEACHER CANDIDATE ASSIGNMENTS: CONSTRUCTIVENESS DOMAIN

Constructiveness is the notion that feedback constructs new meaning, progress information, or provides improvement suggestions for the learner. This idea is closely linked to the meaning the recipient makes of the feedback and what that meaning produces. The characteristics of constructiveness include the traits of self-monitoring, intrinsic motivation, and individualized progress monitoring to move the student forward in constructing a new learning goal.

GIVING	What evidence suggests that the instructor considered the following questions in the delivery of this lesson? • Does the feedback consider what is the responsibility of the teacher candidates in the next steps to complete the assignment? • Is the feedback specific to the teacher candidate and includes references that are individualized?
EXHIBITING	What evidence suggests that the instructor considered the following questions in the design of this lesson? • How will teacher candidates make meaning of the feedback provided by the instructor? • What self-regulation will the feedback produce? • Will the feedback connect to prior learning, and is it meaningful to their current professional improvement? • Does the feedback serve to motivate the teacher candidate to continue making progress? • Does the feedback reinforce a partnership between the one giving the feedback and the one receiving it?
TEACHING	What evidence suggests that the instructor considered how to explicitly teach feedback to teacher candidates? • Does the feedback connect the current stage to the progress that is being made toward the goal? • Is the feedback self-referenced and differentiated? • Can the feedback be used to empower the teacher candidate to create their own process for improvement?

Authentic Example 1

Contributed by
Heather Haynes Smith, PhD

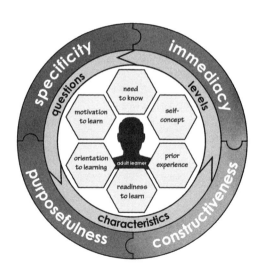

1. Course Details

EDUC 1331: Understanding Learners With Exceptionalities in School and Society. This is an undergraduate introductory course in special education. The course is also a part of the university's liberal arts curriculum and integrates oral and visual communication (OVC) components. This assignment reflects both special education content and demonstration of OVC components, including giving, receiving, and reflecting on feedback.

2. Learning Objectives

- Increase knowledge about and sensitivity toward individuals with exceptionalities.
- Evaluate sociocultural and linguistic factors influencing perceptions of disability, quality of life, and services for persons with special education needs.
- Oral and visual communication objectives are as follows:
  ○ Create and deliver effectively structured oral presentations, using language correctly and appropriately.
  ○ Use visual media that are effective, appropriate, and well integrated into the presentation.
  ○ Analyze and critique oral and visual components of presentations.

3. Assignment Details

Students will select a book with a character or characters with exceptionalities. The IRIS Center list is an excellent resource to aid in the selection of a book (https://iris.peabody.vanderbilt.edu/resources/books/). Students are encouraged to discuss other possible book options with the instructor.

Prepare a three- to five-page written book review. On the selected day of their presentation, students will submit their written review prior to class (using a PechaKucha presentation format) to the class. PechaKucha presentations, in which students present using a storytelling format and 20 slides for 20 seconds each that usually depict only a single related image on each, are explained in more detail and modeled a few weeks prior to the first presentation. Students in the course will reflect, analyze, and critique the oral and visual components of their own presentation and the presentations of others. It is expected that questions will be asked of the presenter after the presentation, and responses will follow OVC guidelines.

Your OVC PechaKucha presentation should both clearly address and provide the following:
a. What exceptionality are you focusing on from the book?
b. Is the portrayal/representation accurate? Provide examples.
c. What significant contributions to your understanding were gained from reading the book?
d. Provide at least two appropriately cited references in American Psychological Association (APA) style (in addition to the selected book and the textbook), connecting the text to peer-reviewed research or evidence-based practices.
e. Reflect the appropriate use of elements of effective oral and visual communication (e.g., eye contact, facial expression, gestures, posture, appearance, enthusiasm, limited vocalized pauses [uh, well], clear topic, visual aids, content, professionalism).

4. Evaluation Criteria

The Book Review PechaKucha rubric is provided in Table 14-5. This is a single point rubric (Fluckiger, 2010). It offers the opportunity for student self-assessment and a focus for more written feedback. The feedback or self-assessment should center around the strengths and explicit examples demonstrated in the first column. In the third column, the instructor can add next steps and opportunities for growth and development or the student can use the space to reflect and set goals for their growth. Instructors can reflect on the domains of feedback to determine what opportunities to focus on, aligned with the learning objectives. For instance, if the focus is on specificity, the instructor might recommend specific vocabulary to use or provide a recommended source for finding additional details for future presentations or conversations about this topic. The single point rubric is also effective for student self-reflection on the assignment.

TABLE 14-5. BOOK REVIEW AND PECHAKUCHA RUBRIC

EVIDENCE OF MASTERY	ASSIGNMENT AND COURSE LEARNING OBJECTIVE	RECOMMENDATION OR OPPORTUNITY FOR CONTINUED GROWTH AND LEARNING
	Paper and PechaKucha addresses exceptionality/disability category (20%) The plot is briefly summarized. Exceptionality/characteristic(s) thoroughly discussed, with evidence (see next item on rubric) given regarding the accuracy of the depiction and sociopolitical considerations. Connection to the week's focus is evident. (Note: Refrain from diagnosis [and focus on characteristics observed] if disability is not clearly stated.	
	Paper and PechaKucha organization, editing, and language (20%) Good overall paper organization, with logically ordered ideas and details. Paper length is on target (three to five pages). Note: Format-wise, the paper follows the same organizational structure as the Movie Review. The PechaKucha has a "key" theme or idea throughout and contains twenty 20-second slides with content. Grammar and spelling are excellent. It is evident that the paper has been proofread. Language is appropriate and respectful in both the paper and PechaKucha. (Note: Contrary to American Psychological Association (APA) style guidelines, a cover page and abstract are not needed for the book review.)	
	Connecting with readings and research (20%) Supporting details, including connections to course text and other materials, are provided as evidence to support the discussion and thesis in the paper and to support the theme in the PechaKucha. All citations and the paper reference list uses accurate APA style. Images in the PechaKucha are attributed to sources when appropriate. Links to the source on the slides are adequate.	

(continued)

TABLE 14-5 (CONTINUED). BOOK REVIEW AND PECHAKUCHA RUBRIC

EVIDENCE OF MASTERY	ASSIGNMENT AND COURSE LEARNING OBJECTIVE	RECOMMENDATION OR OPPORTUNITY FOR CONTINUED GROWTH AND LEARNING
	Explanation of personal learning and growth (20%)	
	Paper and presentation include details about the significant PERSONAL insights and contributions gained from watching the movie. Conclusion in the paper re-states and explains the importance of the problem/thesis to your personal understanding and learning. Mastery is evidenced for both in addressing how your perception regarding ability is deepened or changed as a result of reading this book and what questions you still have about the exceptionality or advocacy for individuals in this exceptionality group.	
	PechaKucha presentation (20%)	
	The presentation tells a story. PechaKucha fully reflects the oral and visual communication skills reviewed in class, including professional attire.	
	Body language and oral presentation skills in both the formal presentation and unstructured panel reflect oral and visual communication concepts. The analysis produces interesting and thoughtful discussion among the audience after the presentation ends.	
	The images/text chosen were appropriate and extremely thoughtful, topical, and conveyed in an excellent manner. The speech by the student was polished and in a professional manner. It was obvious the student had rehearsed the speech, and slide transitions were appropriately timed.	
Other feedback:		

5. Additional Details

What is a PechaKucha? A PechaKucha is the 6-minute, 40-second prepared presentation. The presentation contains 20 slides that are 20 seconds each and advance automatically. A PechaKucha presentation follows a story and aims to both entertain and inform. Guidelines for PechaKucha suggest the use of a theme, relevant visuals, and a focus on audience engagement.

Some resources describing the essential elements of a PechaKucha and providing examples are as follows: https://www.pechakucha.com/ and https://www.wabisabilearning.com/blog/how-to-make-great-presentations-with-pecha-kucha

6. Feedback Reflection

This assignment reflects all three types of feedback: giving, exhibiting, and teaching feedback. It begins a few weeks before the first presentation, with explicit instruction on warm and cool feedback. Refer to the School Reform Initiative Tuning Protocol, Step 6 at https://schoolreforminitiative.org/doc/tuning.pdf. Warm feedback is the positive responses to work, and cool feedback is the constructive criticism provided. The presentations last several weeks and provide multiple opportunities to give peer feedback. Earlier presentations are graded more generously, as they have opportunities to reflect and share about the experience and process, supporting a classroom culture shaped as a professional learning community. As the course instructor, I also exhibit feedback using warm and cool feedback during a question and answer period with all of the day's presenters after the presentations are complete. To address teaching feedback beyond explanation and practice, the design of this course assignment allows additional teaching opportunities because I have presenters provide feedback to me on the overall helpfulness of the class feedback and reflect on the feedback they receive and the impact on their growth and learning. Students in the course are also explicitly taught how to give feedback and provide it for every peer. I collect and review all the feedback forms for a presenter at least two times during the semester. This offers me an opportunity to provide feedback on the feedback peers are giving to one another. My feedback on peer feedback most often focuses especially on the specific, nonattributive feedback. In almost all cases, the presenters receive the feedback immediately after the presentation. If I collect it, they can review it immediately and then pick it up in my office later that day.

Authentic Example 2

Contributed by
Jennifer Porterfield, PhD
Cathy Newman Thomas, PhD

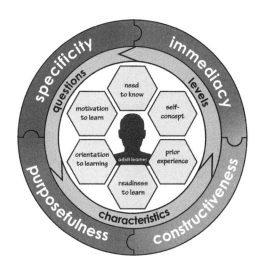

1. Course Details

SPE 4389/5389: Special Education Practicum. This undergraduate- and graduate-level course is required for special education majors at Texas State University after all other special education coursework has been completed and prior to student teaching or internship. This course provides opportunities for application that are focused on best practices in special education and is led by experienced special education teachers, administrators, and supervisors. In this course, each practicum student is placed with a mentor teacher in a local school for 14 weeks and paired with a target student who receives special education services. In this setting, the practicum student has opportunities to practice the knowledge acquired across the program and receive expert feedback from mentor teachers and university supervisors regarding their development and readiness to proceed to student teaching or internship.

The assignment supports future special education educators in developing knowledge and skills in planning for and implementing High-Leverage Practices (HLPs) in special education (McLeskey et al., 2017). The HLPs address 22 evidence-based practices that enhance outcomes for students with disabilities across the categories of collaboration, assessment, instruction, and social-emotional. In this assignment, practicum students select HLPs from the instruction and social-emotional practices and create brief videos of themselves engaging in the specific HLP.

Texas State University College of Education has a license for Sibme, which is a cloud-based video observation and reflection tool that is employed in ways that are compliant with the Family Educational Rights and Privacy Act (FERPA; 1974) and Children's Online Privacy Protection Act (COPPA; 1998). The parents of the target students provide signed written consent for the use of video for the purpose of practicum student learning. Instructional objectives for this assignment are for these future teachers to (a) develop familiarity with the HLPs, (b) practice implementing HLPs with fidelity, and (c) experience opportunities to accept and deliver peer feedback to support reflection on practice. This is a new assignment and the first time we are using Sibme for reflection rather than just observation. We anticipate learning from this first implementation and developing the assignment in response to student outcomes.

2. Learning Objectives

This assignment focuses on one instructional objective for this course—*to observe and recognize implementation of state and national standards in practice in mentor teachers and their own practice.* In this course and other coursework, Texas State University College of Education students are familiarized with their accountability to Texas Education Agency Standards for Special

Education Teachers, the HLPs, and the Danielson Framework. For this assignment, students were placed in groups of three. In the Sibme platform, it is possible to create small groups called "Huddles" for such purposes.

3. Assignment Description

Special Education High-Leverage Practices: Sibme Videos
(10 points each)

In this assignment, you will use the Sibme app to record yourself implementing three of the special education HLPs.

Choose three different HLPs for special educators from the list below and record a short (less than 5 minutes) video demonstrating the HLPs. Please be sure to include at least one HLP from the Instruction column and one from the Social/Emotional/Behavioral column (Table 14-6).

Part 1 (7 points)

TABLE 14-6. HIGH-LEVERAGE PRACTICES FOR SIBME VIDEO	
INSTRUCTION	**SOCIAL/EMOTIONAL/BEHAVIORAL**
HLP 16: Use explicit instruction. Example: • Lesson opening with objective and rationale in student-friendly terms • Modeling • Guided practice with scaffolding	HLP 7: Establish a consistent, organized, and respectful learning environment. Example: • Setting up expectations during a lesson • Teaching a routine or procedure • Practicing a routine or procedure
HLP 19: Use assistive and instructional technologies. Example: • Teaching a student how to use an assistive technology device • Interacting with a student who is using an assistive technology device • Completing an activity with a student who is using an assistive technology device	HLP 8: Provide positive and constructive feedback to guide students' learning. Example: • Providing precise praise to a student • Providing student-specific feedback on a correct response • Providing student-specific feedback on an incorrect response
HLP 18: Use strategies to promote active student engagement. Example: • Using multiple means of responding (e.g., response cards, actions, verbal responses)	HLP 9: Teach social behaviors. Example: • Explicitly teaching a student a social skill (asking for help, asking a question, responding to other students appropriately)

Part 2 (3 points):

Step 1: Upload your video to the Huddle created for your group. Post a short comment at the start of your video to identify which HLP you implemented and what we saw you do.

Example: *I implemented HLP 7 (establish a consistent, organized, and respectful learning environment) when I taught my student the procedure for moving into a small group and being ready to start our lesson together.*

Step 2: In the Sibme Huddle created for your group, post some specific feedback to each member of your group. Feedback should be positive or constructive (to help us improve our practice).

Example of Positive Feedback: *Dr. P., I really like how you broke the procedure down into smaller steps for the student and provided her praise as she completed each step. She seemed to understand exactly what she should do!*

Example of Constructive Feedback: *Dr. P., in this video, we saw the procedure for moving into the small group taught and reviewed one time. What will you do to remind the student of the procedure moving forward? Will you have other practice opportunities?*

4. Evaluation Criteria

This authentic assignment is designed to be completed three times, and each video attempt is evaluated separately (Table 14-7). Part of the evaluation is for the feedback, and samples are provided in the previous section. Each submission is worth 10 points, and there must be at least one video that addresses the instruction HLPs in the left column and at least one video that addresses the social/emotional/behavioral HLPs in the right column.

**Special Education High-Leverage Practices (HLPs): Sibme Videos Rubric
(10 points each)**

TABLE 14-7. SIBME VIDEO RUBRIC

COMPONENT	POINTS POSSIBLE	POINTS EARNED
HLP Video #1	7	
HLP Video Comment #1	3	
HLP Video #2	7	
HLP Video Comment #2	3	
HLP Video #3	7	
HLP Video Comment #3	3	

5. Additional Details

The Danielson Framework. The Danielson Framework for Teaching (Danielson, 2007) is used for observation and evaluation of teacher quality and development. The overall scale has been validated (Lash, Tran, & Huang, 2016), although it has not been validated for special education. Validation studies for this purpose are currently being conducted (Jones & Brownell, 2014; Morris-Mathews et al., 2021). In Texas, the Danielson Framework for Teaching is related to the school-based observation Texas Teacher Evaluation and Support System.

High-Leverage Practices in Special Education (https://highleveragepractices.org). The Collaboration for Effective Educator Development, Accountability and Reform Center (CEEDAR; https://ceedar.education.ufl.edu) in collaboration with the Council for Exceptional Children (CEC; https://www.cec.sped.org) researched and identified 22 practices across four categories that are critical for special educators to know and be able to do to improve outcomes for children with disabilities.

Sibme (https://sibme.com). Sibme is a commercial tool that enables video observation and reflection and is especially useful in teacher preparation for the purpose of providing feedback. Video of novice teachers carrying out their planned lessons and activities offers rich opportunities for mentor teachers and supervisors to review teaching in action and provide explicit feedback on teacher candidate performance and impact on student learning. The video record allows teacher candidates to observe themselves as well as reflect on their ability to put their teaching plan into action and the degree to which they implemented the plan with fidelity and as they intended. The removal of real-time enables reviewing and revisiting the implementation of developing teaching skills to observe growth and change.

6. *Feedback Reflection*

In this assignment, the Sibme video platform allows practicum students to practice a self-selected and very specific HLP. The assignment asks peers to offer positive and constructive feedback regarding a practicum student's brief performance of an HLP with the target student in their practicum placement. By using the G.E.T. Model, practicum students have opportunities to *give* feedback to three of their peers on each of their three HLP video practices. Future teachers mostly receive feedback, but, other than end-of-the-semester anonymous surveys of their instructors, have few opportunities to provide or give constructive feedback. This is a gap in our preparation because the skills to provide effective feedback are foundational to the collaborative and collegial relationships they must form with fellow teachers, the relationship with supervisors, and, of course, the relationship and their roles with future students. This assignment also offers opportunities for *teaching* feedback. In preparing students to complete the assignment, the instructors explicitly taught and modeled the characteristics of effective positive and constructive feedback, both with in-class lecture and via the assignment directions and rubric. Both the instructors and practicum students had opportunities to *exhibit* feedback. The instructors modeled examples and non-examples of effective positive and constructive feedback, and the practicum students practiced providing such feedback to three peers on each of their three videos. Small-group and instructor-led discussion focused not only on the quality of the HLP practice but also on the quality and utility of the peer feedback for recognizing effective HLP practice and improving future HLP practice.

AUTHENTIC EXAMPLE 3

*Contributed by
Dennis Cavitt, EdD*

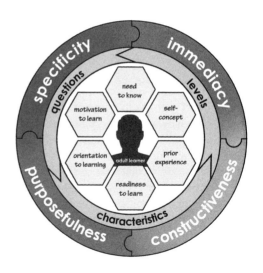

1. Course Details

SPE 3613: Exceptional Individuals. A course for undergraduate teacher candidates.

All teacher candidates must enroll in and successfully complete a survey course in special education. This course covers the laws and processes typically experienced in school districts regarding special education. The federal law at the core of special education law—Individuals With Disabilities Education Act (IDEA)—identifies and defines 13 specific disability categories: autism, deaf-blindness, auditory impairment, developmental disability, emotional disturbance, intellectual disability, multiple disabilities, orthopedic impairment, other health impairment, specific learning disability, speech or language impairment, traumatic brain injury, and visual impairment. A major portion of the course is for the students to learn the definition of the disability category and identify the associated characteristics. Along with learning the defining characteristics of each disability, students will identify evidenced-based educational accommodations.

2. Learning Objectives

Course goals:

a. The teacher candidate will explain the Response to Intervention (RTI) processes and determine various interventions at each tier.

b. The teacher candidate will explain how struggling students move from one tier to another and how they are recommended for an evaluation for potential special education services.

c. The teacher candidate will identify the IDEA disability categories and related characteristics.

d. The teacher candidate will select, adapt, and use a repertoire of evidence-based instructional strategies to advance the learning of individuals with exceptionalities.

3. Assignment Description

This final assignment for the survey course in exceptional individuals is a two-part case study process.

Part A

The teacher candidate will be given 10 case studies that consist of 10 various disability categories. Each case will be made up of primary disability characteristics, including secondary co-morbid disability characteristics. There may also be a case(s) where the student does not meet the criteria for a disability according to the categories in the IDEA. If teacher candidates determine that a student does not meet a disability category, they must thoroughly explain why.

Part B

In-class, small groups will act as an RTI team. Each teacher candidate will, in turn, take on the role of a general education teacher, presenting the case to the other members of the team. In a collaborative process, the RTI team will determine what evidenced-based intervention is appropriate and develop an implementation plan for the intervention. A paper-based intervention plan will account for part of the final. The form for this assessment could be used for multiple meetings. It can be used for initial RTI meetings, review RTI meetings, or dismissal RTI meetings. When complete, the teacher candidates debrief the meetings with the professor, where strengths and challenges are identified and corrected, if necessary.

4. Evaluation Criteria

Case Study Part A

Using the information and sources that were used during the class:
a. Identify the primary disability (50 points per case).
b. List the characteristics identified in the particular case (50 points per case).
c. Identify any secondary or comorbid category (50 points per case).
d. List the characteristics of each disability identified (50 points per case).
e. Identify and list the evidenced-based accommodations, interventions, and modifications that would be appropriate for the particular case study (50 points per case). (Must also include the reference or URL for the interventions.)

The total points for the Case Study (Part A) portion is 250. The grading rubric is presented in Table 14-8.

Part B will be worth 100 points. The grading rubric is presented in Table 14-9.

The total points for the final exam is 350.

Table 14-8. Case Study (Part A) Rubric

TOPIC	UNACCEPTABLE	NEEDS IMPROVEMENT	PROFICIENT	ACCOMPLISHED	SCORE X/250
Identify the primary disability. (50 points)	Identified 7 or fewer disability categories, with no description.	Correctly identified 8 disability categories, with no description.	Correctly identified 9 primary disabilities and included a description of the disability category.	Correctly identified all primary disabilities and included the IDEA description of the disability category.	
List the characteristics identified in the case. (50 points)	Listed characteristics not identified in the case, or no characteristics were identified.	Correctly identified a few of the characteristics in the case.	Correctly listed most of the disability characteristics in the case.	Correctly listed ALL the disability characteristics in the case.	
Identified any secondary or comorbid category. (50 points)	Mislabeled a disability category as secondary.	Correctly identified the disability category, with no description.	Correctly identified the disability and included a description of the disability category.	Correctly identified the secondary disability, if any, and included the IDEA description of the disability category.	
Listed the characteristics of each secondary disability identified in the case, if one was identified. (50 points)	Listed characteristics not identified in the case.	Correctly identified a few of the characteristics in the case.	Correctly listed SOME of the disability characteristics in the case.	Correctly listed ALL the disability characteristics in the case.	

(continued)

Table 14-8 (continued). Case Study (Part A) Rubric

TOPIC	UNACCEPTABLE	NEEDS IMPROVEMENT	PROFICIENT	ACCOMPLISHED	SCORE X/250
Identified and listed the accommodations and modifications that would be appropriate for the case study and other appropriate evidenced-based practices, with reference/citation. (50 points)	Listed 1 accommodation and 1 modification.	Correctly listed 1 accommodation and 1 modification, each an evidenced-based practice, and provided appropriate citations.	Correctly listed 2 accommodations, 1 of which is an evidenced-based practice, and 2 modifications, 1 of which is an evidence-based practice, and provided appropriate citations.	Correctly listed 3 accommodations, at least 2 of which are evidence-based practices, and 3 modifications, 2 of each are evidenced-based practices, and provided appropriate citations.	
Score					x/250

Table 14-9. Part B: Response to Intervention Rubric

TOPIC	UNACCEPTABLE	NEEDS IMPROVEMENT	PROFICIENT	ACCOMPLISHED	SCORE X/100
Description of the problem that was the reason to be brought to the RTI team. (40 points)	Description of a problem not written in measurable or observable terms.	Adequate description of the problem, written in measurable and observable terms.	Thorough description of the problem, written in measurable and observable terms.	Thorough description of the problem, including baseline data, written in measurable and observable terms.	
Goals and settings where implemented. (30 points)	Goals are not measurable.	Goals are written in a measurable way.	Goals are written in measurable terms, with expected mastery.	Goals are written measurably, identifying the setting along with expected mastery statement.	
Interventions. (30 points)	Describes the intervention.	Describes the intervention and provides the URL.	Describes the intervention and includes the training and URL of the intervention.	Thoroughly describes the intervention, including training, cost (if any) of intervention, and URL.	
Total Score					x/100

Part B of the Final Exam:
Response to Intervention Simulation (100 Points)

This collaborative activity occurs during the time scheduled for final exams. Class members are divided into groups of four to six, where each person in the group is given a new fictional case. Each member of the team will have the opportunity to play the role of the classroom teacher presenting the case to an RTI team. The other members of the RTI team will play the role of the campus-based members of the team. Each of the cases in this portion of the final are students who have been receiving services in either Tier 1 or Tier 2 of the campus RTI process. In a collaborative process, the RTI team will determine what evidenced- based interventions (documentation of evidence and URL address of the intervention(s) must be included in the documentations) are appropriate and the implementation plan for the intervention (including the tier, group size, and evaluation timeline). Students are not identifying whether or not the student has a disability but instead are focusing on the educational need for intervention for the academic, behavioral, or social area that the student is presenting as an area for intervention. This process will be completed in paper form and will need to be turned in for documentation of this portion of the final.

5. Additional Details

The following RTI Form and RTI Form Addendum templates are provided to students. These forms were created by the contributor, Dennis Cavitt, EdD.

RESPONSE TO INTERVENTION FORM

RTI TEAM

DELIBERATIONS/INTERVENTION RECOMMENDATIONS/EVALUATION

RTI TEAM MEETING: _____

Name of Student: _____ DOB: _____ Grade: _____

Campus: _____ Teacher: _____

Area(s) of Concern: _____

Team Members:

_____   _____

_____   _____

_____   _____

The RTI team considered the following information:

☐ Completed RTI referral

☐ Teacher information sheet

☐ Classroom observation

☐ STAAR scores of last 3 years if available

☐ TPRI scores for the most current year

☐ Grades for current/past year

☐ Record of disciplinary referrals

☐ Health information

☐ Home language survey

☐ Attendance records

☐ Samples of student work

☐ Other: _____

☐ Other: _____

☐ Other: _____

DISCUSSION:

After reviewing and considering all relevant information, the RTI team made the following recommendation(s):

☐ No Action to be taken at this time. Student will continue to be observed.

Referral to: ☐ Title I program ☐ Language Committee ☐ Reading Specialist ☐ Gen Ed Counseling ☐ Tutorials ☐ PAL Program ☐ Other: _____

(continued)

RESPONSE TO INTERVENTION FORM (CONTINUED)

DISCUSSION (CONTINUED):

☐ Team has determined specific goals and strategies for the student. These goals and strategies will be implemented for the next ☐ 3 weeks ☐ 6 weeks ☐ 9 weeks ☐ Other: _____ and evaluated. The RTI team will meet on: _____ to review.

☐ Other: _____

☐ Other: _____

GOAL(S):

1. _____

2. _____

3. _____

SETTINGS:

1. _____

2. _____

3. _____

Target Date for Goal(s): 1. _____ 2. _____ 3. _____ (*Length of time or Month/Day/Year*)

INTERVENTIONS (INCLUDE THE URL/WEBSITE WHERE THE TEAM IDENTIFIED THE EVIDENCED-BASED INTERVENTION[S])

GOAL NUMBER	STRATEGY/INTERVENTION/WEBSITE LOCATION

(continued)

RESPONSE TO INTERVENTION FORM (CONTINUED)

EVALUATION

RESULT	+3	Much improvement	0	No change	-1	Slightly worse
	+2	Moderate improvement	0	No change	-2	Moderately worse
	+1	Slight improvement	0	No change	-3	Much worse

EVALUATION

ACTION TAKEN	REVIEW DATE(S)			RESULT		
				3 WEEKS	6 WEEKS	9 WEEKS
Goal 1						
	Comments:					
Goal 2						
	Comments					
Goal 3						
	Comments					

Evidence that supports the evaluation(s): _____

_____

EDUCATION CONSIDERATIONS/RECOMMENDATIONS:

☐ No additional recommendations at this time.

☐ The RTI team determines that no further intervention is needed.

☐ Interventions listed continue to be effective to assist the student academically.

☐ The RTI team has determined to continue with interventions.

☐ No action to be taken at this time. Student will continue to be observed.

☐ Referral to: ☐ Title I Program ☐ Language Committee ☐ Reading Specialist
☐ Gen Ed Counseling ☐ Tutorials ☐ PAL Program ☐ Other: _____

☐ Interventions listed have NOT been effective. The RTI team has selected additional interventions for the student. See attached recommendations.

☐ Student will be nominated for the gifted and talented program.

(continued)

RESPONSE TO INTERVENTION FORM (CONTINUED)

EDUCATION CONSIDERATIONS/RECOMMENDATIONS (CONTINUED):

☐ The RTI team determines a need for further evaluation:

☐ Section 504 Evaluation. *Note: This should be done if (a) the team suspects that the student may have a physical or mental impairment that **substantially limits** a major life activity but (b) does not suspect that the student will need adaptations in the content, method, or delivery of instruction.*

☐ Special Education Evaluation. *Note: This should be done only if (a) the team suspects that the student may have a disability that would qualify under IDEA, and (b) the team also suspects that the student may need adaptations in the content, method, or delivery of instruction.*

☐ Other: _____

ADDITIONAL COMMENTS/DELIBERATIONS:

_____

_____

_____

Team Members' Signatures:

_____	_____
Name	Title
_____	_____
Name	Title
_____	_____
Name	Title
_____	_____
Name	Title
_____	_____
Name	Title
_____	_____
Name	Title

RESPONSE TO INTERVENTION FORM ADDENDUM

RTI TEAM INTERVENTION RECOMMENDATIONS/EVALUATION

TODAY'S DATE: _____

ADDENDUM TO RTI TEAM MEETING OF: _____

Name of Student: _____ DOB: _____ Grade: _____

Campus: _____ Teacher: _____

According to the RTI team meeting of _____, the following intervention strategies will be implemented for the next ☐ 3 weeks ☐ 6 weeks ☐ 9 weeks ☐ Other: _____ and evaluated. The RTI team will meet on: _____ to review.

INTERVENTIONS

GOAL NUMBER	STRATEGY/INTERVENTION/WEBSITE LOCATION

EVALUATION

RESULT	+3	Much improvement	0	No change	-1	Slightly worse
	+2	Moderate improvement	0	No change	-2	Moderately worse
	+1	Slight improvement	0	No change	-3	Much worse

(continued)

EVALUATION

ACTION TAKEN	REVIEW DATES			RESULT		
				3 WEEKS	6 WEEKS	9 WEEKS
Goal 1						
	Comments:					
Goal 2						
	Comments					
Goal 3						
	Comments					

Evidence that supports the evaluation(s): _____
_____
_____

EDUCATION CONSIDERATIONS/RECOMMENDATIONS:

☐ The RTI team determines that no further intervention is needed.

☐ Referral to: ☐ Title I Program ☐ LPAC ☐ Read Right ☐ General Education ☐ Counseling ☐ Tutorials ☐ PAL Program ☐ Other: _____

☐ Interventions listed continue to be effective to assist the student academically. The RTI team has determined to continue with interventions.

☐ Interventions listed have NOT been effective. The RTI team has selected additional interventions for the student. See attached recommendations.

☐ Student will be nominated for the gifted and talented program.

☐ The RTI team determines a need for further evaluation:

  ☐ Section 504 Evaluation. *Note: This should be done if (a) the team suspects that the student may have a physical or mental impairment that **substantially limits** a major life activity but (b) does not suspect that the student will need adaptations in the content, method, or delivery of instruction.*

  ☐ Special Education Evaluation. *Note: This should be done only if (a) the team suspects that the student may have a disability that would qualify under IDEA, and (b) the team also suspects that the student may need adaptations in the content, method, or delivery of instruction.*

  ☐ Other: _____

(continued)

RESPONSE TO INTERVENTION FORM ADDENDUM (CONTINUED)	
ADDITIONAL COMMENTS/DELIBERATIONS:	
_____	
_____	
_____	
Team Members' Signatures:	
Name	Title
Name	Title
Name	Title
Name	Title
Name	Title
Name	Title

6. Feedback Reflection

The purpose of this assessment is to help teacher candidates put all the information from the course into a format they can use in their future practice. Feedback is provided to identify where the student is demonstrating misunderstanding of each of the disability categories. Feedback for Part A occurs during the collaborative process. The team debriefs each of the cases on which they worked by using the problem-solving process. Areas of success and challenges are identified and corrected, if needed. Both parts of this authentic assessment provide the teacher candidate with the opportunity to demonstrate the skills necessary to identify potential areas of challenges for their students in their future practice.

AUTHENTIC EXAMPLE 4

Contributed by
Randa G. Keeley, PhD

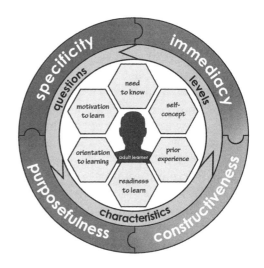

1. Course Details

EDSP 4253: Instructional Strategies for Students With Disabilities. This is one of four special education–specific courses that students seeking a license in special education will complete prior to graduation. The purpose of the course is to teach students to identify and apply instructional strategies and accommodations/modifications for curriculum in oral language, literacy, math, and life and social skills for individuals with disabilities. Upon completion of this course, students will have a knowledge base of strategies for teaching students with disabilities in a variety of instructional settings, with a strong emphasis on evidence-based instructional interventions. The course includes a 15-hour field-based experience.

2. Learning Objectives

Alignment with course objectives:
a. Identify and apply knowledge of the characteristics and needs of individuals with disabilities.
b. Understand and apply knowledge of procedures for planning instruction and managing the teaching and learning environments.
c. Demonstrate how instructional interventions connect with assessments to guide instruction.

3. Assignment Description

Students are to visit an assigned school for a total of 15 hours, with a minimum of three visits. Students are asked to visit a general education classroom that includes students with disabilities and a special education classroom. On at least two separate occasions, students are asked to use the Assessment of the Inclusion for Students With Special Educational Needs and Disabilities (AISSEND; Keeley et al., 2020) observation assessment during a classroom visit. The AISSEND observations are 30 minutes in length and require that students collect data related to the research-based inclusive practices that the respective teacher(s) performs in 5-minute intervals. In addition, students are asked to complete the AISSEND Additional Notes form to include any other information that might provide further context to the observations (e.g., objective, description of activity, classroom design). Prior to using the AISSEND, it is important that the instructor review all the strategies included in the tool to ensure that students understand how to recognize the identified strategies in the classroom setting. This instruction should include additional description of the strategies, modeling of examples and nonexamples of the strategies, and guided practice using the tool.

Upon completion of the observations, students are asked to write a reflection. The reflection must include the following elements:

a. Students must discuss the observed or nonobserved strategies within the context of the following domains: (1) instructional materials/resources, (2) physical environment, (3) teacher activities, (4) student engagement, (5) instructional strategies, (6) culturally responsive strategies, and (7) classroom management strategies.

b. Students must specifically address the following three areas related to course objectives: (1) a description of the specific needs of the students in the classroom, (b) a description of the use of assessment in the classroom, and (3) how the student may or may not apply the observed strategies to their future classroom.

c. Students must include at least two peer-reviewed references in APA format that connect the results from the observation to research or evidence-based practices.

d. Students should submit a reflection that is organized and includes a high level of critical thinking and minimal number of grammatical errors.

e. Students must also submit all completed AISSEND-related forms with the reflection.

4. Evaluation Criteria

The evaluation criteria for this assignment are provided in Table 14-10.

5. Additional Details

The Assessment of the Inclusion for Students With Special Education Needs and Disabilities (AISSEND) graphic is provided in Figure 14-1.

TABLE 14-10. ASSIGNMENT EVALUATION CRITERIA

RATING	CONTENT	ORGANIZATION	CRITICAL THINKING	LANGUAGE USE	WRITING CONVENTION
Proficient (6 points)	___ Topic/purpose is easily identified. ___ Ideas are conveyed clearly and are well-developed. ___ Details are ample, specific, and clearly related to the topic. ___ Information is accurate and consistent with verifiable sources. ___ All required content is addressed.	___ The introduction and conclusion effectively introduce and recap main ideas and are effectively related to the whole. ___ Ideas progress logically and clearly support the purpose. ___ Transitions are used within and between paragraphs to effectively introduce and/or link ideas. ___ Subsections are clearly marked by headings.	___ Collection of information is organized, systematic, and logical. ___ Interpretation of information is accurate, critical, coherent, and in-depth. ___ Synthesis of information generates a new perspective or creative application, leading to insightful conclusions or recommendations.	___ Sentence structures are varied, clear, and complete as well as enhance ideas and increase readability. ___ Word choice incorporates a variety of precise and vivid words. ___ Writing style is expressive and engaging and complements the content of the paper. ___ Effectively writes for the intended audience.	___ No errors in spelling are present. ___ No errors in punctuation are present. ___ No errors in grammar are present. ___ Always cites sources accurately and sufficiently (APA format).

(continued)

TABLE 14-10 (CONTINUED). ASSIGNMENT EVALUATION CRITERIA

RATING	CONTENT	ORGANIZATION	CRITICAL THINKING	LANGUAGE USE	WRITING CONVENTION
Sufficient (4-5 points)	___ Topic/purpose can be identified. ___ Ideas are conveyed clearly. ___ Details are specific and concrete but more are needed. ___ Information is mostly accurate, with verifiable sources. ___ Most required content is addressed.	___ The introduction and conclusion are adequate. ___ Progression of ideas can be followed with minimal effort and adequately supports the purpose. ___ Some transitions are used within and/or between paragraphs to link ideas. ___ Subsections are marked by headings.	___ Collection of information is organized and logical. ___ Interpretation of information is accurate, with some depth. ___ Synthesis of information logically leads to appropriate conclusions or recommendations.	___ Sentence structure is clear and varied. ___ Word choice is clear and exact. ___ Writing style is expressive, even engaging at times, and adds to the content. ___ Although the writing is generally appropriate for the intended audience, some jargon, too little/much information, and/or vagueness is present.	___ Few errors in spelling are present. ___ Few errors in punctuation are present. ___ Few errors in grammar are present. ___ Cites sources sufficiently but inaccurately.

(continued)

TABLE 14-10 (CONTINUED). ASSIGNMENT EVALUATION CRITERIA					
RATING	CONTENT	ORGANIZATION	CRITICAL THINKING	LANGUAGE USE	WRITING CONVENTION
Developing (2-3 points)	___ Topic/purpose is somewhat unclear. ___ Ideas are conveyed but more information is needed. ___ Details are nonspecific or abstract and do not clearly support the purpose. ___ Information is somewhat accurate, with verifiable sources. ___ Some required content is addressed.	___ An introduction and conclusion are present but ineffective. ___ Progression of ideas can be followed with much effort, and support of the purpose is difficult to ascertain. ___ Transitions are infrequently used to link ideas. ___ Subsections are not marked by headings.	___ Collection of information is somewhat organized and logical. ___ Interpretation of information has some accuracy and limited depth. ___ Synthesis of information is limited, leading to some appropriate conclusions or recommendations.	___ Sentence structures are predictable, wordy, and/or repetitive. ___ Word choice reflects vague and/or sometimes repeated words. ___ Writing style is functional but rarely engaging. ___ Consistent use of jargon, too little/much information, and/or vagueness is present.	___ Several errors in spelling are present. ___ Several errors in punctuation are present. ___ Several errors in grammar are present. ___ Fails to cite sources accurately and/or sufficiently.

(continued)

TABLE 14-10 (CONTINUED). ASSIGNMENT EVALUATION CRITERIA

RATING	CONTENT	ORGANIZATION	CRITICAL THINKING	LANGUAGE USE	WRITING CONVENTION
Insufficient (0-1 point)	____Topic/purpose is unclear. ____Ideas are limited and/or repetitious. ____Details are vague or distracting, and connection to purpose is unclear. ____Information is mostly inaccurate and/or sources are not verifiable. ____Little to none of the required content is addressed.	____An introduction and conclusion are not included. ____Ideas do not follow any logical order. ____Transitions are not used. ____No subsections are obvious.	____Collection of information is minimal. ____Interpretation of information has limited accuracy. ____Synthesis of information is lacking, leading to inappropriate or no conclusions or recommendations.	____Sentence structures used are choppy, rambling, awkward, or monotonous. ____Word choice reflects vague, misused and/or repeated words. ____Writing style detracts from the content of the paper. ____Writing is inappropriate for the intended audience.	____Many spelling errors interfere with the reading of the text and credibility of the writer. ____Many punctuation errors interfere with the reading of the text and credibility of the writer. ____Many grammatical errors interfere with the reading of the text and credibility of the writer. ____Fails to cite sources.

Assessment of the Inclusion for Students with Special Educational Needs and Disabilities (AISSEND)

Teacher(s)	
Grade/Subject/Co-teaching Model	
Observer	
Date	
Number of Students (Total)	
Number of SWD	
Number of CLD Students	
Disability Categories	

Instructional Materials/Resources	P/NP	Physical Environment	P/NP
Instructional materials accessible (i.e., visually and auditory)		Classroom set up in manner that would allow student to navigate and obtain all lesson materials	
Instructional materials support the topic/standard		Tables/Desks adjusted for group work	
Instructional materials provided at varying levels of comprehension		Tables/Desks arranged in a way that allows for easy movement	
Instructional materials are culturally responsive		Student work reflecting content is displayed	
Technology used in instruction		Teacher work is posted in accessible areas around the classroom	
*Resource other than the textbook is used to highlight alternate cultural perspectives		*Learning environment promotes respect for other cultures	
		Classroom rules are posted	

Time Interval (Record real time start for each interval)

Teacher Activities	Notes	Instructional Time					
		0-5	6-10	11-15	16-20	21-25	26-30
Teacher uses a checklist, survey, or anecdotal record as an ongoing assessment tool		0-5	6-10	11-15	16-20	21-25	26-30
Teacher attends to academic, social, and/or physical needs of students		0-5	6-10	11-15	16-20	21-25	26-30
Teacher provides time for students to process information		0-5	6-10	11-15	16-20	21-25	26-30

Student Engagement	Notes	Instructional Time					
		0-5	6-10	11-15	16-20	21-25	26-30
Individual student, small group, and/or large group questions asked to assess for student engagement		0-5	6-10	11-15	16-20	21-25	26-30
Interactive activity used to engage students		0-5	6-10	11-15	16-20	21-25	26-30
Student movement is incorporated into instruction to facilitate student engagement		0-5	6-10	11-15	16-20	21-25	26-30
Cooperative learning incorporated for new material to facilitate student engagement		0-5	6-10	11-15	16-20	21-25	26-30
Independent work implemented if student is familiar with the concept to retain student engagement		0-5	6-10	11-15	16-20	21-25	26-30

Figure 14-1. Assessment of the Inclusion for Students With Special Education Needs and Disabilities (AISSEND). NP = not present; P = present. All descriptors marked with an asterisk (*) denote a strategy that is also culturally and linguistically responsive. (Reproduced with permission from Randa G. Keeley, PhD.) *(continued)*

Instructional Strategies

	Instructional Time					
	0-5	6-10	11-15	16-20	21-25	26-30
*Individual student work is incorporated as an instructional strategy	0-5	6-10	11-15	16-20	21-25	26-30
*Small group work is incorporated as an instructional strategy	0-5	6-10	11-15	16-20	21-25	26-30
*Large group work is incorporated as an instructional strategy	0-5	6-10	11-15	16-20	21-25	26-30
Previewing strategy used	0-5	6-10	11-15	16-20	21-25	26-30
Questioning strategy used	0-5	6-10	11-15	16-20	21-25	26-30
Comprehension strategy used	0-5	6-10	11-15	16-20	21-25	26-30
Instructional time is short and incorporates student questioning	0-5	6-10	11-15	16-20	21-25	26-30
Strategy to activate prior knowledge used	0-5	6-10	11-15	16-20	21-25	26-30
Explicit instruction used (e.g., skill breakdown, multi-sensory instruction, examples + non-examples, cueing, etc.)	0-5	6-10	11-15	16-20	21-25	26-30
*Modeling of activity used	0-5	6-10	11-15	16-20	21-25	26-30
*Practice of the activity allowed	0-5	6-10	11-15	16-20	21-25	26-30
Instruction involves a universal theme	0-5	6-10	11-15	16-20	21-25	26-30

Culturally Responsive Strategies

	Instructional Time					
	0-5	6-10	11-15	16-20	21-25	26-30
Instruction discusses differences between individuals	0-5	6-10	11-15	16-20	21-25	26-30
Role-playing used to accommodate for cultural differences	0-5	6-10	11-15	16-20	21-25	26-30
Assignment or activity relates to a community or cultural group	0-5	6-10	11-15	16-20	21-25	26-30
Opportunity to share cultural background given	0-5	6-10	11-15	16-20	21-25	26-30
Clear and consistent wording used in instruction in consideration of English language learners	0-5	6-10	11-15	16-20	21-25	26-30
Artifacts from other cultures are shared	0-5	6-10	11-15	16-20	21-25	26-30

Classroom Management Strategies

	Instructional Time					
	0-5	6-10	11-15	16-20	21-25	26-30
Established routines evident	0-5	6-10	11-15	16-20	21-25	26-30
Classroom rules are enforced	0-5	6-10	11-15	16-20	21-25	26-30
A group oriented contingency system used	0-5	6-10	11-15	16-20	21-25	26-30
Consequence based intervention used	0-5	6-10	11-15	16-20	21-25	26-30
Transition between activity	0-5	6-10	11-15	16-20	21-25	26-30
Precision requests	0-5	6-10	11-15	16-20	21-25	26-30
Planned ignoring	0-5	6-10	11-15	16-20	21-25	26-30

Figure 14-1 (continued). Assessment of the Inclusion for Students With Special Education Needs and Disabilities (AISSEND). NP = not present; P = present. All descriptors marked with an asterisk (*) denote a strategy that is also culturally and linguistically responsive. (Reproduced with permission from Randa G. Keeley, PhD.)

The following AISSEND Additional Notes Form can be attached to the AISSEND Tool:

AISSEND Additional Notes

Teacher(s): _____ Class/Period: _____ Date _____

_____

_____

_____

_____

_____

_____

6. Feedback Reflection

This assignment asks students to identify specific research-based instructional strategies that promote the inclusion of students with disabilities. In addition to teaching and modeling for students' research-based instructional strategies, this assignment asks students to identify the specified strategies in a real-world setting and comment about the use of the strategies in an instructional environment. The observations allow students to reflect on the observed teaching practices and then evaluate those practices for use in their respective future classrooms. Through this assignment, the instructor teaches and models research-based practices for students. Then, for deeper understanding of those practices, students are asked to identify the strategies in real-world settings. Upon completion of the reflection, students receive detailed feedback from the instructor related to their observations.

AUTHENTIC EXAMPLE 5

Contributed by
Lisa A. Finnegan, PhD

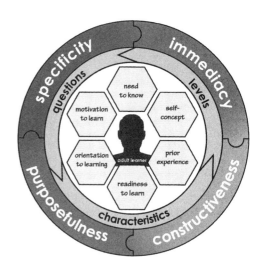

1. Course Details

EEX 4066: Teaching Students With Mild/Moderate Disabilities. This course is an undergraduate course with a co-requisite practicum. The course is part of the Exceptional Student Education teacher education track. This reflection part of the assignment is completed after students have implemented a comprehensive detailed lesson plan and provided instruction. Their lesson plan requires an overall reflection; however, this activity requires a deeper reflection that students complete, based on a set of questions.

2. Learning Objectives

a. Demonstrate knowledge of the hierarchy of developmental skills, which are prerequisites and requisites for academic, social behaviors, and/or life skills.

b. Implement instructional programs to achieve specific instructional objectives.

3. Assignment Description

Students will create a lesson and provide instruction based on the lesson. After the lesson is taught, the students will reflect on the instruction delivery and outcomes of their instruction for the components listed in the outline. Students should reflect on the specifically provided questions as they complete their responses. The lesson and reflection will be submitted to the faculty/instructor. These lessons cannot be the lessons that the student performed for purposes of observation by the cooperating teacher or university supervisor where they received feedback by either the cooperating teacher or university supervisor regarding their instruction that may influence their reflective statements. The instructor/faculty will provide specific feedback connecting back to the lesson itself and the written reflection to the questions. Students are to use the form provided, attempting to connect their lesson preparation and instruction by answering each question on the form, providing the specific evidence from their lesson and what they observed while teaching the lesson.

TABLE 14-11. SELF-ASSESSMENT OF LESSON
(MUST INCLUDE ASPECTS OF THE EFFECTIVE PRACTICES LISTED)

INTENTIONAL INSTRUCTIONAL PRACTICE*	REFLECTIVE COMMENTS: READ, REFLECT, AND RESPOND TO THE QUESTIONS WHEN REFLECTING ON YOUR LESSON. QUESTIONS ARE MEANT TO GUIDE YOUR REFLECTION, NOT NECESSARILY MEANT TO ANSWER EACH ONE INDIVIDUALLY.
Coherent, connected, meaningful learning progression	**Examine how your lesson provided a coherent learning progression.** Assess how the lesson united both skills and knowledge. (Is the instruction accurate? Is the lesson clear and logically sequenced, with a measurable learning objective? How was the continuity of learning connected from one lesson to the next?) **Explicitly indicate how your lesson is connected to both the student(s) and the bigger picture or goal.** (How is the skill or knowledge connected to another skill/concept, or is the skill an isolated skill? How is this learning objective connected to your students' lives? How does this skill impact the student meaningfully or in terms of their life/future?)
Strategies, instructional practices, resources, and technologies that enhance learning for all learners	**Identify your selected strategies and instructional practices used to engage all learners.** (How did you make learning visual and concrete? How were all learners involved and to what extent? Was it effective?) **Elaborate on how the resources and technologies you used provide purposeful learning, enhance engagement, and potentially transform the learning experiences in your lesson/classroom.** (Did the resources/technologies improve the learning or provide an opportunity to be creative? Which SAMR [substitution, augmentation, modification, and redefinition] technology/resource was used and why?) **Identify the principles and guidelines of the Universal Design for Learning framework (UDL) within the lesson.**
Safe, respectful, well-organized learning environment (strong tier 1 of PBIS [Positive Behavioral Interventions and Supports])	**Evaluate how the learning progressed throughout the lesson.** (How do you begin and end the lesson? How did you move learning from you (direct instruction) toward the student (independent)? Distinguish clear routines and procedures within the lesson from those that were unclear?) **Explain how interactions in your classroom be improved through better classroom management.** (What are the classroom expectations for the lesson? What is your presence?) **Align any connection between the design of your lesson, engagement, behavior, and interactions of your students (or a particular student). On a scale of 1** (*needs improvement*) **to 5** (*smooth running*), **rate your PBIS tier 1 classroom structure.** (What structures are in place to provide a continuum of support and expectations? How might the lesson be connected/extended to the students' family?)

*Adapted from Teacher Intentionality of Practice Scales (Marshall, 2016) and aligned with CEC High-Leverage Practices (McLeskey et al., 2017).

SAMR – substitution, augmentation, modification, and redefinition; substitution—drill and practice (Quizlet, Google search); augmentation—interactive (Google docs, PowerPoint slides); modification—narrated animation project (Nearpod, Edmodo, Google+); redefinition—interactive and creative (Padlet, 3D printing, website creation, VoiceThread).

4. *Evaluation Criteria*

Please refer to the Self-Assessment of Lesson (Table 14-11) for the evaluation criteria.

5. Additional Details

Description of Lesson Plan Preparation and Implementation Reflection Assignment: The student will develop a comprehensive and detailed lesson that they will teach. The student will implement the lesson and reflect on the instructional delivery and management of the lesson by responding to specific questions on identified effective practices. The grading rubric is provided in Table 14-12.

6. Feedback Reflection

This assignment reflects on exhibiting feedback and providing feedback. Students evaluate their instruction and management of student engagement after lesson delivery. The instructor reviews both the lesson details and the post-lesson reflection, providing feedback to the student by further connecting areas to be addressed in the reflection questions to the course content as well as provides suggestions to improve lesson plan preparation and delivery. In addition, the instructor may question other aspects of the lesson, enhance the development of the student in providing a coherent, connected learning progression, using strategies, resources, and technologies that enhance learning, and establishing a safe, respectful, well-organized learning environment. Students are to review the feedback and address the feedback by improving their lesson preparation, instruction, and reflection on their next lesson. Students complete four lessons in this format throughout the semester, with a goal of enriching their reflective practices while also improving on their lesson preparation.

TABLE 14-12. LESSON PLAN PREPARATION AND IMPLEMENTATION REFLECTION ASSIGNMENT

ASSIGNMENT VALUE	EXEMPLARY (90% TO 100%)	SATISFACTORY (73% TO 89%)	EMERGING (64% TO 72%)	UNSATISFACTORY (0% TO 63%)	NO SUBMISSION
10 points	Teacher makes a thoughtful and accurate assessment of a lesson's effectiveness and the extent to which it achieved its instructional outcomes, citing many specific examples from the lesson and weighing the relative strengths of each; drawing on an extensive repertoire of skills, teacher offers specific alternative actions, complete with the probable success of different courses of action. Reflection includes more than one type of specific evidence to address questions listed, providing: 1. Coherent, connected, meaningful learning progression 2. Strategies, instructional practices, resources, and technologies that enhance learning 3. A safe, respectful, well-organized learning environment	Teacher makes an accurate assessment of a lesson's effectiveness and the extent to which it achieved its instructional outcomes and can cite general references to support the judgment. Teacher makes a few specific suggestions of what could be tried another time the lesson is taught. Reflection includes at least one type of specific evidence to address questions listed, providing: 1. Coherent, connected, meaningful learning progression 2. Strategies, instructional practices, resources, and technologies that enhance learning 3. A safe, respectful, well-organized learning environment	Teacher has a generally accurate impression of a lesson's effectiveness and the extent to which instructional outcomes were met; teacher makes general suggestions about how a lesson could be improved. Reflection somewhat includes pieces of evidence in a general sense to address questions listed, providing: 1. Coherent, connected, meaningful learning progression 2. Strategies, instructional practices, resources, and technologies that enhance learning 3. A safe, respectful, well-organized learning environment	Teacher does not know whether a lesson was effective or achieved its instructional outcomes, or teacher profoundly misjudges the success of a lesson; teacher has no suggestions for how a lesson could be improved. Reflection minimally includes evidence to address questions listed, providing: 1. Coherent, connected, meaningful learning progression 2. Strategies, instructional practices, resources, and technologies that enhance learning 3. A safe, respectful, well-organized learning environment	Failed to submit or failed to submit on time.

Authentic Example 6

Contributed by
Anni K. Reinking, EdD

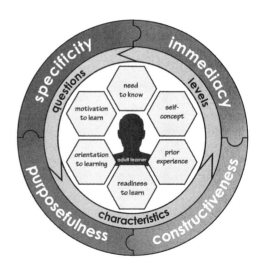

1. Course Details

CI 568:002: Trauma Informed Practices K-12. In this graduate course, students focus on a trauma-informed curriculum in the early childhood field (PreK-12). We will discuss brain development, adverse childhood experiences, strategies, classroom/school tools, and risk factors. This course is not included in any specific course of study but rather is offered as an option to fulfill various requirements in the graduate program. In addition, this course is completely online only.

2. Learning Objectives

Aligned course objectives:
a. Develop knowledge and skills to identify problems in teaching or learning, use resources to address those problems, and evaluate the results of an intervention.
b. Refine understanding of the impact of school organizations and cultures on supporting teacher development during times of change.
c. Develop the knowledge and skills needed to facilitate collaborative teacher learning through frameworks, such as Lesson Study, professional learning communities, and others.

3. Assignment Description

Students will learn about various curricula and programs focused on creating trauma-sensitive schools. Numerous ideas and programs are available to study that focus on all students or specific age bands of students.

When a program is chosen, the student becomes an "expert" on the program/curriculum through research and investigation. The goal is to simulate the research phase of curriculum analysis in a district to adopt or not adopt a program/curriculum.

When the gathering stage is complete, the student prepares a multimedia presentation of their choice. The presentation must include:
a. The curriculum/program
b. Pros and cons of the program
c. Research to support findings
d. A recommendation to adopt or not adopt (in a fictitious district or the district they are currently working)

TABLE 14-13. CURRICULUM PRESENTATION RUBRIC

CRITERIA	0 POINTS	5 POINTS	10 POINTS
Focus on a curriculum from the course			
Included references from the course			
Included references from outside/own research			
Presented in a multimodal way			
Engages listeners with questions, reflections, and handouts			

4. Evaluation Criteria

Please refer to the curriculum presentation rubric (Table 14-13) to assess the assignment.

5. Additional Details

What "counts" as multimedia? It can be anything such as a Powtoon, a video, a podcast, or a presentation with ThingLink or Knovio. Although this list is not exhaustive, it provides ideas of what multimedia is, which essentially is using artistic ways to communicate. The five defined ways to communicate in multimedia ways include text, image, audio, video, and animation.

6. Feedback Reflection

This assignment reflects various types of feedback. First, the presentations are worked on throughout the semester, with checkpoints identified. The checkpoints include meeting with the professor for feedback and also meeting with peers for feedback. Some of this feedback is then expected to be addressed in the final project. Another type of feedback that is embedded into this assignment is the feedback from the real or fake district (depending on whether the student is currently working in a district). The idea is to present this project to the class, but then also to present the project to the district for real implementation, if they deem it appropriate. The feedback from employers is critical through this learning process.

REFERENCES

Children's Online Privacy Protection Act (COPPA), 1998. 15 U.S.C. § 6501 et seq. (2016).

Danielson, C. (2007). *Enhancing professional practice: A framework for teaching* (2nd ed.). Alexandria,VA: Association for Supervision and Curriculum Development.

Family Educational Rights and Privacy Act (FERPA), 1974. 20 U.S.C. § 1232g; 34 C.F.R. § 99.1 et seq. (2016).

Fluckiger, J. (2010). Single point rubric: A tool for responsible student self-assessment. *The Delta Kappa Gamma Bulletin, 76*(4), 18-25.

Jones, N. D., & Brownell, M. T. (2014). Examining the use of classroom observations in the evaluation of special education teachers. *Assessment for Effective Intervention, 39*(2), 112-124.

Keeley, R. G., Alvarado-Alcantar, R., & Keeley, D. W. (2020). The Development of AISSEND: An Observation Tool to Assess Inclusive Practices. *Journal of the American Academy of Special Education Professionals, Fall*, 122-137.

Lash, A., Tran, L., & Huang, M. (2016). *Examining the validity of ratings from a classroom observation instrument for use in a district's teacher evaluation system. REL 2016-135*. Regional Educational Laboratory West.

McLeskey, J., Barringer, M. D., Billingsley, B., Brownell, M., Jackson, D., Kennedy, M., et al. (2017). *High-leverage practices in special education*. Council for Exceptional Children & CEEDAR Center.

Marshall, J. C. (2016). *The highly effective teacher: 7 classroom-tested practices that foster student success*. ASCD.

Morris-Mathews, H., Stark, K. R., Jones, N. D., Brownell, M. T., & Bell, C. A. (2021). Danielson's framework for teaching: Convergence and divergence with conceptions of effectiveness in special education. *Journal of Learning Disabilities, 54*(1), 66-78.

GLOSSARY

constructiveness: The meaning the recipient makes of the feedback and what that produces. The learner is a participant in creating new meaning from the feedback received.

delayed feedback: Given after considerable time. The delay in the feedback is purposeful and planned. Delayed feedback may provide corrective information, support knowledge objectives, and promote positive progress for the adult learner.

exhibiting feedback: Explicitly modeling how feedback should be given through sharing the "why and how" of delivering feedback.

feedback: Any information that the recipient receives that informs their understanding or restructures their thinking or beliefs related to their performance, knowledge, or skills.

giving feedback: Delivering any information to a recipient that informs their understanding or restructures their thinking or their beliefs related to their performance, knowledge, or skill.

identity: Informs how we view ourselves and the story we tell ourselves about who we are and how we teach.

immediacy: The timing of when feedback is delivered, based on questions, levels, and characteristics.

immediate feedback: Feedback given soon after a task is completed. It can be positive, providing specific details about what a learner has done well and should repeat or build upon, and it can also be corrective, providing an example or details on how to reach an objective. Immediate feedback is often used in response to performance-related tasks.

performance feedback: Positive and corrective feedback is delivered immediately through opportunities to respond, verbal expansions, and behavior-specific praise.

purposefulness: Questions, levels, and characteristics that are progress-related; includes all the language and methods describing what is required to keep moving forward along the learning continuum.

specificity: Questions, levels, and characteristics that are goal-related. The characteristics of specificity include the language used, who is receiving the feedback, and the ways the feedback is clearly stated and fully accessible.

status: Refers to the level of respect, honor, and professional competence and standing afforded to an individual.

teaching feedback: Explicitly teaching what feedback looks like and sounds like in the classroom for K-12 learners.

trust: Harley (2013) suggested that it is essential when giving feedback. Trust is important from both perspectives—the instructor providing feedback and the student recipient.

Reference

Harley, T. A. (2013). *The psychology of language: From data to theory*. Psychology Press.

Elford, M. D., Smith, H. H., & James, S.
GET Feedback: Giving, Exhibiting, and Teaching Feedback in
Special Education Teacher Preparation (p. 311).
© 2022 SLACK Incorporated.

Financial Disclosures

Dr. Reesha Adamson has no financial or proprietary interest in the materials presented herein.

Dr. Dennis Cavitt has not disclosed any relevant financial relationships.

Dr. Kyena E. Cornelius has no financial or proprietary interest in the materials presented herein.

Dr. Donald D. Deshler has no financial or proprietary interest in the materials presented herein.

Dr. Martha D. Elford has no financial or proprietary interest in the materials presented herein.

Dr. Amy Gaumer Erickson has no financial or proprietary interest in the materials presented herein.

Dr. Lisa A. Finnegan has not disclosed any relevant financial relationships.

Dr. Carlos A. Flores, Jr. has no financial or proprietary interest in the materials presented herein.

Dr. John Hattie has no financial or proprietary interest in the materials presented herein.

Dr. Randa G. Keeley has not disclosed any relevant financial relationships.

Dr. Susanne James has no financial or proprietary interest in the materials presented herein.

Dr. Kristin Joannou Lyon has no financial or proprietary interest in the materials presented herein.

Dr. Katie Martin Miller has no financial or proprietary interest in the materials presented herein.

Dr. Cynthia Mruczek has no financial or proprietary interest in the materials presented herein.

Dr. Jessica Nelson has no financial or proprietary interest in the materials presented herein.

Dr. Ruby L. Owiny has no financial or proprietary interest in the materials presented herein.

Dr. Jennifer Porterfield has no financial or proprietary interest in the materials presented herein.

Dr. Felicity Post has not disclosed any relevant financial relationships.

Dr. Anni K. Reinking has no financial or proprietary interest in the materials presented herein.

Dr. Heather Haynes Smith has no financial or proprietary interest in the materials presented herein.

Dr. Cathy Newman Thomas has not disclosed any relevant financial relationships.

Dr. Virginia L. Walker has no financial or proprietary interest in the materials presented herein.

Dr. Wendy H. Weber has no financial or proprietary interest in the materials presented herein.

Margaret Williamson has no financial or proprietary interest in the materials presented herein.

INDEX